THE
WEST

THE
WEST

A New History in Fourteen Lives

———— ◆ ————

Naoíse Mac Sweeney

DUTTON

DUTTON

An imprint of Penguin Random House LLC
penguinrandomhouse.com

LIBRARY OF CONGRESS CATALOGING-IN-PUBLICATION DATA
has been applied for.

ISBN 9780593472170 (hardcover)
ISBN 9780593472194 (ebook)

Printed in the United States of America
1st Printing

BOOK DESIGN BY TIFFANY ESTREICHER

For Gianni and Valentino

CONTENTS

CONTENTS

AUTHOR'S NOTE

I have chosen to capitalise the term "Western Civilisation" throughout this book, to emphasise that it is an invented abstract construct, rather than a neutral descriptive term. Similarly, I have also chosen to capitalise "the West" and "Western" when these words relate to abstract politico-cultural concepts which carry connotations of culture and civilisation rather than serving as purely geographical descriptions. Following the same logic, when I use purely geographical descriptions, I have used lowercase to do so. For example, when referring to the central part of the continent of Europe I have used "central Europe" rather than "Central Europe." I have, however, retained the customary capitalisation for the names of continents.

I have followed a similar principle for racial terminology. Terms such as "Black" or "Yellow" are capitalised, to highlight that these categorisations are invented abstract constructs rather than neutral descriptive terms. Lowercase is used when colour terms are deployed in a purely descriptive manner.

With the spellings of names and places, I have tended to use the commonest Latinate versions for consistency and with the aim of simplifying things for the reader. There are, however, names included in this book which can be rendered in several different ways in the Latin script. In these cases, I have tried to choose the spellings and accentuation that seemed to me to be the most common in the existing Anglophone literature. Unless explicitly attributed, translations are my own.

This book engages with subjects from a range of periods in human history, and from many different cultures and societies. In writing parts of it, I have therefore relied heavily on secondary literature for my research. I have done my best to seek guidance from subject, regional, and period specialists when dealing with areas beyond my own particular expertise. Nonetheless, it is unlikely that all sections of this book will be as accurate, detailed, or nuanced as if they had been written by specialists in each area, and I anticipate that they may contain some errors of fact and interpretation. I do believe, however, that there is value in work such as this book, which aims to offer a broad synthetic overview of a topic. By zooming out to see the bigger picture it is inevitable that sometimes we lose some of the detail and resolution, but there are times when the bigger picture is nonetheless important.

THE IMPORTANCE
OF ORIGINS

O RIGINS matter. When we pose the question "Where do you come from?" what we are really asking is often, "Who are you?" This is true for individuals, families, and entire countries. It is also true of an entity as large and as complex as the West.

This intersection between origins and identity lies at the heart of the culture wars that are currently rocking the West. The last decade has seen the toppling of statues, heated debates over culture and history, and the toxic polarisation of public discourse. The identity crisis within the West is largely a response to wider global patterns. The world is changing, and the foundations of Western dominance are being shaken. In this historical moment we have the opportunity to radically rethink the West and to remake it anew for the future. But we can do this only if we are willing to confront its past. Only by answering the question of where the West comes from can we answer the question of what the West could and should be.

The term "the West" can refer to a geopolitical alignment or a cultural community, usually designating a set of modern nation-states sharing both cultural features and political and economic principles. Amongst these are ideals of representative democracy and market capitalism, a secular state overlying a Judeo-Christian moral substratum, and a psychological tendency towards individualism.[1] Nothing on this list is exclusive to the West or universal across it, yet the regular occurrence of all or most of these attributes together is nonetheless characteristic. The same can be said of many of the more clichéd symbols of westernisation—champagne and Coca-Cola, opera houses and shopping malls. But one particular defining feature of the West is the notion of a common origin resulting in a shared history, a shared heritage, and a shared identity.

The origin myth of the West imagines Western history as unfurling unbroken back in time through Atlantic modernity and the European Enlightenment; back through the brightness of the Renaissance and the darkness of the Middle Ages; back, ultimately, to its origin in the classical worlds of Rome and Greece. This has become the standard version of Western history, both canonical and clichéd. But it is wrong. It is a version of Western history that is both factually incorrect and ideologically driven—a grand narrative that constructs Western history as a thread running singular and unbroken from Plato to NATO,[2] and that is usually referred to by the handy shorthand term "Western Civilisation."

Just to avoid any confusion, this is not a book about the rise of the West as a cultural or political entity. There are a great many books on that subject already, offering a variety of explanations for how the West achieved global dominance.[3] Instead, this book charts the rise of one particular version of Western history, a version that is now so widely perpetuated and deeply ingrained that it is often accepted unthinkingly, and yet which is both morally problematic and factually wrong. This book unpicks and unpacks the grand narrative known as "Western Civilisation."

This version of Western history—the grand narrative of Western Civilisation—is all around us. I remember when I became truly conscious of quite how deeply entrenched it was. I was in the reading room of the Library of Congress in Washington, DC. Looking up by chance at the ceiling I realised uncomfortably that I was being watched, not by the ever-vigilant librarians, but by sixteen life-size bronze statues standing on the gallery beneath the gilded dome. From antiquity there were Moses, Homer, Solon, Herodotus, Plato, and St. Paul. From the Old World of Europe there were Columbus, Michelangelo, Bacon, Shakespeare, Newton, Beethoven, and the historian Edward Gibbon. And from the New World of North America there were the jurist James Kent, the engineer Robert Fulton, and the scientist Joseph Henry. I realised in that instant that the entire setup of the room (not just the statues but also the murals that decorated the walls and even the organisation of the bookshelves) was designed to emphasise one thing— that we at the desks were part of an intellectual and cultural tradition that stretched back though the millennia. And our forebears in that tradition were literally watching over us, perhaps in encouragement, perhaps in judgement, as we worked.[4]

Two troubling thoughts hit me. The first instinctive thought was that I was out of place. I felt that someone like me (female, mixed-race) did not belong in a tradition usually imagined in terms of elite white men. I rapidly dismissed this notion as ridiculous (after all, I was at that very moment sitting in a seat of privilege at a reader's desk), but I was then struck by a much weightier concern. Did these sixteen figures truly represent the past of the West? Was the narrative that linked them an accurate portrayal of Western history?

The standard narrative of Western Civilisation is so omnipresent that most of us rarely stop to think about it, and even less often to question it. Indeed, despite the fact it is being increasingly (and successfully) challenged, this narrative is still all around us. We read about it in school textbooks and works of popular history that, when they set out to explain the history of the West, usually begin it "with the Greeks and the Romans, carry it through the European Middle Ages, focus it on the age of European exploration and conquest, and analyse it closely in the modern world."[5] The language used of Western Civilisation in such works is usually peppered with genealogical metaphors, describing it in terms of "legacy," "evolution," and "ancestry."[6] We hear time and again that "western civilisation is something we have inherited from the ancient Greeks, the Romans and the Christian Church via the Renaissance, the scientific revolution and the Enlightenment."[7] This idea of Western Civilisation as a linear cultural inheritance is drummed into us from an early age. One influential series of children's books prefaces its magical adventures by describing Western Civilisation as "a living force . . . a fire" that first started in Greece; passed from there to Rome; alighted in Germany, France, and Spain before pausing for several centuries in England; finally coming to rest in the United States of America.[8] Origins matter, and where we claim the West came from is one way of characterising what the West fundamentally *is*.

The West's imagined cultural genealogy is invoked explicitly in the speeches of populist politicians, the rhetoric of journalists, and the analysis of pundits. It underlies the symbols and vocabulary deployed by people from across the political spectrum. Amongst these, there is often particular emphasis placed on Greco-Roman antiquity as the birthplace of the West, and allusions to ancient Greece and Rome are frequent in contemporary political rhetoric. When a mob stormed the US Capitol building in January 2021 claiming to defend Western values, they carried flags emblazoned with ancient Greek phrases and placards depicting former president Donald Trump as Julius Caesar, while some wore replicas of ancient Greek helmets, and others dressed in full Roman military costume.[9] When the European Union launched an initiative to tackle irregular immigration and refugee flows in 2014, it settled on the name "Operation Mos Maiorum" as a reference to the traditions of ancient Rome.[10] And when Osama bin Laden proclaimed a holy war against the West in 2004, he called on Muslims to "resist the new Rome."[11] But this narrative of Western Civilisation is not just recounted in historical works and invoked in political contexts. It is also all around us, part of the fabric of our everyday lives. We watch it played out in movies and on television, coded into the choices of casting directors, costume designers, and screen composers. We encounter it enshrined in stone not only at the Library of Congress, but also in the neoclassical architecture of both imperial capitals and colonial buildings around the world.[12] It is so pervasive that most of us simply take it for granted. But is it true?

These were the thoughts that raced through my head that rainy afternoon in Washington, DC. By that point, I had spent the best part of two decades studying precisely these imagined origins of the West, in which is invested so much of Western identity. My particular research focus was on how people in the ancient Greek world understood their own origins, investigating the mythical genealogies they constructed, the ancestor cults where they worshipped, and the stories they told of migrations and foundations. While I felt (and indeed still do feel) privileged to be in my profession, in that moment I was deeply uncomfortable. I realised that I was complicit in upholding an intellectual artifice that was both ideologically and factually dubious—the grand narrative of Western Civilisation. From that point on, I began to repurpose the methods of analysis that I had employed for exploring identities and origins in antiquity, and applying them to the modern world around me. This book is the result.

It argues two things. The first is that the grand narrative of Western Civilisation is factually wrong. The modern West does not have a clear and simple origin in classical antiquity and did not develop through an unbroken and singular lineage from there through medieval Christendom, the Renaissance, and the Enlightenment to modernity. As the academic and philosopher Kwame Anthony Appiah has pointed out, Western identity and culture were not passed down, like a "golden nugget," along this line.[13] Problems with this grand narrative were first identified more than a century ago, and the evidence against it is now overwhelming. Today, all serious historians and archaeologists acknowledge that the cross-fertilisation of "Western" and "non-Western" cultures happened throughout human history, and that the modern West owes much of its cultural DNA to a wide range of non-European and non-white forebears.[14] Yet the nature and nuances of these cultural interactions remain to be fully untangled, and the shape of a new grand narrative to replace that of Western Civilisation is yet to emerge. Contributing to this work was part of my motivation for writing this book. The rest of my motivation came from reflecting on the troubling fact that all the historical evidence amassed and all the scholarly consensus against the grand narrative of Western Civilisation have had relatively little impact on the wider public consciousness. The narrative remains ubiquitous in contemporary Western culture. Why do we (that is, Western societies, broadly speaking) still cling so doggedly to a vision of history that has been so thoroughly discredited?

The second main argument of this book is that the invention, popularisation, and longevity of the grand narrative of Western Civilisation all stem from its ideological utility. The narrative exists—and continues to exist today long after its factual basis has been thoroughly disproved—because it serves a purpose. As a conceptual framework, it has provided a justification for Western expansion, imperialism, and ongoing systems of white racial dominance. This does not mean that the grand narrative of Western Civilisation is the brainchild of some evil mastermind, cynically scheming to engineer a false view of history to further their cause. Quite the opposite. Rather, the weaving of this story was piecemeal and haphazard, owing as much to serendipity as to calculation. It is a grand narrative comprised of many micronarratives, interlinked and interleaved, all of which have been separately deployed in the service of specific political ends. They include the idea of classical Athens as a beacon of democracy, used as a foundation charter for modern Western democracy;[15] the notion of the fundamental Europeanness of ancient Romans as a basis for shared European heritage;[16] and the myth of the Crusades as a simple clash of civilisations between Christendom and Islam, justifying anti-Western jihad on one side and the "War on Terror" on the other.[17] The ideological utility of these individual micronarratives, and others like them, is well documented; each has been told because it fits the expectations and ideals of the particular teller. Individually, these stories are various and fascinating, and I hope that readers will enjoy exploring some of their dazzling diversity in the pages of this book. Collectively, however, they make up the grand narrative of Western Civilisation and serve as the origin myth of the West.[18]

The West is not, of course, the only sociopolitical entity that has retrospectively constructed a narrative of its past that fits its needs and self-image in the present. The politicised reimagining of history is in fact pretty standard practice and has been going on as long as history itself has been written (and probably even long before this, through oral histories and community storytelling). It was said that in Athens in the sixth century BCE, lines were added to the Homeric *Iliad* to imply that Athens had controlled the island of Aegina in the age of heroes. Unsurprisingly, these lines were inserted at precisely the time that Athens was trying to control Aegina.[19] More recently, after the modern nation-state of Turkey was proclaimed in 1923, a complex historical and archaeological programme, known as the "Turkish History Thesis," was put into place to strengthen the identification between Turkishness and the landmass of Anatolia.[20] More recently still, under the leadership of Xi Jinping, a new official narrative about China's role in the Second World War has been aggressively promoted, in ways that may be worrying or encouraging depending on your point of view.[21] And in July 2021, as the Russian army massed at the Ukrainian border in advance of a military invasion, Russia's president, Vladimir Putin, published a treatise arguing the historical unity of the Russian and the Ukrainian peoples.

You do not necessarily have to be malicious or mendacious to want to rewrite history according to your political agenda, nor must you necessarily falsify history to do so. Rewriting the past can also take the form of choosing to include facts that were previously written out of a conventional narrative. In 2020, the National Trust in Britain published a report on the connections between colonialism, slavery, and the historic buildings in the Trust's care, further enflaming tensions in an already-heated national debate about Britain's imperial past.[22] On one side, some argue that uncomfortable histories of colonialism, slavery, and exploitation should feature more prominently in the school curriculum and as part of the public information available at museums and other heritage sites. While these arguments are driven by historical fact, they are also fundamentally political, underpinned by political principles and driven by a political agenda that argues for greater social justice and the recognition of historical wrongs. The opposing argument—that these uncomfortable topics should not be given more prominence, and that emphasis should instead be placed on positive themes—is also driven by a political agenda, albeit one that argues for maintenance of the status quo.

This debate demonstrates two important things. The first is that all history is political. Choosing to rewrite, reconsider, or revise the official history is a political act. But equally, choosing *not* to rewrite it is also a political act. The second important thing is that the historical facts themselves are not always under dispute. Rather, the debate can focus on *which* facts should be emphasised, where, and when. Reflecting on these two points, we must conclude that there is nothing intrinsically wrong with writing history from a political standpoint. Indeed, this is the *only* way that history can be written! But there *is* a problem if the history that you write contradicts the available facts.

This is one of the main problems with the grand narrative of Western Civilisation. The evidential basis for it has long crumbled, and while individual elements can be retained, the overall narrative is no longer consistent with the facts as we know them. Yet some in the West still cling to this grand narrative for its ideological value. This brings us to the second of the big problems with the grand narrative of Western Civilisation: its underpinning ideology no longer reflects the principles of the modern West. The guiding ideologies of Western society in the mid-twenty-first century are different from those of the mid-nineteenth when the grand narrative was at its zenith, and from those of the mid-eighteenth when the narrative was first emerging. For many people within the West today, notions of white racial superiority and imperialism no longer lie at the heart of Western identity. Instead they have been replaced with an ideology based on liberalism, social tolerance, and democracy. (There are also significant numbers of people within the West who disagree, and who would rather regress to the nineteenth-century model of Western identity, but I shall discuss them in more detail in the conclusion.)

We must rid ourselves of the grand narrative of Western Civilisation, putting it firmly aside as both factually incorrect and ideologically outdated. It is an origin myth that is no longer fit for purpose—it provides neither an accurate account of Western history nor an ideologically acceptable basis for Western identity. My aim in this book is therefore to tackle the grand narrative of Western Civilisation, first unpicking the micronarratives that comprise it, and then unpacking the ideological baggage that rests upon it. Due to my particular expertise and background, my focus is primarily on the imagined origins of the West.

Given that its subject is an abstraction (albeit an extremely powerful and significant one), a book like this could easily get stuck in the realms of the theoretical. To avoid this, I have grounded my narrative in the lives of fourteen real historical figures. Some might be familiar names, others less so. But from the enslaved poet to the exiled emperor, and from the diplomatic monk to the beleaguered bureaucrat, their stories give a new shape to Western history. In each chapter, I offer not only the story of one remarkable human life, but also an account of the times and places in which each individual lived, setting them for context in relation to other important figures of their age.

The first half of the book addresses the historical inaccuracies of Western Civilisation as a grand narrative, debunking the fantasy of a pure and unbroken cultural line by examining its supposed origins. The first two lives within it come from the classical world that is assumed to be the birthplace of the West, and demonstrate that neither the ancient Greeks nor the Romans saw themselves as partaking in an exclusively Western or European identity (Chapters 1 and 2). The next three biographies come from the supposed "Dark Ages" of the medieval period, exemplifying how the Greek and Roman legacies were embraced, rejected, and reimagined in its Islamic, central European, and Byzantine contexts respectively (Chapters 3, 4, and 5). The final two lives in this section take us to the Renaissance and the early modern period, where civilisational lines were drawn in various and conflicting ways—dividing the continent of Europe and the larger entity of Christendom in a manner that negates the notion of a coherent West (Chapters 6 and 7).

The second half of the book considers how Western Civilisation has functioned as an ideological tool and traces its emergence and development into the grand narrative that has become so familiar today. Within it, the first three chapters explore how changing ideas in the sixteenth and seventeenth centuries about religion and science, global expansion and imperialism, and the political contract contributed to the gradual emergence of the idea of Western Civilisation (Chapters 8, 9, and 10). The next pair of biographies captures how the idea of Western Civilisation developed into its mature form, providing an anchor for Western imperialism and pervasive systems of racial dominance (Chapters 11 and 12). The final pair of lives exemplify the two main challenges currently levelled at both the West and Western Civilisation—those of internal critics and external rivals—demonstrating the changing realities of the world we live in, and the urgent need for a wholesale rethinking of both the fundamental identity of the West and its origin myth of Western Civilisation (Chapters 13 and 14).

These fourteen lives are my equivalent of the bronze statues that so discomfited me in the Library of Congress. But unlike that particular set of imagined ancestors, the individuals whose lives I recount in this book have not been selected as the most important or influential people of their age. I make no claim in this book to present a "gallery of greats." Instead, my fourteen subjects are all people in whose lives and work we can see something of the zeitgeist; through whose experiences, actions, and writings we can discern changing ideas about civilisational inheritance and imagined cultural genealogies. These are, of course, not the only lives I could have chosen to focus on in this book, and I am sure that you each would choose differently were you to embark on a similar project. They do nonetheless serve to make my point. They demonstrate that the grand narrative of Western Civilisation is both manifestly untrue and ideologically bankrupt. They illustrate, at the scale of the individual human, why we must jettison this grand narrative once and for all. And they suggest a richer and more diverse set of historical lineages in which we should seek a new version of Western history to replace it with.

Chapter One

THE REJECTION
OF PURITY

HERODOTUS

*It is absolutely clear that the woman Europa herself
came from Asia, and that she never set foot on the lands
that are called "Europe" by the Greeks.*

HERODOTUS (LATE FIFTH CENTURY BCE)[1]

A MIGRANT stands on the beach. He looks out to sea, his mind
as well as his gaze reaching out towards his homeland, a continent and a lifetime away. He took his first steps into exile
years ago, sailing away from the rough coast of Turkey on an over-
crowded boat. He had been running from the persecutions of a tyrant

and the fury of a fundamentalist mob, hoping for a bright new future in Europe's most bustling and cosmopolitan city. But when he finally got to the great metropolis, his dreams quickly soured. Where he had once hoped for success, he encountered suspicion, and where he had once imagined opportunity, he found restriction. Later, when the government began to cultivate a hostile environment for migrants and instituted draconian new citizenship laws, he left. And so now here he stands—on another foreign beach, looking for another new start. Maybe this time, he will find what he is looking for.

This story could belong to any number of twenty-first-century migrants, but in this case it belongs to the first of this book's fourteen lives—that of the ancient Greek historian Herodotus. Of course, we can only speculate (as I have here) about how Herodotus felt when he arrived on the shores of southern Italy. Indeed, we know relatively little about the life of the man now widely regarded as the "Father of History." Born in the early fifth century BCE in Halicarnassus (now Bodrum in Turkey), he worked for some years in Athens before living out the final years of his life in the small town of Thurii on the Tarentine Gulf. And it was here, twice displaced and twice resettled, that he wrote his masterpiece the *Histories*.

The *Histories* is widely regarded as the earliest work of historical writing in the Western tradition. In the core of the book, Herodotus recounts how, in the years between 499 and 470 BCE (although he focuses mostly on the period 499–479 BCE), a coalition of Greek states fought off the invading armies of the Achaemenid Persian Empire. The Persians had superior numbers, resources, and organisation, and they controlled a vast empire that stretched from modern-day Bulgaria to Afghanistan, and from Egypt to the Black Sea. In contrast, there were hundreds of tiny independent communities that considered themselves to be (to a greater or lesser extent) Greek, squabbling incessantly with one another and eking out a meagre living from their separate territories. Yet against all expectations, the Greeks prevailed and successfully repelled the Persian invaders. It is a story that has captured imaginations across three millennia and remains enormously popular today.[2]

One of the reasons behind the enduring popularity of the *Histories* is its significance for the imagined history of the West. For many people, it has provided a founding charter for Western Civilisation, offering an ancient precedent for the modern notion of the "clash of civilisations." The opening lines of the prologue certainly seem to fit this script. Herodotus starts the *Histories* by stating explicitly that his aim is to record the great deeds of both Hellenes and barbarians (by which he means non-Greeks). This immediately implies a binary opposition between the two sides—Greeks and barbarians, Europe and Asia, the West and the East (or perhaps more accurately, the West and the Rest). Herodotus then goes on to offer a backstory, reaching into even more ancient history to set the scene for the conflict. It all started, he tells us, when Phoenician merchants abducted a princess from the Greek city of Argos. The Greeks responded by kidnapping a Phoenician princess, leading to a cycle of intercontinental rapes culminating with the abduction of Helen from Sparta, which led to the Trojan War. The ensuing destruction of Troy, according to Herodotus, was a disproportionate escalation, and it was this, he claims, that really set the Asians against the Greeks (Hdt 1:5).

Herodotus's prologue reads like an early version of the Western Civilisation narrative. The two key ingredients are there. First, we have two implacably opposed sides—Greece (for which, read "the West") and Asia (for which, read "the Rest"). Then we have the historical present being projected back onto past—the Persians conflated with the mythical Trojans, and the Greeks equated with the Achaeans who sacked Troy. Herodotus seems to give us not only an ancient account of "the clash of civilisations" but also an early formulation of the cultural genealogy of the West. At least, this is what he *seems* to give us.

Many readers have been taken in by this face-value reading of Herodotus. When Samuel Huntington wrote his controversial best-seller, *The Clash of Civilisations and the Remaking of the World Order*, he defined the key characteristics of a civilisation with reference to Herodotus.[3] According to the political scientist Anthony Pagden, Herodotus's subject in the *Histories* was "the perpetual enmity between Europe and Asia."[4] And when Zack Snyder released his film *300* in 2007, he sparked controversy by portraying Herodotus's Spartans as white-skinned, freedom-loving Europeans and the Persians as Asians and Africans characterised by both moral degeneracy and physical deformity.

That Herodotus has been misconstrued is understandable. There are indeed plenty of bits of the text that suggest a "clash of civilisations"–type of narrative. But there are also plenty of bits of the text that suggest the opposite. If we read Herodotus carefully, we find that he introduces the notion of a clash of civilisations only to undermine it. We discover that Herodotus did not divide the world into the West and the Rest, nor did he understand history as an unending replay of the same eternal conflict. In short, Herodotus did not invent an early version of the Western Civilisation narrative, nor did he see himself and the Greeks as belonging to a geo-cultural grouping that parallels the modern West. Rather, his entire life's work points in the opposite direction. It is one of history's ironies that, two and a half millennia after his death, Herodotus has so often been used to promote the very ideology of "us vs. them" that he tried to discredit.

Father of History, Father of Lies

Although we sometimes know him now as the "Father of History," Herodotus was not the first historian.[5] Mesopotamian historiography predates him by more than a millennium, and the first historical works in the ancient Greek language appeared almost two hundred years before he was born.[6] But while Herodotus did not invent history, he did do a good job of reinventing it. He focused less on the telling of sequential events and more on patterns of historical causality, shifting the emphasis from the "what" to the "why."[7]

The *Histories* do, of course, offer an account of *what* happened in the Greco-Persian Wars, detailing the various events and episodes of the conflict. The story broadly runs thus: The fighting broke out with the Ionian Revolt in 499 BCE, a rebellion against the Persian Empire led by the Ionian Greek cities of Asia Minor and supported by the Athenians (as well as other Greek city-states in the Aegean). The rebellion was eventually crushed, and the Persians began to look westwards. When the Persian king Darius launched an invasion of peninsular Greece in 492 BCE, he was defeated by an Athenian-led force at the Battle of Marathon. With revolts elsewhere in the empire, it was a full decade before the second Persian invasion of Greece was launched, in 480 BCE, this time under Darius's son Xerxes. As it marched down through the Greek peninsula, Xerxes's army was briefly checked at Thermopylae, where three hundred Spartans famously made their last stand. But the Persians eventually reached Athens and sacked it, killing many of its inhabitants and carrying off its greatest treasures. Then in a surprising turn of events, the Persians suffered a catastrophic double defeat—first at sea at the Battle of Salamis, and then on land at the Battle of Plataea. With their forces in disarray and the ruins of Athens smouldering behind them, they decided to cut their losses and return home.

Why did things turn out this way? In order to get at this slippery question, Herodotus found himself expanding his view ever outwards—opening up a broader and broader perspective and setting events in a wider and wider context. You can't really understand why

Persia sacked Athens, he reasoned, unless you appreciate the backstory of Perso-Athenian diplomatic relations. And you cannot fully appreciate Perso-Athenian diplomatic relations unless you know something of the internal political structures of both states. And you cannot really grasp the internal political structures of any state without having some sense of that state's history, its development, and ultimately its origins. As you can imagine, the tendrils of Herodotean explanation reached ever outwards.

As a result, the *Histories* offers us not only an account of the Greco-Persian Wars, but also Herodotus's ideas about Persian history (although some of this is evidently based as much on conjecture as it is on solid evidence), including the foundation of the empire and an explanation of its administration. The narrative also spirals out into vivid ethnographic descriptions of Persian culture and society, as well as individual biographies and character studies of key figures from Persian history. Herodotus offers this rich level of detail not only for the Persians, but also for each of the many peoples who lived within the Persian Empire, from the Egyptians in the south to the Scythians in the north, and from the Indians in the east to the Greeks in the west. Herodotus's treatment of the Greeks is, of course, somewhat different from his treatment of other groups. Writing in the Greek language for a primarily Greek audience, Herodotus did not need to explain the basics of Greek culture and customs. But he did recount the individual histories of several Greek states, discussing their unique trajectories of development and highlighting each nation's particular characters.

This focus on the "why" led to his *Histories* being both grand in scope (its content spanning many hundreds of years and thousands of kilometres) and rich in detail (with anecdotes ranging from the sex lives of kings to the maritime mishaps of fishermen). So while Herodotus ostensibly recounts the story of the Greco-Persian Wars, in the telling of it he treats us to a great smorgasbord of historiographical delicacies, including ethnographic exposition (did you know that the Scythians buried their kings only after wrapping them in wax?)[8] and philosophical debate (such as the time when the Persians discussed the best form of government—interestingly, they eventually decided on monarchy by *voting* for it!),[9] geographical theorising (Herodotus waded in, both literally and figuratively, on the debate about the source of the Nile River)[10] and investigative journalism (thanks to an anonymous source, we hear of secret messages passed by means of hidden tattoos).[11]

The richness and variety of the *Histories* led—perhaps inevitably—to the second of Herodotus's nicknames. While Cicero, writing some four centuries after Herodotus's death, may have called him the "Father of History," some two centuries later still, Plutarch dubbed him the "Father of Lies."[12] Plutarch felt that Herodotus's stories were simply too fantastical, too whimsical, and too unashamedly entertaining to be factually true. On this point, Plutarch is partly right. Some of Herodotus's stories are certainly far-fetched—such as the tale of the gold-digging ants of India, or the rumour that some people living in the Sahara had dogs' heads.[13] Other strange-sounding tales might have originally started off as cultural misunderstandings. One likely candidate for this is the story that Scythians milk their mares by blowing air into their vaginas with bone flutes; another is the idea that Babylonian women all served as temple prostitutes at least once in their lives.[14] But Herodotus himself knew that not all of his tales were factually accurate. He often prefaced his more fantastical stories with elaborate disavowals, presenting them not in his own authorial voice but as a secondhand report. Such passages are peppered with phrases such as "some people say . . ." or "the locals claim . . ." Herodotus did not believe everything he heard, and he did not expect his audience to either.

A healthy dose of critical close reading would not, however, have done much to salve Plutarch's ire. He had a deeper reason for suspecting

Herodotus. Fundamentally, he found the *Histories* far too evenhanded towards the Persians, and far too positive in its portrayal of non-Greeks. Herodotus, according to Plutarch, was quite obviously a *philobarbaros* (a lover of barbarians), and nothing he wrote could ever be trusted. Just as problematic was Herodotus's willingness to criticise the Greeks. For while he described the bloodthirsty madness of the Persian Cambyses and the hubristic cruelty of Xerxes,[15] he also wrote about the selfish ambitions of the Milesian nobleman Aristagoras and the greed of the Athenian general Themistocles.[16] For the patriotic Plutarch, living in a Greece that had been reduced to a province of the Roman Empire, this was an affront to his nostalgic ideal of Hellenism.

So, who was Herodotus really—the Father of History or the Father of Lies? Was he a fantasist, a barbarian apologist, and a wily spinner of tall tales? Or was he a scientific innovator, pushing the limits of human knowledge by reconceptualising the human relationship with the past? Perhaps most importantly for us in this book, did he formulate an early vision of the proto-West that forms the basis for our modern notion of the West today? Did Herodotus give us our blueprint for the grand narrative of Western Civilisation? The answers to these questions lie somewhere between the life story of Herodotus the human and the literary texts of Herodotus the historian. But for all the richness of the biographies he writes in the *Histories*, we know frustratingly little about the life of its author.

We know that Herodotus was born in the mid-fifth century BCE in Halicarnassus, on the Aegean coast of what is now Turkey. Although Halicarnassus was officially a Greek *polis* (city-state), it had a mixed population and also celebrated an indigenous Anatolian heritage.[17] Herodotus's own family offers an illustration of the city's cultural mix. The name "Herodotus" is Greek, as is the name of his mother, Dryo. Yet several other members of the family had names derived from the

Anatolian language of Carian, including Herodotus's father, Lyxes, and his cousin the poet Panyassis.[18]

As a young man, Herodotus may have been more interested in politics than history. He had some kind of disagreement with Lygdamis, the hereditary ruler of the city,[19] and was forced to flee to the nearby island of Samos. At some stage Herodotus returned, became involved in the coup that toppled Lygdamis, and supported the establishment of a new regime in the city. But before long, he was forced out again—this time by the anger of a pro-Lygdamian mob. In the years that followed, Herodotus seems to have made good use of his exile, travelling widely across the ancient world.[20] Peppered throughout the *Histories* we find personal anecdotes and eyewitness stories. Herodotus tells us that he explored the sights of Egypt, sailing down the Nile as far as Elephantine; marvelled at the busy harbours and cosmopolitan markets of Phoenician Tyre; and saw with his own eyes the fabulous decorations of the temples of Babylon. If his writings are to be believed, Herodotus would have been an exhausting travel companion—quizzing tour guides for information, haggling with street vendors, and bothering everyone from local dignitaries to humble water sellers for their stories. Perhaps unsurprisingly, his writing also demonstrates an intimate familiarity with Anatolia, including not only its Aegean coasts in the west but also its northern regions bordering the Black Sea and the area of the Hellespont. On the Greek mainland, he seems to have firsthand knowledge of several areas including Sparta, Delphi, and Boeotia, as well as, of course, Athens.

The Greek world may have been politically fragmented in the mid-fifth century BCE, but Athens was its undisputed cultural capital.[21] This was the age of the statesman Pericles and the philosopher Socrates, the sculptor Pheidias and the dramatist Euripides. The city was home to cosmopolitan intellectuals and political radicals, celebrity courtesans and millionaire playboys. The markets teemed with traders from three continents, the temples were thronged with pilgrims, and craftspeople came from far and wide to work on the lavish new buildings on the acropolis. Like fin de siècle Vienna, New York in the Roaring Twenties, or London in the swinging sixties, Athens in the fifth century BCE was a magnet for the creative and the ambitious. For Herodotus, it must have been irresistible.

When he arrived in the great metropolis, Herodotus seems to have fallen in with the literary set fairly rapidly, developing a particularly close friendship with the tragedian Sophocles.[22] We know that Herodotus staged a number of public readings of his own work, apparently earning the eye-popping sum of ten talents for one especially successful performance (for context, at the time a single talent would have covered a month's pay for the entire crew of a trireme in the Athenian navy).[23] Yet for all his success, he left Athens after only a few years, forsaking his new friends and abandoning his burgeoning career. And this brings him to where we first met him at the start of this chapter—standing on the shores of the Tarentine Gulf in southern Italy, preparing to make his final home at Thurii.

What drove Herodotus to leave Athens, abandoning his dreams of fame and fortune in the big city? Why did he—at the moment when he might be said to have "had it all"—suddenly give everything up and emigrate once more? Of course, any number of personal factors may have influenced his decision. But Athenian politics were likely also part of the equation—a radical new politics built on empire, xenophobia, and the invention of a narrative that looks a bit like that of Western Civilisation.

The Shape of the World

The modern nation-state of Greece is now more than two hundred years old and can boast a rich and colourful history.[24] But modern

Greece is not the same as ancient Greece.[25] At the time that Herodotus lived and wrote in the fifth century BCE, the Greeks were not united within a single state or nation. Instead, the Greek world was composed of thousands of *poleis* (city-states) and microterritories, each with its own independent government.[26] These states were usually fiercely independent and had strong individual identities, with many Greeks thinking of themselves first and foremost as Athenians, Corinthians, Spartans, and so forth. Sometimes, groups of Greek states would join together in regional alliances or federal unions, but they usually maintained their individual identities within them.[27] It was not until the conquests of Alexander of Macedon, about a hundred years after the time of Herodotus, that large numbers of Greeks across broad swathes of territory were brought under a single Greek government (although plenty at the time questioned how "Greek" their Macedonian rulers really were).[28] But even this Greek mega-state did not incorporate the Greeks of the Black Sea, nor those of the central and western Mediterranean.

As well as being politically fragmented, the Greeks of Herodotus's day were also geographically dispersed. In the late fifth century BCE, there were Greek poleis ranged around the Mediterranean and Black Sea, from Spain to Cyprus, and from Libya to the Crimea. Remains of their communities can be found today at Marseille in France and Naucratis in Egypt, strung along the Mediterranean coast of Turkey from Adana to Istanbul, and ringing the Black Sea from Poti in Georgia to Sozopol in Bulgaria.[29]

We might well wonder what held these diverse communities together, given that they were both politically independent and geographically dispersed. Even ancient commentators disagreed over who and what was Greek. According to Demosthenes, the Macedonians were not real Greeks, but then neither were the Athenians, in Herodotus's view, because they were descended from non-Greek "barbarians."[30] To complicate matters further, the ancient Greeks never actually called themselves "Greeks." The term was coined by the Romans, who used the Latin word *Graeci* to refer to them as a collective. Rather, the Greeks used the word *Hellenes*, referring to themselves as descendants of the mythic figure Hellen. (Hellen should not be confused with Helen; one was the legendary forefather of the ancient Greeks, the other was the woman at the heart of the Trojan War.)

The self-definition of Hellenes is therefore genealogical—linked to the idea of a shared history and a shared ancestor. We must be wary, however, of thinking of Greekness as a form of ethnicity in our modern sense of the term. The ancient Hellenes were not a coherent ethnic group, set apart from other ethnic groups by a clear boundary. For the ancient Greeks, genealogies were a means to link people together, with plural origins baked into their fundamental structure.[31] Myths about a shared Hellenic bloodline were therefore combined with claims to alternative, non-Hellenic genealogies. The people of Thebes, for example, named the Phoenician hero Cadmus as their civic founder. The Argives claimed to be descended from the daughters of the Egyptian king Danaus. The Arcadians and the Athenians both made the somewhat strange claim that they were autochthonous—born out of the very land they inhabited. Some Greeks claimed that they shared ancestors with the Persians, the Jews, and the Romans. We shouldn't take these genealogies at face value (nor should we assume that the ancient Greeks necessarily did so). Like all foundation myths, these were deliberate statements of identity and affiliation, shaped by an ideal of what people wanted to be as much as by what they actually were. And yet, these genealogies do tell us something about the ancient Greek mindset. While the idea of sharing a common Hellenic bloodline was certainly important, few ancient Greeks thought of this bloodline as being pure.[32]

Something else that bound the Greek *poleis* together, perhaps even more than the imagined Hellenic bloodline, was a consciousness of common culture. There was the Greek language and script, as well as its attendant literary traditions and a rich body of shared myths and stories. There was the structure of Olympian polytheism, involving similar forms of religious ritual and cult practices from city to city, not to mention similar ideas about what made a suitable-looking temple. And there were shared customs and patterns of daily life, with remarkably similar ideas about things as diverse as the makeup of the nuclear family, social rules, educational norms, architectural traditions, and craftworking practices. A big part of being Greek was about doing Greek things in a Greek sort of way. As the orator Isocrates noted in the fourth century BCE, "the name of Hellene is applied to those who share our culture rather than to those who share a common blood" (*Panegyricus* 4:50). Herodotus himself formulated Greek identity (to *Hellenikōn*) as defined partly by blood, but just as much by "shared speech, common shrines and sacrifices of the gods, and shared lifestyles" (Hdt 8.144).[33]

There were of course local traditions within this broader Greek culture.[34] In such a dispersed and diverse Greek world, how could there not be? While the ideal woman in Athens was quiet and stayed mostly at home, her Spartan counterpart was an outdoorsy athlete. While people in Clazomenae buried their dead individually in beautifully painted terra-cotta sarcophagi, in Corinth they interred them in collective rock-cut chamber tombs.[35] And whereas on Sicily the goddess Artemis was worshipped as a nubile young woman ready for marriage, at Ephesus she appeared as a powerful mistress of the animals, her neck hung with severed bulls' testicles.[36] Many of these local variations stemmed from engagement with non-Greek cultures. We have already seen how indigenous Anatolians were an integral part of the Greek polis at Halicarnassus, but similar levels of interculturalism appear across the Greek world. In Pithekoussai in the Bay of Naples, Greek cultural traits could be found alongside Phoenician, Etruscan, and other Italic elements.[37] And at Naucratis, Greeks from a wide range of home cities rubbed shoulders with Egyptians, Libyans, and Arabs.[38] Hybridised styles, practices, and identities emerged and fed back into the conscious sense of cultural commonality that lay at the heart of Greekness.

Yet we must not fall into the trap of thinking that the ancient Greek world was a utopia of cultural and ethnic pluralism, with space under the broad tent of Hellenism for all. Racism and xenophobia were commonplace, and thinkers as eminent as Aristotle argued that it was natural for Greeks to enslave non-Greeks, because of their inborn superiority. Interestingly, this superiority complex was not structured on a sense of West versus East. Rather, Aristotle felt that the Greek world was distinct from both West and East, superior to both Europe and Asia. He argued that: "The peoples of the cold places and around Europe are full of spirit, but more lacking in intelligence and skill; and so it results that they are free, but are politically disorganized and not able to rule their neighbours. Those of Asia are intelligent and skillful of mind but spiritless; and so it results that they are ruled over and enslaved. But the race of the Hellenes, because they are located in the middle, get the best of both—and are both brave and clever."[39]

Ancient Greek ideas about the continents were, quite evidently, different from ours. They also varied. Not everyone agreed with Aristotle that the lands fringing the Mediterranean and Black Seas (i.e., the lands inhabited by Greeks) lay in the middle space between the continents. Herodotus felt that the whole idea of having continental divisions was ridiculous, as we shall see later.

For much of ancient Greek history, however, the most pressing divisions were not those that separated Greeks from non-Greeks, but rather those that drew distinctions between different Greek groups. It is one of these that I suspect had a profound impact on Herodotus's life, compelling him to leave Athens for the relative peace and quiet of

Thurii. Thanks to the version of history that makes up the grand narrative of Western Civilisation, when we think of Athens, we tend to imagine it as the birthplace of democracy, the place where the rule of the people (*demokratia*) and equality before the law (*isonomia*) were pioneered. While this is certainly in part true, the reality of Athenian democracy fell far short of the modern principles of liberal democracy that we now associate with the West. For a start, women were excluded, as were the thousands of enslaved people on whose labour the Athenian economy depended.[40] Furthermore, while Athens may have professed equality for its own male citizens, it certainly did not do so for anyone else. Whether they were Greeks from other cities or non-Greek entirely, any non-Athenians were treated as foreign outsiders. Classical Athenian democracy was not the inclusive, egalitarian institution that it is sometimes imagined to be. Rather, it was an exclusive boys' club, open only to those born into the "right" kinds of families.

The cultural dynamism of Athens in the fifth century BCE rested not on enlightened political equality but on imperialism.[41] The Athenian empire grew out of the alliance of Greek states that had fought against the Persians during the Greco-Persian Wars. Athens quickly claimed sole leadership of this alliance, leveraging both the sympathy felt by other Greeks after the Persian sack of their city and the gratitude earned by Athenian valour at the Battles of Marathon and Salamis. But leadership of an alliance rapidly turned into control. Annual payments were demanded, and defecting "allies" were treated ruthlessly. The lucky ones had their cities sacked, their walls razed, their politicians exiled or executed, Athenian garrisons imposed, and pro-Athenian puppet governments installed. The unlucky ones, like the island state of Melos, suffered the ultimate punishment—all adult men were killed, and the women and children sold into slavery.[42]

Back home in Athens, the public mood was triumphalist. In 453 BCE, the statesman Pericles erected two giant stone inscriptions on the acropolis, each almost four metres in height, displaying the amounts paid in tribute by each city to Athens. This was Athenian supremacy advertised on a billboard. Two years later, he tightened the law on Athenian citizenship, restricting it to those who could claim two citizen parents (rather than just one, as had been the case previously), at a stroke disenfranchising many people who had been citizens all their lives.[43]

As the fifth century BCE went on, the gulf between Athenians and other Greeks widened. Athenians began to see themselves as different, special, and fundamentally better. We can see this in the reorganisation of the city's main religious festival—the Panathenaia. While Athenian citizens enjoyed the festival, resident foreigners were required to participate in subordinate roles serving the Athenians—as tray bearers, water carriers, parasol holders, and stool holders.[44] Towards the end of the century, the dramatist Euripides staged a play that reimagined Athenian origins. Traditional mythology held that the Athenians were descended from autochthons on one side and from the hero Hellen on the other—thereby making them part of the wider Hellenic family. But in the *Ion*, Euripides revised the mythical genealogy by replacing Hellen with the god Apollo, swapping the Hellenic ancestry of the Athenians for a divine one. In the work of Euripides, Athenian exceptionalism didn't just mean that they were better than other Greeks—it meant that they were not even Greeks at all.

How did Athens get away with this? In addition to its near monopoly on naval force, Athens embarked on an aggressive propaganda campaign to persuade other Greeks that their "alliance" with Athens was necessary. None of the Greeks could afford to let down their guard, the Athenians argued, lest the dastardly Persians return. Athenian naval dominance was necessary, they asserted, to provide the Greeks

with protection against the ever-present Persian threat. Athenian prop-
agandists whipped up hatred of the Persians, promoting a stereotype
of the Oriental barbarian as effeminate, luxury loving, and cowardly,
but also treacherous, deceitful, and wily.[45] In contrast, the Greeks were
manly, tough, and courageous; honourable in their dealings with others; and straightforward in their pursuit of personal liberty. You will
encounter these stereotypes if you pick up a copy of Isocrates's legal
speeches, watch a performance of Aeschylus's tear-jerking tragedy *The
Persians*, or look at the hundreds of red-figure Athenian vases depicting Greek warriors defeating feeble Persian opponents. According to
this stereotype, the Persians were enemies of the Greeks not just in the
present but also throughout history. Persians were consistently presented alongside or as Trojans, melding the legendary past and the
contemporary present of Asia into one.[46] It was fifth-century BCE Athens that pioneered the "clash of civilisations" rhetoric, and it did so as
a tool of Greek-on-Greek imperialism.

If this all sounds familiar, that's because you have heard it before.
In the modern West, it is hard to avoid the stereotypes of effeminate
but cunning Asian people that recur sporadically in popular culture. We see them in the literature of European imperialism, as famously pointed out by Edward Said (for which, see Chapter 13), but
also in Hollywood movies, bestselling novels, and newspaper cartoons depicting Chinese officials (for which, see Chapter 14). In our
modern times, this image of the non-Western "other" is set up in the
mirror image of the idealised Westerner through a series of conceptual oppositions—West versus East, masculine versus feminine,
strong versus weak, brave versus cowardly, light-skinned versus
dark-skinned. In the West today, it is a rhetoric that sits uncomfortably
beneath the surface of acceptable political discourse, occasionally
bubbling to the surface. In fifth-century BCE Athens, this racism was
mainstream.

The mid-fifth century BCE in Athens is rightly seen as a golden age of culture, literature, arts, and democracy. But these achievements were the fruits of empire—an empire built on the backs of other Greeks and justified through racist propaganda that cast outsiders and non-Greeks as dangerously "other" and which created a "brand" for Athens as the epitome of idealised Greekness.[47] Living in Athens, Herodotus must have been acutely aware of this.[48] The environment was becoming increasingly hostile. Toxic subjects such as racial purity, national superiority, and the exclusion of migrants now dominated Athenian politics. Should we really be surprised that someone like Herodotus, a bicultural migrant from Asia, no longer felt at home? Should we be surprised that he set out over the waves once more, coming to rest on the Italian beach where we first encountered him at the start of this chapter? And should we be surprised that when he sat down to write his masterwork, he designed it as a spectacular riposte to the ideologies that had brought him there?

The Enquiries

It must have taken Herodotus years to finish the *Histories*. Indeed, its structure suggests it was composed in several discrete episodes, stitched together later into a larger overarching structure. So while he may have written some sections of the *Histories* in Athens, it was probably in Thurii that Herodotus realised his vision for the work as a whole. This vision is set out in the famous prologue, which we have already mentioned, in which Herodotus introduces what he calls his "Enquiries" (in Greek "*historiē*"):

This is the setting-out of the enquiries of Herodotus of Halikarnassos, so that the things accomplished by people might not fade away

over time, and that the great and wondrous deeds displayed both by
Hellenes and barbarians might not lose their glory—including
amongst other things the cause of their waging war with each other.[49]

The interpretation of these lines might seem pretty clear. We are confronted with the opposition between Greeks and barbarians (i.e., all non-Greeks), an apparent clash of civilisations. As I have also already described, Herodotus then gives us the backstory of intercontinental enmity as a series of kidnappings, culminating in the abduction of Helen and the sack of Troy. So far, so familiar. But it is what Herodotus says immediately after this that we need to look at more closely.

All these stories, Herodotus tells us, are unreliable myths. He explicitly dismisses them in the same way as he will later dismiss outrageous tales from the gold-digging ants to the dog-headed men. Crucially, he does not recount the mythical rapes in his own authorial voice but puts them into the mouths of others, claiming, "Persian writers say it was the Phoenicians who started the dispute." He then casts further doubt on the stories by reporting an alternative tale told by the Phoenicians, telling the audience that "the Phoenicians do not agree with the Persians." For Herodotus, the idea of an ancient hatred rooted in the mythical distant past was not only preposterous but also incoherent—a set of self-contradicting fables spouted by unreliable storytellers, each for their own purposes.

If we really want to understand Greek-Persian enmity, he suggests, we must look to historically verifiable events in the much more recent past, starting with the "first barbarian who subdued the Hellenes and made them pay tribute." This, according to Herodotus, was the Lydian king Croesus, best known today for his fabulous wealth.[50] In contrast to the ridiculous myths told by others, Herodotus is careful to specify that his own enquiries—his own *historiē*—start with this act of imperial domination. At one level, he is of course writing about the suppression of the Ionians of Asia Minor by the neighbouring Lydians. But for his original audience, his choice of language would have had a much more contemporary resonance. In the fifth century BCE, it was not barbarians who had "subdued the Hellenes and made them pay tribute," but the Athenians. The word used by Herodotus here for tribute is *phoros*—a technical term specifically coined by the Athenians to refer to the tribute paid to them by their "allies."[51] The word did not exist at the time of Croesus, a century earlier, and would have stood out as a startling anachronism. It was a choice of vocabulary that would have been political dynamite.

If we read Herodotus's prologue carefully, it is therefore not conflict between Greeks and non-Greeks that emerges as the main subject of interest. The "causes of waging war with each other" are indeed included as a topic, but only "amongst other things." Rather, foremost in his mind, and indeed in the *Histories* as a whole, are the "things accomplished by people"—specifically, the "great and wondrous deeds displayed by both Hellenes and barbarians." The evenhandedness of this statement is remarkable. It is not just Greeks who perform great deeds, but non-Greeks too. And the accomplishments that Herodotus seeks to document for posterity are, fundamentally, those of "people" (or in his own word, *anthropoi*). Not only does Herodotus state this in his prologue, he carries it through across the *Histories* as a whole. In its pages, we hear about the generosity of Egyptian pharaohs and the heroism of Scythian queens, the ingenuity of Babylonian engineers and the attractiveness of Ethiopian men.[52] The main focus of Herodotus's *Histories* is celebrating the great things that people did—*all* people, not just Greeks.

So when Herodotus introduces the idea of an opposition between Greeks and Asians in his prologue, he doesn't do it because he agrees with it. He introduces the idea so that he can critique it, subvert it, and demonstrate with example after example that it is false. The Greeks, he argues, were themselves the recipients of cultural influences from more ancient cultures in western Asia. The oldest of all civilisations, he suggests, was that of the Phrygians of Anatolia, the inventors of the earliest human language (Hdt 2:2). He tells us that another Anatolian people, the Lydians, introduced the Greeks to the idea of coinage and commerce, as well as giving them many of their games and pastimes (Hdt 1:94), whereas the technology of writing and the alphabet was brought to Greece by the Phoenicians (Hdt 5:58). But it was the Egyptians to whom the Greeks owed the most. Knowledge about the gods came from Egypt to Greece (Hdt 2:50), along with a whole host of religious customs (Hdt 2:51), as well as the reckoning of calendars, the science of astrology, and the practice of divination (Hdt 2:81). Greek culture, Herodotus tells us, was anything but purely Greek.

For Herodotus, it was not just the cultural bloodline of the Greeks that was mixed—their biological bloodlines were too. He claimed that the two most powerful Greek states of the time, Sparta and Athens, belonged to different ethnic groups and had distinct genealogies (Hdt 1:56). The Spartans came from the true Hellenic stock but were a migratory people (the word Herodotus uses is *polyplanētos*, or "much-wandering"). In contrast, the Athenians were not really Greeks at all, but were instead descended from the non-Greek Pelasgians (Hdt 1:58). Other Greek city-states, Herodotus claims, had equally hybrid bloodlines. The Ionian cities of his home region were at least as much native Anatolian as they were Greek (Hdt 1:147–48), the Argives were the offspring of Egyptian women (Hdt 2:91, 4:53, 4:182), the Peloponnese owed its name to an immigrant Phrygian (Hdt 7:11), and the Thebans of central Greece were descended from Phoenicians (Hdt 5:182). Equally, some non-Greeks could claim a partial Greek ancestry, including the Scythians (Hdt 4:8–10) and even the Persians, who were sometimes said to be descended from the Greek hero Perseus (Hdt 7:150).

For Herodotus, the Greeks were set apart neither by their culture nor by their blood. Neither were they distinct when it came to their ethics and principles. In the pages of the *Histories*, some Greeks do indeed profess their love for freedom—an ideal we now tend to associate with the modern West. The word for freedom (*eleutheria*) appears several times in the context of Greeks seeking freedom from Persian oppression (e.g., Hdt 1:170, 5:2, 7:135, 8:143, 9:98). And yet it also appears in wholly non-Greek contexts, suggesting that Persians, Egyptians, and other non-Greeks could also be motivated by the love of freedom (e.g., Hdt 1:95, 2:102, 3:82, 7:2). Perhaps most surprisingly, the word is also used in the context of Greek-on-Greek warfare, suggesting that freedom could be lost not only to barbarians but also at the hands of fellow Greeks (e.g., Hdt 1:61, 3:142, 6:5). This word would have seemed especially apt at the time when Herodotus was writing, at the height of the Peloponnesian Wars between Athens and Sparta, when smaller Greek cities often found themselves suffering as collateral damage in the conflict.

Herodotus offers perhaps his starkest objections to the "clash of civilisations" model in his treatment of continental geography. "I laugh," he says dismissively, "at those who draw maps of the world, not using their brains to do it," pointing out that the division of the world into Europe and Asia was particularly ridiculous (Hdt 4:37). The notion of dividing up what he saw as "one world" into separate continents was unnecessary, and the idea of designating these continents by random female names was downright absurd (Hdt 4:45). Herodotus's stance makes sense given that he was himself both a transcontinental migrant and a political refugee. In his experience, Europe and Asia were not so different. Both continents were peopled by the cruel and the friendly, the bigoted and the welcoming. In both continents you could find not only Greeks and non-Greeks, but people who, like Herodotus himself, were a little bit of both.

Herodotus did not describe the world in stark terms of "us and them," instead undermining this distinction from the perspective of culture, genealogy, ethnics, and geography. But there were some ancient Greeks who saw things differently. Plutarch was certainly amongst them, as were the Athenian imperial ideologues of the fifth century BCE. But Herodotus cannot be counted among their number. He painted the world in technicolour rather than black-and-white. With his vision of a rich and plural humanity, marked by cultural complexity and mixing, Herodotus was evoking the world of his own youth in Halicarnassus. But he was also explicitly rejecting the xenophobic world of fifth-century BCE Athens. His *Histories*, with all its dizzying diversity, offers a vision of a much more plural and complex ancient world. It stands in sharp contrast to the picture of Greek antiquity that we find in the grand narrative of Western Civilisation, one that sees the ancient Greeks as the originators of a purely European and racially white civilisational line. Herodotus would have shuddered to think of it.

———————

TO ASSUME THAT the classical Greek world was an early version of the West is to misunderstand it entirely. For a start, the modern West has been historically focused on Europe, the European-descended states of North America, and the wider Anglosphere. In contrast, the ancient Greeks did not think of themselves as Europeans. Indeed, as evident from the writings of both Aristotle and Herodotus, Europe was often associated with barbarity. Another connotation of the modern West, often unspoken in polite society, is of racial whiteness in contrast to non-Westerners, who are often racialised as black, brown, or yellow. In contrast, while ancient Hellenic identity was partly defined by common descent and ethnicity, this was not expressed in terms of physiognomic differences and certainly never by skin colour. Skin colour was simply not as important in the ancient Greek world as it is in our own, and while it was sometimes an identity marker for some groups (Gauls were often noted for their milky-coloured skin, and Ethiopians for their darkness), it did not play an important role in the ancient discourse of Greekness.[53]

One ideological model that is found in both the ancient Greek world and the modern West is that of a binary cultural opposition between "us" and "them." In the ancient Greek world, this was the opposition between Hellene and barbarian, conceived as an ancient conflict that stretched back through the generations, contrasting a brave, virile, freedom-loving "us" with a cowardly, feminized, and subservient "them." Although it might be an extreme characterisation, the same basic conceptual model underlies the modern ideology of an opposition between the West and the Rest. This is not because the modern West has passively inherited its conceptual model from ancient Greece, but because the model does the same conceptual work and fulfils the same political function in both instances—serving an expansionist, racist, and patriarchal ideology. As we shall see in the later chapters of this book, the rise of the West as a concept, and the invention of its history as Western Civilisation, was at the outset also an ideological tool deployed in the service of empire. It has since morphed into different forms and held different social and cultural meanings, but it did originally emerge in an imperial context. The same is true of the politically weaponized Hellenism of the Athenian empire.[54]

This was a vision of Greek identity and of cultural difference that Herodotus rejected, writing his *Histories* as a powerful rebuttal of the Greek-barbarian opposition. Herodotus conceived of a much more fluid and changeable world, where the distinctions that divided people along lines of culture, ethnicity, principles, and geography were blurred. Given his own life experience, this must have been the world as he saw it. And he was not alone. Homer describes the Trojan War not as a clash of civilisations but as a conflict between closely related groups, bound together not only by shared culture and customs but also by intermarriage and family ties.[55] The tragedies of Euripides turn the tables again, asking who is really barbaric in their behaviour, the Greeks or the non-Greeks?[56] And the historian Thucydides describes common Hellenic identity as a relatively recent invention, an uneasy umbrella over groups that had a variety of different origins.[57]

The grand narrative of Western Civilisation posits the origins of the West in the ancient Greek world, but not in the ancient Greek world as it truly was—the vibrant and dynamic world of Herodotus, Homer, and Thucydides. Instead, it adheres to the vision of ancient Greece promoted by Athenian politicians such as Pericles as a justification for its own imperial expansion, a world riven by a great divide between "us" and "them." It was a vision not shared by the subjects of our next chapter, the people who are usually cast as the successors of the Greeks and the next in the genealogical line of Western Civilisation.

Chapter Two

THE ASIAN EUROPEANS

LIVILLA

*In honour of Livilla of the line of Anchises, who is like
the goddess Aphrodite, and who produced the most and
the greatest contributions to this most divine lineage*

INSCRIPTION FROM ILIUM (18–19 CE)[1]

L IVILLA was famously beautiful. She was also ruthless and ambitious, the favourite granddaughter of Rome's first emperor, Augustus. Her life was mapped out in early childhood. She was expected to grow up, marry well, and rule the Roman Empire with her husband at her side. The trouble was that Livilla's husbands had a tendency to die young, and in suspicious circumstances.[2] Not that this explains the inscription at the start of this chapter.[3] Honorific inscriptions are not, in themselves, unusual. Cities across the empire dedicated similar inscriptions to various members of the imperial family in the hope of attracting imperial patronage. But the specific form of this inscription, with its emphasis on lineage and genealogy, is curious. Why would the inhabitants of a provincial backwater in northwestern Turkey erect an honorific inscription that described Livilla in this particular way?

The answer lies in the history of this particular backwater. At the start of the first century CE, Ilium was a small city of little strategic or practical importance, its economy largely relying on its unremarkable agricultural production. By the end of the century, it was a thriving cultural centre as well as a political powerhouse. This change in fortunes was due to the patronage that Ilium received from the ascendant Roman Empire, patronage that stemmed from its illustrious mythological heritage. While this heritage would have been conjured for a Roman audience in the word "Ilium," in the modern world we tend to know the place by its alternative name—Troy.

In antiquity as it is today, the site was a magnet for tourists. The Persian king Xerxes is said to have stopped for a visit while on his way to Greece. Alexander the Great stayed for several days, making sacrifices and holding athletic competitions to honour the fallen heroes of the *Iliad*. And in the middle of the first century, Julius Caesar came to Troy to make a political statement. This statement had less to do with the famous myths of the Trojan War and more to do with the myth of what happened afterwards. The story runs that the survivors of the sacked city fled; that the Trojan refugees, led by the pious Trojan prince Aeneas, eventually ended up in central Italy (after a tragic stay with Queen Dido in Carthage); and that Aeneas's descendants, the twins Romulus and Remus, eventually founded the city of Rome.[4]

This myth might initially seem strange to modern ears. It may seem counterintuitive that the Romans, so often invoked today in the rhetoric of European genealogy in general and that of the European Union in particular, would claim an Asian rather than a European origin.[5] It may seem equally counterintuitive that the Romans, with all their military might and imperial power, saw themselves as the descendants of refugees, the losing side in the most famous war of antiquity. The idea has seemed particularly jarring over the last decade or so, as Italy struggles to cope with the influx of desperate refugees trying to reach its shores seeking safety, prosperity, and a new life. The parallels between these contemporary refugees and the myth of Aeneas and his Trojans are obvious, a fact that has prompted some angry outbursts from Italian anti-immigration groups, protesting loudly that "Enea non sia un rifugiato!" ("Aeneas was not a refugee!")[6] Finally, this idea of Roman descent from Troy is counterintuitive if we look back at history through the lens of Western Civilisation. Per the grand narrative, the Romans, after all, are meant to be the cultural heirs of the Greeks, not the biological heirs of their opponents.

But the Romans had no concept comparable to the modern notion of Western Civilisation. They saw no reason why they should belong to the West rather than to the East, to Europe rather than to Asia. They did not usually think of themselves as the heirs of the Greeks, but rather as their conquerors. Finally, the Romans imagined their own bloodline as fundamentally mixed, with influences both sanguineous and cultural coming from all directions. It is an imagined bloodline that we can see promoted through Livilla's carefully curated public persona.

Mongrel Nation

There can be few empires less concerned with cultural and racial purity than that of the Romans. Even putting the Aeneas myth aside, Rome was said to have been a melting pot from the very start. The historian Livy claimed the city's original population was comprised of immigrants flooding in from all directions, attracted by Romulus's deliberate policy of nondiscrimination. It was this initial openness, Livy asserts, that laid the foundations for the later strength and success of the city (Livy 1:5–6). Romans described their city as multicultural in the generations after its foundation. Tradition held that only a minority of the city's legendary kings were Roman-born, with the others all arriving as immigrants before being chosen for the throne for their virtues and merits.[7] As the empire expanded across three continents, Rome eagerly adopted new cultural influences and absorbed incoming groups—perhaps a little too eagerly for some, who, like the poet Juvenal, complained about the rapid rate of cultural change (Juvenal, *Satire* 3).

Amongst myriad diverse influences that became part of mainstream Roman culture, Greek culture was certainly very influential, with significant overlap and borrowings between Greek and Roman mythology, religion, art, and intellectual life. At no time was this more evident than during the reign of the emperor Hadrian, a self-conscious philhellene whose fetish for fifth-century BCE Athens led to its elevation in Roman literature and art over other periods and regions of the ancient Greek past, and eventually to its being labelled as *classicus* (which lies at the root of our idea of the "classical"—we will come back to this in Chapter 11).[8] However, some traits that we might think of as being exclusively Greco-Roman were actually shared by a much wider set of peoples across the ancient Mediterranean and western Asia. Equivalences between gods, for example, were common well beyond the Greeks and the Romans. The Greek goddess of love, Aphrodite, may have been called "Venus" in Latin, but she was also called "Astart" amongst the Phoenicians and "Ishtar" in Mesopotamia. And the same hero that the Greeks venerated as "Herakles," the Romans honoured as "Hercules" and the Phoenicians as "Melqart."

Indeed, Rome was open to cultural influences from the length and breadth of its empire and beyond. Romans embraced the worship of the Egyptian goddess Isis, the Persian god Mithras, and the Phrygian goddess Cybele. Trade across the empire also brought disparate influences directly to Rome. When Roman families of even the most modest means sat down to dinner, it would not be strange to find them eating bread made from Egyptian grain, seasoned with fish sauce from Portugal, and drizzled with olive oil from Libya, all served on plates made in Gaul.[9] Wealthier Romans aspired to dress in silks imported from China and dye their hair in the fashion of Germans.[10] And at the highest level of society, the roll call of emperors includes not only Italians, but also Iberians, Libyans, Arabs, Syrians, and men from various parts of the Balkans.[11]

Not all this cosmopolitanism was the product of happy coexistence. The experience of Roman imperialism could be brutal, and the Pax Romana was often enforced at the edge of a sword.[12] Not everyone wanted to be absorbed or assimilated. When the Iceni chieftain Boudicca resisted Roman encroachment on her lands in 60 CE, she was flogged and her daughters raped to demonstrate Britain's subordination to Rome.[13] When the Jews revolted a few years later in 66 CE, Rome responded by plundering the Temple in Jerusalem and waging a harsh war through Judea.[14] From the eastern to the western edges of the empire, massacres, enslavement, economic exploitation, and cultural repression were all regular features of Roman rule.[15] Yet for all its brutality, the central ideology of Roman imperialism was not one of cultural, ethnic, or racial exclusivity. Quite the opposite—the mixing of culture and the mixing of peoples was a founding tenet of the Roman state. Indeed, Rome gloried in the idea of itself as a mongrel nation. At the heart of this was the myth of Roman origins, a story of refugees from Asia wandering through first Greece and then Tunisia before finally coming to rest in Italy and establishing a hybrid state by mixing their bloodlines with those of the indigenous people.

From a modern Western perspective, concerned as it is about purity and authenticity, this initially seems discordant with the story that the West tells about itself. But for Rome, its myth of hybrid origins was an imperial charter. It provided the Romans with both historical justification and ideological ammunition, transforming Roman imperialism into a homecoming and recasting the conquest of the eastern Mediterranean as the rightful reclaiming of a long-lost inheritance.[16] The Romans embraced the idea of their refugee Asian identity. Theirs was an intercontinental and multicultural empire, governed by a ruling class who also thought of themselves as equally intercontinental and multicultural.[17] It was an ideology that went all the way to the top. The Julio-Claudian family, Rome's first imperial dynasty, traced their lineage back to Aeneas himself and deployed the myth of Trojan origins not only in the service of empire but also to serve themselves.

The dynasty's founder, Julius Caesar, was as strategic with his public image as he was with his armies. He visited the site of Troy in 48 BCE and granted it a special tax and administrative status. On his return to Rome, he sponsored the building of a forum, at the centre of which was a spectacular new temple of Venus Genetrix—Venus being the mother of Aeneas, and therefore by extension of the entire Roman people, according to mythology. The horse races Caesar instituted to celebrate the opening of this temple were held annually as the "Troy Games" and soon became a fixture in the city's sporting calendar. As if this were not enough, over the next decade the coins issued by Caesar often featured the head of Venus on one side, and in one case depicted the image of Aeneas fleeing Troy that would become iconic.[18]

Caesar had set a trend. Soon, even minor noble families sought to "discover" their genealogical links to Asia. To help satisfy this need, the poets Varro and Hyginus both wrote handbooks entitled "About Trojan Families" (*De familiis Troianis*), setting out family trees and lineages that connected Roman nobility to mythical heroes from the

Trojan War.[19] The grumpy satirist Juvenal, when not complaining about the number of foreigners who had overrun his city, moaned about how the jumped-up middle classes were now giving themselves airs and graces, some even going as far as claiming to be "Troy-born" (*troiugenas*: *Satire* 1, line 110). There was no stigma, for any of these upwardly mobile Romans, in being descended from Asian refugees.

Caesar's adopted son and successor, Augustus, was to take the mythological propaganda up a notch.[20] During his rise to power, he had already copied the designs of some of Julius Caesar's coins, reproducing the by-then famous image that depicted Aeneas fleeing Troy. This scene of Aeneas running away from the flames of his home, bearing his father on his back and grasping his young son by the hand, had become instantly recognisable across the empire. Versions of it were emblazoned on the coins that jangled in the merchants' pockets, replicated as palm-sized terra-cotta votives that were mass-produced for the urban market, and parodied in domestic graffiti.[21] Perhaps most famously, however, the iconic image was reproduced on a monumental scale in Augustus's new forum. The statue of Aeneas that took pride of place there stood nearly four metres tall, equalled only by the statue of Romulus for its prominence.

Perhaps the most famous Augustan engagement with Troy is Virgil's epic poem the *Aeneid*, written under the patronage of Augustus and designed as a celebration not only of the Roman Empire in general but also of the Julio-Claudian dynasty in particular.[22] Throughout the poem, Virgil deliberately blurs the distinction between Anatolia and Italy, Troy and Rome, Asians and Europeans, not only equating them with each other but also describing them in interchangeable and ambiguous terms.[23] For example, when the glorious future of his Roman descendants is revealed to him in a prophecy, Aeneas is told that "glory will come for the progeny of Troy, whose grandsons will be of Italian stock" (*Aen.* 6:756–57). It is not clear from this passage where one bloodline begins and another ends—the descendants of the Trojans will also be the descendants of Italians. But perhaps that is the point—a key factor for Virgil is the mixing of bloodlines (*commixtus sanguine: Aen.* 6:762), from which Rome will draw its ultimate strength. In this same passage, Rome is described as if it were a person with its own genealogy. Rome, we are told, not only will be "born" from Romulus (*Aen.* 6:781), but will also be "lucky in its offspring" (*Aen.* 6:784). Virgil then offers us a simile that compares the city of Rome to the Anatolian goddess Cybele, "rejoicing in her divine offspring, embracing a hundred descendants" (*Aen.* 6:783). The language of ancestry and genealogy is everywhere, and it is deployed expertly to create ambiguity both between the cities of Troy and Rome and between the peoples of Asia and Europe.

Like Caesar before him, Augustus also visited Troy, sponsoring a major renovation of the city including the construction of new public buildings and a face-lift for its temples.[24] Needless to say, the citizens of Troy were vigorous when it came to expressing their gratitude. No fewer than three honorific statues of Augustus were erected, as well as a small temple. Over the years, statues would also appear of Augustus's adopted son and heir, Tiberius, his son-in-law Agrippa, his ill-fated grandson Gaius (Livilla's first husband), and the later emperors Claudius and Nero, as well as a whole host of minor members of the Julio-Claudian dynasty including two Antonias, two Agrippinas, one Octavia, and a Britannicus. It is amongst these that we find our curious inscription for the enigmatic Livilla.

The Ugly Child

"Outstanding in beauty"—this is how Livilla is described by Tacitus, the foremost historian of the day. But, Tacitus adds unkindly, she had been rather ungainly as a child.[25] That fact notwithstanding, her early childhood seems to have been happy. As grandchildren of the emperor Augustus, she and her two brothers grew up in the imperial palace in Rome with their cousins, including the beautiful and charismatic Agrippina (who will pop up again in our story later). Amongst the pack, Livilla enjoyed the special attentions of her grandmother, the empress Livia, with whom she shared a name. Although her full name was Claudia Livia Julia, she was affectionately nicknamed "little Livia," or Livilla, to indicate their closeness.[26]

As soon as Livilla reached puberty she was formally betrothed to her cousin Gaius, although sources disagree over whether the teenage couple ever consummated their marriage.[27] In either case, when the dashing young Gaius left Rome for the eastern provinces soon afterwards, the thirteen-year-old Livilla must have felt a mixture of emotions. On a personal level she may have felt anything from regret to relief at their separation (we are woefully uninformed about the emotions of Roman imperial women, especially as regards their arranged marriages). But in either case, she is likely to have felt some excitement. In the eyes of Rome's political commentators, Augustus's trust in Gaius marked him out as his chosen heir.[28] It all started out so well. Gaius chalked up some major diplomatic successes in Arabia and Mesopotamia, only to suffer a minor flesh wound while quelling a rebellion in Armenia.[29] But then the wound began to fester, his physical and mental state began to deteriorate, and he died on his way back to Rome. Our historical sources neglect to tell us how Livilla felt about the sudden demise of her husband, or indeed how she felt when she entered into her second arranged marriage within a year of Gaius's death. She was just seventeen.

Livilla's new husband was another cousin, the famously irascible Drusus. After Gaius's untimely death, Drusus's father, Tiberius, now emerged as next in line for the imperial throne, which meant that

Livilla had moved from being the wife of the heir apparent to being the daughter-in-law of the heir apparent. At this point, Livilla disappears from the historical record for several years. We know that she dutifully bore a daughter, Julia, and we can guess that she was probably deeply unhappy. Even the kindest sources admit that Drusus was bad-tempered; others say that he was licentious and cruel, as well as prone to violent outbursts in public.[30] We can only imagine how he must have treated his wife and his daughter behind closed doors. Yet for all his anger-management issues, Drusus still looked set to inherit the empire. Tiberius did succeed Augustus to become emperor, but he proved to be unpopular, winning neither the hearts of the Roman people nor the political support of the Roman Senate. Aware of the fragility of his own position, Tiberius groomed Drusus carefully for the succession, encouraging him to work alongside the Senate as a consul and to court the affections of the people by sponsoring gladiatorial games. For a while, this strategy seemed to work. But in 17 CE, everything changed.

Livilla was thirty years old when her brother Germanicus returned to Rome after years of campaigning in the northern provinces of Germania and Illyricum. With him came his wife, their cousin Agrippina. The contrast between these two imperial couples—Livilla and Drusus on the one hand, and Germanicus and Agrippina on the other—was stark. Drusus had stayed in Rome while Germanicus had been pacifying troop revolts and pushing forward the northern frontier. Livilla had given birth to one sickly daughter in the time that Agrippina had produced no fewer than nine strapping children.[31] Germanicus and Agrippina were an instant hit, and the rapturous populace heaped on them the adulation they had so long withheld from Tiberius and his son.[32] Although in reality Germanicus's campaign had met with only limited success, he nonetheless staged a spectacular triumph to celebrate, presenting his exploits as resounding victories.[33]

For Tiberius, Germanicus and Agrippina were a threat to his power. As quickly as he could, he found an excuse to send the young couple away from Rome, inventing the pretext that revolts in the eastern provinces could only be settled by Germanicus's calming influence.[34] For Drusus, Germanicus's popularity was a challenge. Spurred on by Germanicus's success, Drusus headed out on campaign himself, taking up the governorship of the troublesome province of Illyricum and engineering the downfall of an unfriendly German king to secure Rome's northern borders.[35] For Livilla, the options for courting public favour were more limited, and more dangerous. But Livilla was a Julio-Claudian raised in the halls of the palace, and she was to prove herself an able player in the game of imperial Roman politics.

The first thing she did was acquire a lover.[36] The man she alighted on was Sejanus, a decorated soldier and the head of the Praetorian Guard, the corps of the emperor's personal bodyguards. Sejanus came from a modest Italian family but had served in the army with distinction before taking over command of the Praetorians. Trusted first by Augustus, Sejanus had by this time also become one of Tiberius's closest confidants, receiving high honours and lavish gifts from him.[37] The second thing that Livilla did was get pregnant. We cannot be sure whether the father of Livilla's children was Drusus or Sejanus, as the precise sequence of events remains unclear.[38] All that we know for certain is that Drusus left Rome for Illyricum in the latter half of 17 CE, that Livilla gave birth to twin boys in late 19 CE, and that around the same period she also embarked on her affair with Sejanus.

The birth of Livilla's sons was celebrated across the empire with a fanfare that outdid even Germanicus's lavish triumph. Tiberius annoyed the senators by boasting endlessly about his grandsons.[39] In celebration, he ordered images of the two boys and their mother to be produced and spread across the provinces. Commemorative coins were issued in Rome, Corinth, and Cyrenaica.[40] A priesthood was established in their name on Cyprus, and a private cult sanctuary was dedicated to them at Ephesus.[41] It is also around this time that carved gems or cameos were produced bearing Livilla's graceful portrait. One particularly fine example depicts her in the guise of Ceres, the bountiful goddess of the harvest, and includes tiny portraits of her twin sons beneath her, holding a cornucopia to symbolise plenty. Livilla and her twin boys were being actively presented as the future of the empire— the next ruling generation of the imperial dynasty.

The day that Livilla gave birth—the tenth of October—proved fateful in more ways than one. It is reported that on the very same day that her two sons came into the world, Livilla's brother Germanicus left it. Germanicus had contracted a strange and unexplained illness in Syria, an illness that would claim his life. Back in Rome, the street churned with rumour. The gossips whispered that Tiberius had conspired against Germanicus, ordering his agents to use black magic to bring about Germanicus's sickness and eventual death.[42] Many amongst the suspicious populace transferred their loyalties from Germanicus to his children and widow, Agrippina. For Livilla, this must have been a trying time. Not only had she lost her brother in much the same circumstances as she lost her first husband, but in her moment of triumph—the moment when she had finally fulfilled her duty as a Roman matron and produced not one but two healthy male heirs— Agrippina had once again stolen her thunder. The opprobrium of Germanicus's death, mired in rumours of imperial conspiracy and black magic, tainted Livilla even as she nursed her newborn sons.

The battle lines were drawn. The Roman people were divided into two camps—those who supported Agrippina and the children of Germanicus for the succession, and those who supported Livilla and her twin sons. The two women were now pitted directly against each other in what was to prove a deadly contest for power.

The Intercontinental Genetrix

The contest between Agrippina and Livilla was carried out not on the battlefield or on the floor of the Senate, but instead in the unforgiving arena of public opinion. The victor would be the woman who won the support of the Roman people. Her prize would be glory, power, and control of the empire. And in the dangerous game of Roman imperial politics, the penalty for the loser would be ignominy and death.

Drusus was the first major casualty. In 23 CE, when the twins were still only three years old, he died of what initially seemed to be a natural illness. Suspicion quickly fell on Livilla and her lover, Sejanus, although the gossipmongers of Rome disagreed over how the poison had been administered. Some thought that it had been fed to Drusus gradually over the course of several years, and others that it had been given to him in a single spectacular trick. One evening at a family dinner, Sejanus reportedly whispered to Tiberius that Drusus had slipped poison into his wine cup. The mistrustful Tiberius is said to have swapped his cup with that of Drusus to test the story and to have been horrified when Drusus drained the cup and promptly dropped dead. For all its implausibility, this rumour seems to have captured the popular imagination with its caricatured depiction of the imperial circle—the rash drunkard Drusus, outwitted by the wily Sejanus and scheming Livilla, manipulating the fears of the doddery old emperor.[43] The rumours were stoked when Livilla and Sejanus requested permission to marry soon afterwards, only to be rejected by the snobbish Tiberius.[44] Whatever we might think of them as individuals, Livilla and Sejanus's relationship does seem to have been based on genuine affection—it endured for another seven years until, despite the objections of Tiberius and the disapproval of the populace, the couple were eventually betrothed.[45]

In the meantime, Livilla did her best to improve her and her children's public image. She arranged for her daughter to marry Agrippina's oldest son, in an attempt to heal the dynastic rift. Around the same time, depictions of her twin sons began to appear on tesserae—lead tokens distributed to the poor that could be exchanged for grain and other foodstuffs, much like a modern food voucher.[46] It was a move calculated to endear the twins to the populace.

Agrippina was playing a similar game. She cast herself as the tragic heroine, a role designed to elicit sympathy with her status as the grieving widow of the popular Germanicus. Contemporary portraits depict her with a soft and wistful face, framed by dense curls arranged on either side of her head in a flamboyant coiffure that cascades dramatically down the back of her neck.[47] In contrast, Livilla's portraits from the same period portray her in a markedly different way. Her features are sterner, and her hair is pulled back from a centre parting into an austere bun at the nape of her neck.[48] If Agrippina was to be the romantic and sexually attractive widow, Livilla was determined to portray herself as a modest and virtuous Roman mother. If Agrippina dressed herself in elaborate splendour, then Livilla advertised a studied simplicity. And where Agrippina's portraits invite an emotional reaction, Livilla's much more straightforwardly demand respect. Not only were the two women at the head of opposing political factions, but they also set out to embody opposing feminine ideals (although whether either of these women lived up to those ideals is, of course, another matter entirely).[49]

This careful curation of public image brings us back to the inscription from Troy. In a text that is explicitly concerned with family relationships and lineage, Livilla is equated with the goddess Aphrodite, worshipped here not as the goddess of love but as the mother of Aeneas and the maternal ancestor of the Roman people. She is also described as "of the line of Anchises" (*Ancheisiados*)—Anchises being the mortal lover of Aphrodite and the Trojan father of Aeneas. Livilla is therefore being portrayed here as the ultimate genetrix—the mother of the genealogical line. This inscription, erected in the main public square of the ancestral home of the Romans in Asia, singles her out as the symbolic linchpin of Trojan-Roman genealogical connections. This was a powerful ideological position to hold.

That this inscription was dedicated to Livilla rather than to Agrippina is noteworthy, especially given that Agrippina had herself visited the city with Germanicus shortly before his death only a few years previously.[50] We would usually expect to find a flurry of honorific inscriptions for imperial visitors, but at Troy, dedications to Agrippina are conspicuous by their absence.[51] What is more, while this inscription reserves its most fulsome praise for Livilla, it also honours her mother, Antonia, and mentions her brothers, Claudius and Germanicus. Commemorating the dead Germanicus in the same breath as Livilla, without any reference to his widow, Agrippina, was a clear political statement. The citizens of Troy were advertising their support of Livilla's faction against that of Agrippina.

But would the backing of local elites in this one provincial city have had any impact in Rome? When the city elders in Troy enshrined their support for Livilla in stone, did she care? Had this been any other provincial city of the empire, the answer may well have been no. But Troy was different, and Trojan support would have been a valuable political prize. Just as Troy was the ancestral mother city of Rome, Livilla was styling herself as the ultimate Roman mother in two ways—first as the biological mother of the next emperor, but also as the symbolic mother, or genetrix, of the Roman people as a whole.

LIVILLA'S STORY DOES not have a happy ending. In 31 CE, Sejanus was executed for plotting against the emperor Tiberius, and Livilla was imprisoned. She either starved to death or died by suicide while incarcerated.[52] Her rival Agrippina did not fare much better, having been imprisoned on the rocky island of Pandateria some years previously, where she too died of starvation.[53] Although it came too late for her to enjoy it, it was ultimately one of Agrippina's sons, not Livilla's, who eventually succeeded Tiberius—the tyrannical and unstable Caligula. But when Caligula died with no issue, the succession reverted to Livilla's side of the family, and the empire fell to her unassuming and often-overlooked younger brother, Claudius.

Dynasty, genealogy, and heritage. The early Roman Empire was consumed with the idea of bloodlines. For a society so preoccupied with ancestry, the celebration of diverse origins was no accident. Rome's self-consciously intercontinental heritage and its roots in Asian Troy demonstrate that the Roman world was not, in the eyes of those who lived in it and ruled it, a Western or a European one.

Yet despite the overwhelming evidence for the diversity—both ideal and actual—of the Roman Empire, many modern inhabitants of the West still cling to an inaccurate vision of ancient Rome. In particular, those seeking to cast the Romans as the ancestors of the modern West often characterise the Romans as racially white, applying ethnic and physiognomic terms to people who would have categorised themselves in completely different ways. For example, in the summer of 2019, there was controversy in Britain over a BBC cartoon that depicted a mixed-race Roman family living near Hadrian's Wall.[54] The resulting outrage stemmed from the idea that dark-skinned people might have been part of the Roman ruling classes, a fact that is well documented.[55]

Similarly, there remains a tendency to think of the Roman Empire as primarily a European phenomenon. This idea was captured in the pomp, symbolism, and political theatre that accompanied the signing of the treaty that created the European Union in 1957—the Treaty of Rome was signed on the Capitoline Hill, in the Hall of the Horatii and Curiatii in the Palazzo dei Conservatori, a room covered in frescoes depicting scenes from Livy of the foundation and early history of Rome. In 2017, facing Britain's imminent departure from the European Union, the remaining members signed the Rome Declaration in the very same room, an ideological nod to the notion that European unity can draw on a common Roman heritage. In the introduction to this book, we have already noted that the European Union's programme to combat irregular migration and a refugee crisis was named "Operation Mos Maiorum" in an attempt to emphasise the shared cultural heritage of Europe in contrast to the regions from which the migrants originated—Africa and Asia.[56] That Africa and western Asia were integral (and indeed foundational) parts of the Roman Empire, western Asia even being central to the very core of Roman identity, has not altered the ideological significance of Rome for the European project.

Finally, many insist on seeing Rome as the model for the cultural values they claim to be at the core of the West, in particular for certain political principles. For example, before the US Capitol building was stormed in January 2021, supporters of the then president Donald Trump used social media to call for him to "save our Republic," using the hashtag #CrossTheRubicon to spread their message—a reference to Julius Caesar using his army to seize power at Rome.[57] The fact that Caesar used force to overturn a more representative government and establish himself as a dictator seems to have been lost on pro-Trump campaigners, who erroneously claim that they were upholding democracy by protesting against a rigged election.

In short, ancient Rome was not what we often imagine it to be—racially white, geographically European, and culturally Western. It was not, despite the attempts by some to portray it as such, a straight-forward ancient analogue for our modern notion of the West. Livilla's political manoeuvrings, captured neatly by the inscription from Troy, demonstrate this perfectly. Her geopolitical perspectives, like those of Rome itself, were greater.

Chapter Three

THE GLOBAL HEIRS
OF ANTIQUITY

AL-KINDĪ

*We must not be ashamed to admire the trust or to
acquire it, from wherever it comes, even if it should come
from far-flung nations and foreign peoples.*

AL-KINDĪ (C. 870 CE)[1]

AFTER Livilla's death, the Roman Empire waxed and waned.
In the late third century, it was irrevocably split in half: the
western half gradually splintering into myriad independent
kingdoms, and the eastern half developing into the Byzantine Empire.
Some elements of Roman culture and learning were lost, some were

preserved, and some were transformed in radical new ways for a radical new world—the early medieval world.

Traditional narratives of Western Civilisation cast this period as a dark age of backwardness and barbarism. But the medieval period only looks like a dark age if your view is fixed on northern and western Europe. In the eastern Mediterranean, the Byzantine Empire dazzled with splendour and sophistication.[2] The Islamic world, as we shall see in this chapter, stretched from Seville to Samarkand and from Mosul to Mali and enjoyed a period of unrivalled prosperity as well as artistic and scientific advancement. In east Asia, the Tang Dynasty transformed China, and the Buddhist empire of Srivijaya ushered in a golden age for the southeast Asian archipelago. But back in Europe, people hung on to Western Civilisation "by the skin of our teeth," in the words of one popular historian.[3] The traditional narrative claims that the precious classical inheritance was preserved thanks to the efforts of monks and nuns (although mostly monks) labouring in obscure libraries and scriptoria across Europe, squirrelling away the cultural legacy of antiquity for future generations. Yet this view of the medieval period is, to put it bluntly, wrong.

First, research over the last few decades has done much to dispel the myth of a European medieval dark age, bringing to light the scientific and artistic achievements of the time. Many cultural innovations emerged out of the supposedly sterile environment of monasteries, from the treaties of the philosophical friar Roger Bacon to the medical texts of the knowledgeable nun Hildegard of Bingen. The Middle Ages were simply not as dark as once thought.[4] Nor is there anything necessarily middling about them. We talk about the "Middle Ages" as if the key defining characteristic of these centuries is that they were between two more important historical periods. The term "medieval" is only slightly better, although I have retained it as a shorthand in this book for convenience.[5] We should no longer think of people in the medieval period as inhabiting a temporal stopgap, caught in the space after one important era and before another. Their world was busy and exciting, and certainly eventful enough to warrant consideration in its own right.

Second, the monks and nuns of western Europe were not single-handedly responsible for preserving the cultures of ancient Greece and Rome. While many Latin texts were indeed kept and copied in the monasteries, and while some of the more bookish members of the clergy did draw on the scientific and especially the theological thinking of antiquity, they were certainly not the only people doing so. The bloodline that we think of as Western Civilisation did not flow in a single channel from Greece to Rome and from there to western Europe. Instead, it sprayed rather chaotically in all directions, carrying the cultural inheritance of Greek and Roman antiquity to all four points of the compass.

The Heirs of Antiquity

The theory of Western Civilisation posits that people in western and central Europe were the main heirs of classical antiquity. In his infamous book, *The Clash of Civilisations*, Samuel Huntington claims that "the West inherited much from previous civilisations, including most notably Classical civilisation. . . . Islamic and Orthodox civilisations also inherited from Classical civilisation but nowhere near to the same degree the West did."[6] Not everything that Huntington says is wrong—western Europe was certainly one of the areas that inherited some kind of legacy from the Greco-Roman world (as we shall see in Chapter 4). But the central thrust of Huntington's claim—that western Europe was the primary heir of Greek and Roman antiquity, and that the Byzantine and Islamic worlds received only a lesser heritage—is utterly incorrect.

Let's deal first with the bits of the standard narrative that do have some truth to them. Despite the sack of Rome by the Gothic king Alaric in 410 CE and the "fall" of the Western Roman Empire (actually, this was more a case of fragmentation than collapse), there was indeed some cultural continuity into the early medieval period, including significant amounts of Roman law,[7] Roman infrastructure such as roads and bridges,[8] and the Latin language, which remained the dominant language of literature, scholarship, and the church. But while the church happily continued to use Latin, it was suspicious about the more overtly pagan elements of the ancient past. This suspicion sometimes manifested itself in the deliberate destruction of ancient art and literature. In the hagiographic *Life of St. Martin*, for example, we hear that the saint's good works included the destruction or attempted destruction of pagan shrines in several villages in France.[9] But, in the bigger picture, the loss of Greek and Roman culture in western Europe was not really the result of deliberate scheming by dastardly fundamentalist Christians.[10] Rather, the spread of Christianity simply meant that many elements of ancient culture, including works of literature and art forms, became quietly and gradually irrelevant. This was not so much the aggressive burning of books, therefore, as the much more prosaic failure to copy them.

A greater challenge to cultural continuity was the sheer number of successor kingdoms that sprang up in what had been the western half of the Roman Empire—including the Gothic Kingdom of Italy, the Visigothic Kingdom in southern France and Iberia, the Anglo-Saxon kingdoms in Britain, and the Vandal Kingdom in North Africa, as well as the kingdoms of the Franks, the Suebi, and the Burgundians in what is now France. As a result, there was not one Roman tradition in western Europe, but many.[11] Crucially, different elements of the Roman past became mixed with local custom according to diverse local contexts. On the holy island of Lindisfarne in Northumbria, the monk Aldred may have copied out the gospels in Latin, but he illustrated his pages with intricate Celtic knotwork and added an interlinear gloss to the text in Old English.[12] Similarly, although the Roman amphitheatre in Arles was carefully repaired and maintained throughout the medieval period, this happened only because it had been reconfigured as a fortress, complete with four imposing square towers.[13] In addition, the Latin language had developed regional differences, so that Charlemagne in the ninth century complained that even formal letters from educated clerics contained too many dialectical variations.[14] The legacy of antiquity was not dead and ossified, to be preserved without change in museum-like conditions. It was vibrant and flexible, adapting to suit local needs and local contexts through the centuries. And so inevitably in western Europe, the cultural inheritance of Rome gradually became as fractured as its political inheritance.

When it comes to political inheritance, one state could claim an unbroken line with antiquity—the Byzantine Empire.[15] At its zenith in the sixth century CE, the Byzantine Empire controlled the entire eastern Mediterranean, as well as parts of Italy and Tunisia in the western Mediterranean. Its core, however, was Anatolia and the Aegean, with the great city of Constantinople straddling the Bosporus. Politically speaking, the Byzantine Empire was a straightforward continuation of the Eastern Roman Empire, occupying the same territories and using the same structures of governance, law, and administration. Crucially, its people never called themselves "Byzantines" but referred to themselves as *Romaioi*, or Romans (we will discuss this in more detail in Chapter 5). After all, by the time that al-Kindī, the subject of this chapter, was born in the ninth century, peninsular Greece and the city of Constantinople had been Roman for more than a thousand years.

Culturally, the Byzantines drew from Greek as well as from Roman traditions. They spoke Greek, and ancient Greek texts remained a standard part of elite education. Indeed, it was common practice for Byzantine scholars to demonstrate their erudition by imitating the ancient Attic dialect of authors such as Herodotus, Sophocles, and Plato in flamboyant displays of literary anachronism. For example, amongst her other scholarly works, in the twelfth century the Byzantine princess Anna Komnene composed an epic poem called *The Alexiad* in high Attic style, extoling her father's great deeds in battle.[16] At the time, the Attic style she was using would have been about fourteen hundred years old. To put this into context, the modern equivalent would be a twenty-first-century British author attempting to write in Old English—the language used by Anglo-Saxon authors to compose poems such as *Beowulf* in the seventh century CE. Byzantine scholars also mined ancient texts for the technical information they contained. They sifted through reams of ancient manuscripts, collating useful information about everything from cavalry tactics to advice on beekeeping into encyclopaedic reference works such as the tenth-century *Constantinian Excerpts*.[17] The Byzantines may have been the political heirs of ancient Rome, but they were also the cultural heirs of ancient Greece.

And yet the Byzantine engagement with both Greek and Roman antiquity was selective. Like their neighbours to the west, the Orthodox Christians of Byzantium were also wary of ancient paganism. Some ancient texts were actively censored and some artworks destroyed, but as in western Europe many were simply ignored, forgotten, or repurposed. Ancient works of mythology, poetry, and drama were particularly prone to this process, and we know the names of literally hundreds of ancient works of literature that have been lost in this way. The Byzantines might have seen the utility of reproducing Aeneas Taktikos's handbook on siege warfare, the legal speeches of

Demosthenes, and the political history of Thucydides. It was less obvious to them that they should make the effort to copy out the comedic dramas of Hegemon of Thasos, the genealogies of Hekataios, or the erotic poetry of Sappho.[18]

Farther to the east were yet more heirs of Greek and Roman culture. Thanks to the prevailing version of history taught in the West about Western Civilisation, many people do not think of the Indian subcontinent as part of the Greek world, but it was. The conquests of Alexander the Great brought him in 327 BCE as far as the Punjab Valley in what is now northern India. When he left, some of his Macedonian soldiers stayed behind, permanently settling in Bactria (modern-day Afghanistan). In the generations that followed, a number of culturally hybrid Indo-Greek kingdoms emerged in the area of modern Afghanistan, Pakistan, and parts of northern India. This Hellenistic far east was unequivocally part of the ancient Greek world, maintaining regular contacts with the Mediterranean and becoming especially influential in the development of later Greek philosophy.[19]

As for the south of the Indian subcontinent, excavations have yielded thousands of Roman coins and amphorae both in southwestern India and on Sri Lanka, the remnants of a vibrant trade route between the Mediterranean and the Indian Ocean.[20] This trade route is described vividly in a Roman text called the *Periplus of the Erythraean Sea*, which is full of lively local knowledge and sometimes surprising detail. Apparently, according to its author, the wealthy townsfolk of Barigaza (Bharuch in modern Gujarat) were especially fond of Italian wines, and Muziris (on the Malabar coast) was the best place to buy pearls.[21]

The Indian subcontinent, and Bactria in particular, retained some elements of this ancient Greek heritage after antiquity. Gandharan art of the first to fifth centuries draws from Greek as well as central Asian sculptural traditions and often depicts episodes from Greek mythology.

One particularly famous relief carving from the Peshawar District, now on display at the British Museum, depicts the wooden horse being wheeled towards the gates of Troy and the Trojan prophetess Cassandra wailing in grief for the fate of her city.[22] The ancient Greek heritage was felt, not just in the visual arts, but also in language and administration. Greek even continued in use as an official language of the Kushan Empire, whose kings also minted Greek-style coins and adapted the Greek alphabet to write the Kushan language into the fifth century.[23] The Bactrian language, which uses the Greek alphabet, remained in use until the eighth century.[24] The medieval afterlives of the mythical hero Heracles best illustrate the ancient Greek heritage in south and east Asia. In south Asia, Heracles became assimilated to Vajrapani, one of the Buddha's most faithful attendants.[25] But Heracles even travelled as far as east Asia, where several figurines and tomb paintings have been found in Tang Dynasty China (seventh to tenth centuries) of a suspiciously Heracles-like figure wearing a lion headdress and bearing a club.[26]

Sub-Saharan Africa is another region that is not often considered as having a classical heritage, and yet classical culture left its imprint here too. Here, as in south Asia, it was Greek rather than Roman cultural elements that were most readily apparent, but unlike in Asia, these Greek cultural elements were often linked to Christianity. For example, when learned monks of the Abba Garima Monastery in Ethiopia were translating the gospels from Greek into the local language of Ge'ez between the fourth and seventh centuries, they decorated their illuminated manuscripts in typical Byzantine style with the toga-wearing figures of the evangelists.[27] The Greek language continued in use as late as the fourteenth century in Sudan, employed not only in formal and religious contexts such as for the liturgy and inscriptions of gravestones, but also for everyday uses such as keeping track of grain shipments and scrawling graffiti.[28] In the medieval kingdom of Makuria in northern Sudan especially, Greek was a common language of administration and commerce.

The theory of Western Civilisation posits that culture and civilisation moved surely and steadily westwards from Greece to Rome, and from there to medieval western Europe. Yet while western Europe was indeed *one* of the heirs of antiquity, it was certainly not the only one. Cultural legacies from the Greek and Roman worlds were carried not only westwards and northwards, but also eastwards and southwards, as well as remaining and evolving on the shores of the Mediterranean (including those not only of Europe but also of Africa and Asia). And while we have surveyed Greek and Roman cultural survivals in the kingdoms of western Europe, the Byzantine Empire, as well as in south Asia and Sub-Saharan Africa, we have yet to discuss one part of the world that can also legitimately claim to be an heir of antiquity. If you follow the threads of classical scholarship and science down through the centuries from antiquity, you will inevitably find yourself wandering through the streets of medieval Baghdad.

The House of Wisdom

The avenues are wide and shady, lined with the well-watered gardens and mansions of the wealthy. The buildings are built of cool marble, their architecture rising in tall domes and elegant archways, and their walls lavishly decorated with gilded designs and hung with silks and brocades of every colour. On both sides of the river, marble steps lead down to the broad quays, jostling with humble gondolas and Chinese junks, passenger ferries and heavy merchant barges. The goods from these barges stock the city's shops and bazaars, their air heavy with the fragrance of spice and perfume, as well as the reek of discarded street food, pack animals, and hundreds of thousands of people eating, drinking, shopping, chatting, and generally going about their daily business. Founded in 726 CE as the "City of Peace" (Madinat al-Salam), by the middle of the ninth century Baghdad was the largest city in the world, with an estimated population of more than a million.[29] Originally designed on a circular plan, the urban core was built in concentric rings arranged around the central beating heart of the city—the caliph's palace, with its high green dome symbolising heavenly as well as temporal authority. Luxurious suburbs, industrial quarters, and urban slums had quickly sprung up outside the city walls, so that it was already in the ninth century a sprawling metropolis that spanned both sides of the river Tigris.

Baghdad was, after all, at the heart of the medieval Islamic world. This stretched from Al-Andalus in the west, occupying much of what is now Spain and Portugal; to Kashgar in the east, located in what is now the Xinjiang Province of China; and as far south as Timbuktu and the empire of Mali in western Africa, famed for the wealth and sophistication of its king Mansa Musa.[30] But the most powerful of all these medieval Islamic states was the Abbasid Caliphate.[31] At the peak of their powers, the Abbasids controlled an empire that reached from Sicily to Samarkand and dominated the trade routes that crisscrossed the Mediterranean, the Red Sea, and the Indian Ocean.[32] Baghdad was their capital, a cultural as well as a political centre that drew in goods and people from three continents like a magnet. When the young al-Kindī first arrived in the city, still a boy eager to embark on the final phase of his schooling in the early ninth century CE, it must have seemed overwhelming.[33]

Yet Abū Yūsuf Yaqūb ibn Ishāq al-Kindī was probably not easily impressed, even as a child. All his surviving biographies mention his elevated lineage, not only coming as he did from the Kinda—a prominent tribe of central Arabia—but also hailing from a noble family within this tribe. Al-Kindī was even said to be a direct descendant of the legendary al-Ashath ibn Qays, a former king of the Kinda and a personal companion of the Prophet.[34] He was, then, born into the most privileged echelons of Arab society. He enjoyed both status and wealth throughout his childhood, living first in the garrison town of Basra and later in the provincial city of Kūfa, where his father held the position of the region's emir. Coming to Baghdad therefore must have been a cruel shock. In Kūfa, al-Kindī had been the son of the city's esteemed ruler, a pampered youth, and a very big fish in a relatively small pond. But in the imperial capital he would have been just one of a gaggle of ambitious young students, all working hard to gain position and preferment in Baghdad's greatest and most hallowed institution—the Bayt al-Hikma, or the House of Wisdom.

The House of Wisdom was a great library, established by the caliph al-Mamūn in the early ninth century with the express aim of gathering the world's knowledge under one roof to be studied by an international team of the empire's greatest scholars, translators, and scientists.[35] Amongst the scholars associated with it were men like al-Kindī whose roots were in the Arabian peninsula but also Iraqi Arabs such as the Banu Musa brothers, a family of three ambitious mathematicians and engineers whose professional rivalry with al-Kindī very nearly proved fatal. They rubbed shoulders with Persians like Abu Mashar, who had started out as a devout theologian but eventually found fame as a celebrity astrologer; as well as sages from central and south Asia such as the Afghani physician Abu Zayd al-Balkhī, who founded a whole new way of approaching terrestrial cartography; and east Africans such as the talented polymath al-Jāhiz. Alongside these diverse Muslim scholars worked Christians like Hunayn ibn Ishāq, a Nestorian who was personally responsible for preserving many ancient texts for us today; and Jews like the pioneering astronomer Sind ibn Ali, born into a Jewish family in what is now Pakistan.

The House of Wisdom was not just frequented by a diverse and cosmopolitan group of scholars; it also housed texts and scholarly traditions from across the known and the ancient worlds. One could read the Greek mathematical works of Euclid, the Sanskrit medical treatises of Sushrata, and the Persian astronomical texts of Brahmagupta, as well as archaeological discussions on the pyramids of Giza— all written on paper, the latest revolution in information technology, imported from China. Al-Mamūn's vision for knowledge acquisition was nothing short of global—it is said that when he defeated foreign kings in battle, he often demanded tribute from them not in gold, enslaved people, or treasure, but rather in the form of books from their royal libraries.

It was a vibrant intellectual environment that fostered enquiry and creativity, leading to many important advances and discoveries.[36] Pythagorean and Euclidean geometry were combined with Indian concepts of zero, decimal numeration, and the place value system, leading to major advances in mathematics including the invention of algebra. Developments in physics ranged from an improved understanding of optics, including the behaviour of light and the functioning of lenses, to the mechanics of movement, including the calculation of velocity and acceleration. All of these contributed to astronomic breakthroughs, and even today, we still use Arabic names for celestial bodies including the stars of the Ursa Major constellation—Dubhe, Megrez, Alioth, Mizar, and Alkaid. In medicine, insights from Hippocratic and Vedic medical traditions were combined with a new interest in chemistry and pharmaceutical experimentation. From psychiatry to gastric bugs, gynaecology to ophthalmic surgery, new encyclopaedic handbooks of medicine were produced, categorising complaints and recommending treatments. For the natural and the theoretical sciences, it was a golden age indeed.

The House of Wisdom is particularly associated with the "translation movement"—a movement in which philosophical and scientific texts written in ancient Greek (and to a lesser extent in Syriac) were collected in Baghdad and translated into Arabic.[37] Indeed, it is to these Arabic copyists and translators that we owe many ancient Greek texts surviving today, especially scientific works such as those of Aristotle, philosophical writings such as those of Plato, and medical texts such as those attributed to Galen. At a time when ancient Greek was all but lost from western Europe, and when scientific and philosophic works were viewed with suspicion by the devoutly Christian Byzantines, it was in the bustling city of Baghdad, the capital of the Islamic Abbasid Caliphate, that this thread of ancient Greek scholarship was kept alive. While many standard historical accounts present Western Civilisation as a torch passed from Greek and Roman antiquity to the medieval world, that the Islamic world was an important torchbearer is often missed.

It was work that al-Kindī threw himself into with vigour. After arriving in Baghdad, he studied and worked hard for more than a decade to establish himself as a scholar of repute. He must have distinguished himself in his studies, as by his late twenties or early thirties he had risen high enough to enter the caliph's immediate scholarly circle. Indeed, he dedicated his earliest philosophical treatise, *A Letter on Cause and Effect*, to al-Mamūn before the bibliophile caliph's death in 833 CE. Al-Kindī continued to flourish under the next caliph, the bellicose al-Mutasim, and it was in this golden decade between 833 and 842 CE that his standing at the court peaked. We even hear of him serving as the tutor for the caliph's son Ahmad, a position of trust and great honour. It was during this decade that al-Kindī wrote some of his best-known and most important works, many of which were personally dedicated to the caliph.

The volume of his output from this period onwards was prodigious.[38] Unlike other members of his immediate circle, al-Kindī was not directly involved in the process of translating ancient Greek texts into Arabic. He left that to gifted linguists such as his contemporary Hunayn. Instead, he devoted his energies to analysis and commentary, building on the philosophical foundations laid by Greek thinkers. His role, as he saw it, was "to supply completely what the ancients said about this, according to the most direct methods and the procedures easiest for those engaged in this pursuit, and to complete what they did not discuss comprehensively."[39] Al-Kindī's obsession with Greek texts even seems to have made him a figure of fun. One biographer claimed that street pranksters sometimes mocked him by inventing meaningless pseudo-philosophical aphorisms that they pretended were Greek in origin.[40]

Not everything al-Kindī wrote was part of this highbrow tradition. Amongst his almost three hundred known works there are pamphlets on perfumes and treatises on tides, leaflets on lenses and guides to geology. One of his works even addressed the crucial issue of how best to remove stains from dirty clothes. Outside scholarly circles, he was also well-known as a physician, and one anecdote describes how he helped the sick son of one wealthy Baghdadi merchant, despite the merchant having publicly slandered him.[41] But although he may have been variously a doctor, a natural scientist, and an experimental physicist, al-Kindī will always be best known for his theological and philosophical works. In these, he reflected on the workings of the universe, the nature of divinity, and the place of humanity within the cosmic order.

We know almost nothing about al-Kindī's personal life or relationships. We hear of no close friends, no lovers or romantic affairs. One apocryphal story suggests that he may have had a son (and supposedly therefore also a wife), as it reports that he warned his son against music, saying, "Listening to music is a dire illness: for a man hears it and is delighted, spends his money and is extravagant, so that he becomes poor, aggrieved and ill, and then he dies."[42] But as this is the only text that mentions al-Kindī having a family, we might want to take this anecdote with a pinch of salt. Indeed, if we look at the vast majority of the extant literature, the only meaningful people in al-Kindī's life seem to have been his students and scientific associates, who included some of the brightest minds of their time, such as the astrologer Abu Mashar, the engineer Sind ibn Ali, and the cartographer al-Balkhī.[43]

Although they obviously respected him, none of al-Kindī's colleagues seem to have liked him very much. One of them, the lexicographer al-Latif, described him as "a brilliant, intelligent and wealthy shaykh, who enjoyed the favour of the caliph, but who was quite taken with himself and offensive to his company."[44] His colleague al-Jāhiz even devoted an extended section to al-Kindī in his *Book of Misers*.[45] Apparently, when one of his tenants mentioned that he was expecting some guests, al-Kindī promptly increased the rent, defending his action in a long pseudo-philosophical letter in which he explained (in excruciating detail to include the specifics of additional water usage, waste disposal, etc.) the reasons for the increase. Reading al-Jāhiz's version of the letter, I am not sure what would have been more painful for the tenant—the rent rise itself, or reading the reasoning behind it.[46] By all accounts, al-Kindī would have been happy if everyone had just left him alone to his scholarship, his philosophy, and his books.

Unfortunately, medieval Baghdad offered no sanctuary for the bookish recluse. Abbasid scholarship was ruthlessly competitive. Rival researchers vied to come up with the most innovative new theory, to develop the most sophisticated interpretations, and to discover or translate the most exciting new texts.[47] After all, there was much more than intellectual fulfilment at stake—your status in society, your standing with the caliph, and even your financial stability depended on your scholarly output in this society so singularly focused on the pursuit of knowledge. Al-Kindī, with his conspicuous success, was bound to attract more than his share of resentful rivals.

The chronicles recount one particularly dramatic episode during the reign of the caliph al-Mutawakkil.[48] Al-Kindī and his glittering circle were targeted by another scholarly faction led by the Banu Musa brothers, who were hell-bent on gaining preferment at court by fair means or foul. The Banu Musa seem to have conspired against several members of al-Kindī's group, successfully preventing them from visiting the court. With al-Kindī and his faction now isolated, cut off from caliphal patronage and commissions, the Banu Musa set in motion a whispering campaign, persuading the devout al-Mutawakkil to have al-Kindī flogged for his theological deviance. The brothers also confiscated al-Kindī's greatest treasure—his personal library—carrying away all his books and impounding them in a special storeroom that they teasingly called the "Kindiyyah." For al-Kindī, the loss of his library must have been devastating.

Fortunately for him, the Banu Musa's triumph was to prove short-lived. The brothers had secured al-Mutawakkil's favour by promising to construct a grand new canal in his name, but their calculations—as well as those of their collaborators—were wrong. By the time they realised their error, the mouth of the canal was deeper than it should have been, and the water had ceased to flow. Al-Mutawakkil was incensed. Under threat of a (very) painful death, the Banu Musa grovelingly appealed for help to Sind ibn Ali, an associate of al-Kindī's whom they had also previously had expelled. As well as being a gifted engineer, Sind must have also had a strong moral compass, as he refused to help the Banu Musa unless they restored al-Kindī's library.

However, scholarly rivals were only the start of al-Kindī's problems. A much more dangerous threat came from another direction entirely.

Conservative religious thinkers disapproved of his unconventional views, objecting in particular to his radical fusion of theology and philosophy. Demagogues harangued him for not being a proper Muslim, and street-corner gossips whispered about the deviant things he did behind closed doors. Even the enmity of the Banu Musa, while based on professional rivalry, had been dressed up in the rhetoric of religious outrage. But the truth about al-Kindī's ideas was even stranger than the gossips imagined.

Aristotle and Allah

The problem was not that al-Kindī studied ancient Greek texts and authors. There was, after all, no shortage of scholars in ninth-century Baghdad who were engaged in precisely this endeavour. The well-known scientist and satirist al-Jāhiz waxed lyrical about Greek texts: "Our share of wisdom would have been much reduced, and our means of acquiring knowledge weakened, had the ancients [the Greeks] not preserved for us their wonderful wisdom."[49] Even the caliph al-Mamūn is said to have had a dream about Aristotle.[50] In contrast, al-Kindī's comments in his most famous and important treatise, *On First Philosophy*, seem a little tame: "We must not be ashamed to admire the truth or to acquire it, from wherever it comes. Even if it should come from far-flung nations and foreign peoples, there is for the student of truth nothing more important than the truth."[51]

This statement might seem anodyne to use, but for many in ninth-century Baghdad, it would have sounded shockingly radical. Yet al-Kindī was to go even further, arguing not only that Islamic intellectuals could usefully borrow ideas from the ancient Greek thinkers, but that the Greek and the Islamic intellectual traditions were essentially part of the same single tradition. It was not enough for him to study ancient

Greek philosophy and science, selecting useful knowledge and harvesting it so that it could be grafted onto various branches of Islamic scholarship. Instead, al-Kindī wanted to prove that there was no real distinction to be made between the Greek and the Islamic traditions of thought, and that Greek philosophy was actually one and the same as Islamic theology. This claim runs completely counter to the narrative of Western Civilisation, which posits instead that Christian Europe rather than the Islamic Middle East was the primary heir of ancient Greek antiquity.

While the continuation of ancient Greek intellectual traditions and the absorption of ancient Greek intellectual influences were widely accepted in ninth-century Baghdad, the claim that Greek and Islamic culture was fundamentally the same evidently raised some eyebrows, and al-Kindī devoted an entire section of *On First Philosophy* to arguing his case. True knowledge, he claimed, was not bounded by cultural, linguistic, ethnic, or religious limits. If we want to comprehend the single underlying cosmic truth of the universe, he argued, the only way to do so was through building on the cumulative knowledge of centuries of learning. He reasoned that "it has only been possible to collect this knowledge over the course of previous ages, century after century until our own time."[52] This knowledge, then, could not belong to the Greeks alone, or to Muslims alone. It was a heritage that belonged to all humanity.

The rest of *On First Philosophy* puts this theory into practice. Al-Kindī draws on the arguments of Neoplatonic scholars against the world being eternal and uses the scientific classifications of Aristotle to examine the nature of being between multiplicity and unity, before coming to the conclusion (in line with the prevailing Islamic doctrine of the day) that the essence of God is unity or oneness. Al-Kindī's philosophical vision therefore blended Aristotelian science, Neoplatonist philosophy, and Islamic theology in a way that was simultaneously radical and traditional.[53] While he was radical in his conclusion that there was no cultural dividing line between Greek and Islamic thought, al-Kindī was entirely traditional in the method he used to prove it. His approach to reading, commentating on, and developing the ideas contained in the Greek texts followed the long-established traditions of textual commentary. In this respect, his philosophical method was similar to those used by generations of Greek philosophers before him. Just as Plotinus had commented on Aristotle, Porphyry had commented on Plotinus; and just as Porphyry had commented on Plotinus, al-Kindī had commented on Porphyry. Al-Kindī did not just argue for the continuity of culture between the Greek and the Islamic worlds; he performed it through his own philosophical practice.

Inevitably, not everyone was convinced by such cerebral philosophising, and al-Kindī had another strategy for claiming the cultural heritage of ancient Greece for Islam. Perhaps aiming to convince a more popular audience, he invented a mythic genealogy in which he named the eponymous ancestor of the Greeks as a certain Yunan (equivalent to the Greek term "Ionian"). He described Yunan as a brother of Qahtan, the legendary ancestor of the Arabs.[54] Yunan, we hear, parted ways with his brother after a fraternal spat and, taking with him his children, his supporters, and anyone else who was willing, left the family home in Yemen. He went first to the Magreb and established a settlement, from which his descendants multiplied and spread. Inevitably at this point, we are told in a regretful tone, they lost the purity of their language. When, some generations later, Alexander of Macedon campaigned on the fringes of Arabia, this is described as a homecoming of sorts—a return to the motherland of an errant branch of the family. As a result, ancient Greek culture and philosophy were not foreign to the Arabs at all. Quite the opposite. It was their birthright.

The original text of al-Kindī's astonishing genealogy no longer survives, but it was summarised by the historian al-Masūdī about a century later in his universal history, *The Meadows of Gold*. Al-Masūdī presents al-Kindī's genealogy for Yunan after a series of conflicting stories, implying that it is the most reasonable account for the origin of the Greeks by attributing it to "a learned scholar, well versed in antiquity." He contrasts this with a story of Greek origins that he holds to be self-evidently false—that they are genealogically linked to the Byzantines.

Although al-Masūdī grudgingly accepts that the Byzantines occupied the same lands as the ancient Greeks and shared some of the same political structures, he is at pains to point out the differences in principles, philosophy, and language. He writes that "the peoples of Byzantium are nothing but imitators of the Greeks—never will they equal them either in eloquence or in quality of discourse." This idea of the Byzantines as illegitimate usurpers of the ancient Greek legacy seems to have been current also amongst al-Kindī's contemporaries. Al-Jāhiz, for example, gleefully offers a list of ancient Greek authors, stressing that they were neither Byzantine nor Christian, and stridently claiming for the ancient Greeks that "their culture was different from the culture of the Byzantines."[55] He goes on to say that the Byzantines "appropriated the books of the Greeks on account of geographical proximity." Towards the end of the ninth century, a new text began to circulate that recounted the transmission of medical knowledge through a genealogy, not of biological descendants but of teachers and pupils. Through this intellectual genealogy, medical science is described as travelling from Alexandria to Baghdad, rejected by the Byzantine Christians, who were suspicious of all science and philosophy.[56]

There are clear political overtones in texts such as these, which deny the Greek heritage of Byzantium and instead claim ancient Greek culture for the Islamic world. At the time that al-Kindī lived and worked in the mid-ninth century, the Abbasid Caliphate found itself in direct conflict with the Byzantine Empire, fighting over territory in both Anatolia and Sicily. In both regions, the ancient Greek heritage remained (and indeed remains today) a conspicuous and tangible part of local history. In this context, the idea of ancient Greek culture living on in Arab scholarship was a potent one. In this context, Abbasid philhellenism was also a form of anti-Byzantinism.[57]

Yet beyond their immediate political implications, the claims made by al-Kindī and his contemporaries have wider implications for how we imagine the lines of cultural genealogy. For them, contrary to the modern grand narrative of Western Civilisation, which posits a single Greco-Roman cultural unity, the ancient Greek and Roman worlds were distinct. And for them, contrary to the modern grand narrative of Western Civilisation, which claims the cultural legacy of this Greco-Roman cultural conglomeration for Christian Europe, the true heir of ancient Greece was the Islamic Middle East. This can be illustrated, for example, by the vibrant literary traditions surrounding Alexander of Macedon in Arabic, Syriac, Persian, and even Malay,[58] but is also starkly evident in the overt claims of cultural lineage made by al-Kindī and his colleagues. If ancient Greek learning and culture is a torch, then for al-Kindī it was a torch that was passed not westwards but eastwards.

————————

THE PRINCIPLE THAT scholarship might transcend ethnic and political boundaries is one that we take for granted today, in modern universities where international teams of researchers collaborate closely on the burning questions of the moment—often across thousands of miles and state borders, thanks to the communications revolution of recent years. (As an aside, it is also sadly an idea that has more recently come under threat with the rise of politicised nationalism.) But this idea was novel, and even radical, in the time of al-Kindī. He devoted a full section of *On First Philosophy* to a spirited rebuttal of his critics.

His tone in this section is full of bitterness and hatred, suggesting that while he generally tried to avoid public confrontations and endeavoured not to rise to the bait when he was publicly denounced, the attacks must have hurt him deeply.

> *[We must] be on our guard against the pernicious interpretations of many in our own time who have made a name for themselves with speculation, people who are far away from the truth although they crown themselves with its laurels. . . . A filthy envy abides in their bestial souls, which shields the vision of their thought from the light of truth with dark veils. They have set down those who have the human virtues, which they themselves fall short of attaining. . . . They defend the fraudulent positions in which they have undeservedly been installed, in order to achieve supremacy and traffic in religion, although they have no religion themselves.*[59]

There is little question who al-Kindī is writing about in this section—the conservative theologians who had blighted his life and caused him trouble on the streets as well as in the imperial court. Yet despite pouring his bile for them out onto paper, when dealing with them in person al-Kindī did his best to counter their accusations in a civilised manner. When one well-known theologian started to denounce al-Kindī, whipping up the general populace against him, al-Kindī publicly seemed to demur.[60] Then, behind closed doors, he worked to interest the theologian and his friends in mathematics. As the theologian gradually expanded his own intellectual horizons, he found himself borrowing books from al-Kindī and even engaging al-Kindī in learned discussion. The theologian eventually gave up his public attacks and became a well-known astrologer who was once famously flogged for a correct (but gloomy) prediction. His name was Abu Mashar, and he became part of al-Kindī's close scholarly circle.

It is Abu Mashar who was with al-Kindī at the end, and Abu Mashar who records the details of al-Kindī's eventual death from a buildup of phlegm in his knee. Apparently, al-Kindī tried to remedy this first by drinking aged wine (a good remedy for many things, but probably not knee problems), and later by taking "honey juice" (which again sounds very pleasant, but not quite as effective as al-Kindī might have hoped). Nothing worked, however, and Abu Mashar writes that the infection and pain eventually spread to reach al-Kindī's brain, causing him to expire.[61]

Al-Kindī's death was not only an end; it was also a beginning of a legacy that reaches down through the centuries. In the years after his death, his students al-Balkhī and al-Sarakhsī founded a school in Baghdad that was to remain important for another two centuries. Later still, al-Kindī's writings also established a foundation on which future Islamic scholars would build. Although the names of some of these later thinkers—amongst them al-Fārābī, Avicenna, and Averroes—might be better known, their work was made possible only by the pioneering efforts of al-Kindī and his circle. It was this circle who collected and translated hundreds of ancient Greek texts, preserving them for posterity. It was al-Kindī in particular who defined the language of Arabic philosophy and laid out the framework for all medieval science that followed it. And it was al-Kindī who personally defended the idea of philosophy as an intercultural endeavour—an inheritance not passed down through bloodlines or in civilisational blocs, but shared equally by all.

The life and writings of al-Kindī demonstrate that the grand narrative of Western Civilisation is false. The medieval period was not a dark age, where the torch of a single coherent Greco-Roman antiquity might have burned low but was carefully preserved in Europe so that it could be rekindled in later generations. Instead, it was a time in which the ancient Greek and Roman pasts were thought of as being separate and distinct, with different people laying claim to different legacies. In central and western Europe, areas that we now closely associate with the West and which the narrative of Western Civilisation presumes were the primary inheritors of classical culture, the idea of continuity with ancient Rome persisted (we will explore this more in Chapter 4), but there was little interest or engagement with the ancient Greek past. In the lands of the Byzantine Empire, in contrast, explicit claims were made to a Roman political, cultural, and also genealogical heritage, while intellectual engagements with Greek antiquity continued. But in the Islamic world, which is almost entirely absent from traditional narratives of Western Civilisation, people were claiming the legacy of ancient Greece for their own, not only on the basis of intellectual traditions and cultural continuities, but also using mythological genealogies. If we were to draw a family tree that begins with ancient Greece and Rome, then in the medieval period, the Islamic world would be one of its thickest and most flourishing branches.

◆ *Chapter Four* ◆

THE ASIAN
EUROPEANS AGAIN

GODFREY OF VITERBO

*Indeed the nobility of the kings and emperors of the
Romans and of the Teutons comes from the same root—
the king of the Trojans.*

GODFREY OF VITERBO (1183 CE)[1]

GODFREY is furious. He has been locked in this room for days, and the chamber pot is beginning to stink. He gingerly lifts it and, holding it out in front of him at arm's length, walks carefully over to the window, nervous lest some of the foul liquid inside might spill. When he empties it out the window, he allows himself a moment to gaze out upon the view. The gentle slope down to the river is covered in vineyards, the vines hanging heavy with fruit. Beyond them he can see fields, pastures, and the roofs of the small town of Casale Monferrato. Piedmont is beautiful, he admits to himself with a sigh. Leaving the chamber pot under the window, Godfrey wipes his fingers on his dark woollen cloak absentmindedly and returns to his desk. He feels a bit better. A new sheet of parchment lies blank in front of him. One good thing about being a prisoner, he thinks, is that he finally has time to write.

Although this scene is plucked from my imagination, we know that Godfrey did sit down to write around the time of his incarceration, penning a chronicle of world history that sidelined Greek antiquity and instead glorified an axis of power and heredity originating in the Anatolia, developing in the Roman world, and maturing in the Germanic dynasties of central Europe. Over the years, Godfrey had put quill to parchment while riding on horseback, sheltering under trees by the roadside, and even squeezed into the quieter corners of besieged castles. He spent a good proportion of his working life on the road—delivering letters, posting decrees, and passing secret messages for his master the Holy Roman emperor Frederick I of the (in)famous Hohenstaufen dynasty, nicknamed "Barbarossa" because of his red beard.[2] Even when Godfrey was not travelling, his regular duties kept him busy. As a member of the imperial bureaucracy, he would have spent his days drafting and copying documents in the chancery, and as a medieval cleric, he would have been expected to participate in several church services every day. His job, if we believe his complaints, was a demanding one, keeping him "in the constant restlessness and confusion of events, in war and warlike conditions, in the noise of such a large court."[3]

It is perhaps our good fortune that Godfrey—a medieval priest, diplomat, and chronicler—was always so busy. All his varied and exciting life experiences informed his writing. His sweeping account of world history may have begun, ambitiously, with the origins of humanity and ended in his own day of the late twelfth century CE, but his chronicle was pithy and succinct, shaped by the political maelstrom in which he found himself. This makes Godfrey's history especially interesting. He wrote no fewer than three versions over the course of four years, revising and reworking it to suit the rapidly changing political situation. The earliest version was completed in 1183 CE and was dedicated to Barbarossa's son Henry with the title *Speculum regum*. Two years later, in 1185 CE, Godfrey modified the text and renamed it the *Memoria seculorum*, although he retained its dedication to the Hohenstaufens. After this, he revised his history one final time, in 1187 CE, as the *Pantheon* and dedicated it not to his former patrons but instead to their archenemy, the pope. Needless to say, Godfrey altered the contents of the chronicle to suit his intended audience, literally rewriting history between one version and another.

A constant element throughout the versions of Godfrey's chronicle is his vision of the shape of history, which differs dramatically from the genealogy presented today as Western Civilisation. In Godfrey's account, after the mythological murkiness at the dawn of humanity, we hear about three sequential phases of divinely sanctioned human kingship, with each empire inheriting the mantle of temporal rule smoothly and directly from its predecessor. This idea of earthly power being transmitted from one imperial power to the next—known as *translatio imperii*—was very much in vogue amongst European medieval chroniclers. For Godfrey, first in his sequence was the *imperium* of the Trojans. The second was the *imperium* of Troy's descendants and rightful heirs, the Romans. The third was the *imperium* of Rome's descendants and rightful heirs, the Teutons. For Godfrey, history proper began at Troy on the shores of the Hellespont and culminated with the

German Hohenstaufen dynasty—Barbarossa's family—on the banks of the Rhine.

In contrast, the modern narrative of Western Civilisation traces a different cultural lineage. In it, we see the medieval period (the time in which Godfrey lived and wrote) as linking forward in time to us in the modern global West, via the Renaissance and the Enlightenment. But we also see it as linking back in time to the classical world, which comprises a cultural fusion of Greece and Rome. Yet Godfrey and his medieval contemporaries did not see, as we do, the Greeks and the Romans as belonging to a single civilisation. Nor did they see themselves as the custodians of a combined classical heritage, preserving Greco-Roman culture and knowledge for future generations. Instead, they thought of the Greek and the Roman worlds as fundamentally different, separate, and even opposed. For while they considered the Roman past as a central part of their heritage, they were utterly unlike the ninth- and tenth-century scholars of Baghdad in the House of Wisdom, in that they wanted relatively little to do with the ancient Greeks.

Imperator Romanorum

Voltaire famously quipped that the Holy Roman Empire was neither holy nor Roman, or even an empire. There is some truth to his witticism. It was certainly imperial in scale and vision.[4] Lasting for more than a millennium from its first establishment by Charlemagne in 800 CE to its dissolution by Francis II in 1806, the empire at its greatest extent incorporated all or part of the modern states of Austria, Belgium, the Czech Republic, Denmark, France, Germany, Italy, Luxembourg, the Netherlands, Poland, and Switzerland. Yet imperial rule was not direct, with the emperor determining all policy throughout its territories, and the tenuous nature of its power is perhaps what Voltaire was alluding to in his famous comment. Instead, the Holy Roman Empire was a fluctuating collective comprising hundreds of independent states and microterritories, the rulers of which owed allegiance to an emperor who was elected by a fixed panel of seven (later nine) of the greatest princes and prelates in the empire. Yet there were rarely surprises in the *Königswahl* (election of the king). The three spiritual electors (the archbishops of Mainz, Trier, and Cologne) and the four lay electors (the king of Bohemia and the rulers of the Palatinate, Saxony, and Brandenburg) usually selected appropriate members of whichever dynasty was in the ascendancy at the time. Famous ruling dynasties of the empire include the Frankish Carolingians, the dynasty founded by Charlemagne himself; the Salians, whose descendants included the Plantagenets of England; and the Habsburgs of Austria. But in Godfrey's day, the ruling dynasty was that of the Hohenstaufens, or "Staufers," a formidable princely family from Swabia in what is now southern Germany.

Godfrey's employer for most of his career, Barbarossa, was the most formidable of the lot.[5] A gifted soldier, but sometimes also hotheaded and impetuous, Barbarossa was driven by his enormous personal energy and his seemingly boundless ambition. Almost by the sheer force of his will and considerable charisma, he managed not just to bind the powerful rulers of Germany together with the independent-minded princes of Austria and northern Italy, but also to expand his power southwards, establishing Staufer rule as far away as Sicily.

Whatever problems it may have had maintaining its temporal power, the empire had even more trouble claiming spiritual authority. Barbarossa's greatest challengers were not the querulous princes of Saxony or the Norman kings of Palermo, but the popes in Rome.[6] He jostled for primacy with Pope Adrian IV, had a series of run-ins with Pope Lucius III, and clashed with Pope Urban III over the contracting of appropriate dynastic marriages. But his bitterest quarrel was with Pope Alexander III (1159–1181 CE). Barbarossa refused to recognise Alexander as the pope, supporting instead his own candidate, Victor, for the position. It took eighteen years, many bloody battles, and excommunication before Barbarossa finally conceded and accepted Alexander's papacy.

Although the empire was neither entirely imperial nor entirely holy, its emperors certainly presented it as being Roman. When Charlemagne founded the empire in 800 CE, he was crowned by the pope as *Imperator Romanorum* (Emperor of the Romans) and issued new imperial coinage that deliberately replicated that of ancient Rome.[7] Although the title was altered by his successors to *Rex Romanorum* (King of the Romans),[8] the territory they ruled over also contained large areas of what had previously been the Western Roman Empire, brought together again after the political fragmentation of previous centuries. The twelfth century, Godfrey's time, in particular saw increasing interest in the ancient Roman past. More and more ancient Latin texts were being copied and circulated, with Barbarossa himself encouraging a revival of Roman cultural symbols and Roman legal codes throughout the imperial territories.[9] Inevitably, ideas about *translatio imperii* also became more popular around this time, with medieval European chronicles claiming political continuity between the old and the new Roman Empires.[10] Just one generation before Godfrey, for example, Frutolf of Michelsberg drew up a list of Roman emperors from Augustus to his own day as if the line had never been broken.[11] Godfrey was to do one better in his own chronicle, setting out a list of Roman rulers that stretched back from Barbarossa through the Caesars to Aeneas, the legendary founder of the Roman *gens*, or people. The appeal of *Romanitas* for the new imperial administration was strong. It lent the relatively new empire legitimacy, as well as the lustre of venerable antiquity.

The idea that the Holy Roman Empire was a continuation of ancient Roman *imperium* did not sit well with everyone, however. It was a clear slap in the face for the Byzantines, who, as we have already seen in Chapter 3, called themselves *Romaioi* (rather than *Hellenoi*) and saw themselves as the only true heirs of ancient Rome.[12] The Byzantines did have a point. Unlike the Holy Roman emperors, their rulers could trace a genuine and unbroken line of political continuity that connected them with antiquity. Unlike the Holy Roman Empire, they could point to a capital city—Constantinople—that was not only an ancient seat of the Roman Empire, but also still a vibrant and thriving metropolis. In contrast, the Holy Roman Empire had no fixed capital, and Rome itself was the stronghold of the popes, who were often caught in a bitter rivalry with the Holy Roman emperors. To Byzantine ears, the claims of this upstart "Roman" empire must have rung hollow indeed.

Compounding the political tension between the two empires were a number of religious disputes between the patriarch of Constantinople and the pope in Rome. The correct date on which to celebrate Easter, the acceptability of using unleavened bread for the Eucharist, and whether or not one should chant the "Alleluia" during Lent—the points of disagreement were manifold. Behind all these theological questions, however, lay another contest for power. Both the pope and the patriarch claimed primacy, the former as the heir of St. Peter, and the latter on the basis that the transfer of temporal power from Rome to Constantinople marked the transfer of spiritual power too. The relationship between the two entities had always been tense, but things came to a head in the eleventh century. When the pope threatened excommunication for all members of churches in Italy that followed the rites as laid down by Constantinople, the patriarch responded by ordering the closure of all churches in Constantinople that followed the rites as determined in Rome. The following year, a papal legate arrived at Constantinople demanding that the precedence of Rome be officially recognised, and then excommunicated the patriarch on the spot when he (predictably) refused. In that moment, the two great churches of medieval Europe—the Orthodox Church of Constantinople and the Catholic Church of Rome—were born. This final sundering of the Latin-speaking and the Greek-speaking churches is known as the Great Schism.[13] By Godfrey's lifetime, in the late twelfth century, the Great Schism was already old news. Indeed, by this time, the lands of Byzantium and the Orthodox Church had become "the East," and the lands of the Holy Roman Empire and the Catholic Church had become increasingly synonymous with the term "Europa."[14]

It is worth stopping to note that medieval ideas about the location "Europa" are not the same as our modern notion of "Europe." To the east, concepts of medieval Europa did not usually stretch as far as the Ural Mountains and the Caspian Sea, as the modern continent of Europe does. To the north and west, the rhetoric of Europa paid little attention to its Baltic and Atlantic fringes, which were for the most part culturally as well as geographically peripheral. Instead, the notion of Europa in Godfrey's day was closer to the contemporary Germanic concept of "Mitteleuropa," with its focus on the area now occupied by the modern states of Germany, Austria, Switzerland, northern Italy, eastern France, Hungary, Slovakia, and the Czech Republic.

This was a continental vision that had emerged from the Carolingian court of the ninth century, in which Europa was equated with the realm of the Holy Roman Empire.[15] In the famous *Paderborn Epic*, an encomiastic poem composed in the early ninth century to commemorate the meeting between Charlemagne and Pope Leo, Charlemagne is given the epithet *"rex, pater Europae"* (king, father of Europe).[16] When the Scottish grammarian Sedulius described Charlemagne in the middle of the century, he called him *"Europae princeps"* (the ruler of Europe), while the evocatively named Notker the Stammerer credited him with bringing "*tota Europa*" (all of Europe) together.[17]

In the time of Godfrey, nearly two centuries later, "Europa" was widely understood not as the name of a continent, nor as a cultural label for a civilisation, but rather as a term of politico-religious geography. It referred to the area of central Europe occupied mostly by Latin Christians and (notionally at least) under the spiritual authority of the pope in Rome. And it was deployed, with increasing frequency, to set apart the sphere of influence of the Holy Roman Empire in central Europe from that of its Byzantine rival in eastern Europe and northwestern Asia. Both the Holy Roman emperor and his Byzantine counterpart claimed to be the true heir of Rome's Caesars, and both competed to have their own empire recognised as the one true and universal Christian empire.[18] Not that the competition was very heated in this period. From the perspective of the Staufers, the Byzantine Empire did not pose much of a threat. Beset internally by dynastic struggles and externally by the Seljuks, a Turkic dynasty originally from central Asia who attacked it from the east, the Byzantines seemed barely able to maintain their core territories. In contrast, the ascendant Holy Roman Empire under Barbarossa was on a trajectory of external expansion and internal consolidation. Small wonder that as the Latin chroniclers of the time became increasingly interested in the Roman heritage of their own empire, they began to belittle the Byzantine emperor as the *Rex Graecorum* (the King of the Greeks).[19]

It would be attractive to locate the birth of the modern West in this period, aligning it with the flourishing Holy Roman Empire. After all, some key elements that we think of as being central to Western identity were already in the frame—Christianity, a geographic focus on Europe, a sense of a Greco-Roman heritage. And yet none of these three elements sits comfortably in this picture. The Holy Roman Empire of this period was mired in religious schism and conflict, rather than standing for a united Christendom. While the Holy Roman Empire was certainly a European power, its lands were concentrated in central Europe, considering as peripheral three areas that we now think of as being crucial to Western Civilisation—Hellenic southeastern Europe, where Western Civilisation supposedly emerged in antiquity; Atlantic western Europe, where it supposedly ushered in modernity; and Scandinavian northern Europe. And finally, while the Holy Roman Empire claimed to be the heir of Rome, it vociferously rejected the ancient Greek legacy. Denizens of the Holy Roman Empire like Godfrey did not imagine the world as being divided into the West and the Rest and, crucially for the purposes of this book, saw themselves as part of a cultural genealogy that was markedly different from that of Western Civilisation. It was a cultural genealogy that Godfrey helped to refine and promote, through his ambitious chronicles, which claimed to recount the universal history of humanity.

The Diplomatic Priest

Godfrey of Viterbo was born in the 1120s, some two centuries after the golden age of al-Kindī and his circle in Baghdad. He came from the city of Viterbo in central Italy, a favourite haven for deposed popes and political exiles from Rome. We know very little about Godfrey's family background, but it seems that he was born to a respectable local family of mixed German and Italian heritage.[20] His social position was certainly elevated enough for him to have come to the attention of the Holy Roman emperor Lothar III while he was still a child. Lothar recognised in Godfrey the makings of a scholar and arranged for him to attend the elite cathedral school in Bamberg in what is now Bavaria. Godfrey was evidently a bookish and somewhat precocious child and must have relished the chance to study in one of the leading intellectual centres of twelfth-century Europe. But the young boy was probably also very homesick. We know from his later work that Godfrey remained fiercely attached to his home city, eventually retiring in Viterbo at the end of a long and distinguished career in the imperial service.

Although he owed his education to imperial patronage, Godfrey's first job was not in the imperial court, but back in Italy in the service of the pope. Detailed analysis of Godfrey's surviving manuscripts reveals that he used certain elements of what is known as "papal cursive"—a form of shorthand handwriting that was developed and used exclusively in the papal curia.[21] He can only have learned this while working in the papal administration as a teenager or young man. It may have been at this time also that Godfrey decided to be ordained as a priest. For young men of his social standing, taking the cloth was as much a professional as a spiritual decision, as membership in the clergy offered opportunities for social advancement and employment that would not otherwise have been available to the son of a respectable but modest provincial family.

It was not long, however, before Godfrey was lured back into the imperial fold, this time under a new and more vigorous dynasty—the Staufers. Godfrey joined the growing ranks of imperial bureaucrats employed by the Staufers to administer their unruly empire. As in so many large bureaucracies, both historical and modern, the top jobs in the imperial chancery were political appointments—distributed to nobles and minor princes who enjoyed the status of trusted advisers. Most of the real work was done by notaries, who beavered away to write the treaties, laws, proclamations, and other documents required for the governance of the empire.[22] Some, but not all, of these notaries would have been priests, and there was considerable overlap in personnel between the chancery and the imperial chapel, as we can see from Godfrey's own career.

It is amongst these humble cleric-notaries that we first discover

Godfrey in the imperial chancery, copying documents during the reign of Conrad III. At this stage of his life, Godfrey had not risen to the level of signing his work or witnessing important documents (although this was to come), and scholars have been able to identify him only though painstaking analysis of his handwriting. Who knows what lured him away from Rome to the itinerant imperial court, but in the years that followed, Godfrey was to show a deep loyalty to the Staufer dynasty, becoming disenchanted with them only at the very end of his life. It was Barbarossa, the second and the most famous of the Staufer emperors, who was the focus both of Godfrey's greatest hopes and of his greatest disappointments.

We have already met Barbarossa, whose raw charisma, bravery, and seemingly boundless energy all marked him out as a man to be reckoned with. This was fortunate because there was quite a lot of reckoning to be done. Keeping the princes of Germany, France, and Austria in line involved some delicate footwork, but Barbarossa was more than up to the task. Dealing with the Italians proved somewhat harder, especially as some were liable to align with the papacy against the imperial cause. Barbarossa launched no fewer than five military campaigns into Italy, between which a near-constant traffic of embassies and delegations shuttled back and forth between the imperial court and northern Italy, seeking diplomatic solutions to stave off the next conflict.

Godfrey, with his Italian upbringing and his German education, became suddenly very useful. During the early years of Barbarossa's reign, he began to take on roles of increasing seniority and appears to have risen through the ranks of the imperial chancery. Handwriting analysis once more allows us to identify key documents that were penned by Godfrey and to trace the trajectory of his career. These include the feudal constitution of 1154 (renewed in 1158); the first European charter for scholars and universities, signed in 1155 (known as the *Authentica Habita*); and, perhaps most importantly of all, the Treaty of Constance.[23] This treaty was agreed between Barbarossa and Pope Eugene III in 1153 and laid out the terms for Barbarossa's accession; it had to be reconfirmed in 1155 when a new pope, Adrian IV, came to power. The change in Godfrey's status between the first and the second versions of this treaty is interesting. Although he acts as a witness and signatory for both documents, in 1153 he is described as *Gotefredus Viterbiensis Capellanus regis* (Godfrey of Viterbo, chaplain of the king); while a mere two years later he is described more affectionately and informally as *Gotifredi capellini nostri* (Godfrey our chaplain). It seems that Godfrey worked his way into the imperial inner circle fairly rapidly after Barbarossa's accession to the throne.

But Godfrey was not destined to spend much time drafting and witnessing charters, and before long he was out on the road as a diplomatic envoy. He also seems to have accompanied Barbarossa on at least three of his Italian military campaigns: rejoicing at his side when Naples capitulated in 1162; bearing witness to the horror when Barbarossa's army was struck by plague in Rome in 1167;[24] and struggling to guard the house of one of his informants when Barbarossa's army was set loose to sack the city of Susa in Piedmont in 1174.[25] These years must have been busy ones, leaving precious little time for rest or repose. Looking back on them later, Godfrey described his life at the time as a never-ending round of work and travel:

> As a chaplain I was occupied every day around the clock in the mass and all the hours, at table, in negotiations, in the drafting of letters, in the daily arrangements of new lodgings, in looking after the livelihood for myself and my people, in carrying out very important missions: twice to Sicily, three times to Provence, once to Spain, several times to France, and forty times from Germany to Rome

and back. More was demanded of me in every exertion and restless-
ness than from anyone else my age at the court.[26]

Godfrey may have exaggerated his importance and status,[27] but it is clear that he was an experienced and trusted diplomat who had seen more than enough excitement in his time. One of his adventures was perhaps even a bit too exciting. It was 1179, and Godfrey was travelling on legation for Barbarossa across the fertile hills of Marche in central Italy. Without warning, he was captured by Barbarossa's first cousin and sworn enemy, Conrad of Montferrat, who held Godfrey prisoner until Barbarossa arranged for his release.[28] We do not know how long Godfrey was in captivity, or what the conditions of his confinement might have been—my speculative sketch at the start of this chapter is plucked purely from my imagination. What we do know is that Godfrey was there for longer than he would have liked, as he complained about it pointedly later. Perhaps his experience was similar to that of the archbishop of Mainz, another of Barbarossa's officials who was captured in the same year by Conrad, and who languished in captivity for more than a year.[29]

His incarceration was to prove a turning point for Godfrey. After this, there is no more evidence for diplomatic missions or for activity in the imperial chancery. He would have been in his early sixties, and would inevitably at some stage have stepped back from the hectic life he had been leading for the last four decades. But the experience of captivity seems to have shaken Godfrey deeply, as well as his feeling of abandonment and disappointment when Barbarossa failed to help him. Exhausted and disaffected, Godfrey decided to retire.

Fortunately, he had already planned for his retirement. In the decade before his capture, Godfrey had secured a number of grants and privileges from Barbarossa, which would support him in comfort for years after he stopped working. Amongst them was a palazzo in Viterbo, which Barbarossa had bestowed on Godfrey, his brother Werner, and his nephew Reiner as a hereditary imperial fief. In addition to this, Godfrey received a regular income from the cathedrals of Lucca and Pisa in Italy, and from the cathedrals of Speyer in the Rhineland, all of which paid him a portion of their annual revenues.[30] With his financial future secure, Godfrey withdrew to Viterbo and devoted himself to composing his chronicle. A good portion was completed by 1183, when Godfrey tentatively titled it the *Speculum regum* (the *Mirror of Princes*). It was ostensibly dedicated to the young prince Henry, Barbarossa's heir apparent, and professed to offer Henry a mirror onto the past, so that he could see historical models for his own future kingship. Contrary to what we might expect, the model of ideal kingship that Godfrey laid out was not one that derived from Greek or Roman antiquity. Instead, for Godfrey, models of kingship were to be sought in western Asia.

The Progeny of Priam

Thus begins the Speculum regum, *composed by Master Godfrey of Viterbo, chaplain of the imperial court, dedicated to Lord Henry VI, King of the Romans and the Germans, son of Lord Frederic the Emperor, who is sprung from the line of all the kings and emperors of the Trojans and Romans and Germans from the time of the Flood to the present day.*[31]

It was a bold way to start. The first sentence of Godfrey's world chronicle set out his position in no uncertain terms. This was an unashamedly political history of the world, structured as a genealogy of successive empires—the earliest being that of the Trojans, the next being that of the Romans, and the current being that of the Germans. We have already seen in Chapter 2 how the Romans took great pride in tracing their ancestry back to Troy. It should come as no surprise, therefore, that when the Holy Roman Empire claimed descent from ancient Rome, it also adopted the idea of Trojan origins.

We have already discussed how the idea of *translatio imperii* bolstered the legitimacy of imperial rule, at the same time both explaining and justifying the Holy Roman Empire with reference to ancient Roman *imperium*. But the question of Trojan origins is a little more sensitive. By the late twelfth century, the Holy Roman Empire was increasingly being characterised as "Western" and "European" when compared to its Byzantine rival. As we have learned, the identification with Europe had begun as early as the ninth century, with an anonymous poet describing Charlemagne as the "Father of Europe" following the establishment of the Holy Roman Empire. But this trend had intensified over the course of the eleventh and twelfth centuries, given the ongoing confessional disputes between Rome and Constantinople. Against this background, the idea of Asian origins (Troy was, after all, located in what is modern-day Turkey) might seem like a strange choice for an empire that was firmly rooted in central Europe. It may seem particularly odd to modern observers, who are usually conditioned to think of history in terms of Western Civilisation, and to view Europe as being demarcated from Asia not only by geography but also by culture, civilisation, and race. Godfrey's perspective, like those of many of his contemporaries, was quite different.

For Godfrey, the origins of kingship and the root of the Staufer family tree were unequivocally to be found in the "*genus imperii Troianaque*."[32] Before this imperial race of Trojans, Godfrey acknowledges that there were some people of interest in prehistory—for example, the biblical peoples of Babylonia, the Israelites, and a quasi-mythical version of the ancient Greeks (amongst which, strangely enough, the king of the gods, Zeus, makes an appearance as the human ruler of Athens). But for him, the start of "real" history is at Troy.

Godfrey's focus on Troy was, as we might expect from a seasoned diplomat, calculated for political effect. In the *Speculum regum*, the Trojan heritage was not about general cultural continuities or broad civilisational inheritance, but a very specific claim about the blood-lines of the Staufers. Henry, Barbarossa, and the entire Staufer dynasty were—according to Godfrey—the direct descendants of the house of Priam. Godfrey was not alone in tracing a genealogical line between a noble family of medieval Europe and the Trojan royal palace. Discovering such links was all the rage in the twelfth century, as it had been nearly a millennium earlier in Caesar's Rome, and we find similar claims in the works of historians from across the continent.[33] The Normans, the Saxons, the Franks, the Teutons, the Venetians, the Genoese, the Paduans, and even, according to the Icelandic author of the *Prose Edda*, the Norse gods were all said to be descended from Trojans.[34] By the end of the century, the English chronicler Henry of Huntingdon wryly remarked that most of the people of Europe now traced their ancestry back to Troy.[35]

These historical chronicles and noble genealogies were only part of the picture. The story of Troy was also the stuff of pop culture, with tales of chivalric romance composed in the various vernacular languages of Europe set against the dramatic backdrop of the Trojan War. Benoît de Sainte-Maure's *Roman de Troie* was published around the same time that Godfrey first began composing the *Speculum regum* and rapidly became an international bestseller. It was quickly translated from the original French into Latin, German, Dutch, Italian, Spanish, and modern Greek. With it, an entire new genre of literature exploded onto the cultural scene, focused on romantic stories set in or around the "Matter of Troy." As one modern scholar has put it, around this time there was "a pan-European fashion for the wildly popular and ideologically powerful bestsellers with a Trojan theme."[36]

Amongst all these Trojan tales, Godfrey stands out from the crowd, both for the clarity of his genealogical vision and for the ingenious nature of its political implications. In rollicking rhyming Latin verse, Godfrey describes how the Trojans scattered after the fall of Troy, some travelling by sea to Italy[37] while others out overland to the banks of the Rhine.[38] This division of the Trojans was crucial for his story, and he was at pains to stress that:

The progeny of Priam then split in twain;
One in Italy chose to remain,
The other founded the German domain.[39]

The Italians and the Germans were, according to Godfrey, like brothers—each sprung from their own branch of the same Trojan tree. This was a genealogical sleight of hand that spoke to the political situation of the time. Godfrey had spent the best part of the last three decades trying to smooth over relationships between the proud princes of Italy and their German emperor, sometimes (as we have seen) suffering personally in the process. While a fragile peace between Barbarossa and the pope had been reached in 1177, the Lombard League of northern Italian cities continued their campaigns against the emperor for several more years. It was not until 1183, the very same year that the first version of the *Speculum regum* was completed, that the Peace of Constance was signed, which finally reconciled the two sides. The Trojan lineage in Godfrey's *Speculum regum* was therefore a form of kinship diplomacy, encouraging the Germans and Italians towards fraternal solidarity.

There was also a personal edge to the genealogy. It spoke not just to Godfrey's experience as a diplomat working to bring the two sides together during a protracted conflict but also to his family background. Godfrey was born in Italy and strongly identified with his hometown of Viterbo but at the same time had Germanic ancestry and had spent his formative years studying in Germany, as well as owing his education and current status to Germanic emperors. He found himself caught between the two worlds personally as well as professionally. While Godfrey's Trojan genealogy might have been a statement about Barbarossa's Italian wars, we can imagine that it also may have struck a chord with him personally.

As an added bonus, the Trojan genealogy was also an opportunity to put the Franks in their place. Like so many European noble houses at this time, the leaders of the Franks claimed to be descended from Trojan royalty. They claimed that their legendary ancestor, the eponymous Francio, was the son of Troy's greatest hero, Hector. Godfrey revised the story so that the Franks—whom he calls the "Francigenae," or "Franklings"—now became a minor offshoot of the main German stemma. This splinter group, he claims, crossed the Rhine to live in a region around Paris that he patronisingly dubs "Little Frankia."[40] We can only imagine how Godfrey's readers would have responded to this jibe, their brows creasing in humour or in frustration depending on their standpoint.

As well as a symbolic snub, the idea of the Franks being an offshoot of the Germans was important because it allowed Godfrey to claim Charlemagne—the founder of the Holy Roman Empire—as a Teuton. Charlemagne's father, Pepin, could be described as hailing from the Teutonic line of Franklings, and therefore Godfrey could assimilate him within the Germanic branch of his Trojan genealogy. Godfrey also detailed the ancestry of Charlemagne's mother, Bertha, who he claimed was descended from the Italian stem of the Trojan line. According to Godfrey, therefore, Charlemagne united the two Trojan bloodlines, bringing them back into a single lineage.

The Trojan family (in two divided)
Fused when Pepin and Bertha collided—
Troy reunited within their son.
If for the line of Troy you care
In Charles you'll find its ultimate heir;
With his Teutonic dad and Roman mum.[41]

Through the blood of its founder, Charlemagne, the Holy Roman Empire was therefore the heir of the Trojan *imperium* twice over. But crucially for the Staufer imperial claim, the Germanic line is represented as being superior to and dominating the Italian, just as the patriarchal thinking of the time would have assumed Charlemagne's father, the Germanic Pepin, as superior to and dominating his mother, the Italian Bertha. This also allowed Godfrey to build an acknowledgement of Germanic origins into his narrative. These traditions of Germanic and northern origins were also an important parallel thread running through medieval historiography at the time.[42] Of course, the blood of Charlemagne also ran, Godfrey claimed, in the veins of the Staufers, making them the living embodiments of the ancient heritage of Troy. All of human history (in Godfrey's version of it anyway) had led up to this point—the Staufer dynasty at the helm of the Holy Roman Empire. It was nothing less than a political bombshell.

And yet, the *Speculum regum* was not the final version of Godfrey's chronicle. Over the next four years, Godfrey expanded on his history, adding lengthy sections about the more recent past. But he also changed and even deleted large chunks of what he had written for the *Speculum regum*. By the time of Godfrey's final draft, genealogical exposition was out and biblical history was in, and being a savvy political thinker, Godfrey would have known to alter his work to fit the times. Along with this came a change in the dedication of the work. No longer addressed to Barbarossa and his son Henry (whom he had originally described as the culmination of the line "of all the kings and emperors of the Trojans and Romans and Germans"), the new version of the chronicle, known as the *Liber universalis* or the *Pantheon*, was dedicated to the pope. In some manuscripts the name given is that of Pope Urban III, while in others we find that of his successor, Gregory VIII, but in all cases the shift of Godfrey's allegiance is clear. After decades of service, he was no longer exclusively the emperor's man.

Scholars have suggested a range of reasons for this change. Did Godfrey meet with only a lukewarm reception when he unveiled the *Speculum regum* at the imperial court, leading him to tout his talents elsewhere?[43] Did he succumb to bitterness over Barbarossa's neglect of him during his captivity? Or did he, as an older man settling down to retirement, begin to turn his mind to the spiritual life, repenting of the years he had spent in an administration that had defied the church? We may never know. One thing that we can be sure about is the political realignment of the chronicle in its final form.

While the *Speculum regum* had been more inward looking, concerned with promoting unity between the Germans and the Italians, the *Pantheon* was more outward focused. It made a point of driving a wedge between two halves of Christendom—on the one hand the Latin church of the pope and the Holy Roman Empire, and on the other the Greek church of the patriarch and the Byzantines. Godfrey's treatment of both the ancient Greeks and his Byzantine contemporaries is dismissive. While in the *Speculum regum* the ancient Greeks had at least made an honourable appearance as a semi-mythical race of prehistoric people, in the *Pantheon* their role has been reduced to the odd casual mention. The Byzantines appear only slightly more often and are described almost contemptuously.

> *The kings of the Greeks we should mention again,*
> *As over Italy they once thought they'd reign,*
> *But what was once Greek is now Italy's domain.*[44]

Charlemagne makes an appearance too, this time as the man responsible for the demise of Greek power by the establishment of his *imperium*. Interestingly enough, Godfrey never uses this word in relation to the Byzantines or Greeks. The title of "empire," or *imperium*, belonged only to those realms and peoples that Godfrey included in his civilisational genealogy—the Trojans, the Romans, and the Germans. In his worldview, the Greeks belonged to another civilisation altogether.

———

STANDARD ACCOUNTS OF Western history today place the ultimate origins of the West in the ancient Greek world, which is assumed to have provided a foundation on which the complex edifice of Western Civilisation was built. Today, modern Greece is an integral part of Europe, both politically and culturally, and we would always define the modern Greek people as belonging to the West. But it was not so for Godfrey. In the medieval world of the twelfth century, the Greeks belonged neither to Europa nor to any embryonic concept of the West. For the peoples of Godfrey's Europa, there was relatively little interest in the cultural legacy of ancient Greece.

This legacy was preserved and even furthered by scholars such as al-Kindī in the Muslim world (Chapter 3) and intellectuals in the Byzantine Empire such as Theodore Laskaris (Chapter 5). But both these men came from societies that were seen as being on a fundamentally different civilisational trajectory from that of central Europe. For Godfrey, sitting in his Italian palazzo and trying to make sense of history, the Asian antiquities of Troy and the Bible seemed far closer and more familiar than the strange and hostile world of the Hellenes. For Godfrey, our modern notion of cultural genealogy as set out in the theory of Western Civilisation would have seemed bizarre. Why the focus on Christendom when it was obvious that there were many opposed and plural Christianities? Why the claim for a conjoined Greco-Roman antiquity when it was clear that the Romans had from their earliest Trojan origins always been in conflict with the Greeks? And why the insistence on continental primacy, when it was evident that boundaries within Europe were just as important as those at its edges?

◆ Chapter Five ◆

THE ILLUSION OF
CHRISTENDOM

―――――

THEODORE LASKARIS

When are you going to come to Hellas from Europe?

THEODORE LASKARIS
(EARLY THIRTEENTH CENTURY CE)[1]

R ELIGIOUS wars are often extremely bloody, and the Crusades
were no exception.[2] They lasted for almost two hundred years,
from 1095 to 1291, and claimed the lives of countless men,
women, and children across three continents. These were wars driven
by religious fervour, as Christians from western and central Europe
fought to claim land from the surrounding infidels and pagans. In the

Iberian Peninsula, the Reconquista was waged against the Moorish kingdoms of Al-Andalus. In northern and eastern Europe, campaigns were conducted against the pagan Slavs. And perhaps most famously in the Holy Land, Christian and Muslim armies fought for control over territories that were sacred to both faiths.

If you mention the word "Crusade," most people will automatically think of these latter wars, fought mostly between Latin Christians and Muslims in the Levant and eastern Mediterranean during the twelfth and thirteenth centuries. They have now become iconic, acquiring a symbolic cultural status in hindsight that outweighs even the (admittedly significant) political and economic importance they had at the time. The idea of a crusade—a fiercely fought conflict where one side is incontrovertibly in the right and the other in the wrong—has become a commonplace metaphor. As early as 1784, Thomas Jefferson wrote about a "crusade against ignorance,"[3] and Dwight D. Eisenhower's 1948 memoir of the Second World War was titled *Crusade in Europe*. More recently, there have been crusades against drugs, cancer, HIV/AIDS, and domestic violence. Yet despite its broad current usage, the term still retains a sense of derogatory Islamophobia—a sense that came to the fore during the so-called War on Terror in the early twenty-first century. The Crusades therefore still stand in the public imagination as a defining chapter in the history of Western Civilisation—a chapter in which Christendom was forged in the heat of battle against the Muslims and tempered in the cooling air of Pan-European collaboration. The Crusades loom large in the imagined cultural genealogy of Western Civilisation. Unsurprisingly, they also feature prominently in the rhetoric of right-wing groups and the self-proclaimed defenders of the West, who use Crusader imagery and symbolism to lend their campaigns historical legitimacy.

But we shouldn't make the mistake of seeing the Crusades in the historical sense (religious wars waged by Christians in the twelfth and thirteenth centuries CE) as being crusades in the metaphorical sense (simple moral conflicts between clearly differentiated sides). They were much more complicated than that. The historical Crusades in the Levant were neither a straightforward contest between Christendom and the Caliphate nor a showdown between Christianity and Islam, but rather a series of complex and bloody power games in which religion was sometimes more and sometimes less important. And crucially, they could also be fought between different Christian groups as well as between Christians and non-Christians.

The man at the heart of this chapter knew this fact only too well. Towards the end of the year 1221, the Fifth Crusade had ended in ignominious defeat for the Christian armies led by Leopold of Austria and Andrew of Hungary. The Abbuyid sultan of Egypt, Al-Kamil, had trounced the Crusaders as they marched towards Cairo, reclaiming the port of Damietta, which had been occupied earlier in the campaign, and imposing an eight-year truce. At precisely the same time, in the imperial palace at Nicaea in what is now northwestern Turkey, an emperor was born in exile. His name was Theodore Laskaris.

Christendom in Pieces

One of the biggest misconceptions that people can have about medieval Christendom is that it existed as a coherent entity. There were certainly many peoples and realms that identified as Christian during the thousand or so years that we tend to call the "medieval period," but there was precious little unity between them. The discerning would-be convert could potentially choose from many different flavours of Christianity. Gnostics, Nestorians, Waldensians, Paulicians, Bogomils, Chaldaeans, and Lollards all offered different approaches to Christian theology and worship—and all were viewed, at one stage or another, by one authority or another, as heresies.[4] Over time, larger and more established churches emerged, the leaders of which spilled much ink in philosophical debate and much blood in forcible conversions to preserve their dominant ideology. Yet true Christian unity remained elusive, and Crusades were waged against heretics as well as against nonbelievers. The genocidal destruction visited on the Cathars of southern France between 1208 and 1229, for example, was justified by the Cathars' confessional deviance. They espoused a dualistic approach to the divine, with separate cosmic forces of good and evil, and therefore found themselves at odds with the rigorous monotheism of the mainstream Latin church.[5] The massacres of the Albigensian Crusade were their reward. Even the most zealous pruning of heresies by the most dominant of churches could not root out all dissent, and divergent Christian practices and beliefs continued to develop.

The diversity of medieval Christianity was not just confessional. It was also geographical, racial, and cultural. The grand narrative of Western Civilisation tends to depict medieval Christianity as primarily a European phenomenon, conveniently forgetting that the faith also thrived in both Africa and Asia. Medieval Christian communities spoke their prayers and wrote their scriptures not only in Latin, the language of the Church in Rome, but also in Byzantine Greek, Coptic, Ge'ez, Aramaic, Arabic, Armenian, classical Persian, various Turkic and Mongol dialects, and Chinese.

One of the strongest and longest-lived of these extra-European churches was the Ethiopian.[6] Christianity had become the state religion of the kingdom of Aksum in modern-day Ethiopia in the fourth century CE, around the same time that it became the official religion of the Roman Empire. By the medieval period, Christianity was therefore not only the state religion in Aksum, but also the prevailing faith of the population at large. The beautifully illuminated Garima Gospels, painstakingly produced by skilled Ethiopian monks in the early medieval period, recount the life of Christ in the elegant language of Ge'ez, and the spectacular rock-cut churches of Lalibela, built to be "New Jerusalem" after the Muslim conquests of the Holy Land, are now inscribed on the UNESCO World Heritage List.

But just as ancient as the Ethiopian church were the Coptic church of Egypt, the Syriac churches of the Levant and Mesopotamia, and the Assyrian churches of Iran and Turkmenistan, all of which were firmly established by the fourth century.[7] The Xi'an Stele even attests a Nestorian Christian community in northwest China in the eighth century (although Christianity seems to have died out in China in the tenth century, only to be revived again in the thirteenth).[8] William of Rubruck, a Flemish monk travelling though the Mongol Empire in the mid-thirteenth century, complained that the Christians he encountered there drank too heavily, spent too much time fraternising with Buddhists and other nonbelievers, and even indulged in polygamy, yet he grudgingly acknowledged that they were Christians nonetheless.[9] While these eastern churches did not enjoy the protection of being part of an official state religion, their longevity and the strength of their traditions are significant. The Christians of Africa and Asia deserve their place in the history of medieval Christianity, which can sometimes be too Eurocentric in its focus.[10]

And yet, Christian Eurocentrism was a phenomenon of the medieval period too. This medieval Eurocentrism looked quite different from its modern counterpart, largely because medieval ideas about "Europa" were quite different from the modern definition of "Europe" (as we have seen in Chapter 4). The term "Europa" was not much used to articulate the opposition between the Christians of continental Europe on the one hand and the Muslims and pagans of Asia and Africa on the other. Instead, Europa was more commonly used to describe the lands where the Catholic Church and the Holy Roman Empire held sway, contrasting these with the jurisdiction of the Orthodox

Church and dominion of the Byzantine Empire (see Chapter 4). The relationship between the Latin and the Greek churches mirrored that of the two empires, which both claimed descent from Rome—the Holy Roman Empire in central Europe, and the Byzantine Empire in southeastern Europe and Anatolia. For centuries, this relationship had been strained but mostly peaceful. The rivalry was to erupt again in the late twelfth century amidst the Crusades, with catastrophic consequences.

The trouble began with Venetian merchants.[11] Outstanding sailors and extremely commercially savvy, the Venetians dominated the maritime trade networks of the eastern Mediterranean and maintained a substantial presence in Constantinople. The Byzantine population were frustrated by the Venetians' wealth and power, as well as by the way they conducted themselves within the city. Substantial groups of merchants from Pisa and Genoa also lived within the city, trying to compete with the Venetians for trading routes and market share within the Byzantine Empire. The umbrella term "Latin" was used for all these communities, in reference to their adherence to the Latin-speaking church of Rome. When inter-Latin rivalries turned violent in the 1170s, with raiding and street battles between the Venetians and the Genoese, the Byzantine authorities saw an opportunity to crack down. The expulsions, arrests, and confiscations of property that followed set Venice and the Byzantine Empire on a footing for violence. The tension sent the relationship between the eastern and western branches of Christianity spiralling deeper and deeper into chaos.

With the gloves now off, in Constantinople popular resentment against the Latin merchants boiled over. The year 1182 saw rioting culminating in a full-scale massacre of the city's Latin inhabitants, with thousands killed and the survivors sold into slavery. Retribution was brutal. In 1185, the Latins sacked the city of Thessaloníki, all but destroying the Byzantine Empire's second largest city. The cold war between the two main churches of Europe had turned very hot indeed, and sporadic conflict between the sides continued for another two decades. But the ultimate blow came in 1204 and the Fourth Crusade.[12]

The Latin armies of the Fourth Crusade were *supposed* to be headed for Egypt, with the aim of reducing the greatest Muslim maritime power in the Mediterranean. But when the fleet assembled at Venice and found themselves unexpectedly short of cash, their plans changed. The Crusaders sailed east rather than south and besieged Constantinople. The siege itself lasted ten months, from July 1203 to April 1204. It culminated in the sacking of the city; the murder, rape, and expulsion of many of its inhabitants; and the systematic looting and destruction of its churches, monasteries, and palaces. The Byzantine court was forced to evacuate, fleeing the bloody streets of Constantinople for the safety of western Anatolia and the provincial capital of Nicaea.

After the sack of Constantinople, the Crusaders set about dividing the spoils. Not only was the city of Constantinople in their hands, but so too was much of the Greek peninsula. Venice, as the leader of the campaign, claimed three-quarters of the plunder taken from the city as well as three-quarters of the Byzantine territory now in Crusader hands. The remaining booty and lands were divided amongst the various Frankish princes who had also taken part in the Crusade, and a new Latin emperor and patriarch were established at Constantinople.[13] This ushered in a period of more than three centuries during which much of the Greek peninsula was controlled by a colonial Latin ruling class—a period still referred to as the "Frankokratia."[14] The Duchy of Athens, for example, was established by a minor knight from Burgundy and remained under Latin rule until its conquest by the Ottomans in 1458. We don't usually think of Greece as being under the colonial rule of western Europeans, but for more than three hundred years, it was.

After the Crusaders had grabbed what they could, there was precious little left of an independent Byzantine Empire.[15] The core of the rump state was in western Anatolia—the Franks ruled the Greek peninsula and Aegean islands; the Seljuks, a Turkic dynasty with origins in central Asia, had established control of central and eastern Anatolia; and southern Anatolia was controlled by an independent Armenian kingdom. The Byzantine Empire found itself dramatically reduced almost overnight. The Fourth Crusade was, in the words of historians, a "cosmic cataclysm."[16] And it had happened at the hands not of the supposed Muslim enemy but of other Christians.

This was the thirteenth-century world of Theodore Laskaris—an emperor destined to be born, live out his life, and die in exile. His parents had fled the blood and the fire of the Crusader onslaught on Constantinople, and Laskaris himself was born in Nicaea in northwest Anatolia. He spent his life consolidating what little was left of the Byzantine territories and attempting to retake the "Queen of Cities" from its Latin occupiers.[17] He might not have lived to see the day that the Byzantines eventually reclaimed Constantinople in 1261 (although despite their best efforts they were never able to oust the Latins from the Greek peninsula), but Laskaris did leave one important legacy. He fostered the idea of the Hellenic nation as an ethnically and culturally Greek political entity—an idea that had not existed in antiquity, when the notion of the Greeks joining into a single political unit would have seemed completely bizarre (see Chapter 1). Laskaris's vision of the Hellenes forming a single ethno-political unity might have been novel in the thirteenth century, but it proved remarkably long-lived.[18] When the celebrations for the two hundredth anniversary of modern Greek independence were staged in 2021, they were rooted in the idea of Hellenism as both political force and national identity. They were rooted in ideas that were to a significant extent popularised by Laskaris.

And yet, Laskaris would be puzzled by the staunchly European nature of modern Greek identity. He had been born into a world where there was little love lost between eastern Europe and western Asia on the one side, and central and western Europe on the other—a world forged by the rift between Greek and Latin Christianity. The hatred between these two sides burned hot and fierce, flying in the face of any notions of a united Christendom. Looking back at the medieval period and the Crusades today, we might be tempted to overlook the schism between Greek and Latin Christianity, viewing the divide as a temporary falling-out between two groups of coreligionists who ultimately had more in common with each other than they had with their shared Muslim adversaries. But we would be wrong. This was no fraternal spat. In the early thirteenth century, the gulf that lay between the Greek and Latin worlds sometimes seemed as wide and as unbroachable as that which lay between Christians and Muslims.

Letters from Exile

Theodore II Laskaris was named for his grandfather, Theodore I Laskaris—the ill-fated Byzantine emperor who had been forced to flee the invading Crusader armies in 1204 as they sacked his city.[19] When our Laskaris first drew breath, therefore, it was not the sea breezes of Constantinople that filled his lungs but rather the soft zephyrs of inland Anatolia.

As a result, he does not seem to have had much emotional attachment to the old capital. A prolific writer, he often waxed lyrical about the "beloved ground" of his "mother Anatolia" in the hundreds of letters, orations, and theological essays he composed.[20] But whatever his personal feelings about his homeland, the shape of his life was crucially determined by the Latin conquest of Constantinople and the expulsion of the Byzantines. He would have been painfully aware that his was a dynasty in exile, biding its time in western Anatolia only until it could reclaim its ancestral seat on the Bosporus.

Laskaris's parents, on the other hand, remembered Constantinople perfectly. His father, John Vatatzes, had been a young nobleman from a distinguished military clan that often intermarried with the imperial family. He became the third husband of Irene Laskarina, the oldest daughter of Theodore I Laskaris.[21] Both Irene and John would have been children in 1204 when Constantinople fell—Irene most likely aged between five and ten, and John between ten and fifteen—but both remembered the event vividly, as well as the excruciating process of setting up the new court in exile at Nicaea.

In the generation after the fall of Constantinople, Nicaea quickly became a bustling and prosperous city.[22] It was peopled by the cream of Byzantine nobility and senior members of the Orthodox clergy who had followed the emperor and his family into exile. For many, it was a city of wistful nostalgia, where the older generation cast their melancholy eyes westwards and clung to the memory of glories now gone. But Nicaea was also a city of new beginnings, and Laskaris grew up at the head of an energetic new generation who did not remember the old capital. This generation dreamed of not a return to a glorious past, but rather the forging of a new future.[23]

Laskaris enjoyed a happy childhood. He was an only child, as after his birth his mother, Irene, suffered a hunting accident that prevented her from having any more children. This must have made him even more precious in the eyes of his parents, who lavished him with affection. Frustrated tutors found that whenever the young Laskaris misbehaved, his parents were more likely to indulge rather than to discipline him. Irene was an especially strong influence during his formative years. She was the linchpin that allowed the succession to pass from her father to her husband, and as a result she wielded a significant amount of power. She also controlled a number of estates in her own name, which meant that she had economic power in addition to political clout.

From a young age, Laskaris was groomed for kingship. Rhetoric, logic, mathematics, and music supplemented a core curriculum based on holy scripture and ancient Greek literature. In all fields, Laskaris excelled. His written works as an adult bear testament to the habits he learned as a child, with erudite allusions and sophisticated wordplay being particularly characteristic of his style.[24] He was eventually to present himself as a "philosopher-king" in the mould prescribed by Plato for an ideal ruler, and wrote lengthy treatises on morality, theology, and cosmology.[25] But equally important for the young prince was physical and military training. Horsemanship was improved by hunting and by playing polo—a game that had been popular in Constantinople before its fall. Laskaris seems to have been especially fond of polo, later in life writing about the joy of the game in detail and describing his feats on his "beloved exercise ground."[26]

But an excellent physical and intellectual education was not enough. The heir to the Byzantine Empire also needed to be married, as a guard against rival claimants making a bid for the throne. And so at thirteen, Laskaris was wed to Elena, a twelve-year-old princess from Bulgaria, in an arranged marriage designed to seal the alliance between the two realms.[27] Despite the youth of the partners and their lack of choice in the matter, the union seems to have been a happy one, with Laskaris later describing his wife as "the springtime of my soul" and their marriage as a "bond of incomparable love." The couple would eventually go on to have five children. When Elena died suddenly of an unknown illness in 1252, Laskaris responded angrily to advisers who counselled him to remarry, composing an elaborate scholarly essay in riposte, titled "Response to Some Friends Pressing Him to Find a Bride." With the passing of his wife, he declared, the only women in his life would be *Sophia* (wisdom) and *Philosophia* (philosophy).[28]

His education, training, and marriage—all of this was designed to prepare Laskaris for power. He was proclaimed a co-emperor with his father while still a child and was performing duties independently on an equal footing by his early twenties.[29] Laskaris worked tirelessly to stimulate the Byzantine economy, focusing in particular on textile production and overland trade. And although the city of Nicaea would always be Laskaris's home, he spent much of his time travelling through the rest of western Anatolia, ensuring the efficient functioning of both the tax and legal systems, stamping out corruption, and cultivating a close relationship with his subjects.[30]

As well as strengthening his rule at home, Laskaris also enjoyed diplomatic and military success abroad. He supported his father in establishing a defensive alliance with the Seljuks against the Mongols and cultivated a personal relationship with the Seljuk sultan ʿIzz al-Dīn Kaykāwūs II, eventually offering him sanctuary at the Byzantine court when he was temporarily deposed by his brother.[31] Indeed, Laskaris was quick to exploit the turmoil within the Seljuk sultanate, extracting more Anatolian territories from ʿIzz al-Dīn as the price of Byzantine support. But Laskaris did not restrict himself to one alliance. Hedging his diplomatic bets, Laskaris also entered into direct diplomatic relations with the Mongols. Embassies were sent between the Mongol and Byzantine courts, and a marriage alliance between the two empires was ultimately reached. The Byzantine historian Pachymeres recounts how Laskaris received the Mongol envoys in splendid but theatrical fashion. While the Mongols were led through mountainous territory to the designated meeting point, Byzantine soldiers dressed in full regalia took shortcuts so that they would appear in sight at several points along the way, to give the impression that the Byzantine army was much larger than it actually was.[32]

Relationships to the west were more fraught than those to the east.

Laskaris was successful in a number of lightning military campaigns in Thrace and Macedonia.[33] Along with his father, he managed to retake substantial tracts of land in what is now northern Greece from the Latins. They even managed to bring the Byzantine armies right up to the walls of Constantinople and besiege the city, eventually agreeing to a peace with its Latin rulers when it became clear that they were unable to reclaim the city itself. After his father's death, Laskaris was also responsible for major territorial gains in the Balkans, soundly defeating the king of Bulgaria to take control of much of what is now the Republic of Macedonia, despite the familial link through his wife, Elena. Laskaris can therefore add expanding the Byzantine-controlled territories both eastwards and westwards to his list of achievements.

The long years of co-ruling ensured that when his father died in 1254, Laskaris was already experienced in both military campaigns and civil government, and the transition of power was smooth. The smoothness of the transition was fortunate, as despite Laskaris's and his father's best efforts at both consolidation and expansion, the Byzantine Empire continued to struggle. The empire would need leaders with competence, vision, and a decent helping of guts to save it. Fortunately, Laskaris's father, the first of the Byzantine emperors in exile at Nicaea, was nothing if not competent, and Laskaris's eventual successor, the indomitable Michael Palaiologos, had guts to spare. It was up to Laskaris to provide the vision.

The Heritage of Hellas

Laskaris's vision played a crucial part in changing the way the Byzantines thought about themselves and about their place in the world. In short, he helped to transform his people from Romans into Greeks.

Until this point, the Byzantines usually referred to themselves as *Romaioi*, that is, Romans. After all, Constantinople had been a capital city of the Roman Empire on an equal footing with Rome, and Roman government and administration had endured here unbroken after the fall of the Roman Empire. The same could not be said of Italy and the old city of Rome, which had been conquered by the Goths in the fifth century and seen significant cultural change over the centuries. Even more significantly, the imperial vestments of the western emperor had been sent to Constantinople in 476 CE, when Odoacer, the general who deposed the last Western Roman emperor, decided to style himself as "King of Italy" rather than "Emperor of the Western Romans."[34] In the eyes of the Byzantines, therefore, only *they* remained true Romans, with their western compatriots having relinquished all claims to the Roman identity. In their eyes, the language of real Romans was Byzantine Greek rather than medieval Latin, and the unbroken traditions of culture and custom that had been maintained within the Byzantine court were more Roman than the fragmentation of Italy and central Europe. And because the Byzantines thought of themselves as *Romaioi*, they did not tend to think of themselves as *Hellenoi*, or Greeks.

Part of the problem was that the word "Hellene" had, for many Byzantines, pejorative connotations and associations with paganism. The Orthodox Church in which they worshipped was not, in their view, a "Greek" Orthodox Church as some Western commentators might describe it today. They held their church to be universal and free from the taint of pagan Hellenism. Some Byzantine authors even stripped the term "Hellene" of all ethnic associations, using the word "Hellene" to refer to all non-Christians, whether they were Arabs, Persians, or Chinese.[35] In a society that was both deeply and performatively Christian, this association with paganism was a taint to be avoided. Byzantine writers before Laskaris use the word "Hellene" mostly in a historical sense, rarely if ever applying it to the living Byzantine population. Although ancient Greek texts were still read and ancient Greek literature still studied by scholars and specialists, this did not filter through to the mainstream, and a conscious sense of Greekness was not the basis of Byzantine ethnic or national identity.

Laskaris played an important role in changing this. The old identity of *Romaioi* no longer fitted the reality in which Laskaris found himself. He was a Byzantine born outside Byzantium, a Roman emperor who ruled neither the "old" Rome on the Tiber nor the "new" Rome on the Bosporus. What was it, he must have pondered as he surveyed the fertile rolling hills that surrounded Nicaea, that lay at the ideological core of his empire if not the *Romanitas* of Constantinople? What made it special and gave it meaning? In his quest to forge a new national identity, Laskaris returned to what he had learned as a precocious child from his long-suffering tutors—the cultural legacy of ancient Greece.[36]

This was a legacy that can be clearly seen in his writings. References to Plato and Aristotle abound, occurring alongside quotations from less well-known ancient philosophers such as Thales of Miletus and Heracleitus of Ephesus; mathematicians such as Pythagoras and Euclid; and the geographer Ptolemy and the medic Galen. But the poetry of Homer seems to have provided Laskaris with particular inspiration. He mentioned Homer by name in several of his letters[37] and made a number of more complex allusions to key passages of the Homeric epics. Writing to the diplomat and chronicler George Akropolites, Laskaris commented at length on the famous episode in Book 1 of the *Iliad*, in which Agamemnon rejects gifts offered to him in exchange for the captive Chryseis. Given that this rejection brought plague and suffering on his people, Laskaris observed gravely, Agamemnon should have accepted the offer.[38] Laskaris even sought comfort in an Iliadic reverie following the death of his wife, Elena. Writing once more to

Akropolites, he describes his excitement at a planned visit to the famous site of Troy and hopes that the trip will distract him from his grief.[39]

Laskaris was not, of course, the first Byzantine ruler to get excited about Homer. We have already mentioned in Chapter 3 how the Byzantine princess Anna Komnene composed epic poetry in the style of Homer, a century before Laskaris put pen to paper. But Laskaris was the first Byzantine emperor to make Hellenism political. For Laskaris, Hellenism could be applied more widely than to the erudite musings of grammarians. It belonged to all his subjects as the basis of their ethnic and national identity. In a letter written to his friend George Mouzalon in 1255, for example, he proudly described the "Hellenic bravery" of his "Hellenic armies" while they were on campaign in the Balkans.[40] Another letter to Mouzalon discussed the position of power that Laskaris found himself in when he granted sanctuary to the deposed Seljuk sultan 'Izz al-Dīn. All his Byzantine subjects, Laskaris claimed—the entire "Hellenic tribe"—were rejoicing at this diplomatic victory.[41] For Laskaris, the people of his empire were certainly still Romans,[42] but they were—perhaps for the first time—also Greeks.[43]

As well as using his writing to transform his subjects into Greeks, Laskaris also referred to his realm as "Hellas," or Greece.[44] But Laskaris's vision of Hellas was not the same as our idea of modern Greece. Today, we automatically assume that Greece is part of Europe and that the ancient Greek world belongs in the genealogy of Western Civilisation. But for Laskaris, Hellas was located not in Europe but in Asia. In a letter to the diplomat Andronikos, he asks, "When are you going to come from Europe to Hellas? When might you glance at Asia from the inside after passing through Thrace and crossing the Hellespont?"[45] And in one of his letters to the bishop Phokas, he discusses the return of the bishop of Sardis "from Europe to the Hellenic realm (*to Hellenikōn*)."[46]

In fact, Laskaris's ideas about the geography of Greekness were even more complex. While the Hellenic realm was—due to the political practicalities of the moment—located in Asia Minor, in Laskaris's more philosophical writings, the conceptual space of Hellas was expanded to encompass everywhere that ancient Greek culture and people were once found. In an especially powerful treatise, the ideologically compelling *Second Oration against the Latins*, Laskaris sets out a vision of Hellas that included not just the Aegean, but also Sicily, the Adriatic, the Persian Gulf, and the Black Sea.[47] In it, he follows Aristotle's geographical scheme whereby Greece did not belong to any of the continents, but instead sat between them in the middle of the world (for which, see Chapter 1). Carefully drawn diagrams in the surviving manuscripts of the *Oration* illustrate this vision starkly. The *oikoumene*, or the inhabited world, is represented as a circle, divided into quarters. At the centre of the circle lies Hellas, equidistant from each of the four poles, represented by Britain in the northwest, India in the northeast, Spain in the southwest, and Egypt in the southeast. Its geographic centrality, claimed Laskaris, meant that Hellas produced the healthiest and most vigorous people. Only the land of the Hellenes, since it has the most central climatic zone and the good air quality that comes from the sea, has the best mix of airs. It is from this mostly that the great vigour of our bodies comes from.[48]

The Hellenes, according to Laskaris, belonged in neither the east nor the west, the north nor the south, but occupied a privileged position in the centre of the world. In this vision, Laskaris was following the characteristically Aristotelian notion of the Greeks existing outside the standard continental scheme. But of all the points on the compass, I suspect Laskaris would have been especially loath to have

Hellenism linked with the west. It was men from the west, after all, under the banner of Latin-speaking Catholic Christianity, who had conquered and were still in occupation in Constantinople. And it was westerners, even more than the Seljuks or the Mongols of western and central Asia, who were the most hated of Byzantine enemies. In the decades before the catastrophic events of 1204 CE, some Byzantine writers and statesmen had, in the spirit of reconciliation and diplomacy, referred to the Latins as *Romaioi* and acknowledged some kind of shared cultural heritage between themselves and their European neighbours. But after the Fourth Crusade, this goodwill evaporated, and westerners are only referred to dismissively as *Latinoi* or *Italioi*.[49]

These *Latinoi* or *Italioi*, Laskaris argued forcefully, had no claim on the cultural heritage of Hellenism. This point is made especially strongly in the *Second Oration against the Latins*. The speech was written in the autumn of 1256 CE and delivered in a series of debates held in Thessaloníki between the Byzantine patriarchate and a papal embassy sent from Rome. In it, Laskaris warns his audience to reject any notion of compromise or fellow feeling with the Latin foe and encourages them instead to feel pride in their own Hellenic heritage. He confronts his interlocutor with a long list of the cultural achievements of Greek antiquity, from the poetry of Homer to the mathematics of Pythagoras—an intellectual and cultural legacy to which the Latins, he asserted vigorously, had no claim.

> *Please, run back to school and learn that philosophy belongs to the Hellenes, who have since ancient times inhabited the middle of the climatic zones; and that the scientists belong to us, and indeed all of their sciences are ours. Learn too, that the air they had back then belongs to us now, that we have the Hellenic language, and are sprung from their blood.*[50]

According to Laskaris, the Hellenes had furnished the world with not only philosophy and geometry, but also astronomy, arithmetic, music, the natural and medical sciences, as well as theology, politics, and rhetoric.[51] All these intellectual and cultural achievements were the inheritance of the Byzantines, thanks to their Hellenic identity, and not shared by the Latins of the west.

Laskaris's *Second Oration against the Latins* is an astonishing piece of political rhetoric, not just because of the power of its language or the dramatic nature of its claims. It is also remarkable for a modern Western audience because it flies in the face of conventional wisdom concerning the history of Western Civilisation. We hear that the heritage of ancient Greece belongs more to Anatolia than to Europe—and that the barbarous Latins of central and western Europe have no claim to Hellenism's cultural legacy.

WE THINK OF the Crusades today as a time characterised by the clash of civilisations, with East pitted against West, Asia against Europe, the Muslim world against Christendom. There certainly was plenty of this kind of rhetoric around in the medieval period, with Islamophobic literature circulating widely in Europe and caricatured depictions of dastardly infidels proliferating as propaganda against Muslims. But it was only part of the picture.[52] The medieval Crusades were fought on multiple fronts by multiple protagonists, sometimes—as in the case of the Fourth Crusade against the Byzantines—pitting one group of Christians against another. Christian unity was illusory, and the oft-vaunted concept of medieval Christendom, frequently associated with emergent ideas of the West, had no tangible reality.

The rifts between different groups of Christians were particularly evident in the time of Laskaris, when animosity between Byzantine

Orthodoxy and Latin Catholicism shaped medieval geopolitics. For Laskaris as for other Byzantines of his time, the idea of Western Civilisation as a cultural construct that took in both the Greek and the Latin traditions would not only have been risible; it would have been offensive. For them, the Hellenic world was fundamentally different from, and fundamentally superior to, the Latin Europeans. Conversely, the Latins of central and western Europe did not seek to trace their cultural lineage back to ancient Greece, which they understood as the ancestor of an enemy and a rival. As we saw in Chapter 4, their interest was in a Roman rather than an ancient Greek heritage, and they preferred to trace their origins back, via Rome, to Troy and ancient western Asia.

Laskaris himself died an untimely death in 1258 at the age of thirty-six, struck down by a mystery illness that is still the subject of scholarly speculation today.[53] At the time, in no small part thanks to Laskaris's own efforts, the Byzantine state had rallied after the catastrophic loss of Constantinople and was growing slowly stronger, still nursing a deep hatred for the westerners of Latin Europe. As we have seen in Chapter 4, the feeling was, for the most part, mutual. But things would soon change. A mere century after Laskaris wrote his *Second Oration against the Latins*, a young Italian poet named Petrarch set about excitedly investigating the ancients. A particular triumph was his rediscovery of several lost orations of Cicero in a codex in Liège, much to the vexation of generations of students around the world who have been forced to read Cicero ever since. But Petrarch's interests went beyond the Roman authors commonly studied in western and central Europe at the time—they included ancient Greece. Although he never learned to read ancient Greek himself, he arranged to import a codex of the Greek text of Homer to his home in Florence and commissioned the Calabrian scholar Leontius Pilatus to translate the Homeric poems into Latin in 1360.[54] Laskaris would have been furious with what he would have seen as the Latin appropriation of Hellenic culture. But he would have been powerless to turn back the cultural tide. Petrarch and his contemporaries had unleashed the Renaissance.

Chapter Six

THE REIMAGINING OF ANTIQUITY

TULLIA D'ARAGONA

Go to the west, and your ancestry will be
discovered by you.

TULLIA D'ARAGONA (1560)[1]

TULLIA D'Aragona was, in many respects, a "Renaissance man." She was a brilliant polymath, a published poet, and a celebrated philosopher whose glittering salon attracted the leading intellectuals of the day. In the mid-sixteenth century, she was a familiar face in the palaces of Florence, Venice, and Rome, associating with dukes and diplomats as well as sages and scholars. But of course, D'Aragona was not a Renaissance man for the simple reason that she was a woman.

If you seek information about D'Aragona today, you will likely stumble upon an array of viewpoints. In my research I found salacious gossip about her activities as a courtesan, earnest analyses of her lyrical love poetry, and detailed assessments of her philosophy from a feminist standpoint. While reading any of these will tell you a great deal both about the woman herself and about the world of Renaissance Italy more generally, D'Aragona's poetry also tells us about the birth of Western Civilisation as a grand narrative. If we want to learn about how the ancient Greek and Roman worlds became stitched together into the uneasy hybrid that we now call "Greco-Roman antiquity"—a hybrid that would have seemed not only bizarre, but actually downright objectionable to the subjects of our previous three chapters; or if we want to explore how Renaissance thinkers started to construct a cultural genealogy linking themselves to this Greco-Roman cultural conglomerate—a lineage that, as we have seen already in this book, was in reality neither singular or unbroken; in short, if we want to discover the first traces of the narrative of Western Civilisation emerging, then D'Aragona's extraordinary oeuvre is an excellent place to start.

Birth or Rebirth?

We use often the term "Renaissance" to refer to the extraordinary flowering of artistic, literary, and scientific activity that took place first in Italy and then elsewhere in Europe between the fourteenth and sixteenth centuries.[2] It was a flowering that was based on two essential principles. The first was humanism, a trend that from a philosophical standpoint elevated human rationality and agency and from an intellectual standpoint placed a high value on human emotional experience and cultural expression as well as more traditional forms of technical knowledge such as law, grammar, and rhetoric. The second principle was a conscious mindset of intentional archaising across a range of cultural production, deliberately harking back to Greek and Roman antiquity. It is this latter principle, crucial for the subject of this book, that forms the basis for the very term "Renaissance."

Of course, not everyone at the time thought of themselves as living through a "Renaissance." The term itself is heavily loaded. It is fundamentally predicated on the idea of a later age receiving a cultural legacy from an earlier one, the cultural ideas and traditions of the ancient past being "reborn" into the Renaissance present. One of the problems with the term is that it foregrounds the rediscovery or reanimation of old ideas at the expense of the new, implying that this was a time of repetition and conservatism rather than of novelty, radicalism, and invention. Another problem is the type of relationship implied with antiquity. The implication is that European societies of the fourteenth to sixteenth centuries did not simply draw inspiration from the ancient world or engage with its traditions, but that the two were fundamentally the *same* thing, linked by a cultural continuity that we now think of as Western Civilisation. If the original "first" birth of this cultural complex was to be located in classical antiquity, the implication was that it had subsequently lain dormant through the darkness of the medieval period, ready to be reactivated, or "reborn," in the correct conditions.

As we have already seen in this book, this idea simply doesn't hold water. In Chapters 1 and 2, we saw that both the Greek and the Roman worldviews differed from our own, and how in neither was there a prevailing sense of a proto-West. In Chapters 3, 4, and 5, we saw that the cultural legacy of Greek and Roman antiquity had not been dormant through the medieval period at all. Rather, it was embraced in different ways in the Islamic and Byzantine worlds, while central and western Europe claimed a heritage that was composed of Trojan and Roman rather than Greek and Roman antiquity. In this chapter, we shall see that people in the sixteenth century did not necessarily think of themselves as living through a rebirth of Greco-Roman antiquity, but instead actively debated their relationship with the ancients. From Castiglione's celebrated *Book of the Courtier* to the works of Tullia D'Aragona, sixteenth-century writers imagined antiquity and their own connection to it in various and diverse ways.[3]

The periodization of history and the labelling of these periods tends to happen retrospectively, and the Renaissance is no exception. The term "Renaissance" was popularised only in the mid-nineteenth century, by the Swiss historian Jacob Burckhardt with the publication of his 1860 book, *The Civilisation of the Renaissance in Italy*. In this book, Burckhardt argued that the spirit of the age could be seen through its culture—in its art, literature, and music, as well as in its manners, morality, politics, and religion. The cultural revolutions of the Renaissance, he argued, represented much broader psychological and social revolutions in the human condition. In the "new monumental spirit that was distinctive of the age of the Renaissance," he argued, one could identify the development of individualism, the rise of sophisticated and impersonal structures of state governance, and the impulse towards scientific enquiry. It was therefore the Renaissance that dispelled the darkness of the medieval mentality, released the shackles of superstition and religion, and ultimately ushered in the modern world. "[T]he Italian Renaissance," he concluded his final chapter triumphantly, "must be called the leader of modern ages," serving as the transformative fulcrum between the medieval world and modernity.[4]

If under Burckhardt's scheme the Renaissance marked the birth of modernity, then engagement with Greco-Roman antiquity was modernity's midwife. Burckhardt does, as an aside, admit that some of the transformations of the period might have been conceivable without the influence of antiquity, and that the idea of "rebirth" has indeed been "one-sidedly chosen as a name to sum up the whole period."[5] And yet, he maintained that the inspiration and influence of the classical world were of vital importance. He argued that "culture, as soon as it freed itself from the fantastic bonds of the Middle Ages, could not at once and without help find its way to the understanding of the physical and intellectual world. It needed a guide, and found one in ancient civilisation, with its wealth of truth and knowledge in every spiritual interest. Both the form and the substance of this civilisation were adopted with admiring gratitude; it became a chief part of the culture of the age."[6]

Crucially however, this was not a matter of introducing alien influences to Renaissance Italy, but rather "the alliance of two distant epochs in the civilisation of the same people." This was a reawakening of something preexisting, rather than the insertion of something foreign, the rebirth of old cultural forms rather than the incorporation of new ones.

Although he did a great deal to popularise it, Burckhardt did not invent the term "Renaissance." Its popular French form was first used by the historian Jules Michelet a few years before Burckhardt published his seminal work, and the Italian form of the word had been around even longer. As early as 1550, at the height of the Renaissance itself, the Italian artist and scholar Giorgio Vasari referred to the "*progresso della sua rinascita*" of the arts following the centuries of the "*media aetas*" in his famous biographical work, *The Lives of the Artists*. However, Vasari's notion of a *rinascita* was not the same as our (or Burckhardt's) idea of the Renaissance as an historical period. Rather, it was a development of older and more generic ideas about cultural decline and rebirth as cyclical, rather than fixed in a linear progression through history.[7] The difference is between talking about *a* cultural renaissance (or even renaissances) and talking about *the* Renaissance as a single discrete period of history. Vasari, D'Aragona, and their contemporaries might have recognised that they were living through the former, without characterising the times in which they lived as the latter.

One thing that D'Aragona and her contemporaries *were* very conscious of was the inspiration they drew from antiquity. As we have already seen in this book (Chapter 3), elements of the Greek but more usually Roman cultural traditions had lingered in central and western Europe throughout the medieval period and continued to be a source of intellectual and political legitimacy and stimulation. Nowhere is this more evident than in the establishment of the Holy Roman Empire, which drew explicitly from ancient Roman cultural symbols both ideologically and artistically.[8] Yet this practice of deliberately harking back to antiquity was transformed, both qualitatively and quantitatively, during the period that we now call the Renaissance. In architecture, Andrea Palladio was inspired by a trip to Rome to design buildings based on symmetry and Vitruvian mathematical proportions, in contrast to the highly ornamented and Gothic styles of the previous generations. In art, Michelangelo studied the realism of Roman sculpture as a model for his own portrayals of the human body, from the taut musculature of the *David* to the luxurious textile folds of the *Pietà*. In literature, Dante's *Divine Comedy* relies on close stylistic borrowings from four Latin poets—Virgil, Statius, Lucan, and Ovid—while also narrating extended encounters between the protagonist and these poets over the course of the poem.[9] The fourteenth to sixteenth centuries saw a proliferation of engagements with the ancient past, deeper and closer than those of the preceding centuries.

Not only did this period see an increase in the quantity of engagements with antiquity; it also saw qualitative changes in what parts of antiquity were considered worth engaging with. Through the centuries, Italian culture had used models taken from the ancient Roman past, while drawing on genealogies from Troy and the biblical world of ancient western Asia. Until this point, the ancient Greek world was considered to be fundamentally "other"—the cultural ancestor of the peoples of eastern and southeastern Europe, who lived under the control of the Byzantine Empire and who adhered to the Orthodox rite of Christianity. Greek antiquity was emphatically not considered to be part of the cultural heritage of central and western Europe, in the lands where the Latin church dominated and the Holy Roman Empire held sway. And yet, in a radical departure from previous practice, from the fifteenth century onwards in Italy, there was an increasing tendency to construct antiquity, not as the combination of Rome and western Asia, but as the combination instead of Rome and Greece. The concept of the Greco-Roman world as a single entity—the basis for classical antiquity—was born, not reborn.

The emergence of Renaissance philhellenism was gradual. We have already met Petrarch (at the end of the last chapter), the scholar and poet who first imported a codex of the Homeric poems to Italy and arranged for their translation into Latin in 1360. But Petrarch was not alone in his Hellenic interests. Along with his contemporary and correspondent, the prose writer Boccaccio, Petrarch was one of several Italian intellectuals who cultivated an interest in the ancient Greek past as early as the mid-fourteenth century.[10] By the mid-fifteenth century, both knowledge of and interest in the ancient Greek world had become common amongst the educated elites of Italy. There was a new Platonic Academy in Florence, founded by no less a figure than Cosimo de' Medici. The Platonic Academy attracted scholars and artists from across Europe and was instrumental in furthering the study of Greek philosophy and antiquity within the Latin world.[11]

Individuals such as Petrarch, Boccaccio, and Cosimo de' Medici all played crucial roles in stimulating this new Italian interest in ancient Greek culture, but several key events effectively supercharged the process. Tension between the Greek and Latin churches had eased enough for them both to send representatives to meet peacefully together, along with delegates from the Coptic and Ethiopian churches, at the Council of Ferrara-Florence from 1437 to 1439, with the aim of healing the Great Schism.[12] Although the council never managed to reach an agreement, the process of discussion itself was only possible thanks to an improvement in the relationship between the churches after centuries of conflict. A loosening of political as well as confessional tensions followed with the fall of Constantinople to the Ottomans in 1453, effectively nullifying the Byzantine Empire as a political force and ending the rivalry between it and the Holy Roman Empire.[13] From this point onwards, no real reason remained for central and western Europeans to see the ancient Greeks as the unsavoury ancestors of a denigrated enemy, as in the days of Godfrey of Viterbo (Chapter 4) or Theodore Laskaris (Chapter 5). Finally, the conquest of the Emirate of Granada in 1492 brought about the final fall of Al-Andalus and the end of Muslim rule in the Iberian Peninsula.[14] The Latin church now straddled Europe triumphantly from Spain to Slovakia and from Sweden to Sicily. Although its dominance was soon to be challenged (which we will discuss in Chapter 7), there was little to shake its confidence during the early Renaissance period.

Political events always have cultural consequences. The fall of Constantinople to the Ottomans also meant that many Byzantine scholars fled westwards, bringing with them their learning and knowledge of ancient Greek literature and philosophy. Many of these settled in the powerful city-states of Italy, finding support from wealthy patrons. Amongst these was John Argyropoulos, a passionate humanist who settled in Florence and eventually died of eating too much watermelon (according to our sources), although not before spending many years at the Platonic Academy, where he taught, amongst others, the young Lorenzo de' Medici and a promising fledgling artist called Leonardo da Vinci.[15] With the fall of Al-Andalus, ancient Greek texts from the libraries of Granada fell into the hands of Spanish Christians, along with centuries' worth of Arab scholarship that developed and expanded on these texts. At the moment that Granada fell, the library of the Nasrid sultans at the Alhambra counted more than 250,000 books in its collection, many of which, it has long been presumed, were destroyed in the book burnings of the early sixteenth century, purportedly organised by Cardinal Cisneros to promote the Christianisation of the region. However, manuscripts from the royal library have recently been discovered in Spain, the Vatican, and Morocco, demonstrating that the Islamic libraries of Granada and the invaluable scholarship they contained were not entirely lost.[16]

It is no coincidence that knowledge of the ancient Greek language and interest in ancient Greek texts, for centuries the primary preserve of Islamic and Byzantine scholars, began to spread across central and western Europe. Not only were the raw materials of such study more readily available than ever before, but Greek culture had shed the toxic connotations that had surrounded it when the Byzantine Empire had been a political rival. Now that Hellenism had lost its fangs, it became a much more attractive prospect for cultural appropriation. The ancient Greek world now became grafted onto the historical consciousness of central and western Europe, being cast in the role of a cultural ancestor alongside ancient Rome, Troy, and biblical western Asia. The twinning of Greece and Rome in the modern imagination is so pervasive that it can be hard to imagine a time when the two were not automatically linked. Yet it was only the Renaissance that made them so, splicing the two together to form a coherent "Greco-Roman" past.

Yet this combined Greco-Roman history had not yet assumed the status of "classical" antiquity, to the exclusion of other ancient civilisations, nor had it yet been posited that central and western Europe should be considered the sole and exclusive heir of this combined legacy. The grand narrative of Western Civilisation had yet to emerge. This was to come later, as we shall see in Chapter 9. Yet by the height of the Renaissance in the sixteenth century, all the pieces were in place: a Christendom slightly less riven than in previous centuries; an area of political and cultural coherence focused in central and western Europe; and an historical orientation to an antiquity that encompassed both Greece and Rome. But still at this point, the antiquity that Renaissance thinkers drew inspiration from was wider than just Greece and Rome—it expanded to encompass also the Etruscan, Egyptian, and Mesopotamian cultures. The sense of cultural exclusivity that accompanies the idea of the West had yet to set in. We can see this clearly in the work of Tullia D'Aragona, a woman who was remarkable as a scholar, writer, and historical figure, but in this respect—in her treatment of antiquity as centred on Greece and Rome but also including other cultures—was characteristic of her age.

"A Wise and Chaste Soul"

For Tullia D'Aragona,[17] as is the case for many women through history, most of what we know about her life is drawn not from formal records or her own testimony, but rather from the romanticised and idealised writings of her male contemporaries.[18] Girolamo Muzio—a courtier, poet, champion of the Italian vernacular language over Latin, and seemingly D'Aragona's greatest supporter—composed a pastoral poem in her honour entitled *Tirrhenia*, an archaising name for the region of Italy immediately to the north of Rome.[19] Within this poem lie several clues that pad out what we know from official records about her biography.

D'Aragona was born in Rome sometime between 1501 and 1504. Her mother, Giulia Pendaglia, originally came from Ferrara in northern Italy and may have worked in Rome as a high-class courtesan before eventually settling down to respectable married life with the Sienese nobleman Africano Orlandini.[20] At some point before these happy nuptials, however, Giulia gave birth to a daughter—Tullia, who took the surname D'Aragona from her father. It is not clear to which D'Aragona Tullia owed her paternity—Muzio implies in the *Tirrhenia* that her father was a cardinal, leading some modern scholars to suggest this might have been Cardinal Luigi D'Aragona, an illegitimate grandson of the king of Naples. A later document, however, lists Tullia's father as Costanzo Palmieri D'Aragona, a lowly member of Cardinal Luigi's retinue. Scholars remain divided on the question of who Tullia's father really was. Did the cardinal arrange for his servant to claim paternity of his illegitimate daughter to save himself from scandal? Or is the whole idea of a link with the cardinal nothing more than gossip and rumour? We will likely never know the truth. All we know is that D'Aragona spent her childhood between Rome and Siena but returned to the Eternal City in her mid-teens. Although she would spend periods of her adult life in various northern Italian cities, she would always come back to Rome, and it seems that this was where she felt most at home. She rapidly became a figure in high society, with the visiting French musician Philippe Verdelot composing two madrigals that refer to her explicitly by name in 1523–24, praising her beauty. Around the same time, D'Aragona seems to have begun a relationship with the famous Florentine aristocrat and banker Filippo Strozzi—a relationship that was set to last for more than a decade.[21]

During this time, D'Aragona seems to have moved between Rome, Venice, Florence, and Ferrara, with her name being linked to various noblemen and other cultural figures, as well as to Strozzi. These were D'Aragona's prime years as a courtesan, in her late teens and early twenties, and she quickly gained a reputation for her intelligence as well as for her looks. One gossipy courtier commented approvingly that she was not only "extremely courteous, discreet, astute, and graced with excellent, sublime manners," but also talented in music and extremely well educated. It was said that she "seems to know everything and can speak with you about any material that you please," that "her house is always full of virtuosi," and that "in conversation she is unique."[22] Other commentators were impressed that she could quote Petrarch and Boccaccio by heart, as well as the work of several Latin poets.[23] But while these admiring words might suggest a glamorous lifestyle, we should not forget that at a fundamental level D'Aragona was engaged in sex work, with all the dangers and social stigma that this entailed. The cultivation of an intellectual persona may have also been part of her personal "brand," and indeed in the infamous *Pricelist of the Whores of Venice*, published in 1535, we find the following reference to her, suggesting that her poetic and cultural accomplishments were considered to be part of her sexual appeal:

> *Gentlemen: Now about the case of Tullia D'Aragona*
> *whose half a palm of intestine*
> *the Spring of Helicon washes when pissing.*
> *She wants ten* scudi *to take it in the ring* [anus]
> *and five in the cunt and this you will leave*
> *for the greatest whore of the brothel.*[24]

Amidst the crude references to urination and anal sex, we hear that D'Aragona is washed internally by the "Spring of Helicon"—a reference to the mountain on which the Muses were said to live. This aura of educated elegance may perhaps have contributed to D'Aragona being considered "the greatest whore of the brothel."

One of the occupational hazards that sex workers faced was

pregnancy, and it has been suggested that D'Aragona took a few months' break around the time that the *Pricelist* was published in 1535 to give birth to a daughter, Penelope, although it remains unclear whether Penelope was actually her daughter or her sister.[25] In either case, D'Aragona was back in Rome within a few months of Penelope's birth, and a significant change seems to have occurred in her life around this time. In her twenties, she had been a witty and learned courtesan. Now in her thirties she became a woman of letters, a poet, and a scholar who happened to take paying lovers on the side. Most of D'Aragona's poetry seems to date from this period, taking various forms including sonnets, dialogues, and an epic poem, *Il Meschino* (*The Wretch*).

For the most part, D'Aragona's work was circulated informally, not published until later in her life. Yet this did not prevent it, and D'Aragona herself, from gaining renown in Italy's literary circles. Sperone Speroni, a renowned humanist and dramatist from Padua, included her as a named character when he wrote his *Dialogo d'amore* in 1542. The famous Mantuan poet Ercole Bentivoglio dedicated poems to praising her poetic skill and "learned words." D'Aragona also engaged in debate with the radical theologian Bernardino Ochino, composing a thoughtful sonnet to him that contemplated the nature of free will. It was also around this time that D'Aragona first encountered Girolamo Muzio, whose support and influence would be crucial in this next phase of her career, just as Strozzi's had been through its early years.

In 1544, around the age of forty, D'Aragona registered her marriage to the otherwise unknown Silvestro Guicciardi, an event that seems to have had relatively little impact on either her professional or her intellectual activities. Professionally, she is recorded five years later in a register of sex workers in Rome, all of whom were required to pay 10 percent of their annual rent to help fund the repair of the Santa Maria

Bridge (interestingly, even in her mid-forties, D'Aragona was in the top 11 percent of Roman sex workers according to the lavishness of their accommodation).[26] Intellectually, D'Aragona was ramping up her literary production.

D'Aragona saw her *Dialogue on the Infinity of Love* published in 1547, which proved popular enough to warrant the publication of a second edition in 1552. Her anthology of poetry, *Rime della Signora Tullia D'Aragona*, was also published in 1547. This included a number of standalone sonnets but was also partly arranged as a series of dialogues with poems penned by D'Aragona matched with poetic responses from various friends and correspondents. The list of correspondents and dedicants appearing in the *Rime* reads like a who's who of Italian literary society of the time and included the Roman aristocrat Tiberio Nari (*Rime* 27); the poet and cardinal Pietro Bembo (*Rime* 15); the Spanish diplomats Don Luigi of Toledo (*Rime* 13) and Don Pedro of Toledo (*Rime* 14); and even the redoubtable Maria Salviati, Cosimo de' Medici's mother (*Rime* 12). The volume as a whole, however, was dedicated to Eleonora, the duchess of Florence and wife of Cosimo de' Medici.

D'Aragona's marriage did bring with it some benefits. Her certificate of marriage made her exempt from a law in Siena that served to mark courtesans out from married women through their clothing. When she was denounced for wearing a luxurious *sbernia* cloak, the judges grudgingly acknowledged that as a wedded woman she was legally entitled to wear whatever she liked. Two years later, D'Aragona ran afoul of a similar rule in Florence, which required all sex workers to wear a yellow veil or handkerchief to set them apart from "honest" women. However this time, she had no need to prove her marital status to avoid retribution since she was enjoying the patronage of the most powerful family in Florence at the time—the Medicis. A special decree on the authority of the duke Cosimo himself records that, thanks to her "rare knowledge of Poetry and Philosophy," D'Aragona was granted "a particular and new privilege"—that is, "to be exempted from all obligation as regards her dress, clothes, and behaviour."[27]

D'Aragona was in Rome when she eventually died in 1556, in her early fifties, leaving behind small bequests to various friends and acquaintances, poor orphans, and repentant prostitutes (as required by the law, she notes drily in her will). The remainder of her belongings, including a small library of books in both Italian and Latin, went to her young son Celio. We do not know when Celio was born, or who his father may have been; we know that D'Aragona consigned him to the care of Pietro Chiocca, a servant and designated meat carver of Cardinal Alvise Cornaro.[28]

Playing with Plato and Arguing with Aristotle

D'Aragona's published works illustrate the new Renaissance vision of antiquity perfectly. The Latin world of ancient Rome is taken for granted, a constant and dependable backdrop against which action can be set. When D'Aragona wanted to praise Cosimo de' Medici, she likened him to the mythical Roman king Numa Pompilius (*Rime* 4); when she wanted to appeal to the double-edged nature of fate she referred to the Roman god of doorways Janus (*Dialogue*); and when her supporter Muzio wrote the long pastoral poem *Tirrhenia* in her praise, he composed it in the style of a Virgilian eclogue.

But if Rome formed the backdrop for D'Aragona's work, then ancient Greece often provided the plot. D'Aragona's *Dialogue on the Infinity of Love* dramatises not only a philosophical discussion on the nature of love but also a contest between Platonic and Aristotelian philosophies. In it, D'Aragona presents her own take on a contemporary literary trend—the writing of love treatises, often in a dialogic form that was borrowed from Plato, who used it to construct a literary image of a Socrates who brings insight to his interlocutors through discussion. As well as engaging with antiquity, therefore, D'Aragona's *Dialogue* draws on the works of several of her earlier contemporaries, including Marsilio Ficino, Leone Ebreo,[29] and Sperone Speroni, who, as we have already noted, included D'Aragona as an interlocutor in his own *Dialogo d'Amore* five years earlier, albeit with a very different characterisation than D'Aragona would later fashion for herself.[30]

The *Dialogue* is a dramatisation of a fictional evening at her quarters in Florence during which D'Aragona and her guests engage in an elevated philosophical discussion on the nature of love. D'Aragona herself appears as a central character in the text, directing discussion and enlightening her listeners. Her main interlocutor is the republican idealist turned earnest man of letters Benedetto Varchi, although interjections are also made by Dr. Lattanzio Benucci and other unnamed gentlemen. Over the course of the *Dialogue*, the interlocutor Varchi proposes a number of Aristotelian theories, including on the semantic separation between "love" as a noun and "to love" as a verb, and the relationship between form and matter. But the Aristotelian theory that interests D'Aragona most is his idea of the natural inferiority of women. In a famous earlier lecture in the Academy of Florence, Varchi had appealed to the authority of Aristotle when he described the role played by women in procreation as a passive one and pointed to the intellectual inferiority of women when compared to men. Throughout the *Dialogue*, D'Aragona challenges Aristotelian notions of the inferiority of women, assuming the intellectual and sexual equality of women and men throughout, and exemplifying them in the speech and actions of the fictionalised version of herself that she uses as the dialogue's main character.[31]

Yet D'Aragona also challenges Platonic theories of love, questioning why Plato argued that a true love was possible only between men. Why, she asks her interlocutor Varchi, should we assume that women can only engage in the baser, more physical forms of love? In the *Dialogue*, both D'Aragona and Varchi express their revulsion at the idea of male homosexual sex, Varchi arguing for the nobility of the "pure" love that Plato and Socrates felt for young men (in real life, Varchi had been criticised for becoming overly attached to several young boys). Yet the cerebral nature of Platonic love, D'Aragona suggests, means that no one is barred from it by virtue purely of their physical form, and therefore it should not preclude women. The dialogue concludes with both parties agreeing that love can change over time, transforming from vulgar and physical to pure and spiritual, and varying also from person to person.[32]

D'Aragona's *Dialogue* therefore draws heavily on ancient Greek texts, relying on a series of Aristotelian rhetorical principles as well as a Platonic format and genre. Yet when it comes to the underlying ideas and eventual conclusions of her work, D'Aragona is neither a Platonist nor an Aristotelian. Instead, she rejects both theories of love and posits her own, developed from personal experience and firsthand knowledge. For D'Aragona, Hellenism provided her with a stylistic template and a philosophical foundation, but not with all the answers.

As engaged as D'Aragona was with Greco-Roman antiquity, her cultural view also expanded beyond these bounds, as is evident from her final work, published only posthumously in 1560. *Il Meschino*, or *The Wretch*, is an epic poem comprising more than twenty-eight thousand lines of verse arranged into thirty-seven cantos (for comparison, the *Iliad* is not quite sixteen thousand lines long).[33] The basis for the epic poem was a prose romance composed by Andrea da Barberino in the fourteenth century that had enjoyed some popularity in D'Aragona's time, even being translated into Castilian Spanish.[34] Yet

D'Aragona's reworking of the tale and her rendering of it into epic metre represent a significant creative achievement.

It is not hard to understand the story's appeal—it was a rollicking tale. D'Aragona's poem draws from Barberino in recounting the tale of Guerrino, the son of one of Charlemagne's knights, who has the misfortune of being captured by pirates as a baby, enslaved, and given the name "meschino," or "wretch."[35] Sold into slavery in Constantinople, Guerrino becomes a servant of the Byzantine emperor, falls in unrequited love with the emperor's disdainful daughter, and undertakes great feats of heroic prowess against the "Turchi" (Turks). But just as he is poised on the brink of glory and success in Constantinople (as well as winning over the princess's heart), the young Guerrino rejects the earthly pleasures of Byzantium and sets out on a quest to find out where he came from. His journey from this point on is a swashbuckling whistle-stop tour of the known world (complete with the obligatory sojourn in the underworld), full of fantastical beasts and mythical figures, all topped off with a reassuring happy ending. Yet Guerrino's quest for his origins also reads like an extended metaphor for the broader Renaissance interest in establishing a cultural ancestry.

Guerrino sets out on his journey eastwards into Tartary (central Asia), where he battles giants and monsters. From there, he sails to Armenia and defeats a treacherous king; then travels to Media, where he rescues a virginal young queen from her attackers and politely turns down her offer of marriage. Continuing on his way, he is taken prisoner by the lascivious king of Solta in Persia, who, when Guerrino spurns his advances, marries him instead to his daughter. Coming thence to India, Guerrino consults the oracle of Apollo at the Trees of the Sun and the Moon, which reveal to him his true name and tell him to travel westwards in search of his true ancestry (providing the quote at the start of this chapter). Boarding a ship to Arabia, Guerrino is kindly received by the sultan and visits the tomb of Muhammad before falling in love with Antinisca, the daughter of the king of Persepolis, and waging a series of heroic wars to secure her throne. Yet despite his great love for Antinisca, Guerrino will not abandon his quest for his roots, and leaves Asia for Africa.

In Africa, Guerrino encounters giants and dragons before meeting the king of Ethiopia, Prester John, who rules over an idealised Christian realm of wealth and refinement, and for whom Guerrino fights as a champion for a time.[36] From there, his journey continues to Egypt, where he becomes a general in the sultan's armies fighting against the Arabs. In Egypt, a chance encounter reunites Guerrino with a boyhood companion from his days enslaved in Constantinople, spurring him to continue on his quest. Travelling westwards across Libya, Guerrino fights giants, converts and befriends a local king, and rejects the advances of a local princess (having murdered her own brother so she can offer Guerrino the throne, the princess then dramatically dies by suicide).

The by-now weary Guerrino then sails to Sicily and Italy, where he seeks out the Sibyl, an otherworldly prophetess who demands that he stay with her for an entire year, during which she tests his resolve against temptation. On his release, Guerrino journeys to Rome, where the pope imposes a penance on him for consulting two pagan oracles— he is to visit purgatory, accessing it via St. Patrick's well in Ireland. After an overland journey through France and a detour to northern Spain to clear the brigands that plague the pilgrim's trail of Santiago de Compostela, Guerrino sails first to England and thence to Ireland. The trip into the well affords Guerrino an appropriately Dantesque vision of hell and purgatory, as well as a glimpse of his true parents. With Guerrino finally granted knowledge of his true identity, the conclusion of all of these adventures is pure Hollywood—he rescues his parents from the dungeon in which they had been languishing all these years; campaigns successfully against the "Turchi" (Turks) across the northern Mediterranean; and marries his true love Antinisca in Persia, converting all her people to Christianity as part of the package and living happily ever after.

The *Meschino* fits many of the conventions of Renaissance Italian epic. Like other examples of its genre, it blends classicising epic heroism with the chivalric romance of the medieval chansons de geste. Like other examples of its genre, it was written in the metre of *ottava rima*: a form of rhyming stanza organised in groups of eight lines that was also employed by Giovanni Boccaccio as early as the mid-fourteenth century for his *Filostrato* (which provided the inspiration a century later for Chaucer's *Troilus and Cressida*), as well as by other sixteenth-century poets, such as Ludovico Ariosto in his chivalric fantasy *Orlando Furioso* (whose eponymous hero was adopted by Virginia Woolf for her gender-bending modernist novel in the early twentieth century).[37]

Like other examples of its genre, the *Meschino* also made liberal use of motifs drawn from ancient Greek and Roman epic poetry. As in Virgil's *Aeneid*, D'Aragona's hero takes a tour of the underworld. Like Circe in the *Odyssey*, the figure of the Sibyl in the *Meschino* is both a frightening witch and an attractive sexual prospect. And like Odysseus battling the cyclops and escaping the land of the Lotus Eaters, D'Aragona's hero is sent to the remote ends of the world on his adventures (Ireland in one direction and India in the other), and is pitted against griffins, unicorns, and a tusked, long-necked creature called the centopochus.[38] Indeed, D'Aragona seems to have inserted several additional Greco-Roman references into her text that were not present in other, earlier versions of the *Meschino* story—she mentions Cato and Ovid; makes reference to the emperor Titus's siege of Jerusalem; and includes a range of divine mythological figures including the god Apollo/Phoebus and the Muses Euterpe and Clio.[39]

Yet while it uses the Greco-Roman world as a source of cultural capital and locates the realm of the Sybil in Italy, the *Meschino* does not assume that the Greco-Roman heritage belongs exclusively to Europe. Apollo's oracle is located in India, and the inhabitants of Mecca are described as reverencing Apollo as well as the prophet Muhammad. Similarly, Christianity is not the preserve of Europeans either. Guerrino encounters Christians regularly during his journeys in Asia, and Ethiopia is the location of the exemplary Christian realm of Prester John. There are also idealised and virtuous figures amongst the pagan inhabitants of Asia and Africa, including Guerrino's Asian betrothed, Antinisca, and his African friend Artilafo, although these more often than not end up converting to Christianity. D'Aragona therefore does not present us with a vision of the world divided into a civilized European Christendom on the one hand and the pagan barbarians of Asia and Africa on the other.

This is not to say that D'Aragona makes no distinction between the three continents—she does, and Asia is described especially negatively. At one point Guerrino is told, "You have searched Asia, along with Greater India, and in the whole great circuit of the earth there is no place worse than that, and anyone who thinks otherwise is wrong, and not just slightly" (*Meschino* 16:84).[40] In contrast, Europe and Africa seem to rank more equally in her estimation. D'Aragona writes, "There is Europe, and Africa, which are densely inhabited, and there your bad or good behaviour can either injure or help you, according to how you choose to guide yourself" (*Meschino* 16:86). Guerrino does find himself battling both monsters and human foes in Asia and Africa, but he also faces bandits, the supernatural power of the evil Sibyl, and enemy armies in Europe too. While D'Aragona does present her readers with almost Herodotean descriptions of exotic people and places in Asia and Africa (in many cases, drawing on her earlier versions of the Guerrino story to do so)—we hear, for example, how pepper grows in India (*Meschino* 11:25–26), and about the correct method for taming elephants in Ethiopia (*Meschino* 18:54–59)—she also describes the oddities of Europe, such as the strange practice amongst Irish priests of taking wives (*Meschino* 27:49), and the wild landscapes of southern Italy comprising "uncultivated country and stabbing thorns, amid cliffs and strange labyrinths" (*Meschino* 24:51).[41]

At the same time, D'Aragona was also interested in describing human difference and inserts several racialised descriptions of Asians and Africans into her narrative. In Asia, for example, the women of Solta in Persia are "black, but otherwise beautiful" (*nere, ma del resto belle*; *Meschino* 10:15); the men of Sotora near India are "strong and dark, and smaller than average" (*uomini forti, e sono bruni, E meno di grandezza che communi*; *Meschino* 10:81); while in Africa, the Ethiopian subjects of Prester John have "red eyes, they have black skin and very white teeth" (*han occhi rossi, La pelle han nera, e bianchissimo "l dente"*; *Meschino* 18:53). In contrast, racialised descriptions do not appear of European peoples, who are instead usually portrayed as being culturally familiar. In a time of increasingly European exploration and expansion, with the Spanish sending ever more expeditions to the Americas and the Portuguese to Africa and India, this is perhaps to be expected (we will discuss the issue of European imperialism in Chapter 9). Of course, as indicated by the quote at the beginning of this chapter, it is perhaps significant that Guerrino can only discover the truth about his origins in the far distant west. Yet it is neither race nor geography that ultimately furnishes D'Aragona with her main axis for dividing humanity, but religion.

Guerrino's most intractable foes on each continent are Muslims, from the Persians of Asia and the Arabs of Africa to the Turks of Europe. At several points in the narrative, Guerrino shows his scorn for Islam, thinking to himself that donkeys made better music than the priest of Muhammad (*Meschino* 13:53), and poking fun at what he sees as stupid traditions (*Meschino* 13:70).[42] D'Aragona was not alone

amongst her contemporaries with her Islamophobia. Indeed, the fifteenth and sixteenth centuries saw a surge in Islamophobic rhetoric
amongst European writers, often appearing in poetic accounts of the
Crusades, but in reality shaped by a much more immediate and contemporary concern—fear of the Ottomans' growing power in the
Mediterranean and southeastern Europe.

Indeed, the ideology of crusading, the nature of Islam, and the issue of Ottoman expansion were all crucial topics of interest amongst
Renaissance humanists, who devoted extensive tracts to debating
these questions.[43] Most of these writings offered a highly stereotyped,
speculative, and defamatory view of Islam, casting it in binary opposition to the European and Christian civilisation that they claimed for
their own by this time. We can see such stereotypes at play in popular
epic poems such as Matteo Maria Boiardo's *Orlando Innamorato* (published half a century before *Il Meschino* in 1495), in which his hero faces
down hordes of invading Saracen warriors; Torquato Tasso's *Gerusa-
lemme liberata* (published just two decades after *Il Meschino* in 1581),
which recounts the exploits of the Christian armies; and another
female-written epic poem, Margherita Sarrochi's *Scanderbeide* (published nearly half a century after *Il Meschino* in 1606), which celebrates
the victories of an Albanian warlord against the Ottomans.

Not all depictions of cultural opposition featured an Islamic enemy, however. Another epic poem penned by an Italian woman of letters, *Enrico, or Byzantium Conquered*, by Lucrezia Marinella (published
in 1635), revisited the theme of the Crusades that had become popular
in Renaissance literature. Marinella did not, however, frame her Crusader epic in terms of a clash of civilisations between Christians and
Muslims, Europe and Asia, West and East. Instead, she chose to write
about the Fourth Crusade and the conquest of Byzantium by the Latins, portraying the Asian enemy as Greek rather than Ottoman.[44]

The existence of Renaissance Islamophobia does not necessitate an early form of a Western Civilisation–type grand narrative. There may indeed have been a prevailing view that a combined Greco-Roman antiquity was the cultural ancestor of Europe, but as the example of D'Aragona's *Meschino* shows, Europe was not necessarily seen as being the sole heir to the Greco-Roman legacy. Nor was the Greco-Roman past assumed to be the only fount of European culture. Giorgio Vasari, the art critic who famously first wrote of an artistic *rinascita* (see earlier in this chapter), drew a line of artistic tradition not only back from his own day to Greece and Rome, but also back farther still to ancient Mesopotamia and Egypt, whilst also paying tribute to the artistic genius of the Ethiopians and Etruscans.[45]

THE GRAND NARRATIVE of Western Civilisation posits the Renaissance as a crucial turning point in Western history. It asserts that this was the time when the original and exclusive cultural roots of the West in ancient Greece and Rome, which had lain forgotten and neglected for centuries, were finally rediscovered. It claims that it was this period of revival that set the West back on its inevitable path to enlightenment, modernity, and world domination. The grand narrative is not entirely wrong.

The Renaissance was indeed a crucial turning point. The new interest in Hellenic antiquity on the part of central and western Europeans and their enthusiastic incorporation of ancient Greece into their pantheon of cultural ancestors constituted a radical change from previous practice. Antiquity was completely reimagined, with the new Greco-Roman cultural compound at its heart. The amalgamation of the Greek and Roman worlds into a single conceptual entity took place over the course of several generations between Petrarch in the fifteenth century and D'Aragona in the sixteenth, and has remained with us ever since.

But as I hope is by now evident from previous chapters, contrary to the claims of the grand narrative, the original roots of the West do not lie exclusively in this Greco-Roman cultural conglomerate, nor is the Greco-Roman world the exclusive heritage of Europe. This was acknowledged by many Renaissance writers like Vasari, who imagined a much broader and more diverse antiquity than we usually attribute to them, and like D'Aragona, who took the Greco-Roman heritage of Asia for granted. In addition, these writers did not merely reanimate Greco-Roman traditions that had long lain dormant but were instead more creative and innovative than the grand narrative allows. While they may have taken inspiration primarily from the Greco-Roman world, they took it from elsewhere too, and used these varied influences and inspirations to develop their own new traditions in literature, philosophy, and art—rather than simply copying what had gone before.

The grand narrative is also wrong in its assumption that the intellectual flowering of the Renaissance necessarily led to future Western hegemony. While it is possible to discern the seeds of this hegemony already sown in the fifteenth and sixteenth centuries, it was by no means inevitable that these seeds (and not other seeds) would germinate and grow. At the time that Tullia D'Aragona wrote in the early and mid-sixteenth century, the shape of history was still unclear and the narrative of Western Civilisation, while it had begun to emerge, was not yet firmly fixed. This was to remain the case for no longer than a generation, into the lifetime of our next subject.

Chapter Seven

THE PATH NOT TRODDEN

SAFIYE SULTAN

*His Majesty Sultan Murad . . . the exalter of the empire, the
Khan of the seven climes . . . the emperor of the lands of Rome*

SAFIYE SULTAN (1591)[1]

THE room quivers with whispers and hushed exclamations. The gift is obviously broken, damaged by damp on the long sea voyage from London to Istanbul. Its metal pipes are warped and the finely carved panels of wood have split apart, the glue that had originally held them together now completely dissolved. The courtiers murmur to one another, wondering if this really is the cutting edge of English technology, the best that the distant island kingdom can offer.

This jumbled mass is supposed to be a clockwork organ—an astonishing automaton that chimes the hours and can even play pieces of music by itself, thanks to a slow-release valve mechanism.[2] It is a gift designed to impress the Ottoman sultan Mehmed with its ingenuity and sophistication. But the organ is broken. Fortunately, there is a second present. In the courtyard stands a glittering ceremonial carriage, covered in gold and encrusted with jewels. Its value is estimated at six hundred English pounds—a significant amount by the standards of the time, as much as a skilled workman would earn in four years. Unlike the organ, the carriage has survived the journey from England fairly well, and now it stands in the courtyard of the palace, ready for service. Yet this is a gift not for Mehmed, but for his mother, the indomitable Safiye Sultan.

In 1599, when these English gifts arrived in Istanbul, Safiye was at the height of her powers. As mother of the reigning sultan, she was the *valide sultan*—a position that carried much weight at the Ottoman court. But Safiye's influence extended far beyond her formal position. Her son, the twentysomething Mehmed, left the details of government largely in her capable hands, and Safiye was widely acknowledged as the guiding power behind the throne. It was a position to which she was well accustomed. She had been similarly influential as the *haseki sultan* (the formal consort) of Mehmed's father, Sultan Murad III, who had held her in high esteem as an adviser on both domestic and foreign policy. By the time the English ambassador presented the golden carriage and the clockwork organ in Istanbul, Safiye had been at the heart of Ottoman government and diplomacy for nearly two decades.

The English diplomats sent to accompany these diplomatic gifts would have been used to formidable women. They served none other than Elizabeth I, who had by this time been on the throne of England for nearly forty years. Elizabeth had been corresponding with Safiye for the last five of these, the two women sending letters and small gifts back and forth to each other to grease the wheels of Anglo-Ottoman trade. But now, Elizabeth wanted more from the Sublime Porte (the name given to the Ottoman imperial administration) than the mutual profits of commerce. Protestant England sought a military alliance with the Muslim Ottomans, combining forces against their common Catholic enemies.

The English were not the only Europeans courting the Ottomans. In the late sixteenth century, the Dutch, the French, the Venetians, and the Genoese were all seeking to develop closer links with the Sublime Porte. The lavish gifts of the clockwork organ and the glittering carriage were designed to further English interests in this competitive diplomatic environment. The English envoys would have watched carefully for Safiye's response to the carriage. The success of their mission hung on the balance of her opinion.

Luckily for the English, Safiye was indeed charmed by the carriage and in the weeks that followed she and her son were often seen riding in it around Istanbul. Even better, the clockwork organ would eventually entrance the court with its automated musical performances, as it was repaired by Thomas Dallam, the Lancashire craftsman who accompanied it to Istanbul. (Thomas gained great favour in the Ottoman court and kept a diary of his travels which makes for compelling reading today, before returning to build many organs in England, including that of King's College, Cambridge.[3])

Although no one could have known it at the time, the unveiling of the clockwork organ and the sumptuous carriage in 1599 marked the height of Anglo-Ottoman relations. At this moment, an accord struck between Muslims and Christians seemed no less unlikely than one between Protestants and Catholics—the political gulf between faiths not necessarily greater than that between denominations. This was a geo-cultural configuration dramatically different from the one proposed in the last few generations by Renaissance ideologies of an emergent West (Chapter 6). Instead, it was a geo-cultural configuration more similar to that into which Theodore Laskaris was born in the thirteenth century (Chapter 5), when the cultural distance between the Greek and the Latin churches seemed greater than the one between the Greeks and their Seljuk neighbours. We can only speculate on what the shape of world history might have been, had a full military alliance been forged as the English had planned. The Catholic powers of central Europe would have been caught, pincerlike, between the Protestants of the north and the Muslims of the south. It is hard for us to imagine today the implications—not just the effects it might have had on the political history of Europe and the wider world, but also the cultural and social changes that would have come along with it. Despite the conceptual foundation laid in the Renaissance (Chapter 6), the grand narrative of Western Civilisation would have looked quite different in such a world—indeed, it might not have developed at all.

Rather Turkish than Papist

When Safiye looked northwards and westwards, she would have seen a Christendom that was riven by bitter divisions. The old schism between the Greek and Latin churches might have been partly patched over in the Council of Ferrara-Florence (see Chapter 6), but new rifts had already opened in its wake. When the German priest Martin Luther nailed his Ninety-Five Theses to a church door in Wittenberg in 1517, he lit a spark that would ignite the flames of confessional conflict across Europe. Within the space of a generation, the movement that we now call the Reformation resulted in the emergence of a myriad of new Christian sects, from Lutherans and Calvinists to Anabapists and Zwinglians.[4] But if the early sixteenth century saw the birth of Protestantism, it also saw the rebirth of Catholicism, reinvigorated and with a new sense of identity and purpose in the face of what it saw as Protestant heresies.[5]

By the time Safiye Sultan was born in 1560, a few years after the death of Tullia D'Aragona, the battle lines had already been drawn. By and large, Protestant states were concentrated in northern Europe. Elizabeth I had ascended the English throne two years earlier, at the head of her own Church of England. The Baltic Sea was ringed by Lutherans in Prussia, Saxony, Denmark, and Sweden. An even harder Protestant line was taken in Scotland and the Netherlands, where Calvinism was favoured. In contrast, southern and central Europe were dominated by Catholic countries. These included France and the various principalities of Italy, but also the territories ruled by the Habsburg dynasties of Spain and Austria.

In the following decades, confessional tensions only grew. In France, the Wars of Religion raged, with millions killed and displaced in a bloody internecine conflict between Catholics and the Protestant Huguenots. In the Low Countries, William of Orange led the Dutch Revolt against the Spanish Habsburgs, winning both political and religious freedom for the largely Protestant Netherlands. And in Britain, there were crackdowns on Catholics, a dynastic challenge from the Catholic Mary, Queen of Scots, and the ever-present threat of Spanish invasion. The papacy was also no stranger to heavy-handed tactics, excommunicating not only Elizabeth I of England in 1570, but also Henry IV of France in 1589. While the former excommunication may have done the Catholic Church precious little good, the latter certainly had the desired effect—although raised as a Protestant, Henry converted to Catholicism, famously quipping that "Paris is worth a mass."[6]

Given the mutual blood spilled by Catholics and Protestants in the middle decades of the century, it was small wonder that for some Protestants, the prospect of an alliance with Muslims seemed more likely than a rapprochement with their coreligionists. In 1569, William of Orange wrote to Istanbul requesting Ottoman support for the Dutch Revolt and received a warm promise of reinforcements in return.[7] As the revolt got underway, the ships of the Dutch revolutionaries were decorated with pennants in "Turkish" colours—red with a crescent—and one popular wartime slogan was *Liever Turks dan Paaps* (Better Turkish than Papist).[8] After the Netherlands became independent, medals for heroes of the revolt were even minted in the shape of silver crescents bearing the catchphrase.[9] For the Dutch nationalists, an alliance with the Muslim Ottomans was preferable to courting Catholicism.

For some Christians, it was not even clear whether the faith of the Muslims was entirely different from their own. After all, Muslims worshipped the same god, acknowledged Jesus as a prophet, and shared many of their religious principles. In a world where divergent visions of Christianity were multiplying and there was precious little consensus about what would constitute a unitary Christian faith, the differences within and between the religions could be subjective. For some Catholic polemicists, both Protestantism and Islam were repugnant heresies of a similar nature, with Calvinism in particular often likened to Islam.[10] For some Protestants, on the other hand, it was almost comforting that Islam could be framed as a sort of Protestantism. This idea, as we shall see later in this chapter, was especially favoured by English Protestants seeking to build diplomatic bridges with rulers in the Islamic world. One such English agent, sent from Elizabethan England to establish trade links with Morocco in 1577, wrote back claiming that the Moroccan king Abd al-Malik was "a very earnest Protestant of good religion" who regarded the Catholics with an appropriate amount of "mislike."[11]

This is not to say that all European Protestants were comfortable with the idea of an alliance with the Ottomans. Sixteenth-century racism and xenophobia directed against Muslims is well documented, and there are certainly many negative portrayals of the Ottomans in particular to be found in the pamphlets, plays, and political rhetoric of the age. Martin Luther himself wrote about the Ottomans as a scourge sent by God to punish Christians for straying from the correct path, describing the sultan as "the Devil's servant" in 1528–30.[12] Just over a decade later, in 1542, the English priest and Protestant reformer Thomas Becon described the sultan as "that mortal enemy of Christ's religion, that destroyer of the Christian faith, that perverter of good order."[13] Indeed, church bells were rung across Protestant England after the Catholic forces of the Holy League defeated the Ottoman navy at the Battle of Lepanto in 1571.[14] Hostility to Muslims in general and to the Ottomans in particular was therefore widespread through sixteenth-century Europe. And yet, such hostility was only part of the story. The relationships between European Christians and their Ottoman neighbours were complex and changeable, and far more complicated than a simplistic notion of a "clash of civilisations."[15]

From the Ottoman perspective, there was nothing particularly strange or novel about dealing with Christians.[16] After all, a substantial proportion of the empire's population belonged to churches that we would now recognise as either Greek or Russian Orthodox, and Ottoman law formally regarded both Christians and Jews as *dhimmi*, or protected groups.[17] Beyond their borders, the Ottomans had longlasting trade agreements with the Venetians that stretched back over a hundred years; and their mercantile dealings with the Genoese were almost as long established.[18] A military alliance had even been agreed in the early sixteenth century with France, resulting in some joint Ottoman-French naval actions in the Mediterranean in the 1530s and 1540s before the alliance fell into disuse.[19] The Ottomans, then, were certainly prepared to collaborate with European Christian states if and when it suited their interests.

Ottoman interests included anything that would weaken one or other of the dynasty's two great rivals—the Safavids of Persia in the east and the Habsburgs of Austria in the west. It is the Habsburgs that are of particular interest to us in this book.[20] This dynasty bestrode Europe, dominating the politics of the continent for more than three centuries. One branch of the family, based in Spain, ruled a dominion that included what is now Belgium and the Netherlands, part of Italy, and expanding territories in the Americas. The other branch was focused in Austria and Hungary but controlled a much wider swathe of central Europe as rulers of the Holy Roman Empire (for the earlier history of which, see Chapter 4).[21]

For the Ottomans, these Austrian Habsburgs were an especial source of annoyance.[22] On a practical level, they were located directly on the northwestern frontier of the Ottoman Empire, frustrating attempts at further overland expansion. Two unsuccessful sieges of the Austrian capital, Vienna, a century and a half apart—the first in 1529 and the second in 1683—illustrate just how tough a nut the Habsburgs were to crack. The sixteenth century also saw a number of other major clashes between the Ottomans and Habsburg-sponsored coalitions, including the Siege of Malta in 1565[23] and the Battle of Lepanto in 1571, and losses at both stymied Ottoman maritime expansion in the Mediterranean.

The Habsburgs were just as galling on an ideological level. They claimed to be the only truly universal world empire, and the rightful successors of the Roman Empire by papal designation. For the Sublime Porte, this was an affront. The Ottomans also claimed that theirs was the only legitimate world empire, with rights to universal dominion and a potentially global reach.[24] They also claimed to be the heirs of Rome—a legacy that had first been won on the battlefield through their conquest of the "New Rome" of Constantinople in 1453, but which was also claimed, as we will see later in this chapter, through narratives of both genealogical and cultural inheritance. Competing not just for territorial control but also for historical legitimacy, it was per-

haps inevitable that the Habsburgs and the Ottomans would be implacable enemies.

And so when, in the final quarter of the sixteenth century, the Ottoman Sultan Murad III began enthusiastically to support European
Protestants, we should imagine that he was motivated more by geopolitical than by theological concerns. The Habsburgs were dedicated
Catholics, sworn to defend the primacy of the pope in their capacity as
leaders of the Holy Roman Empire. To complicate matters, the Spanish branch of the dynasty controlled territories in northern Europe
with resentful Protestant populations—the Netherlands, and also
England for a few years when the Spanish king Philip II was married
to the English queen Mary I. The confessional conflicts raging across
Europe therefore presented Murad with a golden opportunity to form
an alliance with the power to damage the Habsburgs. It is no surprise,
then, that it was during Murad's reign (1574–95) that relations with
Elizabethan England began to blossom.

But the English weren't the only European Protestants to come
knocking. It was to Murad that the Protestant King Henry IV of
France appealed in 1594 when he struggled to take control of his country in the face of Catholic opposition (although, as we have already
seen, Henry eventually chose to make his own life easier by converting). And it was Murad who famously wrote to the Lutherans of the
Netherlands at the height of the Dutch Revolt, bringing succour to
William of Orange. In this letter, Murad deftly manipulates common
religious rhetoric, both to stress the similarities between Muslims and
Protestants, and to heighten the contrast with their common Catholic
enemy. Muslims and Protestants, he argued, had both "banished the
idols and the portraits, and bells from churches," unlike "the faithless
one they call Papa" (i.e., the pope). The pope, Murad claimed, was engaged in "worshipping idols and pictures which he has created with

his own hands, thus casting doubt upon the Oneness of God."[25] If sixteenth-century Protestants felt they would rather be "Turks than Papists," the sultan was certainly not going to dissuade them.

Murad wrote this remarkable letter in 1574, the same year as his accession to the throne. But he did not write it alone, driven by his own personal vision of an anti-Catholic alliance with Protestants on the distant northern fringes of Europe. Rather, his thinking on this point was influenced by his beloved consort and trusted adviser, Safiye Sultan.

From *Haseki* to *Valide*

Safiye was not her real name. History has not preserved the name that was given to her at birth, but records only that the name "Safiye" (meaning "pure" in Ottoman Turkish) was bestowed on her when she was thirteen years old. The new name came with a new identity, and almost all trace of her life until this point has been effectively erased. The reports penned by various Venetian ambassadors furnish us with some of the gossip circulating in the courtly circles of Istanbul at the time, which whispered that she had been born in a small village in Albania, high in the mountains of the Ducagini.[26] The gossips had less to say about the details of her enslavement or her early training in the imperial harem. But it is clear that her striking looks combined with her sharp intelligence made her stand out, even amongst the cultivated beauties of the palace, so that she was handpicked as a companion for the young crown prince Murad in 1563. It is at this point that the unnamed girl became the remarkable woman Safiye—the woman who would rise from enslaved child to empress within the short space of eleven years.

Murad and Safiye were both teenagers when they met—she was

thirteen and he sixteen. They must have hit it off immediately, and their relationship was evidently not only sexual, but also emotional and intellectual. Crucial in this were Safiye's personal as well as her physical qualities. Those who met her commented that she was not only outstandingly beautiful but also calm, wise, and extremely patient.[27] Evidently deeply attached to Safiye, Murad broke with custom and took no other concubines, maintaining a strictly monogamous relationship with her for nearly two decades. Within three years of their meeting, the young couple had produced a son—the future sultan Mehmed III, who would receive the English clockwork organ some twenty-four years later. Four more children followed, unfortunately for Safiye, all of them girls. It was this lack of other sons, making the succession precariously dependent on a single male child, that eventually drove a wedge between the couple.

Things came to a head when Murad's father died, ten years into the relationship in 1574, and Murad himself became sultan. Safiye moved into the New Palace and was given the title of *haseki sultan*—the sultan's chief consort. As *haseki*, Safiye might have expected to enjoy great power and influence, as well as occupying pole position within the imperial household. Unfortunately for her, this spot was already occupied. Murad's mother, the redoubtable Nurbanu, had controlled the harem for the last decade and had also been critically involved in ensuring Murad's smooth ascension to the throne.[28] While Safiye may have been the *haseki sultan*, Nurbanu was the *valide sultan*—the queen mother, and she was disinclined to relinquish her position as the most powerful woman in the Ottoman Empire.

As much as he loved Safiye, Murad was also deeply devoted to his mother and in the early years of his reign found himself heavily reliant on her. A seasoned politician in her own right, Nurbanu now took a prominent public role advising her son on matters of state. It seems that Murad was grateful for her help, and we have records from this period of Nurbanu conducting international diplomacy, administering the imperial estates, and settling affairs in the provinces.[29] With Nurbanu so dominant on the political stage, Safiye had to manoeuvre carefully. Slowly but surely, she developed her own network of agents and contacts in the imperial capital, building relationships of patronage or mutual support with key officials such as the Grand Vizier Koca Sinan Pasha, a fellow Albanian. Perhaps inevitably given the strength of their individual ambitions and characters, the rivalry between the queen mother and the chief consort grew. Five years into Murad's reign, the court was effectively split into two hostile factions—that of Nurbanu and that of Safiye. Murad found himself caught between his mother and his de facto wife (it remains unclear whether he and Safiye were ever officially married). The scene was set for a dramatic showdown.[30]

In this dangerous game of harem politics, Nurbanu had a trump card. She had always objected to the monogamous nature of Murad's relationship with Safiye and had frequently encouraged him to take other concubines. With Murad now a mature man in his thirties, his sexual activities ceased to be a private matter. Nurbanu began to worry loudly and openly about the line of succession, bemoaning the fact that Murad had only one son—the crown prince Mehmed. Even worse, the young prince Mehmed had not yet proven his fertility, and so it was not yet clear whether the dynasty could be continued through his line. Nurbanu argued with her son that he must produce more male offspring in order to ensure the succession. Eventually, in 1583, nine years into his reign and twenty years into his relationship with Safiye, Murad conceded.

What happened next is the stuff of gossip and hearsay.[31] Some Ottoman histories claim that even when presented with the most beautiful girls, Murad found himself inexplicably impotent. Others suggest that this impotence was the result of black magic cast by Safiye to keep

Murad faithful to her. Yet others go further to report that it was only the charms of two particularly accomplished Circassian concubines, specifically their skills in music and dancing, that eventually broke the spell. Some even claim that these myriad stories were nothing more than mere rumours, put about by Nurbanu to wrest Murad from Safiye's clutches. What we do know is that Safiye was sent away in the second half of the year 1583, quietly banished to the Old Palace, that her servants were imprisoned and tortured for information, and that her agents were exiled. Murad, in contrast, found himself miraculously cured of his impotence and in the years that followed went on to father no fewer than forty-seven children with other concubines. Nurbanu, overseeing this parade of sexual partners, enjoyed a brief period of unrivalled influence over her son.

But sex isn't everything, and Safiye was clever enough to know it. Although she must have been smarting from her defeat at the hands of Nurbanu and was likely also suffering pangs of jealousy caused by Murad's newfound voracity, Safiye tried a new strategy. She began to seek out the most beautiful and the most accomplished enslaved women, choosing only those whom she knew would appeal to Murad. She outdid her mother-in-law by procuring the most desirable girls that the Ottoman slave markets had to offer, trafficking in the same trade that had brought her to Istanbul as a child.

Murad was delighted. In the late autumn of 1583, Safiye was welcomed back into the New Palace, her servants released, and her agents recalled. Around the same time, Nurbanu contracted a mysterious illness. By the end of the year, she was dead.[32] These tumultuous events marked a watershed both in Safiye's life and for the empire as a whole. For Safiye, this was victory. She now moved into a new post-sexual role as the sultan's undisputed main adviser and closest personal companion. For the Ottoman Empire, a new diplomatic era opened.

Later historical sources sometimes confuse Safiye with Nurbanu, for quite understandable reasons. Both women started out enslaved in the Ottoman harem, rose to power as royal consorts, and went on to exercise considerable power first through their husbands and later through their sons. But the two women pursued different policies when it came to the empire's international relations. Nurbanu tended to be pro-Venetian in her outlook, having been born into a noble Venetian family before her enslavement.[33] Under her influence, Venetian traders were offered favourable terms and Venetian ambassadors were particularly honoured at court, much to the chagrin of the French and the English, both of whom were also seeking to strengthen relations with the Ottomans.[34] Neither the memory of the previous Franco-Ottoman alliance nor a series of personal letters written to Nurbanu by the French queen mother, Catherine de' Medici, could sway the Ottomans in this period to look more favourably on them.

In contrast, Safiye may have encouraged a somewhat more open foreign policy, and the period of her influence seems to have coincided with increased diplomatic traffic between the Ottomans and a wider range of European states. She appears to have looked with particular favour on Elizabethan England, which, having suffered some years of rather tense interaction with the Sublime Porte, finally installed an official ambassador in Istanbul in 1583.[35] In 1586, this ambassador successfully lobbied his contacts in both the palace and the harem to prevent the Ottomans from agreeing on a nonaggression pact with the Spanish Habsburgs, which would have left the Spanish navy free to attack England.[36]

After Murad died of natural causes in 1595, Safiye acted swiftly to install her son, Mehmed, on the throne. Murad's voracious sexual appetites in his later years meant that he left Mehmed nineteen younger brothers, all of whom could have potentially staked a claim to the Ottoman throne (with succession passing down the male line, his many sisters were not an immediate threat). That none of them did so was not the result of their remarkable fraternal loyalty or an overriding ethos of dynastic harmony, but was because Safiye ensured that all nineteen of them had been summarily executed before they could cause any trouble.[37]

Once Mehmed was sultan, Safiye's grip on power only strengthened. As *valide sultan*, she guided the ship of state with a sure and steady hand. The relationship with Elizabethan England prospered, with Safiye showering favours on two English envoys who particularly caught her fancy—the fiery and charismatic Edward Barton, official ambassador to the Sublime Porte in the early 1590s, and the handsome young Paul Pindar, who delivered the glittering gold carriage to her in 1599.[38] But perhaps the most enduring of Safiye's English liaisons was not her patronage of either of these young men, but instead the surprising epistolary relationship, sustained over several years, with the English Queen Elizabeth I.

The Mars-like Sovereign

We do not know precisely how many letters were exchanged between Safiye and Elizabeth, but we have at least three surviving missives that were sent directly from Safiye to the English queen.[39] The gendered use of language in these letters is remarkable. Safiye is careful to praise Elizabeth in feminine terms, exalting her for her womanly virtues— she is "the support of Christian womanhood," as well as the "crowned lady and woman of Mary's way." Even the nature of Elizabeth's rule is unmistakeably feminine—Safiye flatters Elizabeth by claiming that "skirts of glory and power" trail behind her.[40] One of these letters, sent after the receipt of the golden carriage, thanks Elizabeth for the costly gift and describes the presents that Safiye was sending to Elizabeth in return, most of which seem to be conspicuously feminine

in nature—a robe, a girdle, a sleeve, two gold-embroidered handker-
chiefs, three towels, and a crown studded with rubies and pearls.[41] The
self-consciously gendered relationship that Safiye seems to have constructed between herself and Elizabeth must, at one level, have been
the product of the social norms and expectations of the time. But there
may also have been something else afoot.

The official letters written by the two royal women were only one
part of their interactions. Communication was also carried out by
means of human intermediaries. At one level, the various English ambassadors and envoys to Istanbul would have fulfilled this function,
but at another, messages were also passed via Safiye's trusted female
agent, the Spanish-born Jew Esperanza Malchi.[42] Malchi also wrote
her own letters to Elizabeth, supplementing the more formal correspondence of her mistress. In one such missive, there is a curious reference to an exchange of a much more personal and private nature.
Malchi writes, "On account of Your Majesty's being a woman I can
without any embarrassment employ you with this notice, which is that
there are to be found within your kingdom rare distilled waters of
every kind for the face and odiferous oils for the hands."[43] The letter
continues by requesting that Elizabeth send these items directly to
Malchi to pass to Safiye, rather than via ambassadors or through
Mehmet's court, on account of them being "articles for ladies." The
relationship being built here is one that is explicitly and self-consciously
female, deliberately bypassing the traditional male-dominated channels of communication.

The intimacy and complicity implied in the relationship is, at first
glance, touching. We seem to have here one middle-aged woman reaching out to another across the barriers of geography, faith, and language.
And yet, the message is also faintly ridiculous. Can we really imagine
Elizabeth dutifully collecting face creams to send to her Ottoman pen
pal? Perhaps the key here is not the cosmetics themselves, but rather

the manner of their conveyance—conducted in privacy and secrecy, handed clandestinely from woman to woman rather than passing through official diplomatic channels. Any messages and information travelling along with these "articles for ladies" could have effectively flown under the radar. We can only imagine what intelligence was shared and what plans were hatched in this way. While the surviving historical documents are therefore witness to Safiye's crucial role in Anglo-Ottoman diplomacy, they probably capture only part of a bigger and unwritten story.

This bigger story included the framing of a civilisational history that saw Protestants and Muslims as culturally and genealogically connected, both set in a fundamental opposition to the Catholic world of central Europe. We have already seen how, in the middle decades of the sixteenth century, some Protestants advertised their preference for being "rather Turkish than Papist." We have also seen how similarities between Islam and Protestantism were sometimes drawn, placing them in closer confessional proximity to each other than to Catholicism. We have yet to see, however, how the lines of historical heritage were drawn across Europe at this time, and the part played by Safiye Sultan in drawing them.

The Ottomans did not see themselves as fundamentally Asian, belonging to and representative of an East that was eternally and inevitably opposed to the West. Rather, they saw themselves at the head of a universal world empire, spanning three continents and embracing a myriad of peoples, languages, and religions. They were just as much European as they were Asian, ruling from a capital city that straddled both continents. Indeed, to underscore this point, Suleiman the Magnificent added "Sultan of Two Continents" to his official titles.[44] The Ottomans consciously thought of themselves as the heirs not only to the glories of the Abbasid Caliphate and the medieval Muslim world (Chapter 3), but also to the splendours of the Byzantine Empire and its

Greco-Roman heritage (Chapter 5).[45] In 1538, Suleiman the Magnificent set out his vision of his place in the world: "I am God's slave and sultan of this world. By the grace of God I am head of Muhammad's community. God's might and Muhammad's miracles are my companions. I am Suleiman, in whose name the *hutbe* is read in Mecca and Medina. In Baghdad I am the shah, in Byzantine realms the Caesar, and in Egypt the sultan; who sends his fleets to the seas of Europe, the Maghrib and India."[46]

While Suleiman may have been sultan, he was also caesar and heir to all the lands once occupied by the Byzantine Empire by right of conquest. But the right of conquest was not the only way in which the Ottomans could claim the legacy of Rome. There was a long-standing tradition, traceable throughout the medieval period, that posited a genealogical link between the ancient Romans and the "Turchi" (Turks) of central and western Asia. Both groups, this tradition claimed, were descended from Trojan refugees, fleeing from the sack of Troy.

We have already encountered the medieval genealogies linking various peoples of Europe with refugee Trojans in Chapter 4 of this book. What I didn't mention at the time was how these genealogies extended beyond Europe to include the peoples of western and central Asia, and in particular the "Turchi" (Turks). The Turchi, according to the chronicles of the seventh-century monk Fredegar, were descended from the Trojan hero Francio, who also happened to be the progenitor of the Franks.[47] The story persisted, being retold in one medieval chronicle after another, for seven centuries, until the Ottoman conquest of Constantinople in 1453. For some commentators, the fall of Constantinople to the Ottomans was a frightening event that confirmed their ideas about a fundamental opposition between Islam and Christianity. This was certainly the case for the Italian authors of several Renaissance epics, as we saw in Chapter 6. But for others who were more anti-Byzantine in their outlook, it was historical payback.

Just as the mythical Trojan ancestry of the Latins was used to justify their sack of Constantinople in the Fourth Crusade (see Chapter 5), in the fifteenth century the mythical Trojan ancestry of the Turks was put to precisely the same use. The Ottomans, like the Franks, the Normans, the Germans, and the British, were said to be the descendants of Trojan heroes. The Ottoman victory over the Byzantine Greeks was, therefore, no more than rightful vengeance for the expulsion of their own forefathers from Troy. One French jurist described Mehmed II, the conqueror of Constantinople, as "the great avenger of Troy who, in revenge for the death of Hector, along with his armed companions breached those walls attacked by Mars."[48] An Italian poet wrote that the Byzantines might not have found themselves in such trouble "if you Greeks had not oppressed the Phrygians [another word used in ancient Greek and Latin texts for Trojans] with so much slaughter."[49] According to one Byzantine scholar who stayed on to serve in the court after the Ottoman conquest (and even ended up being appointed governor of his native island of Imbros), the Ottoman Sultan Mehmed II himself took the time to visit the site of ancient Troy, claiming that "God has reserved for me, through so long a period of years, the right to avenge this city and its inhabitants."[50] A century later, Safiye Sultan was to revive the same rhetoric in the service of her own diplomatic ends, with one specific target audience in mind.

By the late sixteenth century, the idea of Trojan origins had largely gone out of fashion in central Europe. Although it had been wildly popular during the medieval period (see Chapter 4), this popularity had by now waned. A new way of thinking about antiquity had emerged during the previous two centuries, during the period that we now call the Renaissance.[51] People had gradually come to think of the ancient Greek world as being fundamentally linked to the ancient Roman one, and to think of a combined Greco-Roman antiquity, peculiar and distinct from the rest of the ancient world (see Chapter 6). The spread of these ideas did not mean, however, that central and western Europeans immediately switched their imagined genealogies from focusing on Troy to focusing on Greece. Although the mature narrative of Western Civilisation had yet to emerge, the sixteenth century ancient Trojan glories no longer glowed as brightly in the eyes of most Europeans as they had in the medieval period, and the idea of noble genealogies traced back to Troy quietly faded away.

Only the British, so often treading a different path from continental Europe, continued to celebrate the myth of their emphatically Trojan origins.[52] Indeed, it was a myth that the Tudor dynasty seemed especially keen to promote. According to Edmund Spenser's extended panegyric poem, "noble Britons sprang from Trojans bold, and Troynovant was built of old Troye's ashes cold" (Spenser, *The Faerie Queene* 3:9, stanza 38). The Tudor dynasty specifically was said to be descended from the Trojan prince Paris. Spenser memorably put the following words into the mouth of his cipher for the queen: "From him my Lineage I derive aright, Who long before the ten Years Siege of Troy, While yet on Ida he a Shepherd hight, On fair Oenone got a lovely Boy" (Spenser, *The Faerie Queene* 3:9, stanza 36). In visual art, Elizabeth was portrayed in the place of the Trojan prince Paris, tasked with choosing which of three immortal goddesses was the most desirable—although of course, while Paris's choice of Aphrodite was to lead to the events of the Trojan War, Elizabeth is depicted as surpassing all three goddesses herself and thereby avoiding conflict.[53]

But the story was popular even outside official court circles, especially in the latter part of Elizabeth's reign. Trojan-themed plays appeared, such as Shakespeare's *Troilus and Cressida* (1601) and Marlowe's *Dido, Queen of Carthage* (1594). Other poetic works also drew on Trojan inspiration, from George Peele's *The Tale of Troy* (1589) to the post-Elizabethan (just) *Troia Britannica* by Heywood (1609). The first English-language translation of the *Iliad* was also produced during this period by George Chapman, with the first instalment published in 1598.[54] Even lawyers seemed to want in on the action, with the renowned jurist Edward Coke (for more about whom, see Chapter 8) seeking to establish the origins of English common law in a Trojan past.[55] The English revelled in the idea of their Trojan origins—origins that, according to some medieval chronicles, they shared with the Ottomans.

Safiye was not one to miss a diplomatic opportunity when it fell into her lap. And the idea of the Ottomans and the English sharing a common ancestry was a ripe plum of an opportunity. Written in 1591, her first letter to Elizabeth revives the idea of the Ottomans as the legitimate heirs to Rome, although it does so only subtly, as if Safiye were testing the waters to gauge the nature of Elizabeth's response. The letter opens with an invocation to God, before Safiye introduces herself as the mother of the crown prince as well as the consort of the reigning sultan, describing him in the process as "His Majesty Sultan Murad—may God perpetuate his good fortune and majesty!—the monarch of the lands, the exalter of the empire, the Khan of the seven climes at this auspicious time and the fortunate lord of the four corners of the earth, the emperor of the lands of Rome."[56]

The introduction is followed by a formal greeting of Elizabeth, replete with its own flowery titulature, in which Safiye wishes Elizabeth "a salutation so gracious that all the rose-garden's roses are but one petal from it and a speech so sincere that the whole repertoire of the garden's nightingales is but one stanza of it."[57] Safiye then explains how she was contacted by Elizabeth's ambassador, following his audience with Murad, whom she describes at this point as the "felicitous Padishah of Islam and the Marslike sovereign." She goes on to reassure Elizabeth of her support and undertakes to champion her cause with the sultan, whom she describes in this final section of the letter as "the Lord of the fortunate conjunction and the sovereign who has Alexander's place."[58]

Safiye was treading carefully, opening a new line of diplomatic communication with a new correspondent. References to Greek and Latin culture are dropped casually into the letter, interspersed with religious and gendered language. Amongst other things, the sultan is described as the emperor of the lands of Rome, the heir of Alexander the Great, and comparable to the Roman god of war, Mars. No explicit claims about ancestry are staked here, but there is an implicit statement being made about the cultural as well as political legacy of the Greco-Roman world—that it belongs to the Ottomans. She must have wondered about how Elizabeth would respond.

Safiye did not have long to wait. The two women exchanged a number of gifts and letters in the years that followed, culminating in the spectacular English embassy of 1599, which brought the sultan his automated clockwork organ and Safiye her jewel-encrusted coach. But Elizabeth was no less subtle than Safiye and was equally adept at deploying diplomatic symbols. Her assent to the idea of a common ancient past was implied in the name of the ship that brought these fabulous English gifts to Istanbul in 1599. It was named for the crown prince of Troy, the greatest warrior of the Trojan army, and arguably the true hero of the Homeric *Iliad*. It was called the *Hector*.

AFTER THE SUCCESS of the *Hector* and its multilayered political messaging, Anglo-Ottoman relations went rapidly downhill. Within four years, both Safiye's son Mehmed and Elizabeth had died, to be replaced by new rulers with radical new ideas about international politics and cultural orientation.

In the case of James I of England (who was also simultaneously James VI of Scotland), this new direction meant a rapprochement with Catholic Spain and a pivot away from eastern connections in favour of western colonies. The establishment in 1607 of Jamestown, Virginia, as the first permanent English settlement in the Americas was a statement of ideological as well as political intent. For the Stuarts, the future of the newly united kingdom lay not in the East but in the West. At the same time but on the other side of Europe, Ahmed I embarked on a diplomatic policy that mirrored that of James. A religious conservative, Ahmed sought to distance himself from his grandmother and her network of western alliances, although he was careful to maintain some European trade and diplomacy. His attention, and that of his son, Sultan Murad IV, was focused eastwards rather than westwards, and in particular on relations with Safavid Persia.

As the seventeenth century progressed, the political imperatives and economic interests that had once connected Protestants and Muslims began to fade. Perhaps inevitably, ideas about a shared civilisational inheritance and a common past faded with them. Gone were the allusions to a single genealogy shared by Ottoman sultans and English queens. Gone were the narratives of a universal antiquity. Instead, there was increasing convergence around an alternative worldview— one that had existed in the medieval period but had not been dominant (Chapters 4 and 5), and that had grown in popularity during the Renaissance (Chapter 6). This view cast Europe and Christendom as a single conceptual entity in direct and binary opposition to Asia, Islam, and the rest of the world beyond. It is a view that is still with us today, often referred to as the clash of civilisations.

In the sixteenth century, Habsburg ideology and propaganda unashamedly followed this view, prompted in no small part by the intense political rivalry between the Ottomans and the Habsburgs.[59] It was in Habsburg interests to promote the idea of a coherent European and Christian front in opposition to the Muslim world, an idea that would bring the diverse Protestant groups under the leadership of the Catholic Habsburgs. At the zenith of Anglo-Ottoman relations in the final decade of the sixteenth century, when Elizabeth and Safiye were sending letters and gifts to each other from opposite sides of Europe, the

Habsburg spin doctors were cranking up their efforts. In particular, they sought to portray the Battle of Lepanto, fought between the Ottoman navy and the Habsburg-sponsored Holy League in 1571, as a heroic struggle between fundamentally opposed civilisations—Europe versus Asia, Christendom against the infidel.[60]

The Habsburgs squeezed every last drop of political mileage out of Lepanto. Letters and proclamations flew around Europe, claiming that the success of the Holy League was a sign of divine favour. The artist Giorgio Vasari (for more on whom, see Chapter 6) painted three frescoes of the battle in the Vatican for Pope Pius V. The Spanish Habsburg king Philip II commissioned a painting from his favourite artist, Titian, to commemorate the event. A series of large-scale paintings and tapestries depicting the battle, produced from cartoons by Luca Cambiaso, adorned palaces and stately homes in Madrid, Genoa, and London.

Amongst the cacophony of Lepanto-related triumphalism in the final decades of the sixteenth century, the scholar and poet Juan Latino composed an epic poem, the *Austriad*, to praise the deeds of John of Austria, the Habsburg general who had commanded the Holy League's fleet. Latino's epic is remarkable because it uses the rhetoric of the Christian-Muslim divide to hedge against racial prejudice and discrimination. Latino himself was black; born to west African enslaved parents in Baena, Spain; and spent his youth attending Don Gonzalo Fernández de Córdoba, the Duke of Sessa. Freed while still a young man, Latino pursued a life of scholarship, eventually being appointed as the professor of Latin grammar at Granada Cathedral. Latino's verse made sophisticated use of classical models and metaphors to draw a contrast between the Christian armies of the Habsburgs and those of the Ottomans. The contrast was emphatically one of religion rather than of race. Latino asserts the importance of personal choice and conversion in the acceptance of faith, highlighting his own experience of being baptised rather than born into the Catholic Church.[61] Latino had obvious and entirely justified motives for writing against what was, at the time, a rising tide of racialised thinking and race-based discrimination in Europe (this was also the period in which the Atlantic slave trade was picking up in earnest, for more on which, see Chapter 9). But it tells us something about the changing zeitgeist that the fashionable rhetoric of Islamophobia and an East-West clash of civilisations became such a valuable tool in his literary arsenal.

In reality, the Battle of Lepanto was fought between a multiethnic, multifaith empire that spanned three continents (the Ottomans) on the one hand, and an alliance of Catholic states bankrolled by the Habsburg king Philip II of Spain on the other. And in reality, while it was a decisive victory for the Holy League and resulted in the large-scale massacre of Ottoman troops, the battle was little more than a costly and embarrassing setback for the Ottomans, who went on to wrest Cyprus from the Venetians two years later and to conquer Tunis a year after that.[62] But reality rarely gets in the way of a good story, especially when that story serves a political purpose.

The correspondence between Safiye Sultan and Elizabeth I is testament to a path in world history that was not taken, a route that was not eventually followed. We can only wonder: What if the alliance had held, and what if the Catholic Habsburg core of Europe had been encircled by a Protestant-Muslim accord? Would the modern notion of the West have developed fully, becoming the unassailable geopolitical bloc that defines the shape of the world today? And would the grand narrative of Western Civilisation have ever developed?

We could indulge endlessly in the what-ifs of history, but in this case I suspect that by the time Safiye Sultan came to power, the writing was already on the wall. The correspondence between her and Elizabeth was perhaps a last-ditch attempt to turn the tide, a final Parthian shot to slow the pace of trends that were already emerging a generation earlier. After this point, it was not long before the story of civilisational clash that grew out of Habsburg anti-Ottoman propaganda came to eclipse the myths of shared ancestry that had once served to bolster the Anglo-Ottoman alliance. The prevailing narrative shifted.

A new narrative became dominant. A sense of "us" focused on the notion of Christendom, a concept that papered over the bloody sectarian conflict between Protestants and Catholics of the previous century and which conveniently forgot about the chasm that had separated the Latin and Greek churches of centuries before. This imagined Christendom became increasingly identified with Europe, engaging in a kind of wilful amnesia in order to ignore the existence of the ancient churches of the Middle East, Asia, and Africa. This imagined Eurocentric Christendom also came to be seen as having a single common origin in Greco-Roman antiquity, a shared history to which it could attribute the shared elements of its culture and political orientation. The world of the past, as well as the world of the present, increasingly came to be seen as divided into two fundamentally opposed and eternally divergent sides—us and them, Christian and non-Christian, Europe and beyond, the West and the Rest.

◆ *Chapter Eight* ◆

THE WEST AND KNOWLEDGE

FRANCIS BACON

*For only three cycles and periods of learning can rightly be
counted: one among the Greeks, the next among the Romans,
and the last among us, that is, the nations of western Europe.*

FRANCIS BACON (1620)[1]

THERE are not many people who will be remembered by history
for excelling in several diverse fields. Some might immediately think of Leonardo da Vinci, Gottfried Leibniz, or Frank

Ramsey. Others might call to mind Alexander Borodin, Hedy Lamarr, or Arnold Schwarzenegger. But in the roll call of historical polymaths, I am sure most of us would find a place for Francis Bacon. Not to be confused with the homonymous twentieth-century artist, the subject of this chapter was a pioneering philosopher of science, influential jurist, and prominent English politician during the late sixteenth and early seventeenth centuries. Bacon's remarkable life therefore spans the transition from the sixteenth-century world of Elizabeth and Safiye to the seventeenth-century world of James and Ahmed. In his lifetime, he saw seismic shifts in global geopolitics, as well as a transformation in the way the world and its history were imagined. In his lifetime, he witnessed the invention of the West. What's more, he played no small role in the process.

Francis Bacon lived at the time when the concept of the West finally began to crystallise, and when the grand narrative of Western Civilisation started to become the dominant model in Europe for thinking about history. His writings demonstrate the scale of the change that occurred in a single lifetime. He began his career under Elizabeth I in a time when the notion of the West was still embryonic, and when it was therefore still possible to imagine an axis of European alignment where the Protestant and Muslim fringes of Europe were united against its Catholic core. By the end of his career under James I, politics had shifted to such an extent that this kind of alignment was no longer conceivable (although, of course, trade and diplomacy between the Ottomans and other European powers continued). The notion of the West had started to emerge, and despite continuing confessional conflicts and political struggles within it, there was no turning back the clock.

At the same time, ideas about the shape of history had also hardened. It became no longer possible, as it still had been in the time of Safiye Sultan, to think in terms of shared cultural ancestors linking

Europe and Asia. Instead, the only imaginable history was one where the West and the East each had their own distinct cultural genealogy and historical lineage. For the West, this lineage purportedly began in Greco-Roman antiquity, a portion of the human past that was now demarcated as belonging exclusively to European history, its cultural legacies bestowed exclusively on Europeans. This fundamental reimagining of the world and its history was possible only because of wider, rapid changes that were happening at the time.

Exploration and Enlightenment

Francis Bacon lived in a world where the basis of knowledge itself was being radically rethought. Firstly, there were changes in *what* people thought. The humanism of the Renaissance had stimulated new developments in theology, philosophy, and the natural sciences, and this, coupled with the proliferation of new Protestant groups, had encouraged new ideas about faith and religion. But there were also changes in *how* people thought. Bacon, amongst others, was crucial in shifting conceptions about epistemology—what could be known, and how one could come to know it. Bacon, perhaps more than most others, was crucial in pioneering what we now know as the "scientific method."

This is why accounts of the Enlightenment often start with Bacon, although the Enlightenment proper is usually associated with thinkers of the late seventeenth and eighteenth centuries such as Voltaire, Rousseau, and Kant. Bacon was crucial in promoting the notion of the scientific method, where facts could be objectively tested through experimentation and observation. This idea was fundamental to the scientific and technological developments of the Enlightenment, from Galileo's astronomical discoveries and Kant's radical epistemology to

Newton's laws of physics and Descartes's geographical mathematics. This Enlightenment emphasis on science and rationality was built on a foundation of Renaissance humanism and was linked to a greater questioning of religion, a move towards secularisation, and the formal separation of church and state.[2] Elements of these ideas can be found in the Treaty of Westphalia in 1648, which concluded the Thirty Years' War, a bloody conflict ostensibly fought on the grounds of religion (although, of course, the signing of this treaty did not bring about the end of inter-Christian violence and religious persecution in Europe).

A second pillar of the Enlightenment was political philosophy, which pondered human nature and the dynamics of human societies and included Rousseau's formulation of the theory of the "social contract"; Hobbes's notion that human life before the state was "nasty, brutish, and short"; Locke's notion of natural law; Leibniz's political optimism; Tom Paine's call for equality in an early conception of human rights; and Mary Wollstonecraft's radical feminism, which extended human rights to women.[3]

The two key strands of Enlightenment thinking—the scientific and technological on the one hand, and the philosophical and political on the other—both sought inspiration from Greco-Roman antiquity, just as Renaissance humanists had done before them. Galileo and Descartes, for example, developed their mathematical thinking from principles laid out by Pythagoras. Amongst political philosophers, the pull of Greco-Roman antiquity was even stronger. Hobbes used Thucydides as a means to sharpen his ideas about political realism, and Locke's theories of personhood and property contain echoes of Stoicism.[4] Rousseau used in particular the history of Republican Rome as the basis for much of his political thought and claimed that as a child, his mind was "full of Athens and Rome . . . I thought of myself as a Greek or a Roman."[5]

As had been the case for the Renaissance humanists a century earlier, these Enlightenment thinkers did not straightforwardly inherit the ideas of Greco-Roman antiquity, passively receiving them as part of an inborn cultural legacy. Rather, they actively sought out Greek and Roman models and inspiration, combing through ancient texts and harvesting what was deemed useful. Some explicitly called for a selective engagement with antiquity rather than its wholesale acceptance. While Thomas Hobbes drew from Thucydides, for example, he was also critical of other Greco-Roman thinkers, including Aristotle, and developed a political theory that stood in stark contrast to ancient models of republican liberty.[6] Hobbes even suggested that on balance, the reading of Greco-Roman texts had a negative effect on his contemporaries, writing: "And by reading of these Greek and Latin authors, men from their childhood have gotten a habit, under a false show of liberty, of favouring tumults, and of licentious controlling the actions of their sovereigns; and again of controlling those controllers; with the effusion of so much blood, as I think I may truly say there was never anything so dearly bought as these western parts have bought the learning of the Greek and Latin tongues."[7] Through this complex process of adoption, appropriation, and dialogue with Greco-Roman antiquity, European Enlightenment thinkers effectively claimed it as their own, integrating it into the cultural world of their contemporary reality. Through this process, they began to fix and firm the grand narrative of Western Civilisation.

The term "Enlightenment," like its German equivalent, "Aufklärung," captures only a part of the romance evoked by the French term for the period, the "siècle des Lumières." This sense of romance colours the way we think about the Enlightenment today. We are taught that this was an age of both wonder and reason—a pivotal age set apart by the luminosity of its intellectual stars, whose glittering beams of rationality banished the shadows of superstition. According to William McNeill in his bestselling 1963 book, *The Rise of the West,* "we, and all the world of the twentieth century, are peculiarly the creatures and heirs of a handful of geniuses of early modern Europe."[8] From these geniuses (or so the story goes), we have inherited not only the scientific method, but also rationalism and religious scepticism, as well as individualism and humanism. It is they, we are often told, who laid the conceptual foundations of the modern world. In the words of one of the Enlightenment's greatest thinkers, the German philosopher Immanuel Kant, "Enlightenment" meant the liberation of humanity from its self-imposed ignorance.[9]

As Kant indicated, this was indeed a period of significant scientific advancement, and these advancements were indeed accompanied by the rise of secular humanism and radical philosophy. Knowledge was disseminated rapidly in books, which had become significantly more affordable thanks to the transformative technology of the moveable printing press. Ideas were discussed through formal correspondence and in circulated pamphlets, creating an international "republic of letters" (perhaps akin to today's notion of the scientific community) focused on intellectual advancement. Interestingly, this was a community whose common language was Latin, which remained the language of elite education across most of Europe and the Americas.

But the Enlightenment was not a single or unitary movement. Within its broad stream, there were innumerable countercurrents, branching schools of thought, and competing intellectual trends.[10] Some Enlightenment thinkers adopted an almost aggressively sceptical approach to religion, for example, while others managed to reconcile their scientific principles with their Christian faith.[11] The Enlightenment also varied in different places and took different shapes in Scotland and Switzerland, in Bohemia and Berlin. In Russia, it was coloured by the centralising autocracy of Peter the Great, while in north and central America (as we shall see in later chapters) it acquired a decidedly revolutionary flavour.[12] Nor was the Enlightenment confined to Europe and North America, despite the fact that in standard accounts of Western history it is often described as so. Crucially, the Enlightenment was a truly global phenomenon, and while the undisputed core of Enlightenment activity was certainly in Europe, examples of Enlightenment thinking can also be found around the world in cities such as Cairo, Calcutta, Shanghai, and Tokyo.[13]

Indeed, even those scientific and philosophical advances that were made in the heart of Europe were often stimulated by new ideas from abroad. Learning about Chinese systems of government and administration, for example, inspired Europeans to reassess their own notions about the shape of the state. The Chinese example was particularly influential amongst French Enlightenment thinkers, and the famous Sinophile Voltaire even claimed that "the human spirit cannot imagine a better government" than that of the Chinese.[14] Confucianism in particular provided inspiration for political philosophy and was powerfully defended by no less a figure than the German polymath and diplomat Gottfried Leibniz.[15] On a different scale, exposure to and conversations with indigenous Americans may have also prompted a radical rethinking of European traditions. It has been argued that Rousseau's *Discourse on the Origins of Social Inequality*, for example, draws from a popular text circulating in the fashionable European salons of the time that purported to recount the philosophical reflections of Kandiakronk, a statesman of the Wendat Nation.[16] Sadly, the achievements of indigenous American, African, and Middle Eastern scientists and philosophers and their contributions to the development of Enlightenment thinking in Europe were not widely acknowledged at the time (including by the subject of this chapter, Francis Bacon).[17]

The Enlightenment therefore occurred against the backdrop of European exploration and increased engagement with the wider world (not all of it peaceful; see Chapter 9) and owed much to this wider global stimulation. Indeed, Enlightenment and exploration are inextricably linked in a feedback loop of mutual causation. Much of European Enlightenment thinking emerged out of the encounter with the wider world. At the same time—and crucial for our purposes in this book—the developments in Europe that made it possible first to encounter and then to subjugate this wider world relied, to a large extent, on Enlightenment thinking. These developments came in two forms, stemming from the two key strands of Enlightenment thought.

Scientific and technological advances gave Europeans the military edge over others, bestowing on them the practical means with which to dominate the rest of the world. But as I stated in the introduction, this is not a book about the rise of the West per se, and I shall leave it to those better qualified than myself to tease out the complex threads of how a small number of states in central and western Europe came to dominate the rest of the world, first militarily and politically, and later economically and culturally.[18] My interest in this book lies instead in the second of the two strands, and the fact that Enlightenment developments in philosophy and political theory gave Europeans the conceptual as well as the practical tools of empire, providing the intellectual basis on which to conceive of the rest of the world as essentially different and fundamentally inferior.

The origin of Western Civilisation as a historiographical theory therefore lies in this nexus of exploration, Enlightenment, and empire. Somewhere inside this feedback loop between global encounters and intellectual revolutions, the idea of the West's cultural genealogy was invented. One of those who contributed to this was Francis Bacon.

Parliamentarian and Polymath

If the Enlightenment is to be characterised by its intellectual stars, one of the earliest, and certainly one of the most sparkly, would be Francis Bacon. He has been termed "the Father of Empiricism" and "the Father of the Scientific Method"—both monikers that refer to his work to establish a standardised and methodical approach to observing natural phenomena.[19] He set out what is now known as the Baconian Method in the *Novum Organum*—a work that was to prove foundational for the scientific advances of the next century. In it, Bacon argued that we must build our understanding of the world on facts, rather than faith, and described a logical system for the observation and recording of these facts (indeed, he was particularly critical of the role that Christianity had played in holding back the advancement of science). So influential was Bacon that when the Royal Society of London was established in 1660, more than thirty years after his death, they embraced him almost as their patron saint, attributing the birth of British science to him in a poetic eulogy:

> *Bacon, like Moses, led us forth at last,*
> *The barren Wilderness he past,*
> *Did on the very Border stand*
> *Of the blest promis'd Land,*
> *And from the Mountain Top of his Exalted Wit,*
> *Saw it himself and shewed us it.*[20]

Yet Bacon came to science relatively late in life—he published the *Novum Organum* in 1620, at the age of fifty-nine. Before this point, his energies had been expended more often in the political sphere. He served as a Member of Parliament for thirty-six years, as well as in various positions for the English, and then later the British, Crown including attorney general, privy counsellor, and lord chancellor. And he began his career neither in politics nor in science, but in the law.

Francis Bacon was just a boy of fifteen when he enrolled at Gray's Inn Chambers in London in 1576.[21] By this time, he had already completed three years of study at Cambridge (although this might seem relatively young to us, the matriculation of preteens was not unusual at the time) and was ready to embark on a more rigorous legal training.[22] His studies took him to France, Italy, and Spain, until the death of his father in 1579 obliged him to return to London and begin—still aged only eighteen—practising as a lawyer.[23] A painted portrait of the teenage Bacon shows him as a round-faced youth with mousy curls, already wearing the look of cautious scepticism that was to characterise him later.[24]

Bacon entered politics in 1581 as Member of Parliament for Bossiney in Cornwall, but languished in relative political obscurity for more than a decade.[25] During this time, he balanced his parliamentary duties with legal work to pay the bills, all the while tirelessly searching for a surer route to preferment and promotion. He must have thought he had found it when he met the charismatic Earl of Essex. Essex was handsome, dashing, and keenly ambitious. By 1587, he had become the favourite of the queen, who showered him with titles and privileges. Knowing a good thing when they saw it, both Francis and his older brother Anthony worked their way into the earl's inner circle. The Bacon brothers made themselves useful when it came to shaping Essex's political strategies, Anthony by feeding him choice titbits from an extensive network of spies that he had painstakingly cultivated on his travels across Europe, and Francis by advising him on legal and religious disputes.[26] In return, they benefitted from his support within court as well as his patronage outside it. Yet despite Essex's best efforts, he never did quite manage to secure for Bacon the high office that he so desired.

It was not until 1601—a year after the *Hector* had returned from Istanbul, having successfully delivered Elizabeth's clockwork organ and golden carriage (see Chapter 7)—that Bacon got the case that made him. He was assigned as a state prosecutor on the most sensational and scandalous trial of a generation—a treason trial that was all the gossip in the alehouses as well as in the corridors of power. There was only one problem. The man in the dock was his erstwhile friend and patron, the Earl of Essex. After a disastrous campaign in Ireland to suppress an armed uprising, Essex had fallen from the queen's favour and had thought to remedy the situation by embarking on a brief and abortive rebellion against her (whether he ever seriously thought this would return him to her good graces is anyone's guess).

Bacon's role in the prosecution of Essex was controversial at the time, given his former closeness to the earl.[27] Perhaps needing to distance himself from Essex and prove his own loyalty to the Crown, he contributed vigorously to the case, providing some of the strongest arguments for the prosecution. He must have done a decent job of it, because Essex was convicted and beheaded at the Tower of London on February 25. Bacon was even charged with writing up the official account of the trial and rebellion, which he accomplished with methodical equanimity. But however level-headed he might have seemed at the time, Bacon's conscience was clearly troubled by the episode. Later, he claimed that he had done all that he could to plead for leniency or pardons for the earl's household and associates—among them, perhaps his own brother.[28]

But Bacon's star was now indisputably on the rise. With the death of Elizabeth, the new king, James I of England (being also James VI of Scotland), knighted him in 1603 and appointed him king's counsel the year after. For the best part of two decades thereafter, Bacon was at the heart of British politics. He served as solicitor general from 1607, clerk of the Star Chamber from 1608, attorney general from 1613, a privy counsellor from 1616, lord keeper of the seal from 1617, and lord chancellor from 1618. At this point, James conferred on him the title of Baron Verulam in recognition of his service, before granting him the even grander title of Viscount of St. Alban in 1621.

No one rises so far without attracting enemies. Bacon's fiercest rival was the formidable Edward Coke (whom we met in Chapter 7, claiming the Trojan origins of English law), who had been a senior colleague on the prosecution team in the Essex trial. The two gentlemen jurists spent much of their careers jostling with each other for power.[29] Coke was appointed attorney general over Bacon in 1594, a post that Bacon finally claimed for himself after he had orchestrated Coke's transfer to the King's Bench in 1613. Bacon and Coke also went head-to-head in a number of high-profile cases, including the case of Edmund Peacham, a clergyman accused of slandering the king in 1614, and became embroiled in heated public disagreements, such as that over the case of the Earl of Somerset, the king's former favourite who was prosecuted for murder in 1616.[30] But the rivalry between these two was beyond the professional. In November 1598, to the surprise of the London gossips, Coke married Lady Hatton, a wealthy widow whom Bacon had been courting for some months.[31] Although at the age of forty-five Bacon would eventually marry Alice Barnham, the thirteen-year-old daughter of an alderman (this was considered to be relatively young for a girl to marry, even though the minimum legal age was twelve), this highly personal defeat at the hands of Coke must have smarted.[32]

Coke's final victory over Bacon must also have felt personal. Spearheading a popular inquiry into government corruption, Coke accused him of accepting bribes—a charge Bacon protested strongly.[33] But the accusations stuck, and within a few short weeks Bacon found himself condemned in the House of Lords, removed from office, ordered to pay a crippling fine, and imprisoned in the Tower. With Bacon now down and out, stories of other scandals began to emerge. Ribald drinking songs began to pop up that joked about Bacon's sexuality, calling him a *paiderastos* and a "sodomite."[34] Supposed firsthand accounts from his servants and assistants appeared, apparently confirming his homosexuality. Whatever the truth of these tales—and the facts about Bacon's sexuality remain obscure—they were certainly deployed as weapons in the armoury of Bacon's enemies, torpedoing the last remnants of his public image. Even though his imprisonment lasted only four days and his fine was waived, Bacon's political career was over. His reputation was ruined, and he was forced to retire quietly in the countryside, far from the clamour of court that he so loved and the hubbub of the parliament that he had grown used to.

And yet this is not the end of Bacon's story. It was during these years, towards the end of his life, far away from the nonstop demands of king and country, that Bacon really began to write. Although Bacon had always composed essays and treatises, it was at this point that he began to write the longer works for which he later became so famous. These spanned the fields of natural history (including the *Natural and Experimental History*, the *History of the Winds*, the *History of Sulphur, Mercury and Salt*, and the *Abcedarium Naturae*), physics (including the *History of Weight and Lightness*, *Enquiries into Magnetism*, and the *Topical Inquiries into Light and Luminosity*), and history (*Historie of the Raigne of King Henry the Seventh*). It was also during this time that he edited and put the finishing touches to several works that he had first drafted earlier, including the *Advancement of Learning* and the moral and ethical *Essays*.

In these last years of his life, from his fall from power at the age of sixty in 1621 until his death in 1625, Bacon's output was truly prodigious.[35] The complete writings from his lifetime take up a shelf-busting fifteen volumes in the standard edition by Oxford University Press—seven of which (almost half!) were composed during these five short years. Without these years, we might never have had the Baconian Method in its full and mature form, and we might never have had Bacon's final theories about law, society, and politics. One work that would certainly never have seen the light of day without Bacon's early retirement is the *New Atlantis*, an imaginative work in which Bacon describes a fictional ideal society, located on a mysterious island in the Pacific Ocean called new Atlantis, or Bensalem.[36] And it is here, in this fantastical work of philosophical fiction, that Bacon offers us a glimpse of a civilisational history that is finally beginning to look like the grand narrative of Western Civilisation—of a European culture with its origins in ancient Greece but whose culmination, according to Bacon, lay on the coasts of the Atlantic.

Knowledge Is Power

The story of the *New Atlantis* begins with the European crew of a ship lost in the Pacific Ocean who stumble upon an uncharted mysterious island. On this island they encounter a Christian state, hitherto unknown to them and apparently cut off from the rest of the world. The place is a utopia of peace and harmony, with everything working smoothly and everyone being content with their lot. The crew are treated with kindness and generosity, leading them to think of Bensalem as a "happy and holy land" and even "a picture of our salvation in Heaven." The tale then narrates a series of conversations between the crew and various representatives of Bensalem they encounter. Their first interlocutor is the governor of the House of Strangers, where they are billeted.

The crew enquire how Christianity arrived on such a remote island, and learn that a book of scripture and a letter from St. Bar-
tholomew were miraculously revealed to the people of Bensalem in a
divine pillar of light. They then ask how the people of Bensalem gained
knowledge of the rest of the world, given that they are so isolated. The
governor replies that in antiquity, Bensalem's traders circled the globe,
and visitors came to the island from Persia, Mesopotamia, Arabia, and
"all nations of might and fame." Yet this success awoke the predatory
urges of their neighbours in the Americas, who launched an ill-fated
attempt to conquer Bensalem.

The hubris of this act, the governor claims, led to divine retribution
in the form of a great deluge that washed over the Americas, destroying its great ancient civilisation and erasing all trace of it from the
earth. Indeed, the Bensalemites refer to the continent of America as
"great Atlantis," and they suggest that some memory of the event is
preserved even in the histories of Europe (a reference to the writings of
Plato). The governor then describes how following this great deluge,
the wise King Salomon imposed a policy of deliberate isolation on
Bensalem, partly because the island could comfortably support itself,
but also "doubting novelties and the commixture of manners." The
two exceptions to this rule of isolation were the hospitable treatment of
any strangers who should happen, as the crew in this story have done,
to arrive on their shores; and the launching of scientific expeditions
once every twelve years, with the aim of gathering information about
the world without giving away the secret of Bensalem's existence.

In the second section of the text, the crew find themselves invited
to join in the celebrations for "the Feast of the Family," a festival that
honours men who can claim thirty or more direct descendants (women
in the same situation are only permitted to watch the party from behind
a glass screen). At this point, the crew meet Joabin, their second
interlocutor, whom the narrator describes as "a Jew and circumcised."

Joabin explains that in Bensalem, great value is placed on chastity out-side marriage, and fecundity within it, expounding in the course of the discussion a theory of the ideal sexual mores.[37] This section serves to highlight the central organising principle of Bensalemite society—the family, as structured by patriarchy, lineage, and ancestry.

In the third and final act of the story, the narrator is selected by his companions to meet with the head of the "House of Salomon," a learned institution named after Bensalem's ancient lawgiver. The House of Salomon is not only a centre of learning, where the knowl-edge gleaned from scholarly expeditions is studied and preserved; it is also the seat of government, where gentlemen-scholars steer the ship of state according to their scientific principles. The House of Salomon, where policy is governed by pure science, is the embodiment of the idea that "knowledge is power," a principle that Bacon advanced in various of his works. Although Bacon did not actually profess this now-popular aphorism in these particular words, he did write: "*ipsa scientia potestas est,*" or "knowledge itself is power."[38]

At this point, the reader is treated to a description of the various scientific activities that went on within this institution—geological, biological, pharmaceutical, optical, mathematical, and mechanical ex-periments, teaching, and theorising of diverse kinds. The section ends with a description of a long gallery in the House of Salomon, in which the scholars have erected statues of those they deem to be their intel-lectual forebears, including:

> *your Columbus, that discovered the West Indies: also the inventor of ships: your monk that was the inventor of ordnance and of gun-powder: the inventor of music: the inventor of letters: the inventor of printing: the inventor of observations of astronomy: the inventor of works in metal: the inventor of glass: the inventor of silk of the worm: the inventor of wine: the inventor of corn and bread: the in-*

ventor of sugars . . . For upon every invention of value, we erect a statue to the inventor, and give him a liberal and honourable reward. These statues are some of brass; some of marble and touchstone; some of cedar and other special woods gilt and adorned; some of iron; some of silver; some of gold.[39]

This is not the first time in this book that we have encountered a gallery of statues representing the great men of an imagined past. It was a similar gallery, described in the introduction, that first stirred in me the doubts that would eventually lead me to write this book. Many such statue galleries exist today, adorning the grand libraries of universities and the ceremonial halls of state buildings across the world. Yet the function of all such galleries is always the same. They stake a claim on the past, zooming in on one version of history and monumentalising it so that it takes on the mantle of an unassailable canon. These galleries are a powerful way of creating historical orthodoxy. Yet the flaws of all such galleries are also always the same. They all start with imagined genealogies, oversimplifying the intellectual cross-fertilisations that actually occurred through history. The choice of who is "in" and who is "out" is informed just as much by ideology as by fact. (This is of course also true of the "gallery" of historical figures that I am presenting to you in this book, although this book has two important differences. The first is that I am explicit about this, rather than trying to hide it, as many other grand historical narratives try to do. The second is that the "gallery" of this book makes no claim to identify the "greatest" or most important people in history, but instead seeks to showcase individuals whose stories can be seen as representative of their times.)

This is why the sculpture gallery in the House of Salomon is so important. It is located in the beating heart of Bensalem, in the hallowed place where the benevolent scientocracy that governs the island is headquartered. It therefore represents not just the history of Bensalem, but also its identity. Just as bloodlines and biological genealogy are of paramount importance to the people of Bensalem as a whole (as we have just learned by reading the description of the "Feast of the Family" in the second section of the text), so this intellectual lineage is important to their rulers. If knowledge was indeed power, then this was not just a display of Bensalem's greatest intellects, but also an exhibition of the basis of its power.

It is therefore curious that Bacon names so few of the great thinkers honoured in the gallery of statues. Only two can be identified—Christopher Columbus, who is explicitly named; and Roger Bacon, who is not named but is still recognisable from his description as "your monk that was the inventor of ordnance and of gunpowder" (Francis Bacon is also playing games with his own fame here, deliberately not naming this earlier homonymous thinker). It can be no coincidence that both identifiable individuals hail from Atlantic Europe, designated as belonging to the world of the visiting crew with the possessive pronoun "your." The implication is that all the other statues depict men who were not Europeans, and as a result the crew would not have been familiar with them. Indeed, the narrator is told that they have "divers [sic] inventors of our own, of excellent works; which since you have not seen, it were too long to make descriptions of them." This tells us something crucial about the cultural genealogy claimed by the Bensalemites—while it acknowledges the contributions of the rare European individual, their intellectual lineage is mostly populated by people who would not be known by the European crew (or, by implication, Bacon's European readers).

Even beyond the House of Salomon, Bacon describes Bensalem in a way that makes it emphatically not European. Geographically, it lies outside the system of continents and is distinct from not only Europe but also Asia, Africa, and the Americas. Yet if Bensalem were to be aligned with any real-world continent, it would be Asia. Although the island is described as peopled by "natives," we hear that it also has long-lived migrant communities of "Hebrews, Persians, and Indians" and in antiquity played host to visiting "Persians, Chaldaeans, and Arabians." Bacon never refers to its inhabitants in racial terms but does create a vision of cultural otherness, offering descriptions of clothing that hint at the Asian. Each Bensalemite they meet wears "a gown with wide sleeves," a piece of "under apparel," and a "hat, being in the form of a turban, daintily made, and not so huge as the Turkish turbans"—the colour of each of these items varying according to the position and rank of the wearer. For Bacon and his readers, the civilisation of Bensalem—including the shape of its history and its cultural genealogy—is emphatically "other" and thus belongs to a different genealogical line from their own.

What of the civilisational genealogy claimed by the crew, and, by extension, of Bacon and his presumed readers? The two Europeans identified amongst the sculptures in the House of Salomon both hail from the Atlantic west of the continent—Britain and Iberia. Yet when the governor of Bensalem recounts the history of ancient interactions between Bensalem and Europe, he mentions the ill-fated journey of a Bensalemite ship "through the Atlantic to the Mediterrane [sic] Sea," where he postulates that it may have met and been defeated by the ancient Athenian navy. This expedition was, he suggests, the ultimate source of information for the tales of Atlantis reported by Plato—whom he refers to twice as a "great man." The cultural lineage of the crew seems clear. It is European, including in more recent generations Atlantic western Europe but in antiquity hailing back to the ancient Greeks of the Mediterranean. This is the arc of Western history as we now know it. This is the grand narrative of Western Civilisation.

The New Atlantis provides us with a wonderfully picturesque illustration of how the narrative of Western Civilisation was beginning to emerge, informing Bacon's worldview and underpinning his cultural assumptions. But elsewhere in his writings, Bacon was even more explicit about what he saw as his own cultural heritage. One good example of this is the quote used as the epigraph to this chapter: "For only three cycles and periods of learning can rightly be counted: one among the Greeks, the next among the Romans, and the last among us, that is, the nations of western Europe." For Bacon, the lines of Germanic or Celtic cultural inheritance that had been so important in western and central Europe in earlier centuries (see Chapter 4) had already faded into the background.

The quote is taken from the *Novum Organum*,[40] the second part of what was meant to be Bacon's scientific masterpiece, the six-part *Great Instauration*. In it, Bacon refers to a period or cycle of history that is "ours," clarifying the "us" of this statement as "the nations of western Europe" (at the same point betraying his ignorance of scientific advances elsewhere, such as in the medieval Islamic world). At another point in the same work, Bacon writes about "us western Europeans."[41] Both passages also make reference to two historical periods comparable to "ours"—that of the ancient Greeks and that of the Romans. Bacon drew heavily from both of these ancient cultures, and he knew it. After all, he wrote his scientific texts in Latin, the lingua franca of scholarship across Europe since the medieval period, and he acknowledged that "the science we have today comes mostly from the Greeks."[42] His works are peppered with ancient references, both direct and indirect, and replete with discussions, analyses, and refutations of ancient Greek philosophers in particular.[43] He even wrote an entire text, *The Wisdom of the Ancients*, reinterpreting Greek and Roman mythology as extended metaphors for various philosophical and scientific truths.

Yet despite his evident cultural debt to the Greco-Roman world and his acceptance of it as a civilisational ancestor, Bacon warned against uncritically accepting the teachings of the ancients, arguing that scientific knowledge should instead be sought in experimentation and observation. Modern science must surpass ancient science, he argued, and "new discoveries must be sought from the light of nature, not fetched back out of the darkness of antiquity."[44] In this aspect, Bacon can be compared to Hobbes. For these early Enlightenment thinkers, the Greco-Roman world may well have been a cultural ancestor, but it offered neither a model for the present nor an ideal for the future. Yet as we shall see in the next few chapters, by the middle of the eighteenth century, the Greco-Roman world would come to fulfill precisely these roles for many political thinkers and philosophers in Europe and North America.

YET THE TRANSITION from the seventeenth-century claiming of the Greco-Roman world as a cultural ancestor to the eighteenth-century valorisation of it as an ideal was far from smooth. It occurred in fits and starts, and happened at different speeds in different places.

On the one hand, some of Bacon's contemporaries in Britain were very keen to use Greco-Roman antiquity as an explicit source of authority and legitimacy. Thomas Howard, the 14th Earl of Arundel, acquired an enormous collection of Greco-Roman sculpture during his visit to Italy in 1614 and displayed the pieces in a specially designed garden. The practice of creating "museum gardens" quickly became all the rage in the seventeenth century, so that a visitor to London in 1651 commented that wandering in the gardens on the banks of the Thames was like "viewing Greece and Italy at once within the bounds of Great Britain."[45] Neoclassical stately homes, taking as their inspiration the style of the Renaissance architect Andrea Palladio (for whom, see Chapter 6), started to appear in the British countryside. It was a new style enamoured of the Stuart king James I, who in 1619 commissioned a lavish new banqueting house for his palace in White-hall, to be designed by Inigo Jones, the same architect who had worked for the Earl of Arundel just a few years earlier. The new royal banquet-ing house was the first large neoclassical building in London and would have stood out distinctly against the smaller pitched roofs of traditional houses along Whitehall in Westminster. It embodied the new pro-European spirit of James's reign, a conspicuous symbol of cul-tural change on the London skyline signalling Britain's adoption of Greco-Roman antiquity as a cultural ancestor, in line with develop-ments in continental Europe.

On the other hand, there were those in Britain who were more sus-picious of the new Greco-Roman fashions. For some, the Italianate style of James's banqueting house represented the degeneracy of Cath-olic European culture. When Charles I ascended the throne, fears about his close relationship to Catholic Europe came to a boiling point, leading to a civil war between royalists and parliamentarians and ultimately resulting in the trial and execution of Charles I for trea-son. The execution itself was staged on a specially constructed scaffold outside the banqueting house. Charles was made to walk through its great hall and out onto the scaffold through the aperture of a tall first-floor window that had been removed for the occasion, before laying his head on the block. The political theatre of this moment must have been astonishing. It combined the rejection of Charles's style as a ruler and his philosophy of divine kingship, a deep-seated suspicion of crypto-Catholicism and continental Europe, and distaste for a Greco-Roman aesthetic that was viewed by some as tainted by its associations with popery.

Bacon and other thinkers of the early Enlightenment lived in a world where the concept of the West was beginning to emerge, based on a common European geography and Christian identity, as well as around the idea of shared Greco-Roman cultural origins.[46] Indeed, the start of the seventeenth century marks the moment when we can start to talk of the West as a meaningful entity, an emerging cultural bloc that we can discern in the writings of Bacon as having some intellectual coherence. Yet the idea of the West was still hazy in the early seventeenth century, and the term itself had not yet come into general use (we shall have to wait until Chapter 10 for this). While the notion of the West's common cultural origins in Greco-Roman antiquity was now well established, suspicion of this idea still lingered in Protestant parts of Europe, given its association with the Catholic Habsburg axis of power in central Europe.

This was set to change over the next century as the pace of European expansionism increased and the age of European imperialism dawned. Encounters with non-European "others," and the conceptual need to justify their subjugation, led to the crystallization of the West as a concept and the hardening of the borders of Western history. It is no coincidence that, at the very same time, much of western and northern Europe was seized with a mania for the Greco-Roman past, with increasing numbers of aristocrats embarking on a "Grand Tour" of the Mediterranean, neoclassical styles of architecture increasingly dominating the urban landscape of northern European cities, and philhellenic Enlightenment philosophies entering into mainstream public discourse.

◆ *Chapter Nine* ◆

THE WEST AND EMPIRE

NJINGA OF ANGOLA

Who is born free should maintain himself in
freedom, and not submit to others.

NJINGA OF ANGOLA (1622)[1]

G OVERNOR Correia de Souza twitched impatiently, sweating under his richly embroidered velvet clothes. He was waiting for the arrival of the ambassador and the start of peace negotiations. His clothes, his jewel-encrusted chair, and the entire setup of the room were designed to communicate Portuguese power and to assert superiority over the rebellious west African kingdom. But when the ambassador finally arrived, Correia de Souza may well have felt the scales of power in the room begin to tip in the opposite direction. As described in the accounts of eyewitnesses, Njinga of Angola swept into the room with an entourage of richly dressed attendants, herself swathed in brightly patterned textiles, her arms adorned with sparkling precious stones, and her hair dressed with beautifully coloured feathers. She cast a disdainful eye over the velvet cloths that had been spread on the floor for her to sit on and signalled instead to one of her female attendants, who immediately dropped to the floor and knelt on all fours. Sitting on her human chair, seated at the same level as her Portuguese counterpart rather than in a humbling position below him on the floor, Njinga looked Correia de Souza squarely in the eye and began her negotiations.

Encounters such as this one were formative in the making of the West as we understand it today. The British, the Dutch, the French, the Portuguese, and the Spanish may have fought bitterly with one another within Europe, deploying ideological as well as military tools in the process. Yet the farther afield they ventured as the wider world became more accessible, the more they realised they had in common with their neighbours. Correia de Souza's first audience with Njinga must have made him painfully conscious of his own foreignness in west Africa. He would have felt conspicuously European and increasingly aware of the similarities he shared with other Europeans in comparison to the Africans with whom he was negotiating.

A sense of common collective identity often emerges when people are confronted with others who they percieve as markedly different. A group of Manchester United football team supporters may not think much about their sporting allegiance when they are socialising together. But they will feel it keenly when another group walks into the room wearing Manchester City football shirts. Children from the same school might bicker amongst themselves, but they will often band together as a group when confronted with children from a different school. Ethnic or racial categories are rarely defined at the homogenous centre of an in-group, but they gain a most potent meaning at the boundary.[2]

But the encounter between Correia de Souza and Njinga was not simply one of neutral self-realisation and identification. It was also an encounter where power was at stake, and it was set against the backdrop of colonial violence. This asymmetry of power relations was made possible by the scientific and technological, and also by the political and conceptual developments of the Enlightenment (for which, see Chapter 8). Improvements in maritime transport, armaments, and military technology made first conquest and then imperial domination feasible. Innovations in economic systems and structures made them desirable. All that was needed was the ideological novelty of a civilisational grand narrative to make Western imperialism morally and socially acceptable.

The Tools of Empire

If the sixteenth century was a time of Western exploration, stimulating the development of new ideas in Europe that laid the foundations of the Enlightenment, the seventeenth century was the time when this expansionism tipped over into full-blown Western imperialism.

Of course, the European empires of the seventeenth century did not spring into existence ex nihilo. The Tudor king Henry VIII proclaimed as early as 1533 that "this Realme of Englond is an Impire." The Elizabethan period saw a dramatic expansion in English overseas activities, including those that were clearly imperial in nature, such as the subjugation of Ireland in the 1570s; those that were more emphatically colonial, such as the charter for the colonisation of the Americas in 1584; and those that can be characterised as "trade before the flag," such as the incorporation of the East India Company in 1600.[3] But it was in the seventeenth century under the reign of James I that British imperialism really gained momentum. The difficulties faced by the colonists at the first permanent British settlement in the Americas, Jamestown in Virginia, proved little more than a minor setback to what was to become a much broader imperial programme. Colonies were to spring up in the Caribbean, Virginia, and New England before spreading along the eastern coast of North America. At the same time, the Plantation of Ulster saw the large-scale settlement of British Protestants in northern Ireland, and the East India Company was establishing control of "factories" and ports along major shipping routes in both Africa and Asia.[4]

But the British was not the only empire on the rise.[5] The Spanish already controlled vast swathes of both North and South America, while the Portuguese had long dominated a large part of southern America, territories in Africa, and a string of ports in India, southeast Asia, China, and Japan. The seventeenth century also saw French expansion in North America, as well as a significant expansion of Dutch imperial activities, focused in particular on southeast Asia. But even this briefest of accounts of European imperialism cannot be a neutral narrative of political and economic expansion. It is also necessarily a story about human suffering. The subjects of seventeenth-century European imperialism, like the subjects of the other empires mentioned in this book—the Roman, the Byzantine, the Arab, the Holy Roman, and the Ottoman—rarely chose their fates. Collectively, they suffered dispossession, displacement, and genocide. Individually, many of them were the victims of murder, theft, rape, and/or varying forms of enslavement. We should also acknowledge that both responses to and experiences of empire varied. Yet one common feature of these modern European empires was the emerging interplay between imperialism and race.

Race-making is the process through which one group of people defines another as a coherent population; imagines that this population can be identified by characteristics deemed to be natural and embodied; and thinks that these characteristics justify that population's position on the social scale.[6] This process is not the exclusive preserve of the modern West. Around the world and throughout history, different societies have developed their own ways of classifying human difference and using these differences to underpin hierarchies of power. Some racial systems place more emphasis on heredity (bloodlines and descent); others on phenotype (observable physical traits of the exterior of the body); yet others on religion or environment. Racial categories are therefore neither automatic nor natural.[7]

For example, while skin colour is an important feature of most modern matrices of race, pigmentary perception can vary from place to place even in today's globalised world. The same individual may be racialised as "white" in Europe but "brown" in North America; or (as I have experienced on occasion myself) as "yellow" in North America but "white" in Asia. But skin colour was not central to all racial matrices of all societies throughout history, as we saw for classical Greece in Chapter 1. Indeed, in Njinga's world of the seventeenth century, racialised perception of skin tones was in the process of changing. When Japanese emissaries arrived at the papal court in Rome in 1585, for example, European observers perceived their skin tones in remarkably divergent ways: some described them as olive-skinned, some as brown, others claimed that the Japanese were deathly pale, or the "colour of Africans," while yet others described their skin as being the "colour of lead."[8] These observers all saw the same people, but they perceived their skin tone differently. It is evident from this instance that racial categories are social constructs, changeable over both geographical space and historical time. As academic and literary scholar Noémie Ndiaye has put it, "race is not the same thing in the fifteenth and in the twenty-first centuries, or in Spain and in India, but it *does* the same thing: it hierarchizes difference in the service of power."[9]

While race may not *be* the same thing in all societies, it does therefore *serve the same function*—it is, in the words of academic and philosopher Falguni Sheth, a technology for "organizing and managing populations in order to attain certain societal goals."[10] It was a technology that became increasingly important as early Western exploration became expansion, and expansionism turned into imperialism. It was against this backdrop of growing global power that Western ideas about racial distinction and hierarchy began first to emerge and then to crystallise in the sixteenth and seventeenth centuries, although it was not until the eighteenth century that these ideas became more systematic and assumed a "scientific" veneer. We will see how this systematisation happened in Chapter 11 of this book. But in this chapter, we remain in the seventeenth century, before the Western matrix of race had assumed the form that we would recognise today. The life of Njinga illustrates how racialised ideas formed, re-formed, and informed Western imperialism in Africa.

Precolonial Africa has often been characterised by Westerners as being without history. Yet African history is long and rich and complex, and in the last few decades Western historians and archaeologists have begun to make significant strides in understanding it, learning from their African counterparts and colleagues.[11] The medieval and early modern periods in west Africa specifically are best known for the Empire of Mali and for its famously wealthy ruler, Mansa Musa, who visited Mecca on pilgrimage in the early fourteenth century. Musa was, according to an estimate made by *Time* magazine in 2015, the richest person in history, if his wealth and purchasing power are calibrated with those of other world leaders and notable figures of his time.[12] The key to the Malian wealth was the gold mined in west Africa, as well as the trade routes linking west Africa, the Islamic world, and the Mediterranean, which were used to transport and exchange that gold.

Although the kingdoms of west Africa had been linked to both continental Europe and the Islamic world by networks of trade and diplomacy for centuries, more direct contact with Europe began to increase only in the fifteenth century, facilitated by improvements in maritime technologies. Dutch and more commonly Portuguese adventurers, inspired and supported by the charismatic Prince Henrique, began to venture along the Atlantic coast of Africa as well as the islands of the southern Atlantic in the first half of the fifteenth century.[13] They came to west Africa in search of gold, but over time, their main aim increasingly became to acquire enslaved humans. (Interestingly enough, around the same time but on the eastern coast of the continent, the voyages of the Chinese general Zheng He were also establishing new trade and communication routes to Asia, although internal politics within China meant these Sino-African connections would soon fade.[14]) It was the changing dynamics in trade networks, in particular the intensification of the Atlantic maritime networks replacing the old overland Saharan caravan routes, that drove a series of political and economic transformations in west Africa which left its people more vulnerable to European raids, occupation, and eventually colonialism.

The Portuguese rapidly found themselves contending with the powerful kingdom of Kongo, covering parts of what is now the Republic of Congo, the Democratic Republic of Congo, and Angola.[15] Luckily for them, the kingdom of Kongo proved receptive to their overtures, and during the reign of King Alfonso (1509–43), the kingdom became radically transformed. Alfonso himself adopted a Portuguese name and encouraged many noble Kongolese to do the same, sending their children to be educated in Catholic schools, cultivating knowledge of European languages, and converting to Catholicism. Alfonso also rebuilt his capital, Mbanza Kongo, along European lines in splendid luxury, and opened diplomatic links with not only Portugal but also Spain, the Netherlands, Brazil, and the Vatican. Indeed, by playing the Dutch against the Portuguese, Kongo now entered the game of international politics, influencing the balance of power between these two states both in west Africa and in South America. But all of this came at a cost. To pay for his rapid Westernization, Alfonso ceded more and more territory and trading rights to the Portuguese, as well as resorting to trade in enslaved people. As time went on, the demographic and economic power base of the kingdom of Kongo became irrevocably eroded, and the power of its kings weakened.

The scale and rate of enslavement during this period was staggering. Slavery was not, in itself, a new thing in west Africa, just as it was also not new in Europe, north Africa, and western Asia. In west Africa there had for generations been both serfs tied to the land and also people sentenced for their crimes to enslavement, sometimes for set periods of time and sometimes indefinitely. But with the Portuguese demand for enslaved people rising exponentially, there were significant economic incentives to condemn ever-increasing numbers of people to enslavement, and also to turn a blind eye to the practice of kidnapping and enslaving people captured in raids and conquests.[16] After a time, the sheer numbers of people being enslaved damaged the local economy in west Africa by depleting the available workforce and skewing demographic patterns, as well as undermining the social stability of communities and eroding trust in political structures. While the transatlantic slave trade visited an unimaginable level of dehumanization and cruelty upon the people it transported to the Americas, it also had a devastating effect on those who were left in west Africa.

By the time that Njinga held her conference with Correia de Souza in 1621, the economic imbalance between the Portuguese and the west African kingdoms had resulted in a substantial political imbalance to match. The Portuguese controlled a vast swathe of land on the Atlantic coast that included Kongo and the smaller kingdom of Ndongo immediately to the south, although there was ongoing conflict with the rulers of both kingdoms, who sought to reclaim their territories from the Europeans. While the people of the region called the kingdoms Kongo and Ndongo and referred to themselves as Mbundu people, the Portuguese called the area they controlled "Angola," taking this name from the word *ngola*, the title of the ruler of Ndongo.

The first *ngola* of Ndongo to enter into diplomatic relations with the Portuguese was Ngola Kiluanje kia Samba, who sent his own ambassadors to Portugal in 1518 and again in 1520, seeking to open new trading and cultural relations in competition with his larger neighbour to the north, Kongo.[17] It was another forty years, however, before the Portuguese established their first mercantile and religious mission in Ndongo, which was set to last only five years, before the *ngola* of the time decided to close it down and expel its members.[18]

When the Portuguese returned in 1575, they came armed with the self-righteous anger of the wronged, remembering that failed mission, and the appetite for conquest whetted by their successes to the north in Kongo. They were led by Captain Paulo Dias de Novais, who had been one of the expelled members of the original mission and who now set off from Lisbon bearing the grand title of *Capitão-Mor da Conquista do Reino de Angola* (Captain-General of the Conquered Kingdom of Angola) in the full expectation that the title would be prophetic. It was not long before this confidence proved justified. The Portuguese successfully raided and grabbed large areas of land from Ndongo, resulting in many deaths and enslavements. They developed the gory practice of cutting the noses off all corpses killed in battle and taking these back to their capital, Luanda, as grisly trophies. After one particularly bloody battle, they needed twenty porters to carry all the severed noses back to their camp.[19]

Hoping to back the winning side, some Ndongans transferred their allegiance to the Portuguese, including a son-in-law of the reigning *ngola* who converted to Catholicism and changed his name to Dom Paulo.[20] While this strategy kept some safe in their positions, more often the Portuguese transferred control over the lands they conquered to their own colonists. In 1581, for example, Dias de Novais granted the lands of eight local lords who had submitted to him to a single Jesuit priest—Father Baltasar Barreira.[21] Into this maelstrom of conquest and resistance was born the subject of this chapter, Njinga of Angola.

Born to Rule

We know relatively little about Njinga's early life, but we do know she was born in Ndongo in 1582, the daughter of Mbande a Ngola, a Ndongan ruler who spent most of his twenty-five-year reign fighting the Portuguese and struggling in vain to contain the ever-expanding slave trade.[22] Her mother was of the royal lineage, and in the matrilineal Mbundu tradition, this distinguished her from her father's other children. According to her biographers, the Capuchin monks Giovanni Antonio Cavazzi and Antonio da Gaeta (both of whom lived at her court for several years), her birth was a miraculous one because she was born from a breech position. This, Mbundu tradition maintained, marked her out for greatness from the start.

As a child, she was her father's favourite, distinguishing herself from the other children at court by excelling in both intellectual exercises and military drills. She was particularly adept in the use of the battle-ax, a weapon that symbolised royalty and which she would wield to great effect later in her life. In particular, she outshone her brother—also named Mbande, after their father—conspicuously.[23] As a result, her father allowed her to attend his councils, where she learned not only about the customs of the court and the correct forms of ritual, but also about the mechanics of government. She would have heard a great deal about the ongoing wars with the Portuguese and experienced at first hand the loss of life, violence, and instability that came with them. When Njinga was still a baby, the entire court was forced to flee from the Ndongan capital, Kabasa, by the proximity of the Portuguese. Although the *ngola* and his family eventually returned to reclaim Kabasa, this episode illustrates the stress and fear of a childhood set against the backdrop of war, even if that childhood is a royal one.

Despite the conflict raging around her, Njinga grew up to be a confident and powerful young woman. In addition to a small household of attendants, she also kept a number of male concubines, a practice that was customary for royal men but which not everyone approved of for a royal woman. One courtier who was heard to be disapproving of her sexual behaviour just a little too loudly paid a dear price for his criticism—Njinga had his son killed in front of him, before having him killed too.[24] Violence was a standard feature of life for Njinga, both within the court and without.

When Njinga's father died in 1617, it was in combat.[25] Her brother lost no time in assuming the kingship, taking the title of Ngola Mbande unilaterally without going through the formalities of summoning a council and holding an election, as would have been expected. In order to consolidate his position, Ngola Mbande set about eliminating all potential rivals ruthlessly. He murdered several family members, including his older half brother and his mother, as well as all her siblings, and several leading members of the court and officials along with their families. He also killed Njinga's newborn son (whose father remains unknown but was likely one of her male concubines). Although Ngola Mbande did not kill any of his three sisters, he still moved to neutralise any future threat from them, ordering their sterilization. The records claim that oils with soaked herbs were thrown "while boiling onto the bellies of his sisters, so that, from the shock, fear and pain, they should forever be unable to give birth." Although the records of this event all come from Njinga's supporters and so perhaps cannot entirely be trusted, it remains the case that after this point neither Njinga nor her sisters ever gave birth again. Njinga was thirty-five years old at the time.

Ngola Mbande's ruthlessness was of little use when it came to the ongoing war with the Portuguese. During his reign, the Portuguese took control over the western half of Ndongo, planting settlers along the coast, building strong forts to maintain power inland, and kidnapping and enslaving thousands. They were helped in this by bands of bloodthirsty Imbangalas—the collective name for rogue groups of violent mercenary warriors who lived a seminomadic life, raiding and slave trading, and who had a fearsome reputation. Control over the capital, Kabasa, moved back and forth. The Portuguese stormed it in 1619, although by 1621 Mbande had regrouped and retaken the city. But this success was only temporary, and the Portuguese reconquered it, this time capturing and imprisoning members of the royal family. Ngola Mbande gave up. He decided to send an emissary to sue for peace with the Portuguese.

The success of this embassy was crucial. Terms had to be carefully negotiated that allowed Ndongo to continue existence as an independent kingdom, alongside the new Portuguese colony on the coast. The person who led the embassy would have the fate of the kingdom on their shoulders. He called for Njinga.[26]

Since her brother had risen to power, Njinga had retired to the east of the kingdom, where she led her own independent war band defending her territory against the Portuguese. It was during this period that she gained valuable experience in strategy and tactics and forged her reputation as a formidable warrior in her own right. Ngola Mbande must have hesitated to recall her, knowing full well that her loyalty would be questionable after his vicious power grab, and that she would not have forgiven him for her forced sterilization and the murder of her son. The fact that she was his best hope says much about his position. Still, her intelligence and knowledge of the Ndongan kingdom were unquestionable, and she still commanded the respect and allegiance of many nobles whom Ngola Mbande needed to win over. He dispatched messengers to ask for her help and services. And perhaps to the surprise of many, Njinga accepted.

This brings us back to the scene at the start of this chapter. Njinga's arrival in Luanda, the capital of the Portuguese colony, in October 1621 caused a sensation. Betraying their prejudices and assumptions of European superiority, the Portuguese sources wrote in wonder at "the Lady of Angola," marvelling at the size of her retinue, the richness of her attire (Njinga refused to don European costume during the visit and chose instead to wear traditional Mbundu clothes, albeit ones appropriate for her royal stature), and the lavish nature of the gifts she distributed.[27] They also remarked at the elegance of her manners, her regal bearing, and—once the negotiations had begun—her keen legal mind and the forensic skill of her arguments.

One of the Portuguese demands proved to be a sticking point. Njinga firmly refused to pay tribute in the form of enslaved people. She reminded the Portuguese, with some rhetorical sleight of hand, that Ngola Mbande had not technically been conquered. Rather, he was the sovereign king of a neighbouring country who was now opening discussions for a formal treaty of friendship. "Who is born free," she is reported as saying, "should maintain himself in freedom, and not submit to others."[28] Although she was referring to the freedom of one king being impinged upon by sending tribute to another, in the context of the expanding Atlantic slave trade her words have a much wider and sharper resonance. Both sides were stubbornly entrenched in their positions. It looked like the negotiations were about to collapse. Just when things seemed to have come to an impasse, Njinga pulled out her trump card: she offered to be baptised as a Catholic. This clinched the deal, and Njinga managed to secure the governor's agreement to a formal treaty between the Portuguese and Ndongo that excluded a tribute of enslaved people.

There was just the small matter of the baptism. Njinga stayed in Luanda for several months and seems to have thrown herself enthusiastically into the preparations, studying the catechism and engaging in discussions about faith. At the age of forty, she took part in a spectacular public ceremony at the official Jesuit church in Luanda, surrounded by "the nobility and the people."[29] The governor himself, João Correia de Souza, bestowed his own name upon her, so that she adopted the baptismal name Ana de Souza. How Njinga felt about this conversion is unclear, as the only written sources for the event that survive come from either Portuguese commentators or Njinga's later biographers. It is remarked that during her entire stay in Luanda, she never removed the Mbundu religious rings and relics that she wore on her arms and that she continued to take part in Mbundu rituals, and her acceptance of baptism was evidently a shrewd political strategy. But towards the end of her life, Njinga would derive great solace and comfort from the Christian faith and seems to have had a genuine commitment to spreading the church's teachings through her realm.

Njinga returned to her brother's court in triumph. In the years that followed, he began to rely on her more and more, so that by the time he fell gravely ill in 1624, she was already the "de facto leader" of Ndongo.[30] The illness resisted all attempts at a cure, and Ngola Mbande eventually died after taking poison. It is not clear whether he did this willingly or whether Njinga forced his hand. In any case, her Portuguese chroniclers wrote that Njinga "helped him to die with the aid of a poisoned drink." Losing no time, Njinga stepped into the gap and assumed the role of *ngola*, becoming—at the age of forty-two—the first female *ngola* of Ndongo.

As her brother had done before her, she immediately set about eliminating rivals. At the top of her hit list was her brother's son, who had been entrusted by her brother to an Imbangala war captain, Imbangala Kasa, for safekeeping. She got her hands on the boy by seducing Kasa with promises of marriage, and then snatched the boy and killed him at the wedding celebrations.[31] She also had several other members of her own family murdered, including a number of uncles, as well as representatives of alternative factions at court. As horrifying as this behaviour might seem, she had good reason to be wary of potential rivals. Repulsed at the idea of a woman on the throne, the Portuguese sought out other claimants to the throne and refused to honour the agreement that Njinga had negotiated on the basis that it had become obsolete upon the death of her brother. The Portuguese eventually settled on Njinga's half brother, Ngola Hari, whom they installed as a puppet king.[32] But Ngola Hari proved unpopular with the Ndongan population, partly because of his close association with the Portuguese but also because he had been the son of an enslaved woman and so was considered not to be of the same royal status as Njinga.[33] For several years, the Portuguese propped up Ngola Hari as an alternative king, refusing to recognise Njinga's rule.

A turning point came in 1631, when Njinga transformed the nature of her rule entirely. The Imbangalas had for a long time acted outside the legal and social frameworks of Ndongo, serving as a destabilising force and often allying themselves with the Portuguese. They were viewed with terror by the settled Mbundu population, who had often suffered at their hands. They were known for their cruelty in war, cannibalism, and human sacrifice, and terrifying stories about them abounded throughout the kingdom. One such story told of how Tembo a Ndumbo, a founding mother of the Imbangala way of life who set down many of their rules and customs, killed her own infant son and ground up his body in a mortar to make the *maji a samba* (holy oil) that Imbangala warriors ritually anointed themselves with before battle.[34]

At this point in her life, desperate for a breakthrough that would establish her rule firmly despite Portuguese actions to undermine her, Njinga saw an opportunity. As previously mentioned, in 1625 she had married Imbangala Kasa, a notable Imbangala war captain, as part of a political ruse. Although she and Kasa had not gone on to live together as a married couple, the marriage now provided Njinga with a way into Imbangala culture and society. Despite her earlier conversion to Christianity, Njinga had never entirely abandoned traditional Mbundu rituals, and now she added to these by learning to perfection the Imbangala rituals (as she was infertile, she reportedly killed the infant of one of her female concubines to make her traditional Imbangala holy oil, the *maji a samba*), becoming initiated into the Imbangala lifestyle, and assuming the role of an Imbangala war leader as well as that of a traditional *ngola*. She moulded her army along Imbangala lines, training them in the ruthless techniques that had made their war bands so successful and fearsome, and winning other Imbangalas to her cause. With these newly strengthened forces at her back, Njinga was able to consolidate her rule in eastern Ndongo, wresting power back from Ngola Hari, and even conquering the neighbouring kingdom of Matamba, unseating its queen, Muongo.

For the next decade, the Portuguese resisted her overtures for an official peace and alliance, describing her in their letters and documents with a mixture of fear and scorn. To them, the Imbangala customs and rituals that Njinga had adopted were anathema, and she was "a queen dedicated to the most horrendous customs and someone whose most appetizing meal was the hearts of boys and the breasts of girls."[35] Even worse, she was "an infernal woman in all her customs who links herself with all the rebels."[36] Although Njinga's reputation amongst the Portuguese was doubtless shaped by their racist assumptions and prejudices, they were correct in one thing—Njinga was a ruthless leader who did not hesitate to use levels of violence that might seem shocking to modern commentators when it would further her cause. But whatever they might have thought about her, the Portuguese found, to their chagrin, that they could not ignore her.

Giving up hope of forcing the Portuguese to come to an agreement with her by military means, Njinga turned to international diplomacy to find a solution. She courted and received the support against the Portuguese from the kingdom of Kongo, the Dutch, and the Vatican, all of whom she persuaded to acknowledge her right to rule. To them, she stressed how the Portuguese had attacked her, a baptised Christian monarch, with unwarranted aggression. Linked to this wider diplomatic effort, Njinga returned to Christianity after years spent mostly observing Mbundu and then Imbangala rituals, and opened up her realm to Capuchin missionaries. How far Njinga's return to Christianity was politically motivated, and how far it was a matter of personal faith, is unclear. Yet it did bear political fruit. It was not long before she received a supportive letter from Pope Alexander VII that was addressed to "Dearest in Christ our Daughter Anna Queen Nzinga."[37]

The Christianization of Ndongo and Matamba was far from straightforward, and many people continued to adhere to Mbundu religious customs long after Njinga's time. Yet some of the more bloodthirsty Imbangala rituals were outlawed, and many of Njinga's courtiers turned to Christianity. She was aided in this work in particular by two Capuchin monks, both of whom would later write biographies of her for a European audience: Father Antonio da Gaeta and Father Giovanni Antonio Cavazzi.

Facing the practical solidity of Njinga's rule in eastern Ndongo and Matamba, her popularity with the Mbundu population, and her support amongst Europeans who upheld her rights as a Christian monarch, the Portuguese eventually capitulated. In 1656 they officially recognised her authority as queen and concluded a peace treaty that clarified the borders between the colony of Angola and Njinga's neighbouring realm. Njinga's war with the Portuguese was finally over. She had lost a great deal to the struggle—three decades of her life, untold stress and discomfort, and the customs and religion first of her Mbundu ancestors and later of her Imbangala fellow initiates, as well as the lives of many people close to her. But in the end, she did not lose face. When it came to the peace negotiations with the Portuguese governor, she took the same line that she had several decades earlier with Correia de Souza when negotiating on behalf of her brother. She would not, under any circumstances, pay tribute to the Portuguese king. She is reported as saying, "In regard then to the tribute that you claim from me, there is no reason to do so, because having been born to rule my kingdom, I should not obey or recognize another sovereign . . . If the Portuguese want a gift from me every year, I would give it to them voluntarily as long as they equally give me one so that we both would deal with each other courteously."[38]

Njinga died comfortably in her bed on December 17, 1663, at the age of eighty-one.[39] She left behind her a stable kingdom that would be ruled by the descendants of her sister until the mid-nineteenth century, successfully holding off Portuguese encroachment for more than two hundred years. It was only much later, in 1909, that the last corners of what had been Njinga's kingdom were finally conquered by the Portuguese and absorbed into the Portuguese colony of Angola.

Angola via Athens

Today, Njinga features in films, comic books, and poems, and she has become a poster girl for a range of different causes. She appears regularly in lists of important female historical figures within Africa and is popular amongst Afro-descended populations in Brazil, the Caribbean islands, and the United States. She is also honoured in modern Angola as the Mother of the Nation, and a giant monument statue of her now stands in the nation's capital, unveiled only a year after the conclusion of the Angolan Civil War in 2002.[40]

Njinga also has been an icon of resistance and national struggle against colonialism. She was an important symbolic figure for the Angolan independence movement in the 1960s and even before this had long served as a kind of national hero, remembered in Angolan histories and oral traditions as a proud ruler who stood up against the Portuguese. But amongst Westerners, in contrast, for centuries the image presented of Njinga was almost uniformly derogatory, with rampant sexuality, cannibalism, and shocking cruelty all recurrent features of the portrayal. Amongst European Enlightenment thinkers of the eighteenth century, she was the epitome of the "other." For the German philosopher Hegel, she ruled a "female state" that was necessarily "outside history," where indiscriminate violence was perpetrated against men by wanton women. For his French contemporary the Marquis de Sade, she was "the cruellest of women," who routinely killed her lovers and murdered pregnant women younger than her. For such authors—male, white, and Western—Njinga represented everything that they believed to be barbarous and primitive about the imagined African "other." In the late eighteenth century in particular, she was deployed as a justification for Western colonialism, and an exemplum to support the Western notions of scientific racism (we will discuss the emergence of these in Chapter 11 of this book).

These portrayals have their ultimate roots in the biographies written by Gaeta and Cavazzi. The account penned by Father Gaeta offers a broadly positive assessment both of Njinga and of her realm, and was published in 1669 under the celebratory title *The Marvellous Conversion to the Holy Faith of Queen Njinga and of Her Kingdom of Matamba in Central Africa*. More complex and ambiguous is her treatment by Cavazzi, which appeared somewhat later, in 1687, in his book *Historical Description of the Three Kingdoms of Kongo, Matamba, and Angola*. Interestingly Cavazzi's depiction of west Africa and its people changes over the course of this book.

He starts out by characterising them negatively. The land itself is barely inhabitable, he claims, not because of the terrible heat or frightening animals that live there. Rather, the place is almost uninhabitable because of the "horrible, monstrous, inhuman people called Giaga [by which he means the Imbangalas], more cruel than the savage beasts of the woods and poisonous snakes."[41] These people, he asserts, live by laws that are as unnatural as they are inhuman. He proceeds to compare them unfavourably with various peoples of antiquity. All of these, he claims, even the barbarian peoples, attributed their laws to some divine origin, citing the Carthaginians, the Persians, and the Bactrians as examples. The barbarous inhabitants of Africa are therefore even worse than the barbarians of the ancient world because "these inhuman, cruel and godless Ethiopians [an archaising term for all sub-Saharan African peoples] without faith refer their satanic laws or *quixillas* [the Imbangala word for sacred rituals] not to any God but to an inhuman and cruel man and to a barbarous and inhuman woman [i.e., Tembo a Ndumbo], who reformed them, and made herself a legislator, without referring them to any God."[42] Njinga herself, he claims, was especially bad, once more comparing her negatively with even barbarians of antiquity. "Queen Ginga was more barbarous and cruel to children than Herod," he claims, saying that she "was always barbarically and cruelly surpassing even King Pharaoh."[43]

Cavazzi's text contains a range of references to antiquity. There are appeals to Aristotle and Seneca, as well as anecdotes about Caligula and Cicero. This is, in itself, no surprise. Such rhetorical flourishes were common in early modern literature, perhaps even standard and expected. They lent the author an air of distinguished erudition, while also anchoring the narrative in comparisons that would have been familiar to many of its original readers. This was especially the case in the genre of travel writing, which by its very nature sought to introduce its readers to the new, the strange, and the exotic. Crucially, the means by which it rendered the alien familiar was by using references to antiquity. When describing the unfamiliar customs of people in Africa and Asia, for example, Portuguese and Italian authors invoked Herodotean ethnography.[44] Similarly, when debating the correct relationship between Spain and its Amerindian subjects, Spanish writers Fernández de Oviedo and Bartolomé de las Casas used Roman comparisons to strengthen their arguments.[45]

Cavazzi's audience would have expected to be informed about contemporary Africa through comparisons with ancient Greece and Rome, Kongo contrasted with ancient Carthage, Angola held up against ancient Athens. By the late seventeenth century, the practice of appealing to antiquity had become a firm fixture of European travel and early colonial writing.

But there is one specific tendency in Cavazzi's text that is of particular significance for the development of Western Civilisation as a narrative. And this is the gulf in the values imputed to different parts of the ancient world. When seeking to portray Africans negatively,

Cavazzi draws on comparisons from across the ancient world, especially using comparisons with non-Greco-Roman groups such as the Egyptians, the Persians, the Carthaginians, and the Bactrians. Yet when he seeks to cast a more positive light, the comparisons become exclusively Greek or Roman.

Cavazzi's damning portrayal of Angola, its people, and its queen in book 1 of his work serves as an extended drumroll for what he will recount in book 2—the miraculous conversion of Njinga to Catholicism and her transformation from a barbarous savage to a recognisable Christian queen. The more heinous her crimes, the more astounding her salvation; the more satanic her previous practices, the more wondrous her conversion to the paths of righteousness. At the point of this transformation, Cavazzi ceases to connect Njinga with any of the other peoples of antiquity and begins to link her instead with the wise and chaste women of Greece and Rome. His aim, he claims, is

> to follow what the great Plutarch wrote of the wise women in Greece and the chaste ones in Rome in order to make their virtues known to the world, and show that masculine valour reigns also in a womanly breast; for this reason I briefly describe to you the descent of the ancestors of Queen Ginga here in occidental or lunar Ethiopia, her life, her customs, the barbarities and cruelties she committed in the past, so that when her vice is noted, the virtue should also be manifest which she shows at the present time, in contrast to the past. I say she was wise as if she had been one of the Greeks, chaste as a Roman converted to God.[46]

Cavazzi's choice of similes, as innocuous as they may seem, are significant. At the opening of the seventeenth century in the time of Bacon (Chapter 8), Greco-Roman antiquity had become cast as the main cultural ancestor for Europeans. For Cavazzi towards the end of the seventeenth century, it began also to become an ideal. It provided a yardstick against which all contemporary peoples could be measured, and—for colonised societies—found wanting. For Cavazzi, all that was deemed good, civilised, and "Western" amongst colonised peoples could be compared to Greco-Roman antiquity. And for Cavazzi, all that was deemed evil, barbaric, and "other" was imagined in terms of a non-Greco-Roman past. He conceived of a world that was split in two—between the colonisers and the colonised, the West and the Rest, those who had origins in Greco-Roman antiquity and those who did not. But for Cavazzi, unlike for other later authors, it was still possible for individuals and even whole states to move from one side of the divide to the other.

———

THE CONCEPT OF the West, a coherent cultural and political bloc with its own unique history and origins in Greco-Roman antiquity, was embryonic in the time of Tullia D'Aragona and still shaky enough to be conveniently ignored in the time of Safiye Sultan. In the lifetimes of Francis Bacon and Njinga of Angola, however, it became a reality. While its foundations may have been laid by Bacon and his contemporaries in Enlightenment Europe, some of the walls of this conceptual edifice were built beyond Europe, in the wider world that Europeans came to dominate. It was here that the distinction between the West and the Rest gained more tangible meaning, with familiar metaphors from antiquity used to render the non-Western world intelligible, and its people tameable.

Yet even at this point, the basis for Western domination was still disputable—was it racial, geographic, or religious? While a clear, trans–historical line between the West and the Rest has been drawn by the mid-seventeenth century, the criteria for placing people on one side or the other could still potentially be disputed. For Cavazzi in the seventeenth century, Njinga's religious conversion signalled her crossing of the civilisational boundary. Before it, he described her as a savage barbarian, an immoral heathen, who was aligned with a non-Western past. After it, he characterised her as civilized, moral, and aligned with a Western Greco-Roman heritage. For Cavazzi and his readers, Njinga had effectively *become* Western. Neither her geographic location in Africa nor any racial distinction prevented this transition. For Njinga herself, it was a conceptual transition that brought tangible political benefits. Her pivot to Christianity allowed her to argue the illegality of the Portuguese occupation, giving her (in theory) the same rights as a Christian monarch in Europe. It was the basis on which she received support from the pope, and contributed to the reticence of some Portuguese imperialists in their dealings with her.

In the late seventeenth century, it was still possible to say of an African queen, as Cavazzi did, that she was as wise as a Greek and as chaste as a Roman. At this point in time, the fact of Njinga's Africanness was not necessarily enough to exclude her from all Western privilege. But things were already changing. In 1685, only two decades after Njinga's death and two years before Cavazzi published his biography of her, the French traveller François Bernier published an article entitled "Nouvelle Division de la Terre," in which he adopted the radical approach of dividing humanity into discrete "races."[47] In the same year, a law was passed in France and its colonies which restricted the activities of dark-skinned people, whether enslaved or free, purely on the basis of their skin colour. It was known as the *Code Noir*. A generation later in 1735, Carl Linnaeus published the first edition of his *Systema naturae*, classifying humans as part of the wider natural world into four categories on the basis of complexion: *Europaeaus albus* (European pale), *Americanus rubescens* (American ruddy), *Asiasticus fuscus* (Asian dark), and *Africanus niger* (African black)—a classification that he would expand to include different temperaments and behaviours in the tenth edition (published in 1758).[48] As the seventeenth century rolled into the eighteenth, Western identity and Western Civilisation became increasingly racialized.

Chapter Ten

THE WEST AND POLITICS

JOSEPH WARREN

Approving heaven beheld the favourite ark dancing upon the
waves, and graciously preserved it until the chosen families
were brought in safety to these western regions.

JOSEPH WARREN (1775)[1]

The meetinghouse was packed. Soldiers surrounded the pulpit, pressing in on the speaker from all sides. The crowd at the doors seethed, churning with anger and resentment. The air between the two groups crackled with tension. The speaker himself seemed oblivious to the atmosphere of growing menace, carried away by the force of his own oratory. Joseph Warren spoke with both passion and authority. For the last ten years, he had been a leading figure in the American independence movement, the last six months of which he had spent as the elected representative of Boston in the new regional government established by the secessionists. One month after this speech, he would be elected its president. Two months later still and he would be dead—killed by British troops at the Battle of Bunker Hill, a founding martyr for the new United States of America.

Joseph Warren appears only rarely in lists of the USA's founding fathers.[2] His name has echoed more quietly through the centuries than those of his friends and colleagues—men such as John Hancock, Paul Revere, and John and Samuel Adams. Yet as a publicist, strategist, and all-round rabble-rouser, his role in the emerging independence movement was crucial. It was Warren who raised the revolutionary troops in time to meet the British at Lexington and Concord, the first military engagements of the American War of Independence, transforming what might have been a bloody rout into a resounding victory. And it was Warren who corralled public sentiment in favour of the revolution, building support so successfully that he was described by one British officer as "the famous Dr. Warren, the greatest incendiary in all America."[3]

The dramatic speech of March 6, 1775, delivered in Boston's Old South Meeting House to commemorate the fifth anniversary of the Boston Massacre, is a perfect example of his impassioned politics. Warren's performance lit a spark in the city, a spark that within the space of days would ignite into the full blaze of an armed uprising.

How did he do it? How did he whip up the crowd to boil from discontent to revolution? Warren's performances are lessons in the expert deployment of pathos, the virtuoso manipulation of tone and metre, and of course raw charisma. But it was not his technical brilliance that captured his audiences' imaginations. Instead, he sold them an idea.

North America, he told them, was not the colonial outpost of a greater and more illustrious Europe, but rather Europe's ascendant successor. (Central and South America were not part of Warren's vision—we will discuss them later in the chapter.) According to Warren, North America remained unblemished by the decadence of the Old World, and was therefore the rightful heir to millennia of European culture. The newly independent United States of America was to be the final and perfect culmination of Western Civilisation.

Of course, Joseph Warren was not the first to appeal to the concept of an inherited Western Civilisation. As we have seen in previous chapters, he was not the first to conceive of Greco-Roman antiquity as a coherent entity, nor the first to use this Greco-Roman antiquity as a source of intellectual and cultural capital. This was happening already two centuries earlier in the Renaissance (Chapter 6). Between the lifetimes of Tullia D'Aragona and Joseph Warren, while other ways of structuring the world history were still just about imaginable (Chapter 7), the prevailing trend was nonetheless to claim the Greco-Roman world exclusively for the emerging idea of the West (Chapter 8), and to use this imagined genealogy as a conceptual tool to distance the West from the rest of the world (Chapter 9). But while Warren was not the first to frame Western Civilisation as a narrative, he and his contemporaries did play a part in popularising it, giving it an appeal beyond the confines of the educated elite, and in making it a powerful political force to be reckoned with. With Warren, the idea of the West gained a new life beyond the pages of learned treatises and erudite discourses. It became current, tied to a fast-moving political movement, and caught up in revolution. At the same time, the cultural genealogy of Western Civilisation came into clearer focus, lent the urgency of the street and the pulpit. Western Civilisation moved out of the realms of intellectualised discourse and into the real world.

Empire and Liberty

Through Warren's lifetime in the mid-eighteenth century, the thirteen British colonies of North America were unusual when compared to other parts of the British Empire. A key difference was demography. Across most of Britain's Asian, African, and central American possessions, subject populations were governed by a relatively small number of British soldiers and administrators, demarcated not only by imperial politics but also increasingly by racialised boundaries.

In Ireland, the situation was different. More than 150 years of settlement and "plantation" meant that by the middle of the eighteenth century, the population included a substantial number of British-derived Protestants, mostly concentrated in the fertile north of the island. Although today many people tend to think of the Irish as "white" and therefore in the same broad racial category as the indigenous British, the treatment of the indigenous Irish for much of their colonial history falls into patterns that can be considered racial.[4] By the mid-eighteenth century, these patterns had begun to change and new racial constellations had begun to emerge.

In the thirteen American colonies, in contrast, a large part of the permanent population claimed descent from British settlers. As the children of the colonisers rather than the colonised, these inhabitants of the American colonies occupied a markedly different position within the imperial system than most inhabitants of Britain's other imperial possessions. Racialised distinctions, which across most of Britain's empire served to distinguish the imperial elite from their colonial subjects, were not made between them and the British colonial governors that ruled over them. This was not, of course, true for all inhabitants of these colonies—racialised distinctions were very much in operation between these British-descended colonists, people descended from other European migrants, people descended from enslaved Africans, and the American native peoples. The large proportion of the population made up of these British-descended colonists posed particular challenges for the governance of these colonies. By the middle of the eighteenth century, tensions between Britain and its thirteen American colonies were running high. In particular, Britain sought to exercise greater control, regulating trade and imposing taxes on key commodities. The Sugar Act of 1765, the Stamp Act of 1765, the Townshend Acts of 1767, and the Tea Act of 1773—all were met in the American colonies with outrage and rioting and eventually led to revolution.

Yet the revolutionaries faced an ideological quandary. On the one hand, they wanted to argue for liberty and against imperialism. On the other, most revolutionaries did not want to argue for *universal* liberty and against *all* imperialism. Crucially, while colonists of British ancestry sought to establish their own inalienable right to freedom and self-determination, there was relatively little support for extending these same rights to the enslaved African American population. Similarly, while many of these same revolutionary agitators found it intolerable to have imperialism be exercised over them, many did not object when it was exercised over others, especially not the imperialism exercised by white colonists over American native peoples, or indeed by European colonists elsewhere in the Americas, Africa, and Asia. The tension between these two ideological needs—to argue for their own liberties without necessarily supporting the liberties of others, and to decry being the subject of empire without rejecting the notion of empire itself—posed a conceptual problem.

This problem can be seen clearly in the speeches, letters, and published works of the revolutionaries, which contain frequent references

to the British enslavement of the colonists and to the British as imperial invaders. During the course of the War of Independence, George
Washington, the revolutionary general and eventually the first president of the independent United States and a wealthy enslaver of many
African Americans, claimed that the colonists sought independence
from Britain because "the Spirit of Freedom beat too high in us to Submit to Slavery."[5] Similarly, the Fairfax Resolves, signed by Washington
and other leading revolutionaries, claimed in 1774 that the exercise of
power by the British Parliament over the American colonies was "calculated to reduce us from a State of Freedom and Happiness to Slavery
and Misery."[6] For these white revolutionary leaders, the idea of metaphorical enslavement to the British was an abomination.

The tone was similar when it came to British imperialism. In 1777 in
a letter to the revolutionary leader and eventual third president of the
United States, Thomas Jefferson, one local politician from Virginia
complained, "Could we but get a good Regular Army we should soon
clear the Continent of these damn'd Invaders."[7] In the same year,
Washington wrote to John Hancock in a fury that "there can be no
doubt of the British Court's straining every nerve and interest at Home
and abroad to bend us to their insufferable yoke."[8] American revolutionary rhetoric framed the independence movement as a struggle
against slavery and imperialism as imposed on white North Americans
by the British.

Yet these same revolutionaries were more ambivalent about the enslavement of and extension of imperialism over others who were not
descendants of British or other European colonizers. On the one hand,
Washington officially condemned slavery as an institution when he
signed the Fairfax Resolves,[9] and Jefferson is perhaps best known
for writing the Declaration of Independence, adopted by the Continental Congress in July 1977. In it, Jefferson famously wrote that "all men
are created Equal; that they are endowed by their Creator with certain

inalienable rights," building on Enlightenment thinking such as the political theories of Locke. Yet despite their opposition to slavery as an abstract notion, for various reasons neither Washington nor Jefferson outlawed the practice of enslavement when they eventually assumed the presidency, and both men continued to own hundreds of enslaved people until the ends of their lives. It seems that for the North American revolutionaries of the mid- to late eighteenth century, servitude was to be avoided for themselves but could be tolerated for others.

A similar ambivalence can be seen in the rhetoric surrounding empire and colonialism.[10] For all his opposition to British imperial cruelties, Washington had no qualms about characterising the newly independent United States as a "rising empire."[11] Indeed, the night before Britain acknowledged American independence, he addressed his troops, thanking those "who have shared in the toils and dangers of effecting this glorious revolution, of rescuing Millions from the hand of oppression, and of laying the foundation of a great Empire." He continued, "thrice happy shall they be hereafter, who have contributed anything, who have performed the meanest office in creating this stupendous fabric of Freedom and Empire."[12]

The North American Revolution, then, was a struggle against slavery fought by people who tolerated, and in some cases participated in, enslavement.[13] It was an anti-imperial war waged by people who accepted, and in some cases actively wanted an empire.[14] The irony of the situation was not lost on contemporary commentators. Writing in 1775, the British scholar Samuel Johnson complained, "How is it that we hear the loudest yelps for liberty among the drivers of negroes?"[15] The same year, an anonymous pamphlet attributed to the British political theorist Thomas Paine asked North Americans to consider "with what consistency, or decency they complain so loudly of attempts to enslave them, while they hold so many hundred thousands in slavery"?[16] There was an ideological problem at the heart of the revolutionary movement. The twin ideas of the West and of Western Civilisation were to prove part of the solution.

Physician and Revolutionary

Warren, a fourth-generation American from a farming family, had enjoyed a comfortable but not luxurious childhood. At ten he had attended the Roxbury Latin School, and at fourteen he had embarked on his undergraduate degree at Harvard University. (This might sound young to us, but it was not so unusual at the time. Francis Bacon was a similar age when he attended the University of Cambridge; see Chapter 8.) At this point, the young Warren found himself constrained by the traditional class system. Although he was a gifted student (his political opponents would later describe him as "possessed of a Genius that promised Distinction"[17]), the university ranked its students not according to academic performance, but on the wealth and social standing of their parents. As a result, Warren was placed a lowly thirty-one out of the forty-five students in his year and barred from many of the privileges Harvard had to offer.[18] This experience must have been formative. Throughout his adult life, first as a doctor and later as a political agitator, Warren would bristle against class conventions.

A portrait of him painted in 1765 shows a pale young man with soft, features and melancholy eyes. According to one contemporary commentator, "the ladies pronounced him handsome,"[19] and when John Adams, the revolutionary leader and eventually the second president of the United States, first met Warren in 1764, he described him as a "pretty, tall, Genteel, fresh-faced young Gentleman."[20] At the time, Warren was only twenty-three years old, but had already worked for two years as a doctor. It was this work that first gained him a public profile.

The winter of 1763–64 saw Boston in the grip of a deadly smallpox pandemic. While most wealthy Bostonians fled, Warren and his colleagues set up an emergency field hospital at Castle William, a fortified peninsula in the south of the city. As well as providing free care for the sick and the dying, they also embarked on a controversial campaign of inoculations, saving hundreds more lives in the process. When the epidemic waned, the city council decreed that "the Thanks of the Town be and hereby are given [to] those Gentleman Physicians, who in this Season of difficulty and distress have generously Inoculated and carried through the Small-Pox Gratis."[21] The doctors of Castle William became overnight celebrities.

Warren embraced his new public profile eagerly. And in the summer of 1764, within months of acquiring his new celebrity status, Warren had put it to good use—first, by making an advantageous marriage to the society heiress Elizabeth Hooton, and second, by fomenting revolution.[22] In the autumn of that same year, when Boston erupted with popular protests against the newly imposed Sugar Tax, Warren threw himself into the political melee. He publicly defended the man charged with inciting the riots, writing a medical note to exempt him from the legal proceedings on the grounds of a nervous disposition, and became involved in a campaign to boycott British imports.[23]

Warren stepped up his political activities in the spring of the following year, publishing his first piece of overtly political writing in response to the imposition of the Stamp Act. These laws, originally passed in 1765, increased the cost of all paper goods, from newspapers to university diplomas and from playing cards to legal documents. They were, in essence, a tax on intellectual and cultural life. Against a backdrop of protests and riots, Warren's article in the *Boston Gazette* set out the colonial argument. Since North Americans were "descendants of Britain, born in a land of light, and reared in the bosom of liberty," they should therefore not have taxes imposed on them without representation in the British Parliament. He closed his article with an impassioned appeal: "Awake, awake my countrymen, and by a regular and legal opposition defeat the designs of those who would enslave us and our posterity."[24] Warren's use of the language of enslavement echoes that of other founding fathers—like them, he railed against the idea of curbs to his own liberty, at the same time remaining an owner of enslaved people himself.[25]

Despite the repeal of the Stamp Act, Warren ratcheted up his revolutionary activities in the years that followed. He pilloried the British governor of Massachusetts;[26] penned new lyrics for revolutionary songs;[27] and surrounded himself with other radicals, including the cousins John and Samuel Adams, as well as John Hancock. At first, not all of his companions understood the value of Warren's voluminous output. John Adams described Warren's writings as "a curious employment, cooking up paragraphs, articles, occurrences etc.—working the political engine!"[28]

Whipped up by pensmiths such as Warren, anti-British feeling in the city was rising, with Boston set to become the cockpit of the American Revolution. Protests, riots, and run-ins with British troops became everyday occurrences, culminating in the infamous Boston Massacre of March 5, 1770. During this tragic event, British soldiers, feeling threatened by an angry mob, had fired their muskets into the crowd, killing five men and injuring many more. Warren, along with Samuel Pemberton, was responsible for producing an official account of the event, designed to stir up public outrage. The published pamphlet styled itself as: "A short Narrative of the horrid Massacre in Boston, perpetrated in the Evening of the Fifth Day of March, 1770, by Soldiers of the XXIXth Regiment; which with the XIVth Regiment were then quartered there: with some Observations on the State of Things prior to that Catastrophe."[29] Distributed alongside it were copies of an engraving by Paul Revere depicting the event, which remains until today the prevailing popular image of the massacre. Warren also organised an annual public oration to commemorate the event, promoting an exhibition of drawings inspired by the massacre hung in the windows of Revere's house. In 1771, the oration and the exhibition reached an audience of thousands.[30]

Another flash point came in 1773, when Britain passed the Tea Act, designed to shore up the ailing finances of the East India Company (which, despite resorting to torture and extortion, was unable to offset its financial losses after a famine in Bengal). It hoped to do this by removing taxes on the shipping of tea, allowing the East India Company to undercut the prices of tea smugglers. In the North American colonies, the threat to the smugglers (many of whom were established businessmen, such as John Hancock) was seen as yet another imperial imposition.[31] On December 16, a public meeting was convened at Boston's Old South Meeting House. Although the details of the event remain unclear to this day, it is evident that an angry mob made its way to the port and boarded three ships that had recently arrived carrying cargoes of East India Company tea. They proceeded to tip more than 340 chests of tea, worth US$2,000,000 in today's money, into the harbour in an event known as the Boston Tea Party.[32] The revolutionaries responded to the inevitable British crackdown by setting up their own alternative government. The Continental Congress and the more local Massachusetts Provincial Congress (in which Warren was chosen to represent the city of Boston) sat in open opposition to the British imperial administration.[33]

This was the powder-keg environment that surrounded Joseph Warren when we first met him at the start of this chapter, standing up to speak at the Old South Meeting House on March 6, 1775, for the fifth annual oration commemorating the Boston Massacre. The British soldiers who watched the oration that day were, behind the scenes, preparing for what must have seemed like the inevitability of armed conflict. For weeks, British troops had been manoeuvring into position and supplies were being stockpiled. But unknown to them, Warren's spies had been watching and the revolutionaries were also poised for action. In early April, the British decided to make their move. They planned to attack the small town of Concord in the interior of Massachusetts, a base used by the revolutionary militia. On April 18, Warren learned that the British troops were scheduled to set off at first light. That night, he dispatched a series of prearranged signals and messages to alert revolutionaries across New England.

Two of Warren's messengers deserve special attention.[34] William Dawes rode south from Boston, warning the local militias in Roxbury and Cambridge before turning inland. Paul Revere rode north through Charlestown before heading towards Concord. Revere's midnight ride was immortalised nearly a century later in a popular poem by Henry Wadsworth Longfellow, "Paul Revere's Ride"—a poem that has sealed Revere's place in the popular consciousness in contrast to the relative obscurity of Dawes and Warren. Yet without the efforts of both riders, and—even more crucially—without the efficiency of Warren's spy network, the next day would have brought victory for the British and proved a major setback for the revolutionaries.

When the British soldiers set out to Concord the next morning, they found the colonial troops expecting them. A brief skirmish was fought at Lexington, a small settlement on the road towards Concord, and another engagement occurred at Concord itself.[35] Their purpose thwarted, the British began retreating towards Boston. But by this stage, the road back to Boston was a dangerous one. The British troops found themselves set upon along the way by colonial militias pouring in from the Massachusetts countryside. Warren fought in one such company, attacking the British column at the village of Menotomy (now Arlington). When they finally reached Boston, the British retreated behind the city's fortified walls and were besieged by colonial forces. The siege was to last an entire year, ending eventually in a colonial victory. The American War of Independence had started.

Modelling Modernity

Warren was neither theorist nor scholar, but a practical man who knew the power of words. As a revolutionary, he used words with spectacular rhetorical effect. But as a man, there was one moment in his life when his usual fluency escaped him. The moment came in April 1773 with the death of his wife, Elizabeth, who succumbed to a sudden and unexplained illness. At the age of thirty-one, Warren found himself a widower with four small children. Stricken with grief, he sought solace in the two pillars of his early education—the church and Greco-Roman antiquity. On May 17, 1773, a poem was published in the *Boston Gazette*. It was written in Latin and was accompanied by no explanation or attribution. It simply read:

Epitaphium Dominae Elisae War***

Omnes, flete, dolete, cari virtutis amici:
Heu! Nostras terras Dulcis Elisa fugit.
Quisnam novit eam gemitus que negare profundos
Posset? Permagni est criminis ille reus.[36]

The poem is almost certainly by Joseph Warren. It may not occur to you or me to write Latin verse upon the demise of a partner, but then you and I probably do not have an eighteenth-century gentleman's education. For Warren, a man who was usually so articulate, whose greatest triumphs lay in his eloquent manipulations of language in the service of his political cause, it is significant that at this moment,

English was not enough. In these darkest of days, he turned to Latin epic to express himself. For those of us who indeed do not have an eighteenth-century gentleman's education, and for whom composing an epic poem does not come quite so naturally, here is a translation in English:

EPITAPH FOR MISTRESS ELISAE WAR***

Weep, all dear and honest friends, grieve!
Alas! Sweet Elisa has left our earth.
Who can know this and not sigh deeply?
They are guilty of a terrible crime.

This was not the only time that Warren invoked antiquity. His writings, both public and personal, were peppered with Greek and Roman references. Instead of writing under his own name in his early publications, he used the Hellenizing pseudonym Paskalos (all good things) and signed other essays with the tags Philo Physic (nature lover) and Graph Iatroos (the writing doctor), as well as using the name of the legendary Roman nobleman Mucius Scaevola.[37] Warren's classical credentials were already established during his time at Harvard, where he wrote and staged one play called *Cato* about the famously strict Roman senator, and another named *The Roman Father*.[38]

Warren was not alone amongst the founding fathers in seeing himself and his cause through a Greco-Roman lens. Even granted the ubiquity of Greek and Latin in elite education by this time, the extent of Greek and Roman material in the writings of the founding fathers goes beyond the accidents of childhood recollection. Rather, a deliberate classicism infused the entire independence project.[39] After the war was won, constitutional debates between federalists and anti-federalists were carried out using the heightened rhetoric of Greek and Roman orators.[40] In the years that followed, many elements of the new American constitution, from the naming of the Senate to the neoclassical architecture of the Capitol building, were based on Greek and Roman models. In this as with much else, the founding fathers were building on the political philosophies of the Enlightenment, borrowing extensively from Locke, Hobbes, and Rousseau. Faced with the challenge of creating a new political system from the ground up, the founding fathers came to think of it not as a radical new system at all, but merely as a refinement of the political structures of those they saw as their ancient forebears.

Greco-Roman antiquity offered the founding fathers a common language—a shared set of reference points and ideals. Although we might have expected Christianity to fulfil this role, the splintered factionalism of different Christian groups in colonial America militated against this. Within the revolutionary movement itself, Catholics and Anglicans butted heads with Quakers, Methodists, Lutherans, Mennonites, and Presbyterians, amongst others. The confessional differences between these groups were significant and strongly felt—many had chosen to leave Europe for North America in part because they had hoped it would allow them more religious freedom. The Christianity of the puritanical citizen farmers of the north differed radically from that of the grandees on their plantations in the south, which was different once again from the cosmopolitan humanism that could be found in some of the big cities. With religion driving them apart, the idea of a common Greco-Roman past became an important element in holding the founding fathers together.

During the revolutionary campaign, the use of ancient Greek and Roman imagery and references had been particularly pointed. In contrast to the philhellenism that was sweeping through much of continental Europe at the time, the North American revolutionaries tended to style themselves in the fashion of Republican Rome.[41] Austere yet aristocratic, morally restrained yet fiercely defensive of individual liberties, Republican Rome provided the perfect ideological model for the developing independence movement (Roman antiquity had somewhat different connotations in Latin America at this time, as we shall see later). The revolutionaries also considered Rome a better model than ancient Greece because the radical democracy of fifth-century BCE Athens was thought to be dangerously open and inclusive, and therefore vulnerable to demagoguery and mob rule.[42] This might seem counterintuitive from a modern perspective, given the emphasis on liberal democracy in current Western ideology and political rhetoric (we will discuss this in Chapters 13 and 14), as well as counterfactual, given how exclusionary Athenian democracy as Herodotus experienced it in the late fifth century BCE actually was (e.g., excluding women and enslaved people, as well as all residents who could not prove their "pure blood" Athenian ancestry; see Chapter 1). Yet for the North American founding fathers, this was an important factor making Rome rather than Greece a more appealing imagined ancestor.[43]

This ideological interest in Rome is especially evident in the revolutionaries' choice of pseudonyms. At the height of civic unrest in Boston during the years 1770–75, the *Boston Gazette* published more than 120 articles signed by revolutionaries using classical pseudonyms, mostly alluding to Republican Rome.[44] These included "Cato of Utica," "Brutus," and "Civis"; as well as several that can be traced back to Samuel Adams, including "Clericus Americanus," "Sincerus," and "Candidus." After the establishment of a British garrison within the city of Boston, Adams also began to sign his essays with "Cedant Arma Togae" ("let arms yield to the toga," a phrase coined by Cicero to argue for the supremacy of public debate over violence). The revolutionaries were positioning themselves as Romans reborn, the heirs of Cato and Cicero.[45]

The classicism of the founding fathers was deliberate, self-conscious, and by no means innocent. Far from an unthinking result of their education, this was evidence of a political stance—an ideological position. They were appropriating the cultural genealogy of the West. In this book we have already encountered the notion of *translatio imperii* (Chapter 4), and the North American revolutionaries now took this idea to its logical conclusion—the crossing of the Atlantic. Whereas Bacon and his successors had begun to trace the lineage of Western Civilisation from Greco-Roman antiquity to their own Enlightenment world of western Europe, the revolutionaries claimed that the torch of Western Civilisation had now been passed to North America.

The revolutionary generation were not the American originators of this idea. As early as 1713, Benjamin Franklin the Elder exhorted his audience to "show us here that your young Western clime / Out Does all Down unto our present Time."[46] In 1725, the cleric George Berkeley asserted the idea of American ascendancy even more clearly, writing, "There shall be sung another golden age, / The rise of empire and of arts, / ... Not such as Europe breeds in her decay; / ... Westward the course of empire takes its way." The last line of the poem would later serve as inspiration and become the title of the famous painting by Emanuel Leutze that now hangs in the US Capitol building. And in the 1758 edition of his annual *Almanack*, Nathaniel Ames commented that "the curious have observed that the progress of human literature (like the sun) is from east to west; thus has it travelled through Asia and Europe, and now is arrived at the eastern shore of America."[47]

Despite these many references, in the early and mid-eighteenth century, the idea of *translatio imperii* culminating in North America remained a somewhat esoteric metaphor, a poetic and scholarly abstraction. What the revolutionary generation did, in the third quarter of the century, was to transform this into something far more concrete—a political ideology. And on the back of this ideology, a country was built.

The first step was to embrace the idea of North America as consti-
tuting "the West." The younger Benjamin Franklin published an outraged letter in the *Pennsylvania Chronicle* in 1768, accusing the British
of mistreating "us in the West." The following year, he claimed that the
British were crushing liberty, or in any case "the first Appearance of it
in the Western World."[48] A few years later, in 1773, he expressed concern lest "our western People became as tame as those in the eastern
Dominions of Britain."[49] Around this time, George Washington also
wrote about his concern for "matters in the western world,"[50] while in
an address in Philadelphia, John Hancock proudly stated that he
looked forward to a time when there would be liberty "in this western
world."[51] It was a rhetoric that soon spread. In the autumn of 1775, the
Bostonian poet and revolutionary Mercy Otis Warren (no relation to
Joseph Warren) wrote to John Adams that were it not for the efforts of
men such as him, freedom "would long ee'r this have been banished
from the western hemisphere."[52] And in 1776, General Philip Schuyler
wrote to Washington, wishing him divine favour in his work of "ensuring Freedom to the Western World."[53]

The second step was to construct the genealogy of this new North
American West, framing it as the climax of the old lineage of Europe.
For many, the idea of *translatio imperii* meant the new united states
were the ultimate heirs of classical antiquity, and in particular Rome.[54]
This idea was to lie behind the later concept of "Manifest Destiny,"
which underpinned westwards expansion in the nineteenth century,
and has spawned countless books, magazine articles, and op-eds in recent decades discussing whether or not the United States of America
should be considered the "new Rome."[55] We can see this notion already
in the works of Warren, not in the form of scholarly tomes or erudite
chronicles, but in an unabashedly populist tone.

Published in 1770, the lyrics of "The New Massachusetts Liberty
Song," attributed to Warren, set out this new vision of the West with its

own unique heritage. The verses of the song chart out the history of the West, beginning in the first stanza with "That Seat of Science Athens, and Earth's great Mistress Rome." Following the cultural genealogy of Western Civilisation, the second stanza transports us to Britain, which receives the precious inheritance of Greco-Roman antiquity by accepting the yoke of Roman imperialism ("Proud Albion bow'd to Caesar"). The song then reminds us of the other peoples who conquered Britain in the centuries that followed, including Picts, Danes, and Normans, rendering it an unworthy final resting place for power. This eventual zenith of Western Civilisation, we hear in the fourth and central stanza of the song, is instead to be located "beneath this western Sky," where "We form'd a new Dominion, a Land of Liberty." This central and politically charged verse is the hinge point of the whole song. Before it, we have the genealogy of Western Civilisation as an historical prelude. After it, we are exhorted to look to a glorious independent future for North America as the final seat of Western Civilisation.

Warren's vision was even more explicit in his 1775 oration commemorating the Boston Massacre, the speech with which we began this chapter. He begins, as in the "Liberty Song," with an historical preamble about the colonisation of North America. He describes how "Our fathers" decided to leave Europe, resolving "never to wear the yoke of despotism." He then evokes the bravery of that ocean voyage, claiming that: "Approving heaven beheld the favourite ark dancing upon the waves, and graciously preserved it until the chosen families were brought in safety to these western regions." After this historical prelude, Warren moves to the main part of the speech—exhorting his audience to revolution with rousing references to the glorious history of the West. The British Empire is compared with "Roman glory" and, despite conquering parts of the world unknown even to Alexander of Macedon and the Caesars, was judged to be an unworthy heir to the classical legacy on account of its tyranny and greed. It was left to the

Americans, then, to emulate antiquity. Warren encourages his audience not to give up hope, arguing that "it was a maxim of the Roman people, which eminently conduced to the greatness of that state, never to despair of the commonwealth."

But Warren's audience in 1775 would have been just as struck by his sartorial choice as they were by his words. He had chosen to deliver this speech wearing not the standard contemporary attire for a gentleman of his station, but a Roman toga.[56] In the Roman world, the toga was the preserve of citizen men—a formal garment conferred on boys when they came of age, marking them out as members of the political community and, as the empire expanded, the Roman elite.[57] Warren's decision to don the toga at this particular moment was a calculated one. As I already mentioned, the tagline "Cedant Arma Togae" (let arms yield to the toga) was already being used by John Adams to sign off revolutionary pamphlets in occupied Boston. With Warren in his crisp white toga, decrying a military massacre while surrounded by British soldiers, the Ciceronian phrase would have seemed painfully relevant.

Through both the power of his words and the theatre of his appearance, Warren popularised a vision of North America as the ultimate heir of Western Civilisation, the inheritor of a long and storied lineage reaching back through the ages to Greco-Roman antiquity. In the most incendiary and bombastic terms possible, he added North America to the bloodline as a separate entity, distinct and indeed superior to its degenerate ancestors. Only in North America, free from the vices and corruption of the Old World, could the potential of Western Civilisation be fulfilled. Only in North America, heir to an unbroken cultural tradition, could the zenith of Western history be reached. Only in North America could the West take its perfect and ultimate form.

As we have already noted, the North American revolutionary

movement suffered from a stark ideological disjoint. How could the revolutionaries claim to be antislavery whilst remaining enslavers, and anti-empire whilst remaining imperialists? It was an ideological problem that critics of the movement were quick to seize on (see earlier in this chapter) and which alienated some potential supporters of the movement (see Chapter 11). The grand narrative of Western Civilisation offered a convenient way out of this ideological problem. Thanks to the ideas promoted by men such as Warren, the revolutionaries could comfortably agitate for their own freedom on the basis of their Western heritage, without necessarily extending that freedom to others, and they could decry the subjugation of themselves, as Westerners, to imperial oversight, without rejecting the principle of imperialism in itself. The narrative of Western Civilisation offered not only a powerful motivating vision for Americans as they surged forward into a new age of political independence, but also an excuse.

THE IDEA THAT Anglophone North America was the culmination of Western Civilisation became popular in the late eighteenth century, thanks to men like Warren. But it was not an idea that was uniformly popular everywhere, even within the Americas. It was problematic for those residents of the new United States who remained disenfranchised under its rhetoric, as we shall see in the next chapter. It was not the prevailing ideology across the large swaths of land in the north still controlled by Britain, which would eventually become Canada. Nor was it necessarily dominant across the parts of North America with substantial Francophone populations, although French colonial rule on the American mainland had ended in 1763 with the Treaty of Paris (it continued for some time after this in the Caribbean). And it was definitely not a vision shared by the peoples of New Spain (in what is now central America and the southern portion of North America), the Caribbean, and South America.

Across much of Latin America, ancient Rome was closely associated with colonialism. The Spanish in particular had couched their
imperial expansion in terms of Roman antiquity, justifying their
American conquests with reference to Roman imperialism.[58] Throughout the Spanish-controlled Americas therefore, antiquity largely meant
Rome rather than Greece, access to the Latin language was largely me-
diated by either the Catholic Church or the Spanish authorities, and
knowledge about antiquity was bound up with social capital within
the colonial system.[59] So although intellectuals in New Spain were just
as engaged with the Roman past as their counterparts in Anglophone
North America in the eighteenth century (this period has even been
called a "Golden Age" of Latin literature in New Spain),[60] the political
implications were markedly different. While for Warren, Washington,
and Jefferson, Rome provided the template for an independent republican future; for the Guatemalan Jesuit poet Rafael Landívar, Latin
literary conventions helped him to render his homeland comprehen-
sible to European readers;[61] for the Jesuit missionary to Paraguay José
Manuel Peramás, epic Roman heroism was a means to valorise the initial Spanish conquest and his own missionary work;[62] and for the Pe-
ruvian composer Tómas de Torrejón y Velasco, allusions to Roman
myth furnished the backdrop for a lavish operatic celebration of the
Spanish monarchy.[63]

The situation did begin to change, however, around the turn of the
eighteenth into the nineteenth century, as ideas about Greco-Roman
antiquity came to play a complex role in independence movements
across central and South America.[64] Toussaint Louverture, a charismatic leader of enslaved Haitians in the revolution against French colonial rule, was hailed in 1796 as a "Black Spartacus"—a reference to
the famous gladiator who led a revolt of enslaved people in Roman Italy in the first century BCE.[65] A more conscious pivot towards the ancient Greek world appears in the works of Latin American writers after

this point, especially those involved with independence movements and with forging post-colonial national identities. Hellenism provided a way to claim the glories of Mediterranean antiquity and Western Civilisation that was free from taint of association with colonial Spain, and which also set itself in opposition to the strident rhetoric of the United States as the "new Rome."[66]

While the grand narrative of Western Civilisation may therefore have become mainstream by the last decades of the eighteenth century, it was not a narrative that was embraced equally across the Americas. Instead, it was deeply embedded in the political rhetoric of the new United States, providing an ideological basis on which the revolutionaries could argue for liberty and an end to imperialism on one hand, whilst simultaneously preserving internal structures of oppression and colonialism on the other. In the next of our biographies, we shall see how these ideological tensions played out in the life of one remarkable individual. While we should acknowledge the conceptual cancer at the heart of the newly formed United States, we should also recognize its success in creating a new system (albeit an imperfect one) that aimed to balance power between the different states and arms of government, and which enshrined the principle (if not always the practice) of political equality. Similarly, while we should acknowledge that the North American revolutionaries created an ideologically driven historical narrative that served their immediate political needs, we should not see them as particularly scheming or devious because they did so. We have seen throughout this book how people have reimagined history according to the political imperatives of the time and how different visions of history can rise (or not, as the case may be) to dominance only when the wider context permits. In particular, we have seen in earlier chapters of this book how the narrative of Western Civilisation emerged gradually, in fits and starts, over the course of the sixteenth to eighteenth centuries. And we have seen in this chapter how it took the specific ideological needs of the North American revolution in the eighteenth century to move it into the (Anglophone) mainstream.

As for Warren, we have left him on the brink of both glory and disaster. A talented wordsmith and gifted spymaster, Warren changed the course of history by trafficking in ideas and information. He was instrumental in getting the American War of Independence off to a strong start for the revolutionaries, a cause for which he would soon give his life. Amongst the numerous skirmishes and battles that took place during the first year of the war, the bloodiest was the Battle of Bunker Hill in June 1775, where Joseph Warren died in combat.

In death as in life, Warren rallied support for the revolution. Accounts of his heroism were carried in admiring letters to friends and family, but so too were scandalous rumours about the savagery of the British soldiers and the mistreatment of Warren's corpse. These stories spread across the American colonies, becoming more and more gruesome with each telling. Even after the War of Independence was won in 1783, the tale of Warren's demise still proved powerful. John Trumbull's painting of 1786, *The Death of General Warren at the Battle of Bunker Hill*, dramatises the moment of martyrdom and was popular enough to warrant Trumbull making several copies, as well as selling the engraving rights for a hefty subscription fee. The engravings meant that the image went into mass production, and soon there were thousands of copies in circulation. Had he known how his death was put to use to rally support for his beloved cause, Warren surely would have approved.

Chapter Eleven

THE WEST AND RACE

PHILLIS WHEATLEY

Muse! Lend thy aid, nor let me sue in vain.

PHILLIS WHEATLEY (1773)[1]

THE judges have gathered in the courtroom. There are eighteen of them, and amongst their number are some of the most powerful men in Massachusetts. They include the colony's governor, His Excellency Thomas Hutchinson; its lieutenant governor, the Honourable Andrew Oliver; no fewer than seven prominent members of the clergy; and a host of Boston dignitaries, including the trading magnate and revolutionary leader John Hancock (whom we met in Chapter 10). These men are gathered in the courtroom to conduct a trial—not of a crime or legal misdemeanour, but rather to uncover the truth behind a seemingly absurd claim. The subject they are examining is Phillis Wheatley, an eighteen-year-old enslaved African woman, and the claim they seek to test is that she wrote a book of poetry.

When her enslaver, John Wheatley, first told people that she was composing poems, they didn't believe him. When examples of these poems began to circulate, with their sophisticated manipulation of both rhyme and metre and their erudite allusions to classical and biblical literature, the doubts only multiplied. It was impossible, in the minds of many members of white colonial society, for a teenaged black woman to compose literature at this level. And so, when John Wheatley began to seek a publisher for a collection of these poems, there were public calls for verification of their authenticity. A court was convened of "the most respected Characters in Boston,"[2] and Phillis Wheatley was summoned to defend her authorship of the collection, *Poems on Various Subjects Religious and Moral.*

We can only imagine what took place at the trial.[3] Her questioners might have quizzed Wheatley on her knowledge of Latin grammar or Old Testament texts. They might have enquired as to the nature and manner of her education, or the inspiration behind her choice of subject matter. They might even have set her a literary riddle, such as the one solved (in verse, of course) by Wheatley at the end of her published collection of poems.[4] At this moment, everything was stacked against her in the court of public opinion—her race, her age, and her sex—but Wheatley ultimately triumphed. Whatever questions they threw at her, she must have answered convincingly, because when her book finally appeared in print a year later, this confirmatory note signed by the judges appeared in its preface:

We whose Names are under-written, do assure the World, that the POEMS specified in the following Page were (as we verily believe) written by PHILLIS, a young Negro Girl, who was but a few Years since, brought an uncultivated Barbarian from Africa, and has ever since been, and now is, under the Disadvantage of serving as a Slave in a Family in this Town. She has been examined by some of the best Judges, and is thought qualified to write them.[5]

The shock at Wheatley's achievement is clear. In this colonial society, one that had enshrined slavery in law and upheld racism at the core of its belief structure, a person like her (black, enslaved, female, and young) was not expected to be capable of mastering Western high culture. Wheatley's life and works encapsulate the problems with the ideology of Western Civilisation that we saw being promoted by Warren and his revolutionary colleagues in the previous chapter—its framing as a biological lineage, rooted in race. It was therefore shocking that someone like Wheatley, who could not belong to the imagined genealogy of the West, could still gain such mastery over its cultural and intellectual legacy. Wheatley challenged the ideology of a biological West by the simple fact of her existence.

Racial Hierarchy

In Chapter 9 of this book, we defined race and considered its function as a technology for the hierarchical structuring of populations. We also saw how Western ideas about race at the end of the seventeenth century, while already developing and clearly implicated in Western imperialism of the time, had not yet fully crystallised. It was not until the lifetime of Phillis Wheatley in the mid-eighteenth century that Western ideas about race took a firmer form, becoming more systematic and "scientific." Central to this was the combination of Enlightenment thinking and political utility.

One important strand of Enlightenment thinking saw humans as part of the natural world, rather than as divinely set apart from nature. It was an idea that laid the ground for the classification of people, in an analogous way to the classification of different breeds and species of animals.[6] This "scientific" approach, rooted in natural history, prompted much heated debate, but was eventually used to support the idea of a strict racial hierarchy. This was perhaps most (in)famously expressed by the Scottish philosopher David Hume, who wrote in 1753, "I am apt to suspect that the Negroes, and in general all the other species (for there are four or five different kinds) to be naturally inferior to the whites." Similarly, the German philosopher Immanuel Kant opined in 1764 that the differences between Blacks and whites was "as great in regard to mental capacities as in colour."[7] Later in the eighteenth century, as we have already seen in Chapter 9, European thinkers such as Hegel and the Marquis de Sade reimagined historical figures like Njinga in racialised terms, making them seem entirely "other" and antithetical to Western Civilisation.

The political utility of a racial hierarchy is obvious in the context of Western imperialism—it provided a justification for the domination of one group by another. Laws such as the *Code Noir*, applicable in France and its colonies (for which, see Chapter 9), hardened the contours of racial hierarchy and ensured that leaders such as Njinga could no longer use Christian conversion, or other political tools, to their advantage. Their inferiority was now deemed embodied, natural, and immutable. This process of race-making was also underway in colonial North America, as demonstrated by the scholar Theodore W. Allen in his analysis of legal codes.[8] For much of the seventeenth century, Allen argues, legal distinctions were starkest between free people and "bondsmen" (the latter category including both those who were contracted to serve for fixed periods and those who were permanently enslaved), and it was not until the early eighteenth century that "whiteness" became a legal category bearing special privileges. For example, under the Virginia Slave Codes of 1705, even the poorest of indentured white labourers could claim privileges denied to all Blacks (even free Blacks), including ownership of weapons, access to separate courts, and rights to hire or employ others.[9] The result was a system that discouraged the development of class-based solidarity in favour of race-based solidarity. The governor of Virginia at the time explained that the aim of such legislation was "to make free Negros sensible that a distinction ought to be made between their offspring and the descendants of an Englishman."[10]

With the establishment of the United States of America, the concept of racial hierarchy became politically useful in new and important ways. As we saw in Chapter 10, the grand narrative of Western Civilisation was vital to the revolutionaries' ideology, allowing them to claim not only equality but even superiority over their former colonial rulers on the basis of *translatio imperii* and as the final and ultimate heirs of Western Civilisation. Yet if North America was to be the final resting place of Western Civilisation, who amongst its inhabitants could claim to be its rightful heirs? By fusing the idea of racial hierarchy with that of Western Civilisation, the new North American republic could finally solve its intractable ideological quandary. It could celebrate the end of the metaphorical slavery of "taxation without representation" suffered by British-descended colonists, but uphold the continued enslavement within its borders of Africans and people of African descent, as well as the indenture of American native peoples and Asians. It could also logically object to its British-descended citizens being the subjects of imperialism but have no qualms either enforcing or extending its own imperial domination over the native peoples and eventually farther afield in central America and Asia. If the grand narrative of Western Civilisation gave the new United States its justification for independence, the combination of the grand narrative with the idea of racial hierarchy gave it a justification for maintaining a rigid system of inequality. The second half of the eighteenth century in North America therefore saw not only the popularisation of Western Civilisation (Chapter 10) but also its racialisation.

One of the architects of American independence, Thomas Jefferson, published a treatise in 1784, less than a decade after he penned the Declaration of Independence, in which he argued that "African Americans, whether originally a distinct race, or made distinct by time and circumstances, are inferior to the whites in the endowments both of body and mind." Later in the same treatise he wrote that African Americans were "in reason much inferior, as I think one could scarcely be found capable of tracing and comprehending the investigations of Euclid; and that in imagination, they are dull, tasteless, and anomalous."[11] Jefferson's mention here of Euclid is pertinent—in this passage, the teachings of this ancient Greek mathematician represent the intellectual heritage of Western Civilisation as a whole, which he assumed must lie beyond the reach of African Americans. Writing a little later in the early nineteenth century, the US senator from South Carolina and vice president John C. Calhoun echoed this sentiment, claiming that he would refuse to "believe that the Negro was a human being and should be treated as a man" until he "could find a Negro who knew the Greek syntax."[12] Once more, it is knowledge of classical antiquity that is the yardstick by which human intellectual capacity (and for Calhoun, even humanity itself) should be measured. Knowledge of the Greco-Roman world, the imagined foundation of Western Civilisation, was thought to be restricted by race. Just as the system of Western scientific racism was solidifying, challenges to the concept also began to appear with increasing frequency. Many of these challenges were made on the basis of moral and religious objections, as was the case for many early abolitionists,[13] including several prominent Quakers.[14] But by the 1750s the idea of white superiority was also being undermined by the cultural accomplishments of several celebrated black and bira-cial individuals. Amongst these was the formidable Quaker leader and leading abolitionist Paul Cuffe, the freeborn son of a formerly enslaved Ashanti father and a Wampanoag mother.[15]

The African Americans whose accomplishments were often the most controversial were those who had mastered Latin, Greek, or both. There was of course a long history of such individuals within Europe, including the sixteenth-century epic poet Juan Latino, whom we met in Chapter 7. Another notable European example was Anton Wilhelm Amo, who gained a doctorate in philosophy before going on to teach at the universities of Jena and Wittenburg, eventually retiring to live at Axim in modern Ghana.[16] But within the Americas, one of the earliest of these who gained widespread recognition for his classi-cal scholarship was the Jamaican intellectual Francis Williams, who published a poem in Latin in 1759 addressed to George Haldane on his assumption of the governorship of the island,[17] much to the surprise and chagrin of David Hume. But it was Phillis Wheatley, the subject of this chapter, who was perhaps the best-known and most widely cele-brated of these authors, thanks to the 1773 book of poetry that made her an international literary sensation.[18]

An Enslaved Celebrity

Phillis Wheatley is known to us only by the appellation given to her by her enslavers when she arrived in Boston (the same Boston where Joseph Warren was busily working as a physician), combining the name of the ship on which she arrived with their own family sur-name.[19] Born in west Africa, Wheatley was enslaved at the age of seven or eight years old, transported to America, and sold in Boston in 1761. At this time, Boston was the capital of the Province of Massachusetts

Bay, one of thirteen British colonies in North America. Enslavement of Africans and African Americans was common across these colonies, although in New England enslaved people made up a relatively small proportion of the total population—just under 10 percent in comparison to the 40 or so percent in Virginia, for example. Yet this was still a slave-owning society, and the early to mid-eighteenth century saw a substantial increase in the number of enslaved Africans living in New England.[20] Soon after arriving in Boston, Wheatley was purchased by John and Susanna Wheatley.

It was Susanna, along with her adult daughter Mary, who provided Phillis with her unusually broad education. Coupled with her natural aptitude, this instruction enabled Wheatley to become literate in not only English but also Latin by the age of twelve, and soon after to begin learning ancient Greek and, of course, to compose poetry. A survey of Wheatley's surviving poems indicates that she tackled a variety of subjects. But in these early years, she was perhaps best known for a series of verse eulogies marking the deaths first of people within her enslavers' circle of literary Bostonians, and later of more prominent public figures.

In her published works we find commemorative elegies for the deaths of babies and small children, beloved husbands and wives, siblings, and friends. One such poem is entitled "A Funeral Poem on the Death of C.E., an Infant of Twelve Months," and begins, "Through airy roads he wings his infant flight / To purer regions of celestial light."[21] It goes on to exhort the infant's parents to seek solace in their Christian faith, reminding them that they will eventually be reunited with their child in heaven. Serving both as a memorial for the dead and a comfort for the living, a poem like this one might be published in a local newspaper as well as being read aloud at the funeral and other family gatherings. It was one such poem, penned on the death of the

Reverend George Whitefield in autumn 1770, when Wheatley was six-teen or seventeen, that catapulted her to fame.

Whitefield was a popular evangelical preacher who had travelled across the British colonies in North America, winning followers and admirers, as part of a wider religious movement now known as the "Great Awakening."[22] He was a firebrand, preaching against the estab-lished clergy and evangelising not only to the free white population, but also amongst enslaved Africans and the native peoples. In Boston, one of his public appearances attracted so many people that the gallery on which many of the crowd were standing collapsed, leading to a stampede in which five people tragically lost their lives.[23] Whitefield was also no stranger to political controversy. He had arrived in Boston just a few months after the infamous Boston Massacre,[24] and find-ing the city under military occupation, he expressed his sympathy for its population and their predicament.[25] His untimely death made him not only a radical popular preacher, but also an early revolution-ary icon.

Wheatley's commemorative poem for Whitefield caused a stir when it was published in the broadsides of Boston and Newport. It was quickly reproduced in an eight-page booklet accompanied by woodcut illustrations and sold across New England under the following adver-tising blurb, which sets out the reasons for purchasing the booklet: "first, is Remembrance of that great and good Man, Mr. Whitefield, and second on Account of its being worte [sic] by a Native of Af-rica, and yet would have done Honor to a Pope or Shakespere [sic]."[26] Within a few months, copies were being produced and sold in London, where thanks to his charismatic preaching, Whitefield already had a following that ranged from poor labourers to the Countess of Hunting-don. Within the space of a year, Wheatley had won literary recognition on both sides of the Atlantic.

From this point on, things moved fast. More high-profile commissions followed, and Wheatley began to gather a selection of her poems for publication as a book. But while Wheatley's works were widely appreciated, they also prompted controversy, especially from those who simply did not believe that an enslaved African teenager would be capable of such literary achievements. What was deemed particularly suspect was Wheatley's apparent mastery not only of literary techniques associated with English verse, but also of those associated with Greek and Roman literature. Wheatley's poems were influenced in particular by the Roman poets Virgil and Horace, and many of her verses not only made use of classical themes but also manipulated classical conventions of form and rhythm, evidencing a deep understanding of Roman poetry in the original Latin.[27]

But for even the casual observer, Wheatley's verse is heavily classicising. The Christian personification of Providence is described in relation to "Phoebus," another name for Apollo, the ancient Greek god of the sun.[28] When comforting a lady following a bereavement, she encourages her to imagine how her dead brother's spirit flies "beyond Olympus."[29] And when she muses on the topic of "imagination," she makes an appeal to Helicon, the mythical home of the Muses.[30] For some people, this fluency with the cultures of both Greece and Rome would have brought status and recognition. But in the case of Wheatley, it gave rise to suspicion.

Wheatley's scholarly abilities were called into question by her contemporaries.[31] In 1772, a court was convened in Boston to test Wheatley's knowledge and literary skills—the court with which we began this chapter. Amongst the judges sat one of the leaders of the revolutionary movement, John Hancock, and we can only speculate on how Wheatley might have felt about the revolutionary movement and Bostonian politics at this point, given Hancock's role in the proceedings. Yet despite passing this gruelling public examination, proving beyond any doubt her capacity to write complex poetry, Wheatley found that no American publisher would agree to publish her book. Some rejected it on straightforwardly racist grounds, while others worried that it would not find commercial success. But the result in either case was the same—Wheatley's book, it seemed, would not see the light of day.

Into this seemingly intractable situation came the Countess of Huntingdon, the English aristocrat who had also supported the work of George Whitefield. The countess now offered to extend her patronage to Wheatley as well, and smoothed the way for Wheatley to publish her book in London rather than America. With high hopes, Wheatley travelled to London in 1773 in the company of her enslavers' son Nathaniel.[32] Over a period of several months, she oversaw the printing of her book by the London publisher Archibald Bell, and met with several leading lights of the London literary scene, including not only the countess herself but also the poet and statesman Baron George Lyttelton, the millionaire philanthropist John Thornton, and even the American statesman and polymath Benjamin Franklin, who also happened to be visiting London at the time. But Wheatley's English stay was cut short by the sudden illness of Mrs. Susanna Wheatley, and Phillis and Nathaniel rushed back to attend to her.

They returned to a Boston in turmoil. Simply by living in Boston, Wheatley had always had a front-row seat for the American Revolution. As we have seen (Chapter 10), in the 1760s Boston was the epicentre of secessionist agitation, and in the 1770s it provided the arena for the first armed conflicts of the War of Independence.[33] The Boston Tea Party erupted in the winter of 1773, not long after Wheatley had returned to America to tend to Susanna. Wheatley therefore must have lived through the British crackdown that followed the skirmish. Amongst other sanctions, the port of Boston was officially closed, the charter that allowed for limited self-government in Massachusetts was revoked, and town meetings were reduced in number and strictly regulated. But as we have already seen, the harder the British crackdown, the stiffer the resolve of the American revolutionaries to oppose them. Wheatley, still getting used to her new status as an international literary celebrity, was thrown into the heart of the maelstrom.

Despite Wheatley's careful nursing, Susanna died in March 1774, having first released Wheatley from her enslavement. A free woman, Wheatley now began to engage more openly and directly with the revolutionary movement.

The Silken Reins

Wheatley's political interests did not come out of nowhere, and there is evidence for her political thinking at a relatively early age. In 1768, when she was fourteen or fifteen years old, she published a poem dedicated to the British King George III, praising him for repealing the controversial Stamp Act (the very same Stamp Act that prompted Joseph Warren to write his first piece of pointed political invective; see Chapter 10). Not only does this constitute a remarkable action by an enslaved teenager in the political life of the colony, but the poem itself contains a powerful sting in its tail. Specifically, its final couplet offers an ambiguous message:

> And may each clime with equal gladness see
> A Monarch's smile can set his subjects free![34]

Do these lines refer to the American colonists' freedom from the controversial Stamp Act, or to a much more fundamental form of freedom? Wheatley would have certainly been aware of revolutionary rhetoric about slavery and freedom. For her, a newspaper article penned by Warren that same year warning Bostonians against British attempts to "enslave" them (see Chapter 10) must have rung very hollow indeed. The poem that first made Wheatley famous, her elegy for George Whitefield in 1770, also had political undertones. Not only was Whitefield known for supporting American rights against the British, but Wheatley describes him as addressing both "my dear Americans" and "ye Africans" in his preaching. Indeed, when her eulogy was published it would have been one of two politically charged pamphlets written by Bostonian writers doing the rounds in London at the time—the other being Warren's account of the Boston Massacre.

As Wheatley's literary reputation grew, so too did her confidence to make political commentary. Later that same year, Wheatley was commissioned to write a poem in honour of the Earl of Dartmouth's appointment as the British secretary of state for the colonies. The poem, once more, is double-edged. Although ostensibly supporting the British colonial administration, the rhetoric Wheatley employs is very close to that of the revolutionaries. The poem calls for "freedom" explicitly at lines 2, 8, and 21 and includes an extended description of Freedom personified, appearing "as a Goddess long desired" (line 11). Addressing America, Wheatley then proclaims:

No longer shall thou dread the iron chain,
Which wanton Tyranny with lawless hand
Hath made, and with it meant t'enslave the land.[35]

Although the imagery is straight out of the revolutionary playbook, the meaning is evidently not simply talking about British treatment of the white colonists. In case there was any uncertainty about the double significance of her words, Wheatley reminds her readers why she, more than most other poets of the day, has an especial love of freedom:

I, young in life, by seeming cruel fate
Was snatch'd from Afric's fancy'd happy seat:
What pangs excruciating must molest,
What sorrows labour in my parent's breast?
Steel'd was that soul and by no misery mov'd
That from a father seiz'd his babe beloved:
Such, such my case. And can I then but pray
Others may never feel tyrannic sway?[36]

Wheatley explicitly compares the control of the British imperialists over the colonists to the tyranny exercised by white slave traders over the Africans they enslaved. Wheatley's poem to the Earl of Dartmouth looks forward to a new future, where the British would rule America in a more restrained manner, using "silken reins" rather than imposing a harsh yoke. Although this is easily interpreted in the context of revolutionary agitation, what she meant in relation to African enslavement is unclear. She stops short of calling for the abolition of slavery, but of course at this point she too was controlled by silken reins—at the time when she wrote this poem, she was still an enslaved person, dependent on the favour of her owners and on the whims of the slave-owning society in which she lived.

After gaining her freedom, Wheatley lost no time in making her political position clear and publicly criticising the revolutionaries' ideological deficiencies. In March 1774, eight days after the death of Susanna, Wheatley published an open letter addressed to the Reverend Samson Occom, a Presbyterian preacher who was also a member of the Mohegan Nation, in which she thanked him for his efforts in support of "Negroes" and their "natural Rights." In it, she equated black American enslavement with the bondage of the Hebrews in pagan Egypt as described in the Old Testament. She continued with open criticism of the revolutionaries, saying, "I desire not for their Hurt, but to convince them of the strange Absurdity of their Conduct whose Words and Actions are so diametrically, opposite. How well the Cry for Liberty, and the reverse Disposition for the exercise of oppressive Power over others agree, I humbly think it does not require the Penetration of a Philosopher to determine."[37]

Yet one year later, when the revolutionary movement had turned into an all-out war of independence, Wheatley decided to moderate her tone. By this time, the first skirmishes of the war had been fought at the Battles of Lexington and Concord, and significant amounts of blood had been spilled on both sides. She wrote a panegyric poem in praise of George Washington in 1775, at the time the commander in chief of the patriot army.[38] A few months later, in February 1776, Washington invited Wheatley to his headquarters for a personal meeting, seemingly intrigued to meet the formerly enslaved woman who had succeeded in gaining a level of education that he famously had not.[39]

And yet the following year Wheatley had evidently once more become frustrated with the hypocrisy of the revolutionaries. Following the death of General David Wooster, a leading military commander who lost his life fighting the British, Wheatley wrote what was ostensibly a consoling letter to his widow, calling him "a martyr in the Cause of Freedom," enclosing within it a poem extolling his nobility, his Christian virtues, and his "warlike deeds." As the poem progresses, however, Wheatley calls upon God to lift up the new nation and its people, so that they might be forever "Virtuous, brave, and free." Then, with a sudden change of tone, the poem questions whether the new nation is indeed deserving of divine favour:

> But how, presumptuous shall we hope to find
> Divine acceptance with th' Almighty mind—
> While yet (O deed Ungenerous!) they disgrace
> And hold in bondage Afric's blameless race?[40]

Finally, only months before her death in 1784, Wheatley wrote another commemorative poem, this time to mourn the death of the Reverend Samuel Cooper, the pastor of the church in Boston where many prominent revolutionaries worshipped, including John Hancock, Samuel and John Adams, and Joseph Warren.[41] The caustic ambiguities of her earlier poems are missing in this final, heartfelt elegy, which puts aside politics to mourn "a Friend sincere."

By virtue of her time and place in history, once she achieved such widespread celebrity, it was inevitable that Wheatley would cross paths (and metaphorical swords) with the elite white men who led the American revolutionary movement. John Hancock was one of the judges in her trial in 1772, the publications of Joseph Warren overlapped with her own, and she attended the same church as many other leading revolutionaries. It was perhaps inevitable too that she would be by turns both supporter and sceptic of the movement, with an understandable ambivalence that she apparently never quite resolved.

Phillis Wheatley was a product of the same intellectual and cultural milieu that spawned the revolutionaries—she was steeped in the same traditions and literature, and wrote in the same idioms using the same rhetoric. But unlike the revolutionaries, Wheatley's place within this milieu was tenuous and peripheral. She acknowledges this in the virtuoso first poem of her published collection, a verse dedication to her patron, the Countess of Huntingdon. The poem is entitled "To Maecenas"—a reference to the greatest patron of poetry from the golden age of Augustan Rome. In this poem, Wheatley examines a range of poetic models for her own art. Should she model herself on Homer, with his grand passions and epic conflicts, or Ovid, with his mastery of the emotions? Or perhaps she should model herself on Virgil, with his bold and elegant style? Wheatley eventually settles on Terence, a Roman playwright known for his clarity of language. She cites Terence's ability to move the masses as his chief virtue, but her choice depends instead primarily on the fact that Terence hailed from Africa. Wheatley sadly reflects that there is only one African poet within the Greco-Roman canon, writing:

> But say, ye Muses, why this partial grace,
> To one alone of Afric's sable race;
> From age to age transmitting thus his name
> With the first glory in the rolls of fame?[42]

Despite mastering the cultural legacy of the West, and accomplishing through hard work and sheer brilliance a feat that the adherents of the theory of racial hierarchy would have never thought possible, Wheatley still struggles to see herself in the Greco-Roman tradition. Her sex is not the determining factor. The Countess of Huntingdon can stand in the place of the Roman nobleman Maecenas because she is a white Englishwoman, but Wheatley can never position herself as Ovid or Homer. Instead, she can only be the African Terence, her literary choices limited thanks to her race.

A similarly melancholy reflection can be found in a poem dedicated "To the University of Cambridge in New England."[43] Wheatley writes about leaving Africa, "my native shore, The land of errors, and *Egyptian* gloom" (Wheatley's italics), and warns the fortunate students to treasure the time and the privileges they have, saying that "an *Ethiop* tells you" (Wheatley's italics) to beware of the vagaries of fate. Wheatley stresses her explicitly nonclassical origins using classical language, heightening her sense of intellectual isolation. She sensed herself to be forever excluded from the lineage of Western Civilisation.

The loneliness of Wheatley's position is palpable. Her body of work exemplifies the imagined genealogy of Western Civilisation, linking her own eighteenth-century present with the ancient Greek and Roman worlds of antiquity. Yet the racialised features of her physical body marked her out as alien to the West and seems to have excluded her from a place within the grand narrative of Western Civilisation, despite her astonishing intellectual achievements. Unlike Njinga of Angola, who, only a century earlier, could be imagined as an ancient Greek or Roman reborn (see Chapter 9), by the late eighteenth century it seems that Wheatley was barred, on account of the newly racialised vision of Western Civilisation, from being an heir to the Greco-Roman tradition.

———

WHEATLEY'S STORY ALMOST has a happy ending. In 1778, she married a free black grocer, John Peters, with whom she would eventually have three children. But by this time the royalties from her first book were beginning to dry up, and Wheatley's proposal for a second were met by American publishers with either resistance or disinterest. Over the years, the family slid deeper and deeper into poverty, with two of the children dying, apparently from malnutrition and disease. When her husband, John, was thrown into a debtors' prison in 1784, Wheatley took on work as a scullery maid in a Boston boardinghouse in the hope of providing for her one remaining child. But their state of health was such that when Wheatley died later that year at the age of thirty-one, her young son outlived her by only a few hours. It was a tragic end to an extraordinary life.

It was during Phillis Wheatley's lifetime that Greco-Roman antiquity became labelled by its would-be heirs in Europe and North America as "classical." The term "classical" (and various versions of it in different languages) often bears associations of elite and high status.[44] These associations date back as far as the reign of the philhellenic Roman emperor Hadrian in the second century CE, when the orator and aesthete Aulus Gellius described one of his acquaintances as "*classicus*"—using the word in the figurative sense to mean "classy" rather than in its official sense of belonging to the first of Rome's property-owning classes. Extending from the fourteenth into the seventeenth century, the term "classical" was applied to works of literature, ancient and modern, in any language, that were considered to be first-class. In this sense, the term tended to denote "a classic" with exemplary value. It was only in the mid-eighteenth century with the work of scholars such as the German Johann Joachim Winckelmann that this began to change.[45]

For Winckelmann, "classical" designated chronology as well as value. In his *Geschichte der Kunst des Alterthums* (*History of the Art of Antiquity*), published in 1764, Winckelmann articulated a new way of dividing ancient art on chronological grounds—there was first a developing or "archaic" phase, when artistic techniques were pioneered and refined; then there was a "classical" phase, which represented the highest pinnacle of artistic achievement; and finally there was a more degenerate "hellenistic" phase, where overblown bathos marred the perfection of classical proportions. Although Winckelmann did not invent this tripartite scheme ex nihilo,[46] he did formulate it in a way that stuck. If you bring to mind images of "classical" antiquity, you will likely imagine fifth-century BCE Athens. You are far less likely to think of Seleucid Babylon or Iron Age Corinth, which in their day were no less a part of the Greek world than fifth-century BCE Athens. In this, you are to some extent following Winckelmann's schema, under which the "most blessed time" was the forty years or so when Pericles ruled Athens.[47] But such artistic and cultural flowering were not, in Winckelmann's view, the result of pure chance. Superior culture was instead the result of superior political structures. "Art," Winckelmann asserted, "received its life, as it were, from freedom, and must necessarily decline and fall with the loss of freedom in the place where it had particularly flourished."[48] The declining political freedoms that followed the death of Alexander of Macedon, he felt, therefore had a direct negative impact on cultural production.

The transformation of Greco-Roman into "classical" antiquity had implications for the notion of Western Civilisation. The idea of a combined Greco-Roman antiquity as a coherent and bounded entity, distinct from the rest of the ancient world, was developed in the Renaissance (Chapter 6); and it persisted despite attempts in the sixteenth century to put forward alternative grand historical narratives (Chapter 7). This combined Greco-Roman antiquity had then been claimed by the West as a cultural ancestor in the seventeenth century, transformed into a symbolic point of shared origins that was crucial in the definition of both the Western "self" (Chapter 8) and non-Western "other" (Chapter 9). Through this gradual and disjointed process, lasting the best part of three centuries, the grand narrative of Western Civilisation was born.

But if the grand narrative was gestated in the sixteenth century and born in the seventeenth, it was not until the second half of the eighteenth century that it came of age. It was at this point that the story of Western Civilisation gained widespread popularity, entering the mainstream political rhetoric of a new nation-state. That it did so was thanks in part to its political utility, allowing the new United States of America to claim its independence from Britain on grounds of civilisational transfer (Chapter 10). The second half of the eighteenth century was also the period in which Western Civilisation became racialised (this chapter). The oppression of non-Western populations was thought to be justified, not only by their categorisation on supposedly natural and biological criteria, but also by their inability to participate fully in the cultural legacy of Western Civilisation. The racial classifications of the present were assumed to map onto the cultural genealogies of the past.

On top of all this, it was the second half of the eighteenth century when Greco-Roman antiquity became invested with a sense of heightened absolute value, superiority, and status. It was not just different from the rest of the ancient world, not just out of reach for those deemed racially non-Western, but also better, more important, and of universal value. It became "classical."

Chapter Twelve

THE WEST AND MODERNITY

WILLIAM EWART GLADSTONE

In olden time, all Western Christendom sympathized
with resistance to the common enemy.
WILLIAM EWART GLADSTONE (1876)[1]

G LADSTONE lived in a world largely coloured pink. Cheaper
and easier to read from than red (the traditional colour of
empire), pink ink was adopted by nineteenth-century car-
tographers to designate territories ruled by Britain. At its peak, Brit-

ain's empire covered almost a quarter of the world's land surface and spanned four continents, counting nearly a quarter of the world's population amongst its subjects. Thanks to this "empire on which the sun never sets," there was pink in every time zone. When Gladstone looked at the world map, he saw it not only coloured in pink but also unravelled according to the now-standard Mercator projection, which locates Britain in the middle and arrays the rest of the world around it on either side. When he looked at a clock, he read Greenwich Mean Time, against which the rest of the world measured its hours. Settling into No. 10 Downing Street in 1880 when he first became prime minister of Britain, William Ewart Gladstone had the comfort of knowing that he was at the centre of the world.

The British was not, of course, the only European empire at the time. The nineteenth century saw the Austrian Habsburgs and Russian Romanovs occupying vast land-based empires, as well as the aggressive colonial expansion overseas of not only Britain but also France and the newly established European countries of Belgium, Italy, and Germany. These rising powers often sought to win new territories at the expense of older European empires such as those of Spain, Portugal, the Netherlands, and the Ottomans, all of whom suffered dismemberment and decline over the course of the nineteenth century. It was not just Europeans who had imperial ambitions—Japan also sought to establish colonies, only to be rebuffed by European powers who had already claimed hegemony in Asia; and the United States of America would at the end of the century wrest both the Philippines and significant territories in central America from Spanish control. Yet amongst these various imperial rivals, it was the British Empire that bestrode the world most surely.[2]

Central to this was Britain's status as the "workshop of the world." Having industrialised early, by the mid-nineteenth century Britain produced roughly half the world's iron, two-thirds of its coal, and more than three-quarters of its steel, as well as a series of technological and mechanical innovations that prompted a seismic shift in both the economic organisation and social structure of the country.[3] Although the wave of technological innovation quickly spread across other parts of Europe and the Americas, it began mostly in Britain, giving Britain an operational head start. With its imperial possessions abroad and its industrial weight back home, Britain was an economic powerhouse at the heart of the newly interconnected global economy.

Britain also lay at the geographic centre of a geo-cultural bloc that was increasingly being labelled "the West." On one side of it lay the countries of central and western Europe, where early intellectual developments had led to the first emergence of the twin concepts of the West and Western Civilisation (Chapters 6 and 8). On the other lay the Atlantic world and North America, where these concepts had eventually come into sharp focus (Chapters 10 and 11). The West was not, however, simply a geographic entity. It was also defined in racial terms, with the newly developed category of whiteness as a key component marking out those who belonged from those who did not, even amongst the inhabitants of the West (Chapter 11). The West could also be identified by a distinct way of life and the notion of modernity—societies governed by scientific and humanistic principles. Yet for all its avowed humanistic principles, religion was also an important element, with Christianity at its core. This was all tied together in the idea of a shared Western history, the common genealogy of Western Civilisation. Although it had emerged gradually in the seventeenth century and been popularised in its full form in the eighteenth, it was the nineteenth century that saw the grand narrative of Western Civilisation at its most strident.

Something else that defined the West was its power. In the nineteenth century, the global supremacy of the West was unchallenged and absolute. Western states controlled the global economy, Western empires ruled territories across five continents, and Western ideas—

about science, morality, and history—were exported around the world, often replacing local systems of knowledge. The dominance of the West in this moment was so far-reaching and so absolute that it became hard to imagine that it had not always existed. Just as the realities of the nineteenth-century present meant one path for the West (domination) and another for everyone else (subordination), so it became hard to think of the shape of history other than in terms of Western Civilisation.

The West Dominates the Rest

In the eighteenth century, the terms "the West" and "Western" were primarily associated with North America (see Chapter 10), but in the nineteenth century the usage broadened. The conceptual racialisation of Western Civilisation (Chapter 11) meant that the West was now envisaged as including much of Europe and most imperial territories where the demographics were dominated by European-descended colonists. Interestingly, some of the earliest examples of this broader usage come not from people who defined themselves as Westerners, but from Russians debating whether they should follow more of a "Westernising" or "Slavophile" cultural orientation.[4] As a result, when European Westerners did embrace the term, they often used it to draw a contrast with Russia and eastern Europe.[5] This was particularly the case in central Europe, where a Slavic European East was contrasted to an Atlantic European West, and where both were seen as distinct from the Germanic-focused "Mitteleuropa."[6] The terminology of the West was soon adopted in Britain, where it immediately acquired an imperial flavour. When one colonial administrator compiled a report on education in India in 1835, he noted "the intrinsic superiority of the Western literature,"[7] and when Marx commented on British colonialism in Asia in 1859, he contrasted Asiatic systems with those of "the Western world."[8]

With this notion of the West therefore came a much stronger notion of "the Rest"—the sense that all the other non-Western peoples of the world could be thought of as a single conceptual entity, a single group with the same fundamental characteristics. These characteristics were inevitably inferior ones to those exhibited by Westerners. When the English lawyer, economist, and academic Nassau William Senior toured the Ottoman Empire in 1857, he opined that "[for the Turk,] like the Chinese, the Hindoos, and in fact, all the Asiatics, there is a degree, and not a high one, of civilisation which he cannot pass, or even long preserve."[9] In his view, all "Asiatics" were essentially the same, and "the distinguishing characteristic of the real Asiatic is intellectual sterility and unfitness for change . . . An Asiatic had rather copy than try to invent."[10] This sense that all non-Westerners were an undifferentiated mass of inferior peoples is captured by a now-infamous poem published by the English poet Rudyard Kipling in 1899. In it, Kipling exhorts his audience to take up "the White Man's burden"—by which he means the "burden" of colonial rule. This rule was to be extended over the rest of the global population, whom he described as "fluttered folk and wild" and "half devil and half child."[11]

The contrast between the West and the Rest was made starker by further developments in scientific racism.[12] During the early nineteenth century in Vienna, the physicians Franz Joseph Gall and Johann Gaspar Spurzheim developed the pseudoscience of phrenology, producing racial pronouncements, such as "the foreheads of negroes, for instance, are very narrow, their talents of music and mathematics are also in general very limited. The Chinese, who are fond of colours, have the arch of the eyebrows much vaulted, and we shall see that this is the sign of a greater development of the organ of colour."[13] Anatomical approaches were also championed by the Scottish ethnologist Robert Knox, perhaps best-known today for purchasing freshly murdered corpses for dissection.[14] "Race is everything," Knox wrote in 1850. "Literature, science, art, in a word, civilisation depend on it."[15] Over the next few years, the influential French diplomat Arthur de Gobineau's voluminous output married physical anthropology with historical determinism to rail against miscegenation and the disruption of what he argued was a natural racial hierarchy.

As noted in Chapter 11, scientific racism was part of a broader trend of Enlightenment thinking that saw humans as part of the natural world, a trend that also gave rise to evolutionary theories and Darwinism. Debates raged over whether humans had a single common origin (monogenesis) or several origins resulting in the existence of discrete "species" of human or races (polygenesis). On the side of the polygeneticists, campaigners such as the American surgeon Josiah Nott claimed that "Nations and races" had separate origins and therefore "have each an especial destiny: some are born to rule, and others to be ruled."[16] On the side of the monogeneticists, *On the Origin of Species* was published in 1859, and while Darwin deliberately stopped short of commenting on how his theories might relate to race, it was no great leap to apply ideas of evolution and natural selection to human societies. At one end of the political spectrum, social Darwinism was promoted by thinkers such as the American pastor and antislavery campaigner Charles Loring Brace, who used the theory to argue that emancipated Africans and the American native peoples were capable of becoming "civilized," if given the opportunity. At the other end, social Darwinism was also deployed by those seeking to justify colonial rule and an entrenched class system, such as the British banker and journalist Walter Bagehot, who claimed that both Britain's imperial subjects and its working classes occupied a lower rung on the evolutionary ladder than their rulers.[17]

Indeed, as the nineteenth century progressed, increasing inequalities and steeper social hierarchies led to an uncomfortable identification between the non-Western "Rest" on the one hand, and the poor and the disenfranchised within the West on the other. One popular London weekly, the *Saturday Review*, reminded its readers about what it considered to be the proper order of things in 1864: "The English poor man or child is expected always to remember the condition in which God has placed him, exactly as the negro is expected to remember the skin which God has given him. The relationship in both instances is that of perpetual superior to perpetual inferior, of chief to dependent, and no amount of kindness or goodness is suffered to alter this relation."[18]

Indeed, while the nineteenth century might have been an era of unrivalled Western domination across the globe, it was also a time of intense social dissatisfaction within the West itself. Rapid industrialisation had brought with it dramatic social changes, including the creation of a new class of urban poor who were keenly aware of the social hierarchy. The year 1848 was one of popular revolutions across Europe, mostly aimed at securing more democratic and economic rights.[19] A new French revolution toppled the constitutional monarchy, ushering in the Second Republic. The March Revolution in the states of the German Confederation demanded freedoms and popular assemblies. The Habsburgs in Austria struggled with a series of rebellions and attempted secessions, including in neighbouring Hungary. And in Britain, the labour and trade union movements began to gather strength. It was in February of this very same year that the German philosophers Karl Marx and Friedrich Engels published a short pamphlet in London that went largely unnoticed amidst the political turmoil that was sweeping through Europe at the time. Although printed in London, it was initially produced in German with the title *Manifest der kommunistischen Partei*. It was months before translations started to appear in other European languages, and almost two years before an English translation became available as *The Communist Manifesto*.[20] The emergence of Marx and Engels's ideas during this period is indicative of a febrile political environment, marked by widespread poverty and popular dissatisfaction.

In this context, the intensification of racialised thinking and the growing popularity of the West as an ideology gain new meaning. When utilized by the ruling class of the Western world, it became not only a means to justify the subjugation of imperial subjects, but also a means to mollify the internally oppressed. A similar process had happened a century before in North America, with the creation of whiteness as a legal category. In the early eighteenth century, popular protests in Britain's American colonies were forestalled by the elevation of poor and indentured whites above their non-white counterparts, thereby giving them a stake in the social hierarchy (Chapter 11). Now in the mid-nineteenth century, a comparable ideological shift was underway in Europe, not as a result of any deliberate political strategy (unlike in America, where the appeasement of poor whites was a conscious aim of legislators), but through a broad range of interlinked cultural developments. The increasingly binary opposition drawn between the West and the Rest, the rise of racist pseudoscience, and theories of social evolution all had their part to play in this process.

So too did the making of history. The nineteenth century has been described as an age marked by "the invention of tradition," characterised by a new interest in national and local histories, linked to both the forging of empires and resistance against imperialism.[21] Where these histories failed to live up to expectations, they were supplemented with traditions—sometimes "rediscovered" and sometimes openly fabricated—that served to root a contemporary community in the sense of its own past. What Walter Scott and the invention of the Highland tartan did for Scotland, W. B. Yeats and collections of mythology did for Ireland. The "traditional" pomp and pageantry surrounding Queen Victoria's adoption of the title "Empress of India" served a similar function—it gave the present reality (British rule) the veneer of antique respectability.[22]

The nineteenth century—an age when ideas about and narratives of the past were often shamelessly invented—was also the period when the study of the past became a science in its own right. In the early decades of the century, the German historian Leopold von Ranke developed a rigorous new approach to historical enquiry, based on the careful analysis of sources and empirical research. Around the same time, the Danish antiquarian Christian Jürgensen Thomsen developed the three-age system (stone, bronze, and iron) in order to classify prehistoric artefacts according to chronology. Later in the century, archaeology emerged as a science, with its own set of recognised methods and techniques, developed by pioneers such as Augustus Pitt-Rivers working on Roman and Saxon England and Flinders Petrie working in Egypt.[23] Of course, enthusiastic antiquarians continued to build up impressive collections by less-than-scientific means (we might think of Thomas Bruce, the 7th Earl of Elgin, and his removal of the Parthenon marbles from Athens; or of the Egyptomania that swept Europe in the wake of Napoléon's campaign in Egypt), but by the middle of the nineteenth century, both archaeology and history were beginning to emerge as serious professions.

What this new historicising impulse lent to the ascendant West was the sense that its own Western history—the grand narrative of Western Civilisation—was of universal and global significance. Just as Western people were assumed to be better, more elevated, and more important than others, dominating non-Western people in the present; so too were Western origins assumed to be better, more elevated, and more important than non-Western antiquity, eclipsing non-Western people also in the past. After all, only Western origins were imaged to be "classical." These various threads—the imperial, the political, the racial, and the historiographical—can be seen coming together in the life of one man, William Ewart Gladstone.

The People's William

Gladstone was one of the defining figures of his age. His life spanned almost the entire century (he was born in 1809 and died in 1898), and his remarkable political career lasted more than sixty years, during which he was four times the prime minister of Britain and four times its chancellor. Gladstone was nothing if not a creature of the times. He began life as the child of empire. Born in the bustling port city of Liverpool, he was the fourth son of a trader from Scotland who had made his fortune selling sugar, cotton, and tobacco, as well as other proceeds of plantations worked by enslaved people in the Caribbean.[24]

This fortune was such that Gladstone and his brothers were able to attend the prestigious boarding school Eton, where Gladstone already began to exhibit the characteristics that would define him throughout his life. He dazzled his teachers with his academic brilliance, excelling in Latin and Greek and showing a particular aptitude for languages, a skill that would stand him in good stead later in life. But Gladstone was not a happy child, taking little pleasure in the sports and physical activities that were central to English boarding school life, and contending with a deep religious faith that seemed to instil in him more guilt than comfort. When he moved to Oxford University to further his studies at Christ Church College, Gladstone would continue in the same mould, achieving academic success with a double first in classics and mathematics as well as performing impressive feats of oratory in the debates at the Oxford Union, but not always having quite as much fun as his peers. When, one night halfway through his second year, a group of drunken classmates barged into his room, regaling him for being self-righteous and performatively pious, Gladstone lived up to expectations, thanking God for the "opportunity of exercising the duty of forgiveness."[25]

On graduating from Oxford, Gladstone then did what many young people with the means still do today when released from their studies—he travelled. Along with his older brother, Gladstone set out for his own abbreviated version of the Grand Tour, travelling through France to Italy, visiting Turin, Genoa, Lucca, Pisa, Livorno, and Florence in quick succession before spending more time in Rome and Naples. In the Eternal City, Gladstone seems to have been more absorbed by religious reflection than cultural discovery, pondering the schism between the Protestant and Catholic Churches and confirming his preexisting belief in the essential unity of western Christendom. Gladstone then made his way slowly northwards via Ravenna, Bologna, Verona, Innsbruck, the lakes of Garda and Como, and finally Geneva. The entire trip took just over two months.

Gladstone might have explored continental Europe further, had he not received a tantalising offer back home. The Duke of Newcastle, a prominent Conservative Party activist, had identified Gladstone as a potential candidate for Parliament and invited him to stand for election in the Nottinghamshire constituency of Newark. It was an opportunity not to be missed, so Gladstone hotfooted it back to Britain, and with the duke bankrolling his campaign, Gladstone was duly elected. And so it was that on February 7, 1833, at the tender age of just twenty-three years old, Gladstone first entered the British Parliament. He would remain there, in one capacity or another, for another sixty-one years.

One issue occupied him during those early years as a parliamentarian more than any other, as he recalled later: "When I came into Parliament the slave question was uppermost and I was thrust into connection with it whether I would or not, for my father was a prominent West India proprietor."[26] Although slave trade had been abolished in the British Empire in 1807, it was still legal to own humans, and enslaved people remained essential to the imperial economy. The abolitionist movement in Britain, spearheaded not only by parliamentarians such as William Wilberforce but also by formerly enslaved people such as Olaudah Equiano and Ottobah Cugoano, continued to campaign for the complete abolition of slavery as an institution.[27] Public figures such as Gladstone who owed their fortune to enslaved labour found themselves targeted by the growing movement.

Gladstone's response was an attempt to please both sides—arguing that while he supported in principle "that exceedingly desired consummation, the utter extinction of slavery," emancipation should be achieved only gradually, after a programme of moral and vocational instruction, to ensure that enslaved people first achieved "fitness to enjoy freedom."[28] When the issue was discussed in Parliament in 1833, he argued for "a gradual and safe emancipation," involving the financial compensation of enslavers for the loss of property.[29] Gladstone was eventually co-opted onto a working committee to implement abolition, which oversaw compensation payments and further softened the blow to plantation owners by deciding that newly emancipated people of adult age should continue to work for their former owners for twelve years as "apprentices." The pill for the plantation owners was certainly sugarcoated. Gladstone's father alone received in the region of £93,000 in exchange for the freedom of around two thousand enslaved people, the equivalent of nearly £12 million today. Gladstone himself must have felt conflicted throughout, struggling to reconcile his deeply held Christian principles with the assumptions instilled in him by his upbringing and his family's financial interests. Later in life, he expressed some discomfort at his own earlier opinions and speeches, although he maintained that he had not done anything fundamentally wrong.[30]

Over the next two decades, both Gladstone's personal and political fortunes varied. After several dispiriting rejections by women, in 1838 he eventually settled down to seeming marital bliss with Catherine Glynne, the sister of an old school friend, with whom he would eventually have eight children.[31] Yet Gladstone was tortured by his own sexual appetites, describing them as "my chief besetting sin" and setting out detailed strategies in his private diary through which he hoped to control his urges. None of the strategies worked, and during the 1840s Gladstone began to engage in what he called "rescue work" with prostitutes. He also began to self-flagellate, using an array of whips and scourges to inflict "immediate pain" on himself, in the hope of assuaging his guilt and purging himself of his carnal urges.[32]

Given his evident psychological turmoil, Parliament must sometimes have seemed like a refuge. Gladstone belonged to a faction within the Conservative Party led by Robert Peel that championed free trade over protectionism, and his star rose and fell over the 1840s and 1850s with that of the faction. Gladstone argued strongly against the Opium Wars, at least partly influenced by the experience of having an opium addict in his own family—his younger sister, Helen.[33] In Gladstone's eyes, Britain's treatment of Qing Dynasty China— flooding it with narcotics and forcing it to cede control of its economy and yield trading ports including Hong Kong and Shanghai—was a source of shame. He claimed not to know of "a war more unjust in its origin, more calculated in its progress to cover this country with permanent disgrace."[34] He was slower off the mark when it came to responding to the Great Famine in Ireland, interpreting the potato blight, which was to result in the deaths of more than a million people, as a sign of divine displeasure, brought about by "the hand of providence." Perhaps as a result, he supported only grudgingly the repeal of the Corn Laws, which kept the price of grain in Ireland artificially high.[35]

Middle-aged in the middle of the century, in 1852 Gladstone moved from the backbenches into the centre of the political fray, where he would stay until he eventually retired more than forty years later, in 1894. He held the limelight in his capacity as chancellor of the exchequer, but also from 1867 onwards as the leader of the newly created Liberal Party, a political party that had been forged in 1859 by the uneasy alliance of left-wing radicals, the free-trade faction of the Conservative Party, and what remained of the aristocratic Whigs. But above all, Gladstone was at the heart of things during the fourteen years, spread over four separate terms of office, that he spent as the prime minister.

The policies Gladstone championed during this time served to define British liberalism, combining the economic liberalism of the free traders with the social liberalism of the reformers. Economically, Gladstone is known for the loosening of trade regulations and the reduction of taxes on a wide variety of goods, from foodstuffs to paper. Socially, his passion projects included the regulation of better working conditions in factories, the provision of free elementary schooling, and electoral reform. As the beneficiary of a substantial inherited fortune, educated at Eton and Oxford, and prone to high-handed religious moralising, Gladstone made an unlikely champion of the people. And yet, many of his policies were designed to improve the prospects, freedoms, and standards of living of Britain's working poor.

He shocked and thrilled Parliament in equal measure when he called for a wide-ranging extension of the franchise in 1864, arguing "every man who is not presumably incapacitated by some consideration of personal unfitness or of political danger, is morally entitled to come within the pale of the constitution."[36] He supported the establishment of trade unions and spoke in favour of striking dockers and miners, claiming that "as a general rule, the labouring man has been in the right."[37] Indeed, when a march was held for the first international May Day in support of workers worldwide in 1889, he and his wife, Catherine, walked out to meet the marchers, to their general delight. Policies and actions such as these won him widespread popularity, especially amongst the working and middle classes in the north of the country, as well as earning him the affectionate moniker "the People's William."[38]

One issue that particularly troubled Gladstone was the status of Ireland, the oldest and the closest of Britain's imperial dominions. A strong independence movement emerged in the late nineteenth century, the people of Ireland scarred by the trauma of the Great Famine and made hopeful by the wave of popular movements that had swept through continental Europe. Although Gladstone had been unsympathetic to the plight of the Irish earlier in his career, in his later years he became convinced of the need for Irish home rule. Collaborating with Irish politicians, he brought two separate bills to Parliament to bring about home rule—in 1886 and again in 1893, only to see both defeated (the first in the House of Commons and the second in the Lords) and the Liberal Party irrevocably split into warring factions over the issue.

The stiffest opposition to Gladstone's home rule bills came from the Conservative Party, which, in addition to being the official opposition party to his Liberals, was also deeply and fundamentally committed to the maintenance of empire. The Conservative leader and Gladstone's great political rival, Benjamin Disraeli, set out the priorities of his party in 1872 thus: "The first is to maintain the institutions of the country, the second is, in my opinion, to uphold the empire of England."[39] Disraeli derided Gladstone and the Liberals for attempting to "effect the disintegration of the empire," tapping into a popular enthusiasm for empire that allowed even the English working poor to cultivate a sense of superiority. Yet Disraeli's own stance on empire, race, and class was complex.[40] Born into a Jewish family but baptised into the Church of England at the age of twelve, Disraeli entered the high echelons of British society as an outsider and was subjected to aggressive anti-Semitism over the course of his political career. He was in many senses the opposite of Gladstone—not just a second-generation child of an immigrant family where Gladstone was born into the English establishment, but also urbane and witty where Gladstone was simple and dour, flamboyant where Gladstone was severe, a successful author of bestselling novels where Gladstone penned only heavy tomes of obscure textual criticism.

Disraeli's novels capture the driving obsessions of his day and in particular the intersection of race, power, and history that sustained the narrative of Western Civilisation. In his 1847 novel, *Tancred—or The New Crusade*, recounting the tale of a young English nobleman who embarks on an epic journey to the Holy Land, Disraeli famously wrote that "all is race; there is no other truth." And in his final, unfinished novel, *Endymion* (1880), he claimed that race was "the key of history." Race, he argued, connected Jesus and early Christianity more closely to the Jews than to modern Europeans, and he bemoaned the tendency of Europeans in his own day to disavow their own Jewish cultural heritage. He wrote pointedly against those "among the wisest and the wittiest of the northern and western races, who, touched by a presumptuous jealousy of the long predominance of that oriental intellect to which they owed their civilisation, would have persuaded themselves and the world that the traditions of Sinai and Calvary were fables. Half a century ago, Europe made a violent and apparently successful effort to disembarrass itself of its Asian faith."[41] Amongst those whom Disraeli had in his sights with this criticism was, perhaps inevitably, his great rival, Gladstone.

A Bulwark against the East

When it came to his view of history, Gladstone found himself diametrically opposed to Disraeli. A keen classicist at both school and university, Gladstone enthusiastically embraced the by-now canonical narrative of Western Civilisation and was active in promoting it. For Gladstone, the fundamental foundations of Western Civilisation were laid in Greece and Rome, and these were later overlaid by Christianity:

> In the West, we must view the extraordinary developments, which human nature received, both individually and in its social forms, among the Greeks and the Romans, as having been intended to fulfil high Providential purposes. They supplied materials for the intellectual and social portions of that European civilisation, which derives its spiritual substance from the Christian Faith.[42]

As "the two greatest races of the ancient world,"[43] the Greeks and Romans had, in Gladstone's mind, left slightly different legacies to the West. The Romans had given the West its structures of political organization and "the firmest and most durable tissue of law, the bond of social man." In contrast, the Greeks were responsible for Western ideas about "the development of the individual." Of the two, Gladstone was completely clear which was the greater gift—it was the Greeks above all who provided the fount of true Western identity. Westerners knew instinctively, he claimed, the "genial primacy of the Greeks" in the formation of their culture.[44] After all, "It was the Greek mind, transferred, without doubt, in some part through Italy, but yet only transferred, and still Greek both in origin and in much of its essence, in which was shaped and tempered the original mould of modern European civilisation."[45]

So far, so canonical. Yet Gladstone took things one step further by claiming that the classical heritage was such that it negated any possible cultural influences from the biblical world of the Middle East. A decade after Disraeli complained in his *Tancred* about Westerners who wanted to ignore or refute the Asian elements in their own cultural inheritance, Gladstone published a book of his own with precisely this aim in mind. This was his *Studies on Homer and the Homeric Age*—three dense volumes packed with detailed textual commentary and comparative material harvested from across the historical and ethnographic spectrum. The first of these volumes (weighing in at a hefty 576 pages) is devoted to an "Ethnology of the Greek Races," ultimately concluding that the ancient Greeks belonged to the Aryan race and were related to the Germanic races of Gladstone's own day. The second volume (a mere 533 pages) was given over to "the Religion of the Homeric Age," suggesting that the key elements of Christian morality and spirituality were already present in the religious practices of early Greece. The third and final volume (a whopping 616 pages) contains an extended ethnographic comparison of the Homeric Greeks and the Homeric Trojans, arguing that the two groups were fundamentally different in both race and civilisation, with the Trojans being prime examples of Orientals and Asiatics. (Although as we saw in Chapter 1, more recent scholarship on the Homeric epic has disproved Gladstone's theory on this point, and the *Iliad* is a long way from being a clash-of-civilisations narrative.[46])

Despite being couched in scholarly language and framed as a study of Homeric poetry, Gladstone had nonetheless written a deeply political book that sought to justify his worldview no less than Disraeli had in his romantic novels. Gladstone described what he saw as a "struggle of races" that spanned "the whole course of history."[47] On the one side was a people belonging to the Aryan race, the cultural as well as racial ancestors of the West, amongst whom the Christian God had sowed the first seeds of divine revelation.[48] The part that it played in history was, Gladstone argued, divinely ordained, so that "[we should] regard ancient Greece as having a distinct, assignable, and most important place in the providential government of the world."[49] If only, Gladstone reflected wistfully, "had the Messiah been Incarnate, among a people who were in political sagacity, in martial energy, in soaring and divine intellect, in vivid imagination, in the graces of art and civilized life, the flower of their time, then the divine origins of Christianity would have stood far less clear and disembarrassed than it now does."[50]

In contrast with the ancient Greeks, Gladstone argued that the peoples of ancient western Asia had made little or no cultural impact on Western Civilisation, despite Christianity first emerging amongst them. The idea of two diametrically opposed races—the Aryans and the Semites—had already become a standard feature of German neo-romantic scholarship by this time, to a great extent thanks to the work of the French scholar Ernest Renan.[51] Gladstone made things even clearer for his Anglophone audience. He singled out the Jews in particular as not making any contribution to the culture of the West: "They have not supplied the Christian ages with laws and institutions, arts and sciences, with the chief models of greatness in genius or in character."[52] The Hebrew claim to being a chosen people was deployed in support of this argument. "In setting the Jewish people apart for a purpose the most profound of all His wise designs," Gladstone argued, "He removed it, for the time of its career, out of the family of nations."[53] He concluded triumphantly that "Palestine, in a word, had no share of the glories of our race; [instead] they blaze on every page of the history of Greece with an overpowering splendour."[54]

The comment is not so much pointed as it is barbed. Its immediate and personal target might well have been his political rival, but Gladstone was also aiming much higher—he wanted to expunge utterly the taint of Asian influence and to create a past for the West that was purely European. Not only were the ancient Greeks the ancestors of the modern West and the recipients of an early form of pre-Christian divine revelation that cancelled out any cultural influences from the Middle East; they also served as the "effective bulwark against the East," repelling Asiatic and Oriental influence from their uncontaminated civilisation.[55] For Gladstone, "the rivalry between the Hellenic race and the (afterwards so called) βάρβαροι [barbarians] of Asia"[56] was clear, and "the less warlike character of the Trojans, their more oriental manners, and their less multiform and imaginative religion, all point to considerable difference in the composition of the people."[57] While the ancient Greeks were freedom-loving and virile, "the Trojans were more given to the vices of sensuality and falsehood . . . certain fundamental features of distinction which have always been more or less observable, between the European and the Asiatic races."[58] For Gladstone, the mythical Trojans were essentially the same as the Asian peoples of his own day, in his mind sharing their practices of polygamy and licentiousness, in contrast to the Western practice of faithful monogamy,[59] as well as what he saw as their "less developed capacity for political organization" and ideas about the inherited rule,[60] and even assuming them to be of lesser intellect when compared with Western peoples.[61]

Gladstone's characterisation of the mythical Trojans of Homeric epic echoes his description of non-Western peoples of the nineteenth century, and in particular the Ottomans. In 1876, he launched an impassioned campaign criticising the harsh nature of the Ottoman response to a rebellion in Bulgaria. He used it as an opportunity too to disparage Disraeli, suggesting that it was Disraeli's racial sympathy with the Ottomans that prompted his inactivity. Instead, he argued, the sympathies of the West should more rightly lie with the small "handfuls of our race" who were withstanding the onslaught of "the entire weight of the Ottoman army."[62] During this episode, Gladstone resorted to anti-Semitism and Turkophobia by turns, reserving his harshest vitriol for the Ottomans, expressed in racial rather than religious terms:

> It is not a question of Mahometanism simply, but of Mahometanism compounded with the peculiar character of a race. They are not the mild Mahometans of India, nor the chivalrous Saladins of Syria, nor the cultured Moors of Spain. They were, upon the whole, from the first black day when they first entered Europe, the one great anti-human specimen of humanity. Wherever they went, a broad line of blood marked the track left behind them; and, as far as their dominion reached civilisation disappeared from view. They represented everywhere government by force, as opposed to government by law. For the guide of this life they had a relentless fatalism: for its reward hereafter, a sensual paradise.[63]

Gladstone was not alone in his anti-Ottoman sentiments. Edward Augustus Freeman, at the time the Regius Professor of Modern History at Oxford, wrote in sorrow that "in the countries where European civilisation first had its birth, the European has been ruled by the Asiatic, the civilized man by the barbarian."[64] He was referring, of course, to Greece, as Greece had been part of the Ottoman Empire until relatively recently. Gladstone's views, some of which might seem shocking to us now, were much more common in his own day.

There are few people across human history who have held as much power as Gladstone did at his peak—the power to oppress or elevate, to degrade or improve, darken or lighten the lives of millions across the world. Historians and commentators of differing flavours will tot up the balance sheet of his actions differently, but in this book I am not interested in making my subjects into heroes or villains. What I am interested in is understanding the broader worldview that lay behind their actions, and the historical narratives that informed them. For Gladstone, his worldview was unquestionably that of the West and the Rest, locked in an eternal clash of civilisations, with the timeless edifice of Western Civilisation destined, by its inherent superiority, to dominate the world.

———

THE IDEA THAT Britain was the ultimate heir of classical antiquity can be found more widely in nineteenth-century Britain, not just in the obscure writings of one of its more eccentric prime ministers. Comparisons abounded between "Greater Rome and Greater Britain,"[65] with significant interest in "a comparison between Rome and England as conquering powers, and more especially as governors of subject peoples and provinces."[66] In contrast, as we have already seen in Chapter 10, the United States of America claimed the same legacy on a different basis—its political institutions, its Polybian mixed constitution, and its Roman influenced republicanism. Nor was the claiming of classical antiquity restricted to the Anglosphere. In 1809, the German philosopher Georg Wilhelm Friedrich Hegel asserted that the basis for scholarship was "grounded on Greece and Rome" and that in Germany "the foundation of higher study must be and remain Greek literature in the first place, Roman in the second."[67] In the nineteenth century, the grand narrative of Western Civilisation was firmly established in different parts of the West.

The term itself was also beginning to gain traction. Although it is impossible to pin down when the term "Western Civilisation" was first used, the mid-nineteenth century saw its proliferation in both the United Kingdom and the United States, in contexts as varied as political treatises, educational reports, and travel literature.[68] Gladstone himself furnishes us with an early use of the term, referring to the important position of Homeric literature "throughout the entire sphere of Western Civilisation."[69]

Strident in his civilisational thinking and confident in his vision of history, Gladstone illustrates the broader trend perfectly. His politics and his view of history were deeply intertwined, his belief in British and Western superiority both influencing and being influenced by his vision of the past—a past whose contours followed a grand narrative that by this time was explicitly labelled as "Western Civilisation." He believed that the ultimate origins of his own culture lay in ancient Greece and Rome and that this made his culture superior to all others. In the life and writings of Gladstone, we find the acme of Western Civilisation as a vision of history.

Yet even in this moment, at the height of Western power and when the grand narrative of Western Civilisation was at its strongest, other voices could still be heard and other narratives could still be told. Comparisons between Britain and classical antiquity were also sometimes made by colonized peoples and turned on the British as a means of imperial critique. The Indian intellectual and political reformer Bhaskar Pandurang Tarkhadkar appealed to classical antiquity, writing that "to advocate the cause of India with success would require the pen of a 'Junius' or the eloquence of a 'Demosthenes.'" He argued that if the Romans had imposed similar conditions on their subject populations to those visited by the British on the Indians, this would only have served to hasten their ruin. Indeed, even the example of the Roman Empire, he claims, demonstrates that subject peoples rarely if ever submit to their imperial overlords willingly, saying, "It cannot be doubted that the Romans lost possession of their subdued countries owing to the Natives being quite averse to be governed by another nation."[70]

Another nineteenth-century Indian commentator, who wrote anonymously as the "Hindu Writer," published detailed articles analysing the nature of Roman rule and concluding that there was no historical precedent for a subject population ever benefitting from colonial rule, and that in actuality, all had necessarily suffered from it.[71] In Sierra Leone, the nationalist and surgeon James Africanus Beale Horton argued that Africans had made a significant contribution to the classical cultures of Greece and Rome, with many Greeks and Romans coming to Africa in search of wisdom, claiming, "Several came to listen to the instructions of the African Euclid who was at the head of the most celebrated mathematical school in the world . . . The conqueror of the great African Hannibal made his associate and confidant the African poet Terrence."[72] If the grand narrative of Western Civilisation could be deployed in the service of Western imperialism, it would be used to subvert it too.

Further ambiguities can be seen even in the heart of empire. The last volume of Edward Gibbon's *History of the Decline and Fall of the Roman Empire* was published in 1789, and the work as a whole became a runaway bestseller in the nineteenth century. Its apocalyptic view of the collapse of empire tapped into British anxieties about their own imperial overreach, which also manifested themselves in literature such as the twin "Ozymandias" poems published by Percy Bysshe Shelley and his friend Horace Smith in 1818.

But while on the one hand Britain was the new Rome, destined to fall as Rome once had, on the other hand it could simultaneously cast itself as the colonised subject of Rome. Pondering the great edifice of Hadrian's Wall, the local Newcastle historian John Collingwood

Bruce wrote, "The sceptre which Rome relinquished, we have taken up. Great is our Honour—great our Responsibility." Yet in the same booklet, he was also careful to valorise the ancient Britons against which Hadrian had chosen to build his wall, comparing them to the Romans thus: "Though they were their inferiors in discipline and arms, were not behind them in valour and spirit."[73] The monumental bronze statue group of Boudicca and her daughters that now stands at Westminster on the bank of the Thames was commissioned in 1850, to commemorate the queen of the Iceni who rebelled against Rome. Another celebrated bronze statue, that of Caractacus, a chieftain of the Catuvellauni who resisted the Roman conquest, now erected in front on the official residence of the lord mayor in the City of London, was initially unveiled with widespread acclaim. Indeed, it was such a sensation that it was referred to in the Major-General's song in Gilbert and Sullivan's popular comic operetta *The Pirates of Penzance*. The audience, like the voluble Major-General, was expected to know "ev'ry detail of Caractacus's uniform"—a joke, given that the statue portrayed the chieftain heroically naked. While for the most part, nineteenth-century Britain saw itself as the heir of Rome, there were also some instances where people identified with the subjects of Rome.

It was not just in the context of empire that classical antiquity was being used to subvert and undermine the dominant narrative. Classical rhetoric, examples, and learning had been used to argue for the abolition of slavery,[74] the emancipation of women,[75] and the elevation of the working classes.[76] The very qualities that aligned classical antiquity with the establishment—its canonical nature, its association with elites and class, and above all, its status as the cultural ancestor and ultimate origin of the West—were also the things that made it ripe for appropriation. The grand narrative of Western Civilisation may have furnished the West with a powerful ideological tool for its arsenal, but it also provided a range of subaltern voices with a powerful tool for subversion. Originally designed to anchor us backwards with clear roots in the past, the notion of Western Civilisation was now being used to incite radical change, unsettling and rewriting the future.

Chapter Thirteen

THE WEST AND ITS CRITICS

EDWARD SAID

Appeals to the past are amongst the commonest of
strategies in interpretations of the present.

EDWARD SAID (1993)[1]

THE West is under attack. At least, this is what we hear today from some political pundits and cultural commentators, often in shrill and panicked tones. The threat is twofold. Externally, the West is threatened by alternative power blocs seeking to wrest global dominance away from it and to claim it for themselves. We will discuss these rivals of the West in the next chapter. The focus for this chapter is not those external adversaries, but instead the threat from within—the elements within the West that criticise its workings, challenge its assumptions, and question its legitimacy.

There have been a rash of books in recent years that warn against the "suicide of the West."[2] These books argue that the relative decline of Western political, military, and economic power stems from a lack of confidence in the traditional beliefs and principles that originally made Western culture great. Socially liberal trends in society undermine these beliefs, they claim, thereby leading to moral degeneration, social fragmentation, and the weakening of the West. The rhetoric of Western decline due to internal critics has also appeared in mainstream political discourse in recent years, with a prominent British politician claiming in early 2022 that "woke" ideology was a "dangerous form of decadence."[3] For some, this has amounted to a "war on the West," in which it has become accepted practice to "demonize white people."[4]

Anxiety about such internal threats is nothing new. Even at the height of Western global supremacy in the nineteenth century (Chapter 12), there were those—such as the notable British art critic and writer John Ruskin—who warned against its imminent decline due to moral, religious, and racial degeneracy.[5] Others singled out individuals for vilification as "the enemy within"; as we saw in the last chapter, in the latter part of the nineteenth century, the politician Benjamin Disraeli was often targeted as a "secret Jew" who was said to be actively working against the interests of Britain, Christendom, and the West.[6] But just because there is anxiety about an "enemy within," it does not mean that such a threat actually exists; just as the emergence of a conspiracy theory is not always predicated on the existence of an actual conspiracy.

But the anxious would-be guardians of the West have got one thing right—there *are* indeed critical elements within. From the middle of the twentieth century onwards, there have been an increasing number of people within the West who have begun to question the fundamental ideologies on which the West was traditionally based and to challenge the narrative of Western Civilisation. The aims of these critics of the West vary widely. Some, like the Western-born fundamentalist Islamists of Daesh, have sought to bring down the West entirely, explicitly labelling themselves enemies of the West. Others, like the right-wing extremists and terrorists who claim to defend the West by overturning its institutions and attacking its people, seek rather to remake the West anew, purged from elements they consider to be unsavoury. (Many of the loudest voices warning against attacks on the West come from this same camp that is also fundamentally threatening Western values and principles, a point that we will return to in the conclusion of this book.) Yet others, like the subject of this chapter, Edward Said, have sought to make much more modest improvements to the West, critiquing it in order to better understand it and the interconnected world of which it is a part.

While the critics of the West are diverse both in their aims and in their reproaches, they have all emerged out of the same historical process—the relative decline of Western political, military, and economic dominance. The self-professed enemies of the West celebrate this decline, nursing their hatred by cultivating the memories of Western imperial outrages and historical injustices. The self-appointed defenders of the West lament this decline, fuelling their ardour by cherishing nostalgic images of lost Western supremacy. And the questioners of the West (a category to which I consider myself to belong) seek to operate in the new spaces opened up by the changing global landscape, seeing in them opportunities for transformation.

Unthinking the West

Two major geopolitical developments have served to transform the way the West sees itself, rendering the nineteenth-century model of Western identity that was dominant in the time of William Gladstone (Chapter 12) functionally obsolete.

The first is decolonisation, which gained momentum as the global hegemony of the West started to unravel in the wake of two world wars that effectively overturned the old colonial world order.[7] The experience of decolonisation has been highly variable, from bloody and brutal to cordially negotiated.[8] There are also places where decolonisation is not yet complete, and where postcolonial or post-mandate settlements have led to entrenched and ongoing demographic divides, injustices, and bloodshed. But decolonisation is not just a process that happens "out there"; it is underway "at home" too. With the immigration of colonial subjects and the forced movement of enslaved people, the demographic makeup of most imperial heartlands changed forever. I am myself a product of this, with my parents coming to Britain from two different former colonies, and my husband from a third. We are here, to paraphrase the race relations campaigner Ambalavaner Sivanandan famously said, partly because you were there. The dynamics of this are different, of course, in different Western countries. I am writing this chapter at my kitchen table in Vienna, an old imperial capital with a postcolonial demographic very different from that of London, the old imperial capital I grew up in.

Since the middle of the twentieth century, we have seen Western countries coming to terms with these demographic shifts in different ways, from the American civil rights movement of the 1950s and 1960s to the Black Lives Matter and Rhodes Must Fall campaigns of recent years. Yet whether we are supporters of, detractors of, or uncomfortable bystanders to the latest campaign or movement, and whether we are the descendants of the colonisers or the descendants of the colonised, or—as is increasingly the case—descendants of both, these struggles and the demographic changes they are predicated on have changed the way the West sees itself. Crucially, fewer and fewer Westerners still think of the West primarily in racial terms, as Joseph Warren and Phillis Wheatley did in the eighteenth century, or as William Gladstone did in the nineteenth. (There are of course exceptions to this general rule, and we shall discuss them in the conclusion.)

The old racialised way of defining the West has become obsolete in part because it simply no longer works, but also because it runs counter to the principles that most Westerners consider to be central to Western identity today—principles of fundamental human equality and rights, social liberalism, and toleration. (Once more, there are people within the West who do not subscribe to these principles, preferring instead illiberalism and intolerance, but once more, we shall discuss these people in the conclusion.)

These principles have become core to Western self-definition in part because of the second major geopolitical development of the late twentieth century—the Cold War.[9] Today, most people tend to think of the West primarily in economic and political terms. The economic element of this emerged during the Cold War itself, when the rhetoric of the West identified it with capitalism in contrast to communism. This resulted in a stretching of the West geographically. Although its core remained in North America and western Europe, the West expanded to include countries of the global Anglosphere such as Australia and New Zealand, as well as other countries around the world that were "encouraged" to align themselves with the West through a variety of means, ranging from the use of soft power and appeals to shared history to military intervention and the forced installation of pro-Western governments.[10]

After the end of the Cold War, however, capitalism could no longer serve as a defining feature of the West, given that different forms of capitalism had now appeared in former communist states, from the aggressive state capitalism of China to the rapacious oligarchic capitalism of Russia (we will discuss Russia and China as rivals to the West in the next chapter). As a result, the rhetoric of Western self-definition shifted once more, with an increasing emphasis on political systems and in particular on liberal democracy. In my adult lifetime, the West has sought to present itself, and to justify its actions, with reference to liberal democracy more than to anything else. Sometimes the rhetoric of the West as the champion of liberal democracy has been honest and sometimes it has been disingenuous, but for the last thirty years it has been constant. That liberal democracy is, from a modern Western perspective, the ideal and ultimate form of human government has been argued by the historian Francis Fukuyama, who provocatively suggested that the dominance of liberal democracy in the West marked the "end of history."[11] (Of course, history did not end in the late twentieth century, the West has not "won," and there is no global consensus around liberal democracy, as Fukuyama himself admits.)

This reimagining of the West is still incomplete, but it began in a time of dramatic change in the mid- and late twentieth century, when both the geopolitical position of the West and the fundamental basis for Western identity shifted. Over the course of the twentieth century, the racial and geographic definitions of the West espoused in the eighteenth and nineteenth centuries became obsolete, out of step with both the political imperatives and lived realities of the West, and no longer representative of the ideological basis of Western identity. But reimagining the West also involves a radical rethinking of Western history, questioning and challenging the grand narrative of Western Civilisation.

Out of Place

The life of Edward Wadie Said spanned these tumultuous decades during which the West (and the rest of the world along with it) was transformed. Academic, activist, and public intellectual, through his writings Said laid the intellectual foundations on which this book has been built, exploring the constructed nature of cultural identities and their inherently political nature. He also argued that historians, for all their attempts at Rankean objectivism, are products of their time and that their work contributes to ongoing power dynamics. A perfect illustration of his own argument, Said's scholarship was certainly rooted in his own experience of decolonisation, exile, and a near-constant feeling of (in his own words) being "out of place."[12]

Said was born in 1935 in Jerusalem, a subject of the British Empire in the British-controlled territory of Mandatory Palestine. Yet at birth he held American citizenship through his father, who, although originally hailing from Jerusalem, had lived and worked in America for several years before joining the American Expeditionary Forces in the First World War.[13] His mother was a dedicated Anglophile from Nazareth who chose to name her son "Edward" in honour of the then Prince of Wales and went on to select equally English names for her four daughters. The family lived primarily in Cairo, where Said's father owned a flourishing stationery business, but spent holidays and extended visits with their relatives in Jerusalem. In Cairo they were a minority within a minority—Anglicans within a Christian community that was dominated by the Eastern Orthodox Church, and Christians living between two predominantly Muslim countries.[14]

As a child, Said attended elite schools in both Cairo and Jerusalem that were designed in the mould of English public schools, growing up in an environment so completely bilingual that he was never sure, as an adult looking back, whether Arabic or English had been his first language. It was a privileged childhood, in which Said was waited on by servants, attended classical music concerts, and escaped the summer heat in the swimming pools of exclusive members' clubs. Yet Said recalls always being painfully aware of being different from—and somehow inferior to—the white English and Americans who lived in his neighbourhood. "Arabs aren't allowed here," he would sometimes be told, even in the clubs where his family held membership,[15] and he was expected to socialise only with other non-whites, derogatively referred to as "wogs."[16]

He was only twelve years old in 1948 when the British withdrew from Palestine, the state of Israel was declared, and war broke out between Israeli and Arab armies. After a year of the bloodshed and chaos, borders were agreed that separated the new country of Israel from the Jordanian-controlled West Bank, Jewish immigrants poured into their new homeland, and hundreds of thousands of displaced Palestinians fled in what is known as the *Nakhba,* or "Catastrophe." Amongst them were Said's extended family, many of whom ended up in Cairo in abject poverty. Said's father found himself employing as many Palestinian refugees as he could, and Said remembers long afternoons sitting with his aunt, who served as an unofficial one-woman charity: dispensing medical advice, helping children find places in schools, supporting refugees navigating their way through Egyptian bureaucracy, and offering financial support where she could.[17]

The young Said felt painfully conscious that the plight of many Palestinian refugees was a world away from his own privileged existence, moving as he did in cosmopolitan circles that included elite Egyptians, but also Armenians, Greeks, Italians, Jews, Jordanians, Saudis, Syrians, and Turks. It was a social milieu that Said would later remember as "a dancelike maze of personalities, modes of speech, backgrounds, religions, and nationalities."[18] It was perhaps this disjoint, coupled with an academic brilliance that meant he was often bored at school, that led to him being branded—in his own words—a "trouble-maker."[19] During these years, music was to be an important outlet for his emotional as well as intellectual overflows. A gifted pianist, he developed a particularly close relationship with one of his teachers, the Polish Jew Ignace Tiegerman, who helped him establish classical music as one of the constant and calming influences on his life.

But music was not enough to keep Said on the straight and narrow. At the age of fifteen, he was finally expelled from his British-run school in Cairo; his parents decided to send him to the country of his citizenship to complete his education. He was enrolled first in a boarding school in rural Massachusetts, a period which Said later looked back on as "probably the most miserable of my life." The student body was almost exclusively white and American-born and "made no bones about my belonging to an inferior, or somehow disapproved, race."[20] Despite the hostility of both staff and fellow students, Said studied hard and did well and went on to study English and comparative literature first at Princeton University as an undergraduate, and then at Harvard University as a graduate student.

Throughout this time, Said remained relatively aloof from politics. He returned to Cairo regularly, taking family holidays with his parents in Lebanon as he had often done as a child, as well as longer trips to explore continental Europe. Yet he seems to have kept all of this at arm's length from his life as an academic in America. He remembered later that "Princeton in the fifties was un-political, self-satisfied, and oblivious,"[21] and although Said published an article offering an Arab perspective on the 1956 Suez Crisis in the university newspaper, no one seemed to take much notice or interest.[22] At Harvard, Said felt that "the Middle East drifted further and further from my consciousness," as he delved deeper into the Western philosophical and literary tradition, immersing himself in Heidegger, Sartre, and Vico before settling down to a doctoral dissertation on Joseph Conrad.[23] It was while he was a doctoral student that Said met and married his first wife, Marie Jaanus, another doctoral student working towards a PhD in comparative literature.[24] Jaanus was Estonian, but her expertise in German complemented Said's Francophone leanings. Together, they explored the world of European literature, philosophy, and social theory and experimented with writing fiction and poetry.

Said's political awakening came years later, while he was teaching at Columbia University in New York. The Arab-Israeli War of 1967 may have lasted for only six days, but its consequences were long-lived. When the dust lifted, Israel controlled large swathes of new territory, and many more Palestinians found themselves permanently exiled. For Said it was a turning point. At the time, America was swept up with powerful political movements, including protests against the Vietnam War and a civil rights movement to fight against racial discrimination. Hoping to raise awareness of the plight of ordinary Palestinians amongst what he imagined would be a sympathetic public, Said sharpened his pen.[25]

The essay that followed, "The Arab Portrayed," contains many of the elements that would later appear in his best-known works. In it, Said addressed the portrayal of Arabs in Anglophone journalism, trawling through newspaper reports and magazine articles from North America and Britain (with the occasional foray into French publications). He identified recurring themes, including stupidity, sexual degeneracy, and savageness, which meant that "if the Arab occupies any space in the mind at all, it is of negative value."[26] These mental images were not harmless, argued Said, but had serious real-life consequences. They meant that Westerners struggled to see Arabs as victims capable of suffering, and so there was precious little sympathy for Palestinians in comparison to Israelis, who were perceived both as more white and as more Western.

Indeed 1967 proved to be a turning point for Said personally as well as politically. He split from Jaanus, who he felt had never understood his devotion to his family, and met his future wife, Mariam Cortas. Their first encounter was not, on the face of it, very promising. Said was still married and much distraught (he was visiting his sister in hospital at the time, as she had broken her leg), and Mariam was soon to leave New York to return home to Beirut, having completed her finance degree.[27] It took two more years and a gathering of the extended family in Beirut before they eventually became a couple, marrying in 1970 and having their daughter, Najla, in 1974.

Over the next three decades, Said balanced his home life with his scholarship and activism. As an academic, he continued to teach, research, and publish on comparative literature. As an activist, he quickly became a public intellectual, writing for newspapers and magazines as well as appearing regularly on television. His outspoken public support for the Palestinian cause won him both devotees and critics, the former elevating him to iconic status as the poster boy for the victims of colonial oppression, and the latter denigrating him as an enemy of the West and the "Professor of Terror." He was a controversial and polarising figure but contributed to transforming the public discourse in the West so that support for the Palestinians became respectable and even, in some circles, fashionable.

He had more direct political involvement between 1977 and 1993, during which time he held an elected position on the Palestinian National Council (PNC), the legislative body of the Palestinian nationalist movement in exile. Yet here too Said quickly found himself swimming against the current. He criticised Palestinian leaders, including Yasser Arafat, feeling that they were both unrealistic in their expectations and unprincipled in their demands.[28] Even more controversially, he argued against the signing of the Oslo Peace Accord in 1993, an agreement that had been painstakingly negotiated and was much vaunted in the press as offering a peaceful solution to the conflict. Said contended that the agreement was fundamentally flawed and therefore destined to fail. He resigned from the PNC in anger and frustration. Although many of his contemporaries condemned Said for his pessimism, time has sadly proved him right.

By this point, Said had been diagnosed with leukaemia. Although he would live for another twelve years, continuing to work on musical, political, and scholarly projects, he eventually succumbed to the disease in 2003. In his last decade, a heightened awareness of his own mortality prompted him to reflect on his early life, writing memoirs and essays that dwelt on questions of identity, exile, and homeland. He also invested his time more heavily in his musical projects, in particular the West-Eastern Divan Orchestra, a multifaith enterprise that he launched with the Jewish conductor Daniel Barenboim in 1999. The aim of the orchestra was to bring together young people from across the many different countries of the Middle East, allowing them to share a common love of music. Said had always felt that music had transformative potential, and he and Barenboim hoped that cultural cooperation could succeed where politics had failed, promoting peace and mutual understanding.

Said might not have succeeded as a politician, or in his ultimate aim of securing a homeland for the Palestinians, but he did achieve indisputable success in one thing—in showing us that culture and politics are deeply intertwined. Some cultural activities such as the West-Eastern Divan Orchestra can, as Said hoped, promote peace and understanding. Other cultural activities, such as the derogatory stereotypes of Arabs that Said identified and analysed in literature, can serve to sow hatred and alienation. By highlighting this interplay between politics and culture, Said laid the foundations for a reassessment of

Western Civilisation, allowing us to see it for what it really is—an invented social construct, one that is extremely powerful and has far-reaching consequences in the real world, but a construct nonetheless. This is perhaps Said's greatest legacy.

Rethinking Western Civilisation

This legacy means that we can rethink Western Civilisation. Before the late twentieth century, most people thought about civilisational identity as something automatic—a natural and unchanging given. (In fact, many people still do think along these lines today.) And yet, it is obvious from the lives of the subjects of this book that civilisational boundaries and definitions have never been static. We have seen how ideas about the West and Western identity varied between individuals as well as over space and time. Francis Bacon conceived of the West differently from Joseph Warren because they were rooted in different historical contexts, as well as different social and individual circumstances. The cultural allegiances of Britain were imagined differently by Safiye Sultan and William Gladstone for the same reason. From the unique historical standpoint of each of these individuals, the West and Western Civilisation looked different. As a result, the subjects of each of our biographies portrayed and experienced the West differently.

Some, of course, were very deliberate about this. They chose to portray civilisational identities in particular ways, shaped by and tailored to the specific political goals they had in mind. From the biographies contained in this book, Herodotus, Godfrey of Viterbo, and Joseph Warren are perhaps the best examples of this approach. Yet not everyone manipulated ideas of civilisational identity in a conscious or intentional way, and instead simply expressed ideas about civilisational identity that made sense to them given the time, place, and social context in which they were situated. Amongst this latter group we might, from the lives recounted here, include Theodore Laskaris, Njinga of Angola, and Phillis Wheatley. And yet, for an even greater number of people, the truth lay somewhere between these two poles.

Yet all the individuals discussed in this book *did* shape civilisational identities, even if they did so unwittingly. The act of creating or sponsoring cultural products meant that they changed, shifted, nuanced, or reinforced ideas in wider society. The statues and inscriptions of Livilla, for example, not only were born out of dynastic pride in a pluralistic intercontinental identity but also served to promote the idea of an intercontinental dynasty more widely. While the poems of Wheatley expressed her own personal sense of racial alienation, they also strengthened and reinforced the sense of racial distinctions across society more generally. And when al-Kindī began to write about the Arabs as the intellectual heirs of ancient Greece, the criticism he attracted from religious conservatives kicked off a broader public debate. We know that the sociopolitical context shapes culture, but we must also acknowledge that culture in turn shapes the sociopolitical context. The relationship between culture and identity is therefore like a feedback loop—with variation in one producing changes in the other, circling around in a mutual and constant flux.

Thanks to Said, as well as other postcolonial scholars and social theorists of the late twentieth century, we now recognise how this process works. We now acknowledge that identities are socially and culturally constructed, rather than being natural, automatic, and primordial. This might seem obvious to us now, but in the third quarter of the twentieth century, it was dangerously controversial. Said often bore the brunt of this controversy. It was a role that he understood as his duty, almost as his vocation. He wrote that "the job facing the cultural intellectual is therefore not to accept the politics of identity as given, but to show how all representations are constructed, for what purpose, by whom, and with what components."[29]

While this general principle could be applied to all types of identities in all periods, in his academic work Said chose to apply the principle to the two large-scale identities to which he felt he belonged—the Arab world and the West. When his breakthrough book *Orientalism* was first published in 1978, it contained an honest admission of how the personal had influenced the academic. "My own experiences of these matters are in part what made me write this book," he wrote in the introduction.[30] *Orientalism* was a detailed study of literary and scholarly writing produced on subjects related to the Middle East and the Arab world in the English and French languages over the course of the eighteenth, nineteenth, and twentieth centuries. Said argued that such writings framed the Middle East and Arab world as "the Orient," attaching to this a stereotyped image of despotism, splendour, sensuality, and cruelty that was at the same time romantic and prompted a sense of Western superiority. In this sense, the idea of "the Orient was almost a European invention, and had been since antiquity a place of romance, exotic beings, haunting memories and landscapes, remarkable experiences."[31]

But the Orient was not alone in being an invention. The process of inventing the Orient, Said argues, was a crucial element that also contributed to the invention of the West, which increasingly began to understand itself in opposition to the East.

> I have begun with the assumption that the Orient is not an inert fact of nature. It is not merely there, just as the Occident itself is not just there either . . . as both geographical and cultural entities—to say nothing of historical entities—such locales, regions, geographical sectors as "Orient" and "Occident" are man-made. Therefore as much as the West itself, the Orient is an idea that has a history and

a tradition of thought, imagery, and vocabulary that have given it
reality and presence in and for the West. The two geographical enti-
ties thus support and to an extent reflect each other.[32]

Neither the Orient nor the Occident, therefore, had a primordial existence. "Neither the term Orient nor the concept of the West has any ontological stability," Said writes; "each is made up of human effort, partly affirmation, partly identification of the Other . . . These supreme fictions lend themselves easily to manipulation and the organization of collective passion."[33] But, of course, just because something is a fiction does not mean that it has no real-life consequences. For Said, the crucial result of the invention of the Orient, as well as the associated invention of the West, was the ideological justification of imperial rule. Imagining the Orient as fundamentally different from and necessarily inferior to the West made it easier and indeed ideologically possible for Westerners to dominate the peoples of the Middle East. This was a domination that began politically with direct imperialism in the eighteenth, nineteenth, and early twentieth centuries but which Said argued also continued culturally and intellectually into the later twentieth century. "Orientalism can be discussed and analyzed as the corporate institution for dealing with the Orient—dealing with it by making statements about it, authorizing views of it, describing it, by teaching it, settling it, ruling over it: in short, Orientalism as a Western style for dominating, restructuring, and having authority over the Orient."[34]

Said was careful to set out that all of this was not the result of "some nefarious 'Western' imperialist plot to hold down the 'Oriental' world." Instead, countless individual choices, shaped not only by individual circumstances and private interests but also crucially by historical context, went into creating this broader texture of knowledge.

Said's scholarship was almost as controversial as his politics. Some critics condemned Said for what they saw as an unfairly negative portrayal of the West.[35] Others, like the prominent scholar Bernard Lewis, attacked Said for politicising his academic discipline and for misrepresenting Islam, which he continued to argue was locked in an ongoing "clash of civilisations" with the Christian West.[36] Yet others took issue with the narrow limits of *Orientalism* as a book. For example, it did not engage with German-speaking traditions of Oriental scholarship, which were not only vast but also vastly important and influential beyond the German-speaking world.[37] Similarly, it failed to consider Western ideas about Africa, Latin America, and the other parts of the Orient, Central or East Asia—a fault Said partially addressed with his wider-ranging book of 1993, *Culture and Imperialism*. It was pointed out that these regions might offer a different and more nuanced perspective, in particular the case of Japan, which seems to defy Said's binary definitions of Orient and Occident.[38] Yet others pointed out the historical inaccuracies of the book, of which there are many (we will discuss some of these later in this chapter).

Even taking these criticisms into account, the core argument of *Orientalism* remains hard to dispute. The book rapidly became influential across the humanities and remains a classic text read by students across the world today. It was foundational in the development of postcolonial studies as a discipline and has prompted studies in new directions, such as the manifold nature of Occidentalism in both Asia and Africa.[39] This is because, for all its inaccuracies, omissions, and theoretical flourishes, the book's central argument is solid. Cultural products including academic writing both *are* shaped by the historical and political contexts in which they are produced, *and also*, at the same time, go on to shape these contexts as well. This is the feedback loop of culture and identity.

Said may have been right about some things, but he was wrong on others. Ideas about the West were certainly developed in relation to the peoples and societies of the Middle East and in the context of imperialism, but in this book, I have argued that there is more to it than that. The invention of the West and Western Civilisation did not happen purely due to European imperialism. Within the Anglophone world, it also emerged from the ideological sleight of hand required to justify both the American Revolution and the inequalities in North American society simultaneously (Chapters 10 and 11). In continental Europe, it also was coloured by the ideological opposition between a Russo-Eurasian and an Atlantic orientation (Chapter 12). There is also a fundamental flaw in Said's treatment of Western history, and in particular of the grand narrative of Western Civilisation. While he argues that the West itself is a fiction, he tends to accept the narrative of Western Civilisation as an unbroken cultural genealogy, running (in literary terms) "from Homer to Virginia Woolf."[40]

Homer is invoked as the starting point for Orientalist attitudes in the West at several points, and inevitably Said chooses to open his analysis of Western Orientalism with texts from the ancient Greek world. Said exhorts his readers to "consider first the demarcation between Orient and West. It already seems bold by the time of the *Iliad*."[41] This is, as mentioned in Chapters 1 and 12 of this book, not actually true—the Homeric *Iliad* does not recognise any significant ethnic, cultural, or racial differences between the warring parties, and certainly does not offer a demarcation between the Orient and the West.[42] Said subsequently embarks on a discussion of two Athenian tragedies—Aeschylus's *Persians* and Euripides's *Bacchae*—which offer an essentialised and stereotyped vision of the Asian Oriental. And yet, as we saw in Chapter 1 of this book, Athenian literature of the mid-fifth century BCE does not capture the broader zeitgeist of the ancient Greek world, written as it was in the context of (if not in the service of)

Athenian imperial domination over other Greeks. Had Said selected Herodotus for close reading instead of the Attic dramatists, he might have come up with a rather different picture.

These questions of individual source selection aside, on a grander scale, Said adheres to the conventional shape of history as established by the Western Civilisation narrative. He briefly considers Rome, perhaps skating over it as its ideology was too blatantly hybrid for it to fit his overall argument (as we saw in Chapter 2). He dwells for slightly longer on medieval Christianity, medieval Islamophobia, and the Crusades before touching lightly on the Renaissance and finally focusing for the rest of the book on literature of the late eighteenth and nineteenth centuries. In *Orientalism*, therefore, Said broadly accepted the grand narrative of Western Civilisation, using its general framework as a structuring principle to introduce his own work. That even Said, with his sensitivity to politically inflected literature, took it at face value stands as testament to the strength and persistence of Western Civilisation as a narrative. Even at a time when it was not only possible but necessary to reimagine the West itself, it seems that it was somehow harder to reimagine Western history.

SAID HIMSELF ALWAYS acknowledged the specificity and limits of *Orientalism* and went on to tackle the broader complexity of identity making in a later book, *Culture and Imperialism*. In it, he concluded that the very practice of making identities involves an artificial drawing of boundaries and the creation of exclusive categories where exclusivity did not necessarily or naturally exist. Writing about imperialism, he claimed that

> *its worst and most paradoxical gift was to allow people to believe that they were only, mainly, exclusively, white, or black, or Western, or Oriental. Yet just as human beings make their own history, they*

also make their own cultures and ethnic identities. No one can deny the persisting continuities of long traditions, sustained habitations, national languages, and cultural geographies, but there seems no reason except fear and prejudice to keep insisting on their separation and distinctiveness, as if that was all human life was about.[43]

Yet in his own life, Said found it difficult to move beyond the categories that he had grown up with and which had become ingrained in him. Towards the end of his life, his autobiographical reflections returned once more to the idea of an implacable and unbridgeable divide between the West and the Rest, "us" and "them." As a scholar, he had critiqued the opposition, uncovering some of the ways that this opposition had been drawn in the first place. Yet on a more human level, he found it hard to imagine his own place in the world beyond it. One concept recurs time and again in these later writings—the sense of being, as Said put it, always and inevitably "out of place." Said felt himself to be an eternal exile, destined to be an Oriental in the West and a Westerner in the Orient, belonging to none of the societies in which he lived. In one essay, he described the exilic state of being as follows:

Exile is strangely compelling to think about but terrible to experience. It is the unhealable rift forced between a human being and a native place, between the self and its true home: its essential sadness can never be surmounted. And while it is true that literature and history contain heroic, romantic, glorious, even triumphant episodes in an exile's life, these are no more than efforts meant to overcome the crippling sorrow of estrangement. The achievements of exile are permanently undermined by the loss of something left behind forever.[44]

These words would perhaps strike a chord with many people today, if they ever have the occasion to read them. In a world where examples abound of forced displacement, and when refugees from war and tyranny are plenty, they ring with a certain miserable truth. Yet they are grounded in an assumption that does not always hold true in every instance—that everyone necessarily hails from a single "native place" to begin with. To belong *here* is to not belong *there*, and to belong to one category of human is necessarily to *not* belong to another. Yet the very idea of absolute borders being drawn between identities is what Said argues against in his work, asserting instead that humans "make their own cultures and ethnic identities." The contrast between Said's personal feelings and his scholarship arguments is stark. If something is a social construct, this does not mean that it is not real. If something has been invented, this does not prevent it from becoming a meaningful truth that shapes our lives. Just as this was the case for the identities that Said deconstructed, it is also the case for the West.

Living with the idea that your identities are constructed and multiple has become easier in the twenty-first century. The increase in global mobility, biracialism, and intercultural families means that it is more common than ever to belong to more than one group at once, to be at home *both* here *and* there. For some, this plurality of identities is problematic, something that needs to be grappled with, picked over, and explained (away). I have certainly felt like this at times in my own life. Yet for a new generation, this plurality can also be a source of potency and pride. It can be, in the words of the Iraqi-Welsh poet and artist Hanan Issa, "a strength none can take."

MY BODY CAN HOUSE TWO HEARTS

We say 'qalbain for two hearts
Pumping parts through crimson sea
Tied to land's history split
I've tried to fit

Uneasily.
A blazing of blood combined,
Obsess
Rewind
Frustrate me.
Say between two stools I fall
Those boundary walls formed early.
But my body is enough
Gently tough
Stretched agony, growing a love
Embracing
Rejecting patriarchy
No need to
Shame my peers
Or let my fears
Rat-race me
Two hearts my body can hold
So I mould
My legacy
To make space enough for all.
Standing tall
I rise,
Breathe free.
Two hearts—
A strength none can take.
Love's a lake
and the world is thirsty.[45]

Chapter Fourteen

THE WEST AND ITS RIVALS

CARRIE LAM

*I sincerely welcome visitors from all over the world to
come to Hong Kong . . . to immerse themselves in the
extraordinary cultural experience that embraces the
best of both the East and the West.*

CARRIE LAM (2021)[1]

A MOB of violent protesters had stormed the seat of government. Encountering minimal resistance from a nervous police force who were hesitant about where their own sympathies should lie, the mob occupied the legislative chamber, smashing windows, breaking down doors, and graffitiing political slogans across the walls. It was the culmination of months of grassroots protest by a section of the population who felt that both their way of life and their political vision were under threat. The country was split between those who sympathised with their actions, thinking of them as legitimate protestors, and those who condemned them as a mob, outraged by the illegality and violence of the occupation. Around the world, people watched in shock as footage of the events was broadcasted globally in real time, on both traditional news channels and social media.

This is what happened on Wednesday, January 6, 2021, at the US Capitol building, the seat of the American government in Washington, DC, when protestors tried to overturn the results of the recent presidential election and return their preferred candidate, Donald Trump, to power despite his defeat at the polls. This is also what happened on Monday, July 1, 2019, at the Legislative Council Complex in Hong Kong, when protestors sought to prevent the enactment of a controversial new bill that would ease political extraditions to mainland China. There were significant differences between the two events. One major difference was the level of violence involved—the storming of the US Capitol led to five deaths, including that of a policeman who was overpowered and beaten by the rioters,[2] while in contrast, no deaths were recorded as resulting from the storming of the Hong Kong legislature. There are also differences in the protestors' political aims—those in Hong Kong wanted more democracy, and those in America wanted less. Taken together, the two events illustrate how ideas about politics, civilisational identity, and the West are currently changing.

One of the people who must have watched closely the events at the

US Capitol building on January 6, 2021, was Carrie Lam, the chief executive of Hong Kong. At the time, Lam occupied a unique and unenviable position, tasked with administering a territory that had traditionally positioned itself as "the best of both the West and the East" (as per Lam's 2021 speech quoted at the start of this chapter). Hong Kong was part of the British empire for more than a century and a half, an experience that has left a deep imprint on both the culture of the city and the mindset of its people. Britain relinquished its colonial rule only relatively recently, in 1997, when Hong Kong became a special administrative region of the People's Republic of China, with a significant degree of autonomy and its own systems of political and economic governance. It is, as Lam herself has often acknowledged, a place where the cultural, political, social, and economic traditions of the West overlap and interact with those of China. At the start of her term of office in July 2017, Lam celebrated the idea that Hong Kong could encapsulate the best of both China and the West. By the end of it in June 2022, it seemed that such deliberate biculturalism would no longer be possible. The world has changed, and the historical imaginings of both China and the West with it.

As we move into the middle of the twenty-first century, China is the most obvious of the West's various rivals. Much ink has already been spilled discussing the economic, political, and military aspects of this rivalry, and in particular the tensions between China on the one hand and the USA and the Anglosphere on the other.[3] There is another aspect of this relationship, however, which has attracted less attention. This is the divergence between the two geopolitical blocs in terms of the grand historical narratives they espouse and promote. Each has its own vision of global history, and each has its own model for the relationships between cultures and civilisations.

Wars between World(views)

The West no longer bestrides the world in unchallenged global hegemony as it did in the nineteenth and early twentieth centuries (Chapter 12). The West now has rivals.

By a "rival" of the West, I do not simply mean an individual, organisation, or state that positions itself as anti-Western. The West in the twenty-first century is a large-scale, supranational power bloc, containing within it many states that do not always see eye to eye and may on occasion also be competitors, but that nonetheless share a broad overall global outlook and conscious sense of identity. A rival to the West must therefore be comparable—a geopolitical grouping large enough to stand outside the Western-dominated international system, with an alternative international system of its own. For this reason, individual states such as North Korea that lie outside the Western-dominated international community cannot be considered rivals to the West. It is a question of scale—North Korea is simply too small to be a viable global challenger, despite its nuclear capacities.

During the first two decades of the twenty-first century, one external threat often discussed in Western media was militant Islam, and in particular two organisations that both styled themselves as rivals to the West—Al Qaeda and the so-called Islamic State. The idea of militant Islam as a would-be rival to the West erupted violently into the global public consciousness on September 11, 2001. Al Qaeda operatives staged coordinated terrorist attacks in the United States by hijacking commercial airplanes and deliberately crashing them into busy public buildings and key government complexes. These attacks killed thousands, and scarred the lives of many more. Yet rather than sowing fear and disunity within America, and rather than weakening the United States' standing in the world community, they instead resulted in the opposite.

The American president at the time, George W. Bush, declared a "war on terror,"[4] and within a month, declared war on the regime that had sheltered Al Qaeda, the Taliban of Afghanistan, at the head of a broad-based international coalition. This coalition eventually included not just many Western countries but also several countries not always considered to be part of the West, such as Russia, Egypt, Jordan, Bahrain, the United Arab Emirates, Uzbekistan, Japan, and the Republic of Korea. Although some of its members had originally helped to install the Taliban in Afghanistan as a bulwark against communism, the Western-led coalition now overturned the regime, installing a new pro-Western government. But this quick win was not consolidated into a lasting peace. The coalition would spend the next twenty years fighting a bloody guerrilla war in Afghanistan, and when American forces finally withdrew from the country in summer 2021, they left it in poverty and chaos, once again under the control of the Taliban. Despite opposition from within their own countries, Western leaders opened a second front in the "war on terror" with the invasion of Iraq in March 2003, on the basis of claims (later disproved) that it had weapons of mass destruction capable of striking targets in the West at short notice. The course of the Iraq War paralleled in some ways that of the Afghanistan War, with rapid victory and the installation of a pro-Western government followed by a protracted period of insurgency and civil war. By May 2011, however, Al Qaeda had been largely neutralised.

Yet out of the civil war in Iraq emerged a new would-be challenger to the West—the Islamic State of Iraq and Syria, sometimes known by its English acronym, ISIS, or by the term "Daesh," derived from its Arabic acronym and used pejoratively by its critics within the Arab world.[5] In 2014, the organisation began to style itself as a caliphate, claiming to be an alternative international system that was independent of and ideologically opposed to the West. This system was neither global (the reach of Daesh was always geographically limited), nor stable (Daesh was defeated militarily and collapsed within five years), nor entirely independent of the West (for funds, Daesh relied on the export of gas, oil, phosphate, and cement).[6] Yet it claimed, for a short time, to be a rival to the West. At its peak, Daesh controlled most of Iraq north of Baghdad and all but the coastal areas of Syria, and threatened the borders of Turkey. It also laid claim to a number of "provinces" in regions of the Sinai Peninsula, Libya, Yemen, Afghanistan, and Nigeria. Supporters poured in from across the world, eager to fight for the so-called caliphate and to start new lives in what they believed would be a fully religious society. Daesh's success was short-lived. Over the course of 2016 and 2017, it was pushed back by an international coalition of states from Europe, western and central Asia, and Africa, as well as Kurdish fighters who provided most of the "boots on the ground." Like Al Qaeda, Daesh might have aimed to challenge the West but succeeded in uniting both Western and non-Western countries against it. In the first months of 2019, the final remnants of its army were besieged and defeated at Baghuz, a town on the Iraqi-Syrian border.

Militant Islamism might never have been a serious rival to the West on a global scale or in the long term, but it did develop its own civilisational narratives. It embraced the narrative of Western Civilisation as a continuity, stretching back through the medieval Crusades to Greek and Roman antiquity. In a famous speech released by the news agency Al Jazeera on January 6, 2004, the leader of Al Qaeda, Osama bin Laden, called on Muslims around the world to join the militant Islamist cause and to "resist the new Rome" and the "crusader-Zionist onslaught." They should not be, he exhorted, like the ancient Arab dynasty of the Ghassanids, who were "appointed kings and officers for the Romans in order to safeguard the interests of the Romans by killing their brothers, the peninsula's Arabs." Instead, he argued that "honest people concerned about this situation should meet away from the shadow of these oppressive regimes and declare a general mobilisa-tion to prepare for repulsing the raids of the Romans."

Daesh also chose to label its Western enemies as Romans, or "Rum," following the medieval Arabic usage of the term to encompass Byzantine Christians as well as the followers of the Latin church. One of the factors behind the initial growth and success of the organisation was a strong online presence, allowing its leaders to reach audiences far beyond its territorial limits.[7] It published several online magazines in different languages aimed at encouraging Muslims around the world to engage in terrorism. Articles included instructions for bomb making in your kitchen, ways of encrypting messages, and the right kind of vehicle to choose for a vehicle attack. The flagship magazine aimed at an Anglophone audience between 2014 and 2016 was called *Dabiq*, a name drawn from a prophecy by the prophet Muhammad and recorded in one of the Hadiths, which foretells an apocalyptic battle between Muslims and the Rum.[8] In 2016, however, a new Anglophone magazine was launched, entitled *Rumiyah* (*Rome*) as a reference to a prophecy that Muslims would one day defeat and conquer the Roman Empire. Each issue featured the following epigraph: "O muwahhidin [believers], rejoice, for by Allah, we will not rest from our jihad except beneath the olive trees of Rumiyah."[9] These magazines echo the narra-tive of Western Civilisation, although they adopt a hostile rather than a celebratory tone, claiming, "The Roman Empire never fully fell, but merely adopted new names."[10]

This "clash of civilisations" narrative was one of the reasons for Daesh's policy of destruction and vandalism when it came to ancient sites, monuments, and artefacts.[11] Although artefacts and archaeologi-cal remains of all periods of the "idolatrous" pre-Islamic past were at-tacked,[12] there was a particular interest in destroying Greco-Roman antiquities because of their association with the birth of Western Civ-ilisation (of course, this did not prevent Daesh from sometimes seeking financial gain by the sale of illicit antiquities).[13] The topic attracted a lot of attention in the Western press, in particular Daesh's actions in May 2015 when they ransacked the ancient city of Palmyra, a UNESCO World Heritage site and one of the most famous ruins of Mediterranean antiquity. International outrage focused on the destruction with dynamite of the Temple of Bel, the Roman theatre, and other buildings, as well as on the murder of Khaled al-Assad, the site's chief archaeologist.[14]

After Daesh was evicted from Palmyra, its ruins proved to be valuable political capital once more. A scale replica of the triumphal arch was erected in London's Trafalgar Square "in defiance against the barbarians."[15] An international campaign has now been launched to rebuild the Temple of Bel at Palmyra, led in particular by the German Archaeological Institute, in what is being described as an act of "cultural defiance" and "combative reproduction." While this may be in some senses appealing, my own feelings on this point align with those of my colleague in Vienna Professor Andreas Schmidt-Colinet, who excavated at Palmyra for decades and was a personal friend of the murdered archaeologist Khaled al-Assad—any international aid and funding that can be spent at Palmyra should go first to meet the needs of the living community, who should also be consulted on the plans regarding the reconstruction of the site.[16]

It was not just Western politicians and commentators, however, who saw the ruins of ancient Palmyra as a political symbol. A few months after the expulsion of Daesh from the site, the Russian National Symphony Orchestra staged a concert, in May 2016, which included the screening of a video where the Russian president, Vladimir Putin, thanked Russian soldiers for the "rescue of ancient culture" (referring to the parts of the ancient city that still remained standing), a feat that he claimed that "the West was not capable of doing."[17] Such rhetoric is part of a wider discourse of Russia as a rival to the West—a discourse that is familiar from the Cold War in the twentieth century. But in the twenty-first century, it is a discourse that has gained a new lease on life.[18]

This started as early as April 2005, when Putin encouraged Russians to look back on the Soviet Union with nostalgia, saying that its collapse was "the major geopolitical disaster of the century."[19] Since then, he has often evoked the Soviet era as a time of Russian greatness, during which Russia was in a position of strength in relation to the West, and explicitly stated his aim of a return to this situation. Over the last decade and a half, Putin has sought to ramp up anti-Western rhetoric, rekindle national pride in the Soviet past, and reassert Russian influence over countries that had once been members of the Soviet Union—most obviously with the 2022 invasion of Ukraine. As early as 2008, some Western commentators were suggesting that the Putin era marked the beginning of a new Cold War.[20]

As well as the political, military, and economic rivalry between Russia and the West, there is also an opposition in terms of historical grand narratives. In July 2021, just months before launching his invasion of Ukraine, Putin published an extended historical essay on the Kremlin's website in Russian, English, and Ukrainian, titled "On the Historical Unity of Russians and Ukrainians."[21] In it, he argues that Russians and Ukrainians are essentially "one people—a single whole."[22] The basis of this unity, he asserts, lies in a shared language, the shared religion of Russian Orthodoxy, and common culture—all of which stem from a long and glorious shared history. This shared history, he argues, negates the idea of a separate Ukrainian identity and nation. Belief in a distinct Ukrainian nation, Putin claims, has been brought about by a politicised rewriting of "real" history. Thanks to this ideological manipulation by "the Western authors of the anti-Russia project," people "are being forced not only to deny their roots, generations of their ancestors but also to believe that Russia is their enemy." But, Putin concludes, Russia will never allow one of its "historical territories" to be manipulated by the West into becoming "anti-Russia."

In the essay, Putin offers a sketch of what he considers to be a more accurate vision of history, claiming amongst other things that "Russians, Ukrainians, and Belarusians are all descendants of Ancient Rus, which was the largest state in Europe." The nation of Ancient Rus, Putin asserts, included all Slavic peoples and predates the arrival of Christianity. Putin positions the ancient state of Rus almost as comparable to the Roman and Byzantine Empires, suggesting that, "like other European states at the time, Ancient Rus faced a decline of central rule and fragmentation" during the medieval period, although "both the nobility and the common people perceived Rus as a common territory, as their homeland."

This is significant, given the revival of the idea of Russia as the "Third Rome," the successor to both the Roman and Byzantine Empires. Under this grand narrative of history, the lines of civilisational and imperial inheritance did not lead westwards from Rome to central and western Europe (and thence to the North Atlantic world and the wider Anglosphere), but rather eastwards—from the old first Rome to the second Rome of Constantinople, and thence to the glorious third Rome of Moscow. The idea of Moscow as the "Third Rome" first emerged in the sixteenth century, and was neatly summarised by Philotheus of Pskov, the head of a monastery in northwestern Russia, in a letter written in 1523 or 1524: "this is the Russian empire: because two Romes have fallen, but a third stands, and a fourth shall not be."[23] From the outset, the notion was linked both to imperialism (this was a period when Russian territorial expansion was gathering pace) and the Orthodox Church. When an independent Orthodox Patriarchate was established in Moscow in 1589, the decree establishing it made explicit reference to the "Third Rome": "For the old Rome fell through the

Apollinarian heresy [i.e., paganism]. The second Rome, which is Constantinople, is held by the grandsons of Hagar—the godless Turks. Pious Tsar! Your great Rus' tsardom, the Third Rome, has surpassed them all in piety."[24]

The notion of a Russian "Third Rome" gained momentum again in the late nineteenth century when Russian thinkers were seeking to position themselves distinctively in relation both to the Islamic and Asian East on one side, and the Catholic and Protestant West on the other.[25] (Indeed, as we have seen in Chapter 12, it was around this time that Russian authors began to use the term "the West" to refer to central and western Europe.) It is an idea that remained a literary constant throughout the modernist period, 1890–1940, despite the dramatic political changes that swept Russia during this time.[26] The idea is now resurfacing, albeit more subtly, in the Putin era. It was Putin who, in 2001, signed a federal law to create a new coat of arms for Russia. This coat of arms depicts the double-headed eagle of Byzantium, adopted by the tsars in the first "Third Rome" period, and it started to appear on rouble coins in 2016. And it was Putin's video statement, played during the Russian concert at the Roman theatre in Palmyra, that implicitly positioned Russia rather than the West as the rightful heir of classical antiquity.

The first rival of the West discussed in this chapter, militant Islamism, largely accepted the historical narrative of Western Civilisation, turning this narrative around as a means of attacking the West. The second rival of the West discussed so far, Russia, takes a somewhat different approach. It revises the cultural genealogy claimed by the narrative of Western Civilisation, offering a different view of the shape of history, with culture and civilisation moving in an eastern rather than a western direction. Yet it is the third rival to the West considered in this book, China, whose rise causing particular consternation amongst some Western political commentators.[27] And when it comes to historical grand narratives, China takes another approach altogether.

Parallel Civilisations

In the mid-twentieth century in China, there was much heated debate amongst historians concerning the overall shape of world history. When Marx wrote about the "Asiatic Mode of Production" in the 1850s, did he mean that Asia was destined to remain forever in a static state of development, evolving separately from the West along its own parallel civilisational trajectory? Or, as argued Lin Zhichun, a patriotic historian known as the "Red Professor," did the term "Asiatic Mode of Production" refer instead to a stage of economic development through which all societies must at some stage pass? According to Lin, China and the West shared a single historical trajectory and all world history, including the history that the West claimed for itself under the narrative of Western Civilisation, was relevant within a single universalising Marxist model.[28]

With this model of a shared world history, Lin promoted academic research into "Ancient World History," including within its scope not only ancient Chinese and Asian history, but also the study of ancient Greece and Rome. A national centre for this research was established at Northeast Normal University in Changchun in the early 1950s, and in the following decades Lin's grand narrative became increasingly influential in China, especially after the publication of his influential 1979 textbook, *An Outline of Ancient World History*.[29]

Yet a few decades later, the Chinese administration began to promote a different grand narrative of history.[30] Gone was the universal Marxist model of Lin, in which different peoples and countries move along the same global trajectory, albeit at different paces. Instead, this grand narrative envisions humanity as being divided into a number of separate civilisations, each running parallel and unchanging from the ancient past to the contemporary present. In current official government rhetoric, modern China is not the heir of ancient China, but rather its unchanging continuation. This is, in essence, an ahistorical model of history. It rejects ideas of civilisational transfer and transformation, and instead posits civilisational purity and essentialism.

Under this vision of history, China is not the only modern nation-state to embody an ancient civilisation. In April 2017, foreign ministers from ten different countries met in Athens and signed an agreement to establish a new international organisation. Its explicit aim was to use cultural diplomacy as a form of "soft and smart power" to strengthen bonds between their countries, as well as deploying culture "as an agent of economic growth."[31] The organisation was the Ancient Civilizations Forum, an initiative launched jointly by China and Greece, to which were invited representatives from eight other states that they deemed to have "great ancient civilisations"—Bolivia, Egypt, India, Iran, Iraq, Italy, Mexico, and Peru. Since its first meeting in Athens, the Ancient Civilizations Forum has held regular biannual meetings attended by each country's cultural minister, one meeting usually happening in New York on the side of a session of the UN General Assembly, and another in the capital city of one of its member states— La Paz in 2018;[32] Beijing in 2019, by which point Armenia had joined the group;[33] remotely due to the COVID-19 pandemic in both 2020 and 2021, but under the presidency of Peru;[34] and in Baghdad in 2022.[35]

The declaration signed at the first meeting of the forum described the ancient civilisation of each member state as "omnipresent" and "transcending time," asserting that their relevance "remains actual to this day." While these civilisations may therefore be ancient, the members of the forum nonetheless assert that they do not belong only in the past, but have continued their existence uninterrupted from antiquity to modernity. In his speech at the 2021 meeting, the Armenian deputy minister of foreign affairs, Vahe Gevorgyan, claimed: "What gathered us today and unites us is the vast history, culture, traditions and values of our ancient civilisations that we collected and accumulated throughout centuries."[36] Under this model, civilisations are timeless rather than dynamic, and culture is cumulative rather than changeable.

Not only can culture not be changed under this model, but there is also little room for it to be transferred. The idea of *translatio*, the transmission of culture between people across space and time, is central to the narrative of Western Civilisation, but has no place here. In the vision offered by this forum, the relationship between civilisations cannot be one of ancestry or lineage, with one population or group adopting cultural influences from another. Rather, "each individual culture"[37] remains a distinct and separate entity. Under the Chinese model, modern countries such as Germany, Britain, and the United States cannot claim a cultural inheritance from ancient Greece and Rome—instead, these ancient civilisations are seen as belonging exclusively to the modern nation-states of Greece and Italy.

Instead of cultural transfer, adoption, or inheritance, there is a preference for "dialogue between civilisations," as highlighted by the original declaration signed at that first meeting in Athens. The word "dialogue" here implies a certain detachment, avoiding cross-contamination between one civilisation and another. This principle was summed up by the Chinese foreign minister Wang Yi, in a comment to journalists at the first Athens meeting: "We should inherit our traditional cultures, remain confident, and respect and honour each others' social system and development path."[38] In other words, each civilisation should stay in its own lane. The ideology of the Ancient Civilizations Forum, therefore, sees different cultures as parallel and distinct, rather than being interrelated. Rather than cultural genealogy, the rationale of the group is cultural analogy—each "great ancient civilisation" is an analogue of the others: parallel and internally pristine.

While influence, inheritance, and transfer between civilisations are missing from this model, so too is civilisational clash and conflict. Indeed, speaking to the international press in the wake of the first forum meeting, the Iraqi foreign minister, Ibrahim al-Jaafari, said that the group fundamentally rejected the idea "put forward by several intellectuals of a clash of civilisations."[39] He even referred to the author of the infamous book *The Clash of Civilisations* by name, speaking with evident exasperation: "Samuel Huntington came to us with the clash of civilisations . . . What does this mean?" Respecting the diversity of civilisation is a principle that has also featured in the speeches of the Chinese President Xi Jinping, who has claimed that: "diversity among human civilisations is the fundamental characteristic of the world." And that: "Different nations and civilisations are rich in diversity and have their own distinct features. No one is superior or inferior to others."[40] Clashes between civilisations can be avoided, according to Xi and official Chinese policy, by promoting cultural "dialogues" and "mutual learning" through channels such as the Ancient Civilizations Forum.

Of all the forum's members, China seems to have been particularly concerned with developing cultural diplomacy with Greece—the two countries being described by Nikos Kotzias, the Greek foreign minister at the time, as the "twin engines" driving the establishment of the forum.[41] The level of official and state-sponsored engagement with antiquity across the two countries has intensified dramatically in recent years, with 2017 designated by mutual agreement as the year of Chinese-Greek cultural exchange. Museums in the two countries exchanged loan objects and organised travelling exhibitions, including: *EUREKA! Ancient Greek Science, Art and Technology Exhibition* at the China Science and Technology Museum, Beijing (November

2017–May 2018); the *Ancient Chinese Science and Technology* exhibition at the Herakleidon Museum, Athens (September–April 2018); *The Antikythera Shipwreck* at the Palace Museum, Forbidden City, Beijing (September–December 2018); and *From the Forbidden City: Imperial Apartments at Qianlong* at the Acropolis Museum, Athens (September 2018–February 2019). Theatre companies collaborated on the bilingual staging of traditional plays, including a production of *The Orphan of Zhao* in Athens (November 2018) and *Agamemnon* in Beijing (February–March 2019).

There has also been an increase in academic research drawing parallels between ancient Greece and China. The study of ancient Greece, often assumed in the West to be the preserve of Western scholars, is on the rise in Chinese universities.[42] Conferences have encouraged the study of "dialogue" between ancient Greece and ancient China, such as the *Spiritual Dialogue between Chinese and Ancient Greek Civilisation* conference, held in Beijing in January 2022 ahead of the Winter Olympic Games to great fanfare.[43] Academic interactions are also now being fostered by a formal cooperation agreement, signed in October 2021, designed to facilitate exchanges between Chinese and Greek universities, with a particular focus on comparative studies of the two ancient civilisations.[44]

The particular interest in China and Greece as parallel ancient civilisations in "dialogue" is no accident. When announcing the 2021 formal cooperation agreement between Greek and Chinese universities, the Greek minister for education stressed the apt nature of the connection, given that ancient Greece and ancient China were the "cradles of Western and Eastern civilisation respectively."[45] During the 2022 Spiritual Dialogue conference, new translations of ancient Greek texts in Chinese were celebrated because they enabled more Chinese scholars to deepen their "understanding of western civilisation and its historical origin," thereby providing "a comparative perspective of civilisation to rediscover the Chinese classical culture."[46] The parallel is considered to be especially important because ancient China and ancient Greece are thought to represent the "Eastern and Western spiritual cultures."[47]

While this interest in parallels and "dialogue" between ancient Greece and ancient China might seem very academic and of interest only to a few historical enthusiasts, it has some tangible, real-world implications. The cultural diplomacy has been accompanied by a strengthening of political and economic links between the two countries. In 2019, the Greek prime minister, Kyriakos Mitsotakis, visited a business trade fair in Shanghai, bringing with him more than sixty Greek businesspeople in search of economic opportunities. A few days later, Chinese president Xi Jinping made the return visit to Athens, also visiting Athens's port of Piraeus and the archaeological site of the Acropolis. And in May 2022, a series of grand celebrations were staged at the Chinese embassy in Athens to celebrate fifty years of diplomatic relations between China and Greece, culminating in a conference entitled China and Greece: From Ancient Civilisations to Modern Partnership.[48] This modern partnership dates from 2016, when a Chinese state–owned company bought a controlling stake in the port of Piraeus. As the first deep-sea port in the European Union that Asian ships reach on entering the Mediterranean, Piraeus immediately became a central linchpin in China's Belt and Road Initiative, and since then the Chinese state has cultivated a close interest in the Greek economy, drawing Greece closer into its cultural as well as economic embrace.[49]

The Belt and Road Initiative was launched in 2013 as a wide-ranging policy to develop infrastructural connections through Eurasia, reviving the "Silk Road Spirit" and drawing participating countries into closer economic and cultural relationships with China. At the time of writing, estimates place its costs in the region of US$50–100 million per year, and its membership as including more than eighty countries with a population of more than 4.4 billion people, or 63 percent of the world's population.[50] It is a manifestation of China's challenge to the global dominance of the West—a truly independent international network that is already beginning to rival the established Western-backed world order.

Although whether the Belt and Road Initiative is eventually successful may ultimately depend on economic incentives and political imperatives, cultural diplomacy—and in particular the rhetoric of parallel ancient civilisations—has proved a vital ideological tool, providing an imagined justification in the past for the actions of the present.[51] In the Athens Declaration, members of the Ancient Civilizations Forum (sometimes abbreviated in official documents as ACF) committed to "advancing the Belt and Road Initiative" with the aim of "enhancing the sustainable social and economic growth of each ACF member." The link between the forum and the extension of Chinese power was never anything but explicit, with Foreign Minister Wang issuing a statement that "the Ancient Civilisations Forum is in line with the 'Belt and Road' construction and can provide intellectual and cultural support and assistance to the joint construction of the 'Belt and Road.'"[52]

No grand narrative of history is ever innocent. Each is situated within its own particular historical and social context, and each contains within it (whether explicitly or implicitly) a political vision of the world. The grand narrative of Western Civilisation, as we have seen over the course of this book, emerged from a particular historical and social context in the mid-eighteenth century and contains within it a political vision that aligns with this context. The grand narrative of parallel civilisations currently being promoted by Chinese official policy is no different. It has emerged in the particular historical and social context of the early twenty-first century and carries within it a political vision—one that supports a Chinese-sponsored alternative to a Western-led international system.

The civilisational model established in this grand narrative posits that different civilisations should be understood in terms of comparisons, analogies, and parallels, rather than by change and transfer. While there the official rhetoric does encourage "dialogue" between civilisations, it nonetheless views these civilisations as pristine and eternal, with an unchanging essential core. Crucially, each civilisation is imagined as the exclusive preserve of a specific and unchanging population group, rooted in a specific and unchanging place. It is a model which sits ill at ease with the idea of combining culture, or merging East and West. It is therefore a model that offered precious little room for manoeuvre to Carrie Lam, the chief executive of Hong Kong from 2017 to 2022, whose personal vision, as quoted in the epigraph to this chapter, was of a Hong Kong that offered "extraordinary cultural experience that embraces the best of both the East and the West."[53]

Unlucky 777

Carrie Lam (Chinese name: Lam Cheng Yuet-ngor) has lived much of her life between two worlds, embracing both Chinese and Western traditions. The same is true of many of her generation who grew up in Hong Kong as subjects of the British Empire, taking for granted the unique blend of Chinese and Western culture within their city. It was a blend that persisted after the handover of Hong Kong back to China in 1997, but which has come under significant strain in the last decade or so.

Lam was born in Hong Kong in 1957 into a poor family, with her father working on ships to support his wife and five children.[54] Lam recalls living in a flat so small that there was no place where she could do her homework but on her bed. She nonetheless did well academically, attending a Catholic girls' school, where she received a Western-style education that instilled in her both a powerful work ethic and a strong sense of faith. She also seems to have been extremely competitive from the start. She has said she remembers crying only once as a child—when she found out that she did not score the top mark on a midterm examination. Years later, when asked in a radio interview how she responded to this setback, she replied with characteristic bullish assurance: "I took the No 1 place back."[55]

Lam discovered political interests in university, where she switched her focus from social work to sociology, because it allowed her better opportunities to engage in student politics. At this stage of her life, Lam claims to have been "anti-government," joining a sit-in protest at the government headquarters and helping to organise a student exchange with Tsinghua University in Beijing.[56] This rebelliousness was evidently only a passing phase, as on graduating in 1980, Lam took up a job in Hong Kong's civil service, later claiming that she hoped to bring about social change from inside the system.

Lam was remarkably able, and within two years had been sent to the University of Cambridge to take a diploma course in development studies targeted at high-ranking government administrators. There she met her future husband, Lam Siu-por, who was studying for his doctorate in mathematics. Within a few years, the couple had returned to Hong Kong and married—Lam Siu-por teaching at the Chinese University of Hong Kong and Lam herself returning to her civil service work, occupying a range of positions including several in Hong Kong's Finance Bureau. The next two decades were busy ones for the Lams, who were both building their careers as well as caring for their two sons. At the same time, the environment around them was one of tense uncertainty leading up to the political transition of 1997, when Hong Kong ceased to be a British colony and was handed back to China. Many Hong Kongers were suspicious of the "one country, two systems" policy that China had promised, and there was a wave of emigration, in particular to Britain and North America. Although the Lams remained in the city, they took the precaution of acquiring British citizenship through a scheme deliberately designed to allow people born in the colony as British nationals to be awarded full citizenship, including residency rights in mainland Britain.

Despite the fears, everything seemed to go smoothly in the years immediately after the handover, and in the new millennium Lam's career flourished.[57] She held a string of high-profile positions, including director for the Social Welfare Department from 2000 to 2003, permanent secretary for housing, planning, and lands from 2003 to 2004, and permanent secretary for home affairs between 2006 and 2007. She also returned to the United Kingdom between 2004 and 2006, where she served as director-general of the Hong Kong Economic and Trade Office in London. Given this return to the United Kingdom, the fact that both her sons studied at Cambridge, and the British citizenship held by all members of the family, we might conclude that until this point, Lam still saw herself as being part of both worlds—like Hong Kong itself, the beneficiary of two cultural traditions. Indeed, the family's ties with Britain were so close at this time that when Lam Siu-por retired from his post at the university, he chose to spend part of his retirement in Oxford.

His wife returned to Hong Kong, making a dramatic leap in her career, leaving the civil service to take on a role as a politician. No longer serving as an adviser and an administrator, from this point on Lam would be at the heart of government, making decisions about public policy. But the new job came at a personal cost. Lam had to renounce her British citizenship, thereby declaring her exclusive commitment to Hong Kong.

Lam's first political appointment was as the director of the Development Bureau. Here, she gained herself a reputation as a "tough fighter" who brooked no compromise, pushing through controversial development projects.[58] Despite suggesting that she would retire to join her family in Britain at the end of this first political term in 2012, Lam remained in Hong Kong and was appointed chief secretary for the administration—the second-most powerful position in government, after that of the chief executive. Ideologically, she became increasingly aligned with Beijing, introducing a series of controversial policies that would bring Hong Kong into closer alignment with the Chinese mainland, eroding the promise of "one country, two systems." Lam first attempted to introduce a new school syllabus for Moral and National Education in 2012, meeting with considerable opposition from teachers, students, and pro-democracy groups, who were wary of the ideological elements of the new syllabus. The opposition was so great that Lam had to put the implementation of the syllabus on hold, to concentrate on another controversial issue—constitutional reform.

Hong Kong's complex electoral system means that only some lawmakers are directly elected by the general public; the others are selected by the institutional votes cast by representatives of different sectors within the economy and by the Election Committee, a body of unelected individuals drawn from business, civil society, and religious organisations, as well as political appointees. Pro-democracy groups demanding change were growing ever more vociferous, and between 2013 and 2015 Lam led a task force to address the issue. The pro-democracy campaigners were further outraged in August 2014 when she announced a new system for the appointment of the chief executive in which all candidates would need to be approved by an unelected nominating committee.

The protests that subsequently filled the streets culminated in a seventy-seven-day occupation of sites in the city centre. Known as the Umbrella Movement due to the protesters' use of umbrellas to shield themselves from the tear gas and pepper spray used by the police, these protests captured the popular imagination, not only in Hong Kong but also in the West, where significant support was expressed for their cause. Lam, however, remained resolute, eventually ordering the police to break up the occupation. Yet for all her "tough fighter" tactics, Lam was not in the end able to implement the reform, as, mindful of the popular protests as well as international condemnation, the Legislative Council voted against it.

In the wake of this failure, the administration was ruthless in prosecuting those they identified as the main troublemakers, and leaders of the protests were sentenced to short prison sentences. These protestors belonged to an idealistic new generation, born in the boom years after the handover, but who now found themselves facing a future of unaffordable housing and declining job prospects. It is a generation struggling to find a distinct Hong Kong identity, with ambivalent feelings about both their city's old colonial ties to Britain and its current national ties to mainland China.[59] Many members of these new youth movements were extremely young. Joshua Wong and Agnes Chow, leading figures of their generation, were both aged only fifteen when they established the activist group Scholarism and started to protest against the Moral and National Education bill and had not yet turned eighteen when they joined the Umbrella protests. Wong would serve his first prison term in 2017 at the age of twenty-one as a result of these protests.[60]

By 2017, when the election for the chief executive was held, Lam was already a figure of hate for many pro-democracy campaigners. But she still commanded the respect and support of many within Hong Kong, especially businesspeople and establishment figures who saw her as a safe pair of hands. Despite her failure to enact either the constitutional reform or the new school syllabus, she was also Beijing's pre-ferred candidate, and this may have given her the extra edge she needed to land the top job. Lam won a clear victory in the 2017 chief executive elections, with a total of 777 out of the available 1,194 votes of the Election Committee. The number of votes immediately prompted derision from her detractors, as in Cantonese the number "seven" is pronounced *chāt*—sounding remarkably like *chat*, which is slang for an impotent penis.[61] Although she must have been pleased finally to be in the top job, Lam cannot have been so happy with her new nickname—777.

Her inability to push through either the Moral and National Education Act or the planned constitutional reform must indeed have seemed like two cases of political impotence, and Lam was determined to avoid living up to her unflattering nickname. A new wave of popular protests broke out in March 2019, in response to a law that would make it much easier to extradite political dissidents from Hong Kong to the Chinese mainland. The scale of these protests was greater than anything Lam had faced before. Yet despite hundreds of thousands of protestors coming out regularly onto the streets (estimates of the numbers vary, but it has even been suggested that more than a million people attended one of the marches in June 2019), Lam remained unbowed and unapologetic. It was not until October that the law was eventually rescinded, following sit-ins at universities and the airport, as well as the storming of the Legislative Council Chamber on July 1, with which we started this chapter. Lam had been forced to back down for a third time.

In early 2020, the COVID-19 pandemic put Hong Kong's political struggles on pause, as it did to so many other things across the world. In June, during the relative quiet of the lockdown, a new National Security Law was passed, granting the government wide-ranging powers to imprison for life those convicted of fomenting "secession, subversion, terrorism, and collusion with foreign forces," as well as those deemed guilty of "inciting hatred of the central government and Hong Kong's regional government." Administration of this law is to be overseen by officials appointed from the mainland, in a process that will be independent of the normal Hong Kong judicial system. With the city under strict COVID regulations and the details of the new law not disclosed until after it had been passed, Lam could finally chalk up a victory. To cap it off, this was not just any victory; it was a victory that shattered the opposition. The pro-democracy opposition party Demosistō was disbanded on June 30, the same day the National Security Law went into force, to save its members from prosecution and the risk of life-long imprisonment. Arrests spiked, with many prominent critics of the administration being prosecuted. Joshua Wong and Agnes Chow, still only in their mid-twenties, were sentenced to thirteen and ten months of imprisonment, respectively

A bill of constitutional reform was also quietly passed in May 2021, drastically reducing the number of positions on the Legislative Council filled by popular vote, with half of lawmakers now to be chosen by the unelected Election Committee. At the same time, the proportion of seats in the Election Committee filled by Beijing political appointees has been increased and the bill states that only "patriots" will be permitted to participate in government.[62] Considering the political turmoil that characterised her term and the widespread dissatisfaction with her administration's handling of the COVID-19 pandemic, few were surprised in May 2022 when Lam announced that she would not be standing for a second term. She was succeeded in the role on July 1, 2022, by John Lee, a former police officer who stood as the only candidate in the chief executive election, and who had received the official endorsement of Beijing.

Lam herself remains an elusive figure. She has given relatively few interviews to the media, and her speeches have rarely betrayed any trace of personal emotion. A notable exception came in the summer of 2019, when Lam faced the largest protests of her career. During a television address in mid-August, she broke down crying while appealing to the protestors to give up their cause.[63] Although colleagues claimed that she was genuinely "quite shaken" by the personal nature of the criticism she received, her opponents accused her of shedding crocodile tears in a strategy to win sympathy. Whatever the truth behind the tears, Lam's style became more muted from this point on. Journalists and diplomats working in Hong Kong noted that she became increasingly formal in her interactions, her conversation and pronouncements carefully mirroring the language favoured by Beijing.[64] Just a few days after her breakdown on television in August 2019, Lam made a telling slip in a rare unguarded moment speaking to business leaders. She reflected that "the room, the political room for the chief executive who, unfortunately, has to serve two masters by constitution, that is the central people's government and the people of Hong Kong, that political room for manoeuvring is very, very, very limited."[65]

This brief statement cuts to the heart of the problem. For many years, Lam had belonged on a personal level to two worlds simultaneously— that of the East and that of the West. Indeed, she began her career in an environment where such pluralism was not only possible, but encouraged. As a younger woman, she and her family moved between Britain and Hong Kong, operating in a bicultural manner that was evidently seen as desirable by Lam's employers in the Hong Kong administration. This biculturalism seems also to have been central to Lam's vision for Hong Kong.

Throughout her term as chief executive, Lam did her best to position Hong Kong as a place where Eastern and Western cultures met. The epigraph at the start of this chapter comes from a speech Lam gave in November 2021 to mark the opening of M+, a new museum of contemporary visual culture that Lam hoped would give visitors an "extraordinary cultural experience that embraces the best of both the East and the West."[66] M+ is situated within the West Kowloon Cultural

District—a long-anticipated development that featured in her manifesto when she campaigned for chief executive in 2017, where she promised that "the development of the West Kowloon Cultural District will be expedited to underline Hong Kong's position as a cultural hub" (manifesto paragraph 5:44). When Lam addressed the business community in June 2021 on the subject of Hong Kong's role within China's latest five-year economic plan, she told them with satisfaction that Hong Kong was poised to be "a hub for arts and cultural exchanges between China and the rest of the world."[67] This idea of Hong Kong as a venue for cultural exchange recurred through Lam's speeches and policy documents, and it was through the arts and culture above all that she sought to make Hong Kong "an East-meets-West cultural hub."[68]

Lam's hopes of making Hong Kong the best of both worlds, a harmonious hybrid of East and West, was doomed. By the time she took office in April 2017, Chinese policy and the model of parallel civilisations that underpinned it had already been established. Indeed, by coincidence, the first meeting of the Ancient Civilizations Forum had been convened just days before Lam's election as chief executive. In the summer of 2019, it became evident that it was no longer possible for Lam to straddle both worlds, meeting both the demands of Beijing on the one side and those of the pro-Western, pro-democracy protestors on the other. Just as on a personal level Lam had been forced to choose either her British or her Chinese citizenship when she entered public office, the city of Hong Kong as a whole could no longer belong to both East and West simultaneously. Under China's new civilisational model, the city had to belong to one civilisation or another. Cultural transfer, change, and merging was simply not an option.

———————

CHINA AS A whole, Hong Kong in particular, and Carrie Lam personally now all operate under a grand narrative that differs not only in content from that of Western Civilisation, but also in terms of its fundamental structure. Where Daesh embraced a mirror image of the grand narrative of Western Civilisation, and Russia seeks to rewrite it, China has opted to ignore it entirely, creating an entirely independent and qualitatively different model of civilisational history. Rather than seeing a world where civilisation is transferred, inherited, or passed down through a cultural lineage, China sees a world where civilisations are parallel, pristine, and unchanging. This is not only a very different global conception of the present from that imagined in the West, but also a very different model for the shape of history.

This matters for two reasons. The first is that it demonstrates that radically different ways of imagining the shape of history are possible. We have encountered various different grand narratives in this book, with different people drawing the lines of civilisational inheritance in different ways at different times: from Greece to Baghdad by al-Kindī in the ninth century (Chapter 3); from Troy to Rome to central Europe by Godfrey of Viterbo in the twelfth (Chapter 4); from Greece to western Europe and thence to North America by Joseph Warren in the eighteenth (Chapter 10); and from Rome to Byzantium to Moscow by Philotheus of Pskov in the sixteenth (as noted earlier). Yet the grand narrative of parallel civilisations currently being promoted in Chinese state rhetoric posits something entirely and qualitatively different. It offers an ahistorical model of history, positing permanence rather than transformation, accumulation rather than transmission, and an essential and unchanging relationship between a distinct population group, a place, and a civilisation. The idea of such civilisational essentialism runs counter to the available archaeological and historical evidence (as we have noted from the introduction of this book onwards, incontrovertible factual evidence for cultural interactions and transfers is widely documented). This is therefore a vision of history which, like that of Western Civilisation, is inconsistent with the facts as we currently understand them. Yet the very existence of these radically divergent models tells us something. It should prompt all of us, both within and without the West, to question the narratives that we usually take for granted, and to think more openly about the types of narratives that we might possibly build for the future.

China's model of parallel civilisations also tells us something significant about the shape of Western history specifically. The canonical lineage of Western Civilisation is, as we have seen in this book, wrong. But it does have something in common with the other equally wrong civilisational genealogies that we have examined. All of them are predicated on the principles of transmissibility and mobility, relying on the movement of cultural elements between different people and different places. When compared with the Ancient Civilizations Forum grand narrative of stable and parallel civilisations, the common emphasis on civilisational transfer emerges more clearly. Rather than stability, there is change. Rather than accumulation, there is transfer. And rather than continuity, there is variation.

Transmissibility and mobility therefore lie at the heart of all the grand narratives of civilisational inheritance that are enmeshed, in one way or another, with the idea of the West. In all of these narratives, civilisation moves. It moves between people, so that no single population can claim a monopoly on it. It moves between places, so that it belongs exclusively to no single location. Indeed, if we had to identify a kernel at the center of Western Civilisation—a core essence—then this would not be any particular set of cultural traits or ethno-racial characteristics. Rather, the beating heart of Western Civilisation would instead be the principles of cultural transmissibility and mobility. It is around these core principles that a new vision of Western identity should be conjured and a new grand narrative of Western history should be written.

THE SHAPE OF HISTORY

ISTORY is not, in the words attributed to British historian
Arnold Toynbee, just "one damn thing after another." There
certainly are a lot of "damn things" in history, of course—
individual facts that are objectively and verifiably true about the past.
But there is more to history than this. While individual facts should
always be at its foundation, how we select those facts—which we
deem important enough for inclusion and which we discard as less
important—is subjective, and how we order them into chains of causation is even more so. The shape of history is different depending on
your vantage point.

The choice of *who* represents the history of the West is certainly subjective. The ancestors selected by Ainsworth Rand Spofford still adorn
the Library of Congress in Washington, DC, and Francis Bacon decided
which putative forefathers would stand in his imaginary gallery in Bensalem. The biographies I have presented to you in this book are ones I
have selected, based on my own personal experiences and interests. I
imagine that you might select differently should you undertake a similar exercise. This book is therefore necessarily my own subjective interpretation of Western history, focused not on "great men," like those of
Spofford and Bacon, but rather on individuals whose lives I feel encap-
sulated something of the Zeitgeist of their age. But as subjective as this

book is, it is at the same time based on facts. I have, to the best of my ability from the available evidence, compiled facts about these fourteen lives and presented them as a set of discrete biographies. I have then used these biographies to sketch out the basis for a richer and more diverse narrative of Western history that is, to my knowledge, consistent with the facts that we have about the past. This is in stark contrast to the traditional grand narrative of Western Civilisation, which has long been disproved on a factual basis and yet continues to be reproduced in popular culture and political rhetoric.

As we noted in the introduction of this book, origins matter. The grand narrative of Western Civilisation posits that the origins of the West lie in the Greco-Roman world, and modern political rhetoric has made much use of these imagined origins. Yet by examining the life and work of Herodotus, we have found that the ancient Greeks constructed civilisational identities in complex and often contrasting ways. They did not conceive of themselves as predominantly white or European and did not consider themselves to be fundamentally distinct from the peoples of Asia and Africa—Asian Greeks and African Greeks were just as Hellenic as those who happened to live in what we now call Europe. The idea of an unbridgeable civilisational gulf was also alien in the time of Livilla and the early Roman Empire. Claiming descent from Asian Troy and ruling an empire that spanned three continents, the Romans would have objected to being pigeonholed as belonging exclusively to the West. Yet the mirage persists of the Greco-Roman world as a single coherent entity, European geographically and white racially, despite its having been comprehensively disproved. Even those of us who recognise the fallacy of this almost cartoonish notion, acknowledging instead a more diverse antiquity, are conditioned to think of the Greek and Roman worlds as set apart and "classical," aligning them with a particularly Western identity.

It is the grand narrative of Western Civilisation which posits that the origins of the West lie in a culturally pure and internally coherent Greco-Roman world, also asserting that this Greco-Roman world was the exclusive heritage of the West. Once more, this is demonstrably false. In the time of al-Kindī, legacies from Greek and Roman antiquity could be found from Britain in the northwest to Afghanistan in the east as well as Sudan in the south. At the heart of the Islamic world, ancient Greece was viewed as an important cultural ancestor, while in western and central Europe, a separate Roman antiquity was claimed. The writings of Godfrey of Viterbo and Theodore Laskaris illustrate how Roman antiquity was understood as something separate from and fundamentally opposed to Greek antiquity. For them, the notion of a united Christendom rang hollow in the face of bloody and protracted confessional disputes, and the concept of Europe as a single cultural zone would have seemed ridiculous. Their belief in the Latin tradition being entirely different from and antithetical to the Greek was part of a civilisational perspective that was markedly different from that of the modern West.

The conventional story of Western Civilisation then recounts how Europe rediscovered its classical roots during the Renaissance, reviving traditions that had lain dormant. Yet a closer look suggests otherwise. Renaissance thinkers and writers such as Tullia D'Aragona did not revive old traditions so much as create new ones, and were less passively influenced by antiquity than actively involved in its appropriation. While they might have fused the Greek and Roman worlds into a single conceptual entity, they did not imagine this entity as firmly bounded, untouched by influence from other ancient cultures. Although the foundations for Western cultural identity were indeed therefore laid during the Renaissance, the grand narrative of Western Civilisation had not yet taken hold. Even in the early modern period it was still possible to imagine configurations of global geopolitics that aligned Protestantism with Islam in opposition to Catholic central Europe, appealing to an imaginary shared Trojan heritage that rejected the notion of a conjoined Greco-Roman antiquity. Yet the time of Safiye Sultan was perhaps the last moment when such things were possible. With the opening of the seventeenth century, a new world order (and with it, a new conception of world history) was ushered in.

We associate Francis Bacon with the aphorism that "knowledge is power," and from this point onwards the West began to take shape as a coherent entity, held together not only by new Enlightenment ways of thinking but also by an increasingly asymmetrical set of power relationships with the rest of the world. The notion of a common Western identity rooted in a conjoined Greco-Roman antiquity had become entrenched, but was thrown into sharper focus with European expansion and imperialism. Yet the boundaries of this Western identity remained permeable. For individuals such as Njinga of Angola in the late seventeenth century, it was still possible to assume some of the elements of Western identity through conversion to Christianity, and to be viewed through the lens of Greco-Roman antiquity by some Western commentators as a result.

While the grand narrative of Western Civilisation had therefore begun to coalesce in the seventeenth century, it was not until the mid-eighteenth that it crystallized into a fimer form, honed to meet the ideological needs of the American Revolution and popularised so that it became part of the wider public consciousness. In the speeches of men such as Joseph Warren, the idea of the West became closely linked to the new United States of America, whose independence could be partly justified by the notion that it was the historical culmination of Western Civilisation. At the same time, the racialisation of Western Civilisation served to maintain the inequalities that had existed within the old colonial system, and in particular the racial hierarchies that worked in favour of white elites, barring both the native Americans and enslaved Africans and their descendants from power. While individuals like Phillis Wheatley therefore may have engaged with "classical" high culture, the racialised grand narrative of Western Civilisation meant that they were not usually perceived as legitmate heirs to the Greco-Roman heritage.

The writings of William Gladstone furnish an example of how the idea of Western Civilisation operated at its height. It is at this point, in the nineteenth century, when we see the narrative articulated most clearly and powerfully, and indeed when it explicitly received the label of "Western Civilisation." It was imagined as a purely European and racially white cultural lineage, ultimately derived from ancient Greece and Rome without contamination or blemish from "inferior" cultures, but later shaped by Christianity. At the time, given the global dominance of the West, it served both as an origin myth and as a charter for empire.

Questioning this narrative became more common only later, in the second half of the twentieth century. Edward Said was a key figure in launching the challenge, posing difficult questions of the West and revealing the constructed nature of its history. It is a process that is still underway today, and of which this book is a part. The political importance of grand narratives of history and their constructed nature is currently demonstrated by developments in China. The current administration is cultivating its own system of global geopolitics, its own model of civilisational relations, and, unsurprisingly its own grand narrative of world history. A new grand narrative is being promoted not only by China but also by its partners in the Ancient Civilizations Forum. Under this grand narrative of parallel civilisations, cultures cannot blend or merge, inherit or transfer elements. Rather, they endure, solid and stable, through history. This is a static and ahistorical model, positing that both people and culture should be conceived of as belonging to a fixed place and indeed even a fixed political structure—the modern nation state. This model is fundamentally different from the various imagined genealogies recounted in the different historical visions of the West. In Western-related grand narratives, culture is transmissible, moving between peoples and places (although of course the specifics of the people and places vary between different accounts). At their core, these narratives see civilisation as both transferable and mobile. Given this fundamental incompatibility of civilisational models, Carrie Lam's vision of a Hong Kong that encompassed both East and West would always have been problematic.

Where does the West go from here? There are some within the West who would have us go backwards, who peddle a nostalgia for a time long gone. Such nostalgia can be dangerous.[2] The grand narrative of Western Civilisation was constructed and popularised over the course of the seventeenth to nineteenth centuries because it served a particular ideological function. It provided an origin myth for the West—an ideological tool that justified domination and rationalized subjugation on the basis of an elevated and glorious past. Yet this ideological function is now defunct. Most people in the modern West no longer want an origin myth that serves to support racial oppression or imperial hegemony.

As a result, attempts have been made to make the narrative of Western Civilisation fit better with modern Western principles of liberal democracy: emphasizing the democracy of classical Athens; the early modern development of religious toleration; and the Enlightenment celebration of individual freedoms as underpinning contemporary ideals of social liberalism, for example. Yet these attempts have often proved problematic, given the nature of the basic historical material. Classical Athens may have been partly democratic, but it was also racist, imperialist, and sexist, and relied on enslavement. Early modern religious toleration emerged with the Treaty of Westphalia only after horrific wars, bloodshed, and cruelty; and even then did not succeed in ending religious conflict in Europe. And Enlightenment personal freedoms were not always equally applied to all humans, with significant exclusions made on grounds of race and sex. While individual elements and strands within it have been successfully rethought, the grand narrative of Western Civilisation as a whole cannot be adjusted to suit twenty-first-century sensibilities. It is an origin myth that was crucial for the West in the past, but which no longer serves the West in the present.

There are people who argue otherwise, some of whom are in the front line of the culture wars mentioned in the introduction of this book. Once thought of as belonging to the far right, such people have now entered the political mainstream, and they include in their number prominent commentators, campaigners, politicians, and even the heads and ex-heads of some Western states. These people would prefer to turn back the clock on the West, to undo much of the last century of social change, and to restore the West to its supposed glory days of world domination. Those self-styled defenders of the West should actually be numbered amongst its attackers. As pointed out in recent studies on the rise of illiberalism in the West,[3] these people actually stand against the principles at the heart of the contemporary West, promoting instead the outdated principles of a West that belongs firmly in the past. And when they call in shrill tones for us to mount a defence of Western Civilisation, they are, in reality, calling for us to rally to the defence of a morally bankrupt fiction.

Some of these voices can be heard in the current debates about my own academic field, where we are experiencing our own miniature version of these wider culture wars. If origins matter, then the way that we study Greco-Roman antiquity as the imagined origins of the West matter a great deal to the way the West thinks about itself. There are those who seek to uphold a traditional notion of "the Classics" as limited purely to the study of a pristine Greek and Roman antiquity, based on the notion that in them lie the origins of Western Civilisation, their literature and culture being the heritage of the modern West.[4] There are also those who seek to eradicate the discipline entirely, objecting to its historical complicity in systems of oppression, exploitation, and White supremacy.

There are also those (and I count myself amongst their number) who advocate for a reimagining of the field.[5] We acknowledge the problematic history and status of "Classics" as a field of scholarship and accept that we who work within the field have a responsibility to dismantle the various systems of racial, gendered, and class-based discrimination (as well as other forms of discrimination) that still exist within it. But above all, we are committed to uncovering and communicating how diverse, exciting, and colourful antiquity really was—much more so than acknowledged by the grand narrative of Western Civilisation. Our appreciation of Homeric epic is enriched when we realise that it re-imagined themes and motifs from Mesopotamian and Hittite poetry. Our knowledge of Roman religion is deepened when we examine the complex syncretisms that emerged between Roman cults and those of Iron Age Europe. And we gain a much more sophisticated understanding of fifth-century Athens if we consider how engaging in anti-Persian rhetoric went hand in hand with adopting Persian material culture and artistic styles. Like Herodotus, we argue that the most historically accurate (as well as the most interesting) way of studying the ancient world is by embracing it in all of its dizzying diversity.

The debates over "Classics" as an academic field carry wider significance because of the special status that Greco-Roman antiquity has in the grand narrative of Western Civilisation, as the supposed birthplace and imagined point of origin of the West. Moving forward, the West needs to discard the old grand narrative of Western Civilisation and to stop thinking of Greco-Roman antiquity as its singular and pristine origin. It needs to set up a new grand narrative of Western history—one that is, I would hope, a bit closer to the historical facts as we know them. These facts point to a narrative that is more complex, yet all the richer for this complexity; diverse, thereby inviting inclusivity; and crucially characterised by dynamism, thereby embracing change. This narrative, I suggest, aligns more easily with the liberal, pluralistic, and democratic values embraced by many in the West than the grand narrative of Western Civilisation.

This book is not an attack on the West. Instead, I would argue that it is a celebration of the West and its central principles. These principles come into sharper focus when we compare the various genealogies of the West explored in this book with the model of ahistorical parallel civilisations currently being promoted by the Ancient Civilizations Forum and Chinese official rhetoric. Dynamism, innovation, and the creative reimagining of the past—these characterised the *Histories* of Herodotus and the philosophising of al-Kindī, the poetry of Tullia D'Aragona and the speeches of Joseph Warren. What could be more Western than questioning, critiquing, and disputing received wisdom? What could be more Western than engaging in dialogue? And what could be more Western than reimagining the shape of history?

ACKNOWLEDGEMENTS

This book originally grew out of academic research
genealogies of Troy, research that I began as a res
vard's Center for Hellenic Studies in Washin
grateful to the entire team of the Center, a
Gregory Nagy, for creating such a sti
ment. In the years since then, I h
portunity to present my ideas
valuable feedback. I am th
and the organisers of
Association of Gha
2018; Simon So
Departmen
Jew and
His

Kennedy, Julia L. Hairston, Jan Heywood, John McLucas, Andrew
Merrills, Jana Mokrišová, Cosimo Paravano, Josephine Crawley Quinn,
Mira Seo, George Southcombe, and Yana Xue. All of these wonderful
people contributed to this book by reading draft chapters or sections,
generously sharing their expertise and providing helpful comments on
the text, checking or composing translations, suggesting bibliography,
offering sound and helpful advice, and/or kindly sharing their unpub-
lished research and works in progress. This book would be weaker
without you. I am also thankful to Sharon Gauci Mestre, Mary Har-
low, Matthias Hoernes, and Yasmin Yasseri for the support and encouragement. This book might not have been written at all without
your helpful, and often unwitting, interventions.

into the mythic

arch fellow at Har-

gton, DC, in 2017. I am

d especially to its director,

mulating intellectual environ-

ve been fortunate to have the op-

at a number of events where I gained

refore grateful to Michael Okyere Asante

he 2018 inaugural conference of the Classical

 na; Rebecca Rideal and the team behind HistFest

on and the organisers of the research seminar at the

of History at Universiti Malaya in October 2019; Daniel

the organisers of the research seminar at the Department of

ory at the National University of Singapore in 2019; my brilliant

ormer colleagues and students at the University of Leicester, who heard and commented on different bits of the book's core argument at different times; and my fantastic current colleagues and students at the University of Vienna, who have more recently done the same.

To my uncle John Nielsen: Thank you for backing this project from the beginning, for reading every word (often more than once!), for tirelessly checking facts and looking up references, for prompting me to go in new and unexpected directions, and for always being there. To my husband, John Vella: Thank you for holding me steady when my confidence was shaken, and for holding our family steady during the times when I was away working, for the long talks on the long walks when all my best ideas were (and still are) formed, for your intellectual rigour in the editing process, and for challenging my assumptions and telling me what I needed (but not necessarily always wanted) to hear. Above all, thank you for the clay dunes and for the woods.

NOTES

INTRODUCTION: THE IMPORTANCE OF ORIGINS

1. For the argument that Westerners are psychologically conditioned to think in certain ways, see Henrich 2020.

2. "From Plato to NATO" was a phrase widely used to describe a number of broad cultural courses taught mostly in the USA that purported to survey Western Civilisation. It is also the title of a popular book on the history of the West written by David Gress in 1998.

3. If you are looking for a book that deals intelligently with the rise of the West as a multifaceted process, I recommend Morris 2011. A list of other books dealing with this topic, mostly from a triumphalist perspective, is collected in Trautsch 2013, 89nn1–2.

4. See Somma 2010, 321–23, for an analysis of the sculptural programme of the Library of Congress. According to Somma, the reading room is "the primary site for the transfer of knowledge, the active point of intersection between past, present, and future historical time. It is here that the modern visitor obtains direct access to the printed record of human civilisation, the intellectual raw material necessary to fuel the steady progress of Western culture" (321–22).

5. Noble et al. 2013, xxiii. A selection of recent textbooks and popular histories that share the same basic structure could include Cole and Symes 2020; Waibel 2020; Perry et al. 2015; Spielvogel 2005; Drogin 2008; Roger Osborne 2008; Kishlansky, Geary, and O'Brien 2006; Gress 1998.

6. For "legacy," see Roger Osborne 2008; "evolution," Gress 1998; "ancestry," Perry et al. 2015, 9 (for the Hebrews and the Greeks as the spiritual ancestors of the West) and 32 (for Egypt and Mesopotamia *not* being the spiritual ancestors of the West).

7. Roger Osborne, 1998.

8. I refer of course to Rick Riordan's rollicking Percy Jackson stories. This passage about Western Civilisation comes early in the first book of the series, *Percy Jackson and the Olympians: The Lightning Thief,* first published in 2005 and released as the film *Percy Jackson and the Lightning Thief* in 2010.

9. As documented in McDaniel 2021. The rioters also carried Confederate flags and flags bearing Crusader crosses and were dressed in costumes designed to evoke depictions of ancient Germanic warriors. The ancient Greek phrase favoured by the rioters was *molon labe,* which means "come and take them." This was the answer

attributed to the Spartan king Leonidas in response to Persian demands that the Spartans lay down their weapons at the Battle of Thermopylae in 480 BCE. While it is unlikely that Leonidas actually ever said this phrase, it has recently been adopted by the pro-gun lobby in the United States.

10. This was seen as controversial at the time, see Agbamu 2019.

11. Extract from a recording made by Osama bin Laden and first released by Al Jazeera on January 6, 2004.

12. For colonial architecture, see Vasunia 2013, 157–92.

13. The point has been made both in postcolonial studies and philosophy: e.g., Appiah 2016; Appiah 2018, Chapter 6 for the idea of the "golden nugget"; Ahmad 1992, 166; but also within the discipline of Classics, which is so heavily implicated in this discourse: e.g., Futo Kennedy 2019, 2022; Greenwood 2010, Introduction.

14. For a fresh all-round perspective on this, I recommend Quinn 2023. The point was also openly acknowledged in the 1991 edition of McNeill's 1963 classic, *The Rise of the West*. See also Hobson 2004, 2020.

15. Classical Athens was not, as we shall see in Chapter 1, a true democracy, as it excluded women and enslaved people, as well as anyone who could not prove the purity of their Athenian bloodlines, from political participation.

16. The Roman Empire covered large parts of not only Europe, but also north Africa and western Asia, and people from all parts of this empire enjoyed equal legal status as Romans, as we shall see in Chapter 2.

17. Many of the Crusades were fought against European pagans, as well as against those who were considered to be deviant Christians, as we shall see in Chapter 5.

18. Bonnett 2004 argues that the concept of "the West" was invented and perpetuated because of its ideological utility.

19. At least, this is the story told to us in Strabo 9:1:10, writing about the Catalogue of Ships (*Iliad* 2:558).

20. Atakuman 2008.

21. Mitter 2020. Stallard 2022 sees this as a cause for concern, Chang 2022 as a cause for congratulation. See Fan 2021 for a broader perspective on politicized history in modern China.

22. Huxtable et al. 2020. This report was to a significant extent based on research by Corinne Fowler (see Fowler 2021). For an excellent and lively discussion of the debates over Britain's history and its historical self-perception, see Woods 2022.

CHAPTER 1: THE REJECTION OF PURITY

1. Herodotus, *Histories* 4:45.

2. For example, within the last twenty-five years there have been at least seven new English-language editions of Herodotus, meaning that a new edition of Herodotus is published every three to four years. They include Peter Frankopan with a transla-

tion by Robin Waterfield (2020), James Romm with a translation by Pamela Mensch (2014), Paul Cartledge with a translation by Tom Holland (2014), Robert Strassler with a translation by Andrea Purvis (2009), Carolyn Dewald with a translation by Robin Waterfield (2008), John Marincola with a translation by Aubrey de Sélincourt (2003), and Rosalind Thomas with a translation by George Rawlinson (1997).

3. Huntington 1996, 42.
4. Pagden 2011.
5. Cicero, *De Legibus* 1:5.
6. For Mesopotamian chronicles, see Glassner 2004, and for Mesopotamian historiography more generally Finkelstein 1963. For early Greek historical writing in verse, see, for example, Mimnermus's *Smyrneis* (Allen 1993; West 2008).
7. Pelling 2019.
8. Herodotus 4:71.
9. Herodotus 3:80–83.
10. Herodotus 2:25–27.
11. Herodotus 5:35.
12. This moniker ultimately derives from Plutarch's *On the Malice of Herodotus* (*Moralia* 854); see Momigliano 1958.
13. Gold-digging ants (Hdt 3:102); people with dogs' heads (Hdt 4:191).
14. Bone flutes in mares' vaginas (Hdt 4:2); temple prostitutes (Hdt 1:199).
15. In his madness, Cambyses stabbed the sacred bull of Apis in Egypt, so that it bled to death (Hdt 3:29). Xerxes, furious that a storm in the Hellespont had caused the bridges to be broken, ordered that the waters be whipped and branded as a punishment (Hdt 7:35).
16. Aristagoras initiated the Ionian Revolt because he wanted to avoid paying back a debt and losing his status within Miletus (Hdt 5:35). Themistocles used his position to extort money from the island-dwelling Greeks (Hdt 8:112).
17. For cultural hybridity in this region, see Mac Sweeney 2013. For Halicarnassus in particular, see Gagné 2006 and Carless Unwin 2017.
18. *Suda*, s.v. "Herodotus" and "Panyassis." This mix of Greek and Carian names within a single family seems to have been quite common and is recorded in inscriptions of the period (see Meiggs and Lewis 1969, 32; Aubriet 2013). Panyassis is sometimes said to have been Herodotus's uncle.
19. The Greek sources label such a ruler a *tyrannos*, although the modern translation "tyrant" has some more complex associations.
20. On the question of Herodotus's travels, see Asheri et al. 2007, 6–7.
21. For Athens in the fifth century BCE, see Robin Osborne 2008.
22. There are a number of conspicuous similarities between Herodotus's *Histories* and plays such as Sophocles's *Antigone*, suggesting that the two men discussed their work, perhaps even sharing sources and inspiration. Sophocles was eventually

to write a song in honour of his historian friend, suggesting the relationship was personal as well as professional. Compare, for example, Sophocles's *Antigone* 903ff with Herodotus's *Histories* 3:119. Ancient references to their friendship include: *Anth. Lyrica Graeca* I³ 79 Diehl, and Plutarch *Mor.* 785b. See also Chiasson 2003.

23. Public readings of Herodotus's work: Eusebius *Chronica Arm* 83; Diyllus *FGrHist* 73 F3. For the value of a talent in fifth-century BCE Athens, Thucydides 6:8.

24. For this history, see Beaton 2019.

25. For the fraught ideological relationship between the two, see Hanink 2017.

26. For an inventory of these, see Hansen and Nielsen 2004.

27. Beck and Funke 2015; Mac Sweeney 2021a.

28. Engels 2010.

29. For this wider Greek world, see De Angelis 2020. For a history of changing notions of Greekness from antiquity to the present day, see Beaton 2021.

30. For ancient views on Macedonian ethnicity, see Engels 2010. For Herodotus's views on ethnicity and Greekness, see Munson 2014.

31. For genealogies in the ancient Greek world, see Fowler 1999 and Varto 2015.

32. Hall 1997; Hall 2002; Malkin 2001; Vlassopoulos 2013; Mac Sweeney 2013.

33. This definition of Greekness is problematic, as Herodotus does not state it in his own authorial voice. Rather, these words are put in the mouths of Athenian politicians trying to convince the Spartans that they will not defect to the Persian side in the war. We cannot be sure, therefore, whether Herodotus himself defined Greekness in these terms, or whether this is part of his characterisation of the Athenians.

34. For variation in dialect and script, see Colvin 2010. For variation in cult, see Osborne 2015.

35. For Clazomenian sarcophagi, see Cook 1981; for the chamber tombs of the Corinthian north necropolis, see Slane 2017.

36. The identification of the bulls' testicles is debated. Some scholars think instead that Artemis is being depicted with many breasts.

37. Donnellan 2016.

38. Villing et al. 2006.

39. Aristotle, *Politics* 1327b.

40. For demographic estimates of Athens and Attica at this time, see Akrigg 2019.

41. For the Delian League and Athenian empire, see Ma et al. 2009; Low 2008.

42. Thucydides 5:84–116. Thucydides's account of the debate leading up to this event is famously known as the "Melian Dialogue" and has been treated as a foundational work of political theory.

43. Aristotle, *Ath. Pol.* 26:4; Plutarch, *Pericles* 37:3. For the wider implications of Pericles's new citizenship law and a new racialised way of approaching Athe-

nian identity, see Lape 2010. For Athenian citizenship laws in general, see Patterson 2005.

44. For the roles played by metics in Athenian civic religion, see Wijma 2014.

45. This process in the fifth century BCE has been well documented and is famously described as the "invention of the barbarian"; see Hall 2002; Hall 1989.

46. For fifth-century BCE stereotypes of the Persians, see Castriota 2005.

47. Hanink 2017 describes this process as Athens "building its brand."

48. On Herodotus and his relationship to the Athenian empire, see Moles 2002.

49. Herodotus, *Histories* prologue.

50. Herodotus then segues into an ethnographic episode detailing the history and culture of the Lydians (Hdt 1:6–94).

51. See Thucydides 1:96:2 for the Athenian invention of the term. On the resonance of the word *phoros* in Herodotus, see Irwin 2013, 275–76; Ruffing 2018.

52. For the generous pharaoh Amasis: Herodotus 5:172–79; for the heroic Scythian queen Tomyris: Herodotus 1:205–14; for Babylonian engineers and agriculturalists: Herodotus 1:192–93; for Ethiopians as the best-looking people in the world: Herodotus 3:144.

53. Skin colour has, however, played a role in modern discourses about ancient Greekness, with much modern scholarship assuming that the ancient Greeks should be racialised as white. For an excellent discussion of this phenomenon, as well as of the more fluid attitudes to skin colour that could be found in Greek antiquity, see Derbew 2022. For race in antiquity in general, see McCoskey 2021. For distinctions between race and ethnicity in Mediterranean antiquity, see Mac Sweeney 2021b.

54. Although it was not just the Athenians who sought to use this ideology for political gains. Amongst the Greek poleis of Sicily, the Deinomenid tyrants of Syracuse used the rhetoric of Hellenic unity in the face of Phoenician and Carthaginian barbarism in order to justify Syracuse's domination of other neighbouring Greek cities. See Prag 2010.

55. Mac Sweeney 2018; Vlassopoulos 2013, 172; Ross 2005.

56. Said 2001.

57. Thucydides 1:2–3.

CHAPTER 2: THE ASIAN EUROPEANS

1. Frisch 1975, no. 88 = *IGRR* IV.20.

2. For short biographies of Livilla, see Wood 2001, 180–84, and Sinclair 1990.

3. For the archaeology of Troy, see Rose 2013 and Mac Sweeney 2018.

4. Erskine 2001; Wiseman 1995, 2004.

5. Erskine 2001, 6–10, explores the history of this common misconception.

6. Flavio Bartolucci, writing in *Il Primato Nazionale,* January 29, 2019.

7. Wiseman 2004.

8. For the emperor Hadrian, see Birley 1997. For Greek education at Rome, see Bonner 1977.
9. For the hybrid culture of early imperial Rome, see Wallace-Hadrill 2008.
10. For silk imported from China to the Roman Empire, see Hildebrandt 2017; for hair dye in the Roman world, see Olson 2012.
11. From Iberia: Trajan, Hadrian; Libya: Septimius Severus, Caracalla; Arabia: Philip; Syria: Elagabalus; Thrace (Bulgaria): Maximinus Thrax, Galerius; Illyricum (Croatia and Albania): Diocletian, Aurelian, Constantine.
12. For bottom-up approaches to the Roman Empire from the perspectives of conquered peoples and provinces, see Woolf 1998; Hingley 2005; Mattingly 2011.
13. Johnson 2012.
14. Berlin and Overman 2003.
15. This brutality has been highlighted by some of the most recent research on the Roman Empire, e.g., Fernández-Götz et al. 2020.
16. For the uses of the myth in the service of imperial expansion, see Horsfall 1986. For the *Aeneid* in its Roman political context, see Stahl 1998.
17. Schneider 2012.
18. Erskine 2001, 19–20. Caesar's strategy was commented on even at the time (Suetonius, *Julius Caesar* 6:1).
19. Toohey 1984.
20. Erskine 2001, 19. Augustus promoted the idea of his own personal Trojan ancestry widely, and this was noted at the time: Horace, *Satires* 2:5:63 and *Carminae* 4:15-21-32 and *Carminae Saeculae* 50.
21. For the replication of this standard image, see Fuchs 1975; Dardenay 2010, 43–51; and Zanker 1997. See Erskine 2001, 15–23, and Squire 2011 for the ubiquity of the Aeneas story.
22. Casali 2010; Horsfall 2000.
23. Gladhill 2009. Some of this creative ambiguity is put into the mouths of characters within the story, who engage in "genealogical opportunism" to rewrite their own genealogies; see Nakata 2012.
24. Rose 2013, 223–27.
25. Tacitus, *Annals* 4:3.
26. A later decree of the Senate commends Livilla and explicitly mentions the high esteem in which she was held both by Livia and by Tiberius (*Senatus Consultum de Gn. Pisonem Patre* 142–45).
27. Zonaras 10:36.
28. Cassius Dio 55:10:18.
29. For Arabia, see Pliny *Nat. Hist.* 6:32; Bowersock 1994, 56. For Mesopotamia, see Velleius Paterculus 2:101. For Gaius's wound and death, see Cassius Dio 55:10a.8; Velleius Paterculus 2:102.

30. Cassius Dio 57:13:1; Cassius Dio 57:14:7.

31. Livilla's daughter, Julia, was sick in her childhood. On his deathbed, the emperor Augustus is said to have enquired about her ailing health and hoped for her recovery (Suetonius, *Augustus* 99).

32. The historian Tacitus records the strength of popular support for Germanicus and Agrippina around this time, commenting that it was truly "astonishing" (*mirus*: Tacitus, *Annals* 1:7).

33. For Germanicus's spectacular triumph, staged at Rome as a celebration of his northern victories, see Beard 2009, 107–9, and Strabo 7:1:4. For his limited successes, see Tacitus, *Annals* 1:55. For the figure of Germanicus in the writings of Tacitus, see Pelling 2012.

34. Tacitus, *Annals* 2:43.

35. Tacitus, *Annals* 2:62–63.

36. Tacitus suggests that it was Sejanus who seduced Livilla, pursuing personal and political advancement and out of spite for her husband (Tacitus, *Annals* 4:3). However, Tacitus accords very little agency to many imperial women he discusses, and the severe way Livilla was later treated suggests that she adopted a more active role in the affair and in politics than has previously been assumed.

37. Tiberius even went as far as to describe Sejanus affectionately as his "partner in work" (*socium laborum*; Tacitus, *Annals* 4:2).

38. Suetonius, *Tiberius* 62:3.

39. Tacitus, *Annals* 2:84.

40. Rome: BMC 95 (Tiberius), Cohen 1 (Drusus), RIC 42 (Tiberius). Corinth: RPC 1171. Cyrenaica: RPC 946.

41. Salamis: *IGRR* III:997. Ephesus: *Forsch.Eph.* 7:2:4773 = *IvEph* 4337.

42. Tacitus, *Annals* 2:71–73.

43. Cassius Dio 57:22:1–2; Tacitus, *Annals* 4:8; Tacitus, *Annals* 4:10–11.

44. Tacitus, *Annals* 4:39; Sinclair 1990, 250–53.

45. The sources are unclear as to the identity of Sejanus's betrothed, but the likelihood is that it was Livilla. See Bellemore 1995, 259–60, for a discussion.

46. Examples include British Museum R.4456 and Berlin Münzkabinett 18237641.

47. See Wood 2001, 220, for a discussion of the statue types of Agrippina. The standard statue type, produced during her lifetime, showed Agrippina with elaborately curled and styled hair. Later types depicted a simpler style.

48. Wood 2001, 190–200; Varner 2004, 94–95.

49. See Tacitus, *Annals* 4:12, for the cold war between the women.

50. Tacitus, *Annals* 2:43; Suetonius, *Caligula* 1.

51. Rose 1997, 29, notes this absence.

52. Cassius Dio 58:11:7.

53. Suetonius, *Tiberius* 53.

54. Hingley 2019; Moyer et al. 2020, 24.
55. For mobility between Africa and Britain during the Roman period as documented by isotopic analysis of skeletal material, see: Chenery et al. 2011; Eckhardt et al. 2016; Leach 2009.
56. E.g., tweet by Kelli Ward, at the time the chair of the Republican Party in Arizona, Agbamu 2019.
57. E.g., tweet shared by retired general Michael Flynn on December 20, 2020.

CHAPTER 3: THE GLOBAL HEIRS OF ANTIQUITY

1. Al-Kindī, *On First Philosophy* II.4. Translation from Adamson 2007, 23.
2. For an accessible introduction to Byzantium in English, see Herrin 2007 or Stathakopoulos 2014.
3. This phrase was used as the title of the first episode of Kenneth Clark's popular and influential television series, *Civilisation: A Personal View* (1969), and remains frequently repeated and paraphrased.
4. Falk 2020.
5. For a discussion of this problem, see Falk 2020, 2–5.
6. Huntington 1996, 70.
7. For Roman law in today's legal codes, see Zimmerman 2001.
8. For the continued use (and limited maintenance) of Roman roads in the early medieval period, see Fafinski 2021.
9. Sulpicius Severus, *Vita Martini* 12–15.
10. This was the argument of Edward Gibbon in the late eighteenth century, which despite now being roundly disproved is still often repeated.
11. For the various successor kingdoms of the Western Roman Empire, see Heather 2009. For the Kingdom of Italy based at Ravenna, see Herrin 2020; for the Goths, see Heather 1998; for the Vandals, see Merrills and Miles 2010.
12. For Aldred's gloss on the Lindisfarne Gospels, see Brown 2003, 90–204.
13. For the transformation and reuse of Roman public buildings in the early medieval period in western Europe, see Ng and Swetnam-Burland 2018.
14. Heather 2017, chap. 7.
15. Kaldellis 2019b.
16. For Anna Komnene, see Neville 2016.
17. Németh 2018.
18. As Kaldellis puts it, "a work did not have to be seen as dangerous or subversive in order to be denied survival. It merely had to be uninteresting or perceived as not useful" (2019a, 57–58).
19. For the Indo-Greek kingdoms in general, see Mairs 2016; Mairs 2020. For intellectual and especially philosophical traffic between Bactria and the Mediterranean, see Stoneman 2019.
20. Parker 2002.

21. In *Periplus of the Erythraean Sea*, for Barigaza, see sec. 49; for Muziris, see sec. 56.
22. For Gandharan art, see Rienjang and Stewart 2020.
23. Sinisi 2017.
24. Sims-Williams 2022.
25. Galinsky 2009.
26. Hsing 2005.
27. McKenzie and Watson 2016. I am grateful to Dr. Mai Musié for bringing these to my attention.
28. Łajtar and Ochała 2021.
29. For a description of Baghdad at this time, as well as its foundation, see Bennison 2009, 69–71. For the estimation of its population, see al-Khalili 2011, 7.
30. For Muslim Spain and Portugal, see Kennedy 1996, Catlos 2018, and Fierro 2020. For the involvement of central Asia in the Islamic golden age, see Starr 2015. For an exciting new take on the empires of west Africa, see Gomez 2019.
31. For an all-round introduction to the Abbasid Caliphate, see Bennison 2009. For a broader view of world history as seen from an Islamic perspective, see Ansary 2010.
32. For trade in the Abbasid Caliphate, see Bennison 2009, chap. 4.
33. For the details of al-Kindī's life and works, I am largely dependent on Adamson 2007.
34. Ibn Abī Uṣaybiʿah, *The Best Accounts of the Classes of Physicians*, 10:1:1–4. See also Adamson 2007, 4.
35. For the establishment and likely workings of the House of Wisdom, see al-Khalili 2011, chap. 5; and Ansary 2010, chap. 7.
36. For an overview of the intellectual developments and discoveries of the time, see al-Khalili 2011.
37. For the Abbasid translation movement, see Bennison 2009, chap. 5; Gutas 1998; and al-Khalili 2011.
38. Adamson 2007, 6–12.
39. Al-Kindī, *On First Philosophy* II.5.
40. Adamson 2007, 18.
41. Ibn al-Qifti, *History of Learned Men* 1–6.
42. Ibn Abī Uṣaybiʿah, *Best Accounts* 10.1.12. Translation taken from Adamson and Pormann 2012, lxix–lxx.
43. Adamson 2007, 4–5.
44. Ibn Abī Uṣaybiʿah, *Best Accounts* 15:40:3.
45. Al-Jāhiz, *The Book of Misers* 71–78.
46. There is some debate over whether this anecdote referred to the philosopher al-Kindī or to another homonymous person, although al-Jāhiz clearly writes about the philosopher elsewhere in *The Book of Misers* (Adamson 2007, 17–18). It is generally thought that this letter is not genuine, but instead a literary creation by al-Jāhiz for comedic effect. Yet for this to be funny, al-Jāhiz must have been lampooning

well-known aspects of al-Kindī's personality, and there must have been elements of the story that rang true (Adamson and Pormann 2012, xxi).

47. For the competitive culture of Abbasid scholarship, see Bennison 2009, 178.
48. Ibn Abī Uṣaybiʿah, *Best Accounts* 10:1:7.
49. Al-Jāhiz, *The Book of Animals* (translation from al-Khalili 2011).
50. Al-Khalili 2011.
51. Al-Kindī, *On First Philosophy* II.4 (translation from Adamson and Pormann 2012).
52. Al-Kindī, *On First Philosophy* II.3 (translation from Adamson and Pormann 2012).
53. Adamson 2004.
54. Gutas 1998, 88. *Al-Masūdi, Murūj aḏ-Ḏahab wa-Maʿādin al-Jawhar* (Masʿūdī, edition by Barbier de Meynard and Pavet de Courteill, 1861–1917, 2:25:243).
55. Gutas 1998, 87.
56. Gutas 1998, 90–93.
57. Gutas 1998, 83–95.
58. Stock 2016; Doufikar-Aerts 2016.
59. Al-Kindī, *On First Philosophy* III.1–2 (translation from Adamson and Pormann 2012).
60. Ibn Abī Uṣaybiʿah, *Best Accounts* 10:1:6.
61. Adamson 2007, 5.

CHAPTER 4: THE ASIAN EUROPEANS AGAIN

1. Godfrey of Viterbo, *Speculum regum*: prologue 22–23.
2. This nickname was not used by contemporaries but invented in the thirteenth century to distinguish him from his grandson, Frederick II (Freed 2016, xviii).
3. Godfrey of Viterbo, *Memoria seculorum* 22:105:24–36. Translation quoted from Weber 1994, 175.
4. For the history of the Holy Roman Empire, see P. H. Wilson 2016.
5. For the life of Barbarossa, see Freed 2016.
6. For the fraught relationships between the Staufers and the papacy, see P. H. Wilson 2016, 62–67.
7. MacCulloch 2009, 350. For explorations of how the idea of Romanness was (re)imagined in the medieval period, see Pohl et al. 2018.
8. Charlemagne quietly dropped the title to avoid clashes with the Byzantine Empire. For Charlemagne as a successor of the old Roman Empire, see Heather 2017.
9. Petersohn 1992, 2001.
10. It was also an idea that was gaining particular traction in the twelfth century; see Reuter 1992.
11. P. H. Wilson 2016, 37.
12. Kaldellis 2019b.
13. MacCulloch 2010, 374. For the development of the Latin and the Byzantine churches, see MacCulloch 2010, pt. IV (Latin church) and pt. V (Byzantine church).

14. P. H. Wilson 2016, 143; Burke 1980 notes that the term "Europe" at this point was used to emphasize the difference between the Latin West and the Orthodox East.
15. Delanty 1995, 28; Jordan 2002; Ailes 2012.
16. *Karolus magnus et Leo papa* II.529.
17. Sedulius: *Seduli Scotti carmina* ii.14:8. Notker: *Notkeri Balbuli Gesta Karoli Magni imperatis,* in MGH, *Scriptores rerum Germanicum* 12:1:40.
18. Angelov and Herrin 2012.
19. For the rivalry between the two empires, see P. H. Wilson 2016, 138–43.
20. See Dorninger 2015, 16–17; and Dorninger 1997, 33–36, for Godfrey's family background and early life.
21. Weber 1994.
22. For the imperial chancery, see Freed 2016, 107–10.
23. Freed 2016, 109–10. The identification of Godfrey with the scribal hand known as Arnold II.C has been disputed (see Weber 1994) but remains widely upheld (Dorninger 2015, 19; Hering 2015, 55–56).
24. Godfrey of Viterbo, *The Deeds of Frederick*: MGH SS 22:321:37–323:27.
25. Godfrey of Viterbo, *The Deeds of Frederick*: MGH SS 22:326:33–35.
26. Godfrey of Viterbo, *Memoria seculorum*: MGH SS 22:105:24–36. Translation taken from Bumke 1991, 460–61.
27. This is a key argument of Weber 1994.
28. Godfrey of Viterbo, *Pantheon*: MGH SS 22:271:43–45.
29. Weber 1994, 165n71.
30. Weber 1994, 164.
31. Godfrey, *Speculum Regum*: MGH SS 22:21:3–7.
32. Godfrey, *Speculum Regum*: MGH SS 22:31:26.
33. Waswo 1995; Innes 2000; Shepard and Powell 2004; Desmond 2016; Mac Sweeney 2018. For a detailed study of early medieval ethno-genealogies setting the Trojan genealogies in the broader context, see Plassmann 2006.
34. Snorri Sturluson, *Prose Edda*, prologue 3.
35. Henry of Huntingdon, *History of the English* 7:38.
36. Boeck 2015, 264. For this phenomenon more generally, see Aerts 2012 and Desmond 2016.
37. Godfrey, *Speculum Regum*: MGH SS 22:45:47ff.
38. Godfrey, *Speculum Regum*: MGH SS 22:62:40ff.
39. Godfrey, *Speculum Regum*: MGH SS 22:62:4–6. I have translated these lines loosely to capture a sense of the original Latin, with its short rhyming lines.
40. Godfrey, *Speculum Regum*: MGH SS 22:66:5–10.
41. Godfrey, *Speculum Regum*: MGH SS 22:93:4–9. This translation is a bit of a loose one, but it maintains the core of the meaning and communicates a sense of the rhythm and rhyme of the original Latin.

42. Wood 2013 identifies a later trend amongst scholars of the period to emphasize either the Germanic or the Roman origin myths.

43. As suggested by Weber 1994.

44. Godfrey, *Pantheon*: MGH SS 22:203:7–9.

CHAPTER 5: THE ILLUSION OF CHRISTENDOM

1. Theodore Laskaris, *Epistle* 125:25.

2. For a good introduction to the Crusades, see Throop 2018. For an account of the Crusades from the perspective of the Muslim sources, see Cobb 2016.

3. Thomas Jefferson, letter to George Wythe, August 13, 1786, Founders Online, National Archives, https://founders.archives.gov/documents/Jefferson/01-10-02-0162.

4. Ames 2015 explores the idea of heresies in the medieval period more generally, expanding the view beyond Christianity to include heresies also in Judaism and Islam.

5. Pegg 2008.

6. Mackenzie and Watson 2016; Rukuni 2021.

7. For the Coptic church, see Kamil 2013; for the Christians of medieval Syria, Mesopotamia, and Iran, see Hunt 2011.

8. Keevak 2008.

9. *Itinerarium fratris Willielmi de Rubruquis de ordine fratrum Minorum, Galli, Anno gratiae 1253 ad partes Orientales* 14.

10. For example, the generally excellent MacCulloch 2010 devotes a paltry five pages to the Ethiopian church, and nine to the various eastern churches, out of a total of 1,016 pages of text. Indeed, so conditioned is this book by the narrative of Western Civilisation that it begins its history of Christianity in the ancient Greek world, explaining this by claiming that Greek thought provided much of the intellectual foundation on which later Christian thinking was built.

11. For an overview of the changing relationship between the Byzantine Empire and Venice, see Nicol 1989.

12. For the Fourth Crusade, see Throop 2018, chap. 4; Nicol 1989, chap. 8; and Harris 2003, chaps. 10 and 11. The Fourth Crusade has spawned scholarly controversy; see Harris 2005 for a discussion.

13. Nicol 1989, chap. 9.

14. For the Frankokratia, see Chrissis, Carr, and Maier 2014.

15. Angold 2009.

16. Angold 2009, 731.

17. It is hypothetically possible that Laskaris entered the city to conduct negotiations for a peace treaty in 1241 after laying siege to it for several months, but there is no evidence to suggest that this was the case. The negotiations could have just as easily been conducted outside the city walls. See Angelov 2019, 92.

18. For the history of modern Greece and modern ideas of Hellenism, see Beaton 2019.

19. See the excellent and highly recommended Angelov 2019 for the details of Laskaris's life and times.
20. For "beloved ground," see Laskaris, *Epistle* 111:16–17. For "mother Anatolia," see the newsletter appendix to Laskaris, *Epistle* 281:84. More than two hundred of Laskaris's letters still survive today. We must assume that he originally wrote many more. Laskaris's works are collated and summarised in Angelov 2019, app. 1.
21. Angelov 2019, 33. John Vatatzes was also, by blood, Irene Laskarina's uncle.
22. Angold 2009.
23. Angelov 2019, 109, writes about the "youth culture" of the court and contrasts the generation of Laskaris with the "traumatized perspective" of the "humiliated generation."
24. Angelov 2019, 69.
25. For Laskaris as a philosopher, see Angelov 2019, 181–201.
26. Angelov 2019, 76.
27. Angelov 2019, 72–74.
28. For the relationship between Laskaris and Elena, see Angelov 2019, 129–32.
29. Angelov 2019, 61.
30. Angelov 2019, 105–8.
31. Angelov 2011; Angelov 2019, 149. ʿIzz al-Dīn was later restored as sultan, only to be deposed a second time. He lived out the final years of his life at the Mongol court.
32. Angelov 2019, 169–71.
33. Angelov 2019, 152–65.
34. Heather 2017 explores this "fall of the western empire" as well as successive attempts to restore it. See Kaldellis 2019a and 2019b for the tendency amongst Western commentators to ignore the Roman identity of the Byzantines.
35. Kaldellis 2019a, 35.
36. For Laskaris as a proponent of Hellenism as a political identity, see Kaldellis 2007, 327–29; and Angelov 2019, chap. 10.
37. E.g., Laskaris, *Epistle* 30:13; 52:40; 89:10; and 217:61.
38. Laskaris, *Epistle* 51.
39. Laskaris, *Epistle* 59.
40. Laskaris, *Epistle* 204:59–60, 129.
41. Laskaris, *Epistle* 214: 34–35.
42. Laskaris continued to refer to his realm and his people as Romans; see Laskaris, *Epistle* 27:39; 214:30.
43. Laskaris refers to his realm and his people as Greek or Hellenic; see Laskaris, *Epistle* 5:14; 40:19; 40:28; 51:30; 109:48; 125:24.
44. Laskaris, *Epistle* 77:40.
45. Laskaris, *Epistle* 125:52; translation from Angelov 2019, 213.
46. Laskaris, *Epistle* 118:24.
47. For a discussion, see Angelov 2019, 213–15.

48. *Second Oration against the Latins* 4.
49. Angelov 2019, 206–7.
50. *Second Oration against the Latins* 10.
51. Laskaris, *Epistle* 125:24.
52. For the complex rhetoric of otherness during the First Crusade, see Morton 2016.
53. Angelov 2019, app. 3.
54. Prosperi 2019.

CHAPTER 6: THE REIMAGINING OF ANTIQUITY

1. Tullia D'Aragona, *Il Meschino* 12:69. This translation is quoted from D'Aragona, McLucas, and Hairston, forthcoming.
2. Histories of the Renaissance abound. I have found Brotton 2006 and Greenblatt 2012 to be good places to start.
3. I am grateful to Julia Hairston for this point.
4. Burckhardt 1860 [1945 English ed.], 292.
5. Burckhardt 1860 [1945 English ed.], 89.
6. Burckhardt 1860 [1945 English ed.], 91–92.
7. Burioni 2010; McLaughlin 1988.
8. Heather 2017.
9. Brownlee 2007.
10. Signorini 2019; Graziosi 2015.
11. Field 1988.
12. MacCulloch 2010, 492–93.
13. For the Ottoman conquest of Constantinople, see Goodwin 1999, chap. 4; and Baer 2021, chap. 4.
14. For Al-Andalus, see Kennedy 1996; Catlos 2018; and Fierro 2020 (particularly the excellent chapter on material culture by Carvajal López).
15. For Argyropoulos and the watermelon, see Harris 2010. For Byzantine scholars in Italy, see Wilson 2016.
16. Ženka 2018.
17. "A wise and chaste soul" is Alessandro Arrighi's description of D'Aragona, as published in *Rime* 53.
18. For information on D'Aragona's life, I am indebted to the work of Julia Hairston, both as published in her introduction to an edition of the *Rime* (2014), and as will soon be published in a forthcoming book with John McLucas, which will offer for the first time an English translation of *Il Meschino*. I am grateful to Professors Hairston and McLucas for sharing their manuscript with me, for their generous support and encouragement, and also for reading early drafts of this chapter.
19. Hairston 2014, 10.
20. Hairston 2014, 11–14.

21. Hairston 2014, 14–15.
22. Battista Stambellino, report to Isabella d'Este, as quoted in Hairston 2012, 18.
23. Russell 1997, 22.
24. Hairston 2012, 37.
25. Hairston 2012, 17.
26. Hairston 2012, 25–26.
27. Hairston 2012, 24.
28. Hairston 2012, 27–29.
29. Giovannozzi 2019. I am grateful to Julia Hairston and John McLucas for encouraging me to look more widely at D'Aragona's contemporaries and literary influences.
30. The intertextual interplay between these two dialogues is discussed in Smarr 1998. In her own dialogue, D'Aragona appears as a more intellectually driven and rounded character, whereas Speroni reduces her to a caricature of a courtesan and woman overcome with emotions. D'Aragona may have been partly motivated to write her dialogue in refutation of Speroni, his portrayal of women and of her in particular.
31. Russell 1997, 37.
32. Russell 1997, 39.
33. Allaire 1995; D'Aragona, McLucas, and Hairston, forthcoming.
34. For the relationship between D'Aragona's version of Il Meschino and her various source texts, see D'Aragona, McLucas, and Hairston, forthcoming. For the various versions of the tale by different authors, see Allaire 1999.
35. See McLucas 2006 for a summary of the poem.
36. The mythology surrounding Prester John is diverse. Sometimes located in Africa and sometimes in India, he appears in a range of medieval and Renaissance texts as an ideal Christian monarch.
37. Mazzotta 2010.
38. Allaire 1998.
39. D'Aragona, McLucas, and Hairston, forthcoming.
40. All translations of the text of the Meschino are quoted from D'Aragona, McLucas, and Hairston, forthcoming.
41. A particular favourite episode of mine is D'Aragona's description of the people who have only one eye, and this located in their chests (Meschino 11:49), which is reminiscent of one of the tall tales told by Herodotus of the Blemmyes (Hdt 4:191).
42. For the anti-Islamic sentiments expressed in the Meschino, see D'Aragona, McLucas, and Hairston, forthcoming.
43. See the excellent Meserve 2008 on this issue, as well as Frassetto and Blanks 1999.
44. For the life and work of Lucrezia Marinella, see the introduction in Marinella and Stampino 2009.
45. Vasari, Lives of the Artists, prologue.

CHAPTER 7: THE PATH NOT TRODDEN

1. Safiye Sultan, *Letter to Elizabeth I of England*. Skilliter 1965, 131: Document 1 (translation by Skilliter).

2. For more details of this embassy sent from Elizabeth I to Mehmed III and Safiye Sultan, see Jardine 2004 and Brotton 2016, 226–32.

3. See Wood 2015 and Trudell 2020 for the extraordinary clockwork organ sent by Elizabeth I to Mehmed III and also for Thomas Dallam.

4. For the Reformation, see MacCulloch 2010, chap. 17.

5. For the Counter-Reformation, see MacCulloch 2010, chap. 18.

6. Wolfe 1993.

7. Bulut 2001, 111–12.

8. Although classical Ottoman texts use the term "Osmanlı" for the Ottoman ruling class and only employed the term "Turk" pejoratively, contemporary European Christian writers used "Ottoman" and "Turk" interchangeably. See Meserve 2008, "Note on Nomenclature."

9. Brotton 2016, 157.

10. Brotton 2016, 10, 23; Malcolm 2019, 96.

11. Brotton 2016, 75.

12. Malcolm 2019, 83.

13. Brotton 2016, 14.

14. Marshall 2012 collects examples of anti-Ottoman sentiment from Protestant England.

15. For this argument, see Meserve 2008, Brotton 2016, and Malcolm 2019.

16. For histories of the Ottomans, see Baer 2021, Goodwin 2011, and Inalcik 2001.

17. Lewis and Braude 1982.

18. Malcolm 2019, 105–6.

19. For the Franco-Ottoman alliance, see Malcolm 2019, 110–18.

20. For the Habsburgs, see Rady 2020.

21. See also P. H. Wilson 2016 for the history of the Holy Roman Empire.

22. For the rivalry between the Ottomans and the Austrian Habsburgs, see Malcolm 2019, 57ff.

23. For the relationship between the Habsburgs and the Knights Hopitallers of Malta, see Buttigieg 2021.

24. Inalcik 2001, chap. 7.

25. For a fuller excerpt of this letter, see Brotton 2016, 78.

26. For the origins and early life of Safiye Sultan, see Skilliter 1965, 145; and Peirce 1993, 308n2. For the reports of the Venetian ambassadors, see Pedani 2000.

27. As reported by the Ottoman courtier Solomon Usque, originally a Portuguese Jew whose family fled first Portugal and then Italy before arriving in Istanbul (as quoted in Skilliter 1965, 145).

28. Nurbanu reportedly kept the death of Murad's father a secret until Murad could arrive in Istanbul in person, thereby preventing any of his younger brothers from claiming the throne in his absence (Kayaalp 2018, 26; Peirce 1993, 261).

29. For Nurbanu's political activities as *valide sultan*, see Kayaalp 2018; Peirce 1993.

30. For the details of the rivalry between Safiye and Nurbanu, see Kayaalp 2018, 31ff.

31. For this episode, see Kayaalp 2018, 34–36; Peirce 1993, 94.

32. For the death of Nurbanu and its impact on Murad, see Peirce 1993, 238.

33. For the origins of Nurbanu, see Kayaalp 2018.

34. For the complaints of the French envoy, Jacques de Germigny, see Kayaalp 2018, 30. For the frustrations of the English envoy, William Harborne, see Brotton 2016, 99.

35. For Safiye's support for the English, see Peirce 1993, 224. For the installation of an official English ambassador after some years of tense diplomatic relations, see Brotton 2016, 121.

36. Brotton 2016, 145.

37. Peirce 1993, 97.

38. Brotton 2016, 186.

39. For a description, translation, and commentary, see Skilliter 1965.

40. Skilliter 1965, Document 1.

41. Skilliter 1965, Document 2.

42. Baer 2021, 220–23.

43. Skilliter 1965, 143.

44. Malcolm 2019, 67–68.

45. Kołodziejczk 2012.

46. Inalcik 2001, chap. 6.

47. Fredregar, *Chronicle* 4:45–46. For the Trojan genealogies attributed in medieval Latin texts to Turkic peoples, see Malcolm 2019, 25–29; Mac Sweeney 2018, 122–25; Meserve 2008, 22–64.

48. Florentius Liquenaius de Tours; see Meserve 2008, 40.

49. Giovanni Mario Fileflo; see Meserve 2008, 42.

50. Critoboulos; see Meserve 2008, 43.

51. For the start of the Renaissance, see Greenblatt 2012.

52. Adolph 2015; Shepard and Powell 2004. As one modern scholar has put it, "No traditional story was so popular in the Elizabethan age as that of the siege of Troy" (Tatlock 1915, 673).

53. Hackett 2014. See *Elizabeth I and the Three Goddesses*, 1569 (London, Royal Collection, RCIN 403446); *Elizabeth I and the Three Goddesses*, ca. 1590 (London, National Portrait Gallery, NPG 6947). See also George Peele's 1589 play, *The Araygement of Paris*.

54. For the political ramifications of this translation, see Briggs 1981; Sowerby 1992.

55. Coke, 3 *Reports* 4 (1602), preface viii a.

56. Skilliter 1965, 131: Document 1 (translation by Skilliter).

57. Skilliter 1965, 132: Document 1 (translation by Skilliter).
58. Skilliter 1965, 133: Document 1 (translation by Skilliter).
59. Malcolm 2019, 59–63.
60. Stagno and Franco Llopis 2021 offer a survey of the voluminous literature on the multimedia representations of Lepanto, which rapidly assumed the status of myth.
61. For Juan Latino, his epic, and the dynamics of race and literature in early modern Spain, see the excellent Seo 2011 and Wright 2016.
62. Baer 2021, 177.

CHAPTER 8: THE WEST AND KNOWLEDGE

1. Francis Bacon, *Novum Organum* 78. I am grateful to John Nielsen for encouraging me to look into Bacon as a historical figure, and for setting me on the path to learning more about the Enlightenment.
2. Jacobs 2019.
3. There are many books available on the Enlightenment, but I found that a good one to start with is Jacobs 2001.
4. For Hobbes and Thucydides, see Evrigenis 2006; Campbell 2022. For Locke and the Stoics, see Hill and Nidumolu 2021.
5. Lifschitz 2016, 1.
6. Skinner 2008.
7. Hobbes, "Of the Liberty of Subjects," in *Leviathan, or The Matter, Forme and Power of a Commonwealth Ecclesiasticall and Civil* (1651). I am grateful to George Southcombe for bringing this point, and this quote, to my attention.
8. McNeill 1963, 599.
9. This is a loose paraphrase of Kant's famous statement, "Aufklärung ist der Ausgang des Menschen aus seiner selbst verschuldeten Unmündigkeit," in his 1784 paper, "Beantwortung der Frage: Was ist Aufklärung?" (published in the *Berlinischer Monats-schrift*). Criticisms of this view have included the famous argument made by prominent social theorists Theodor Adorno and Max Horkheimer that Enlightenment ideas also contributed to the horrors of the Nazi regime as well as Stalinism (Adorno and Horkheimer [1972] 1997).
10. Outram 2013.
11. See, for example, the healthy academic debate that has grown up around Jonathan Israel's view of the Enlightenment (Israel 2001, 2006, 2009, and 2011; for an interview with Israel on the topic, see Malik 2013).
12. See Porter and Teich 1981 for the particular national contours of the Enlightenment.
13. Conrad 2012. Justin Smith, an historian of philosophy, describes this neatly: "We cannot at all understand natural philosophy and natural history as these developed in Europe if we do not look at them as a regional inflection of global developments" (Smith 2015).

14. Harvey 2012, 42. For the impact of Chinese science and technology on the British Industrial Revolution, see Hobson 2004, 190–218.
15. Ching and Oxtoby 1992.
16. This has been suggested in Graeber and Wengrow 2021, although the point is hotly contested, as it relies on a positivist reading of the text that admits no literary invention.
17. For example, the subject of this chapter, Francis Bacon, did not acknowledge the achievements of Islamic scholars, such as al-Kindī.
18. As stated in the introduction, I would recommend Morris 2011 on this topic.
19. For Bacon as a scientist, see chapters by Rossi, Kusukawa, and Malherbe in Peltonen 1996. For a broader perspective of Bacon's thought and his later influence, see Zagorin 2020.
20. Abraham Cowley, as quoted in Jardine and Stewart 1998.
21. For the biographical details of Bacon's life, see Jardine and Stewart 1998.
22. For Bacon in Cambridge, see Jardine and Stewart 1998, 34–37.
23. For these youthful travels, see Jardine and Stewart 1998, 39–66.
24. Nicholas Hilliard, *Francis Bacon, 1st Viscount St Alban*, 1578, National Portrait Gallery, NPG 6761.
25. Jardine and Stewart 1998, 95.
26. For the relationship between the Bacons and Essex, see Jardine and Stewart 1998, 121; Gordon 2007; Gajda 2012.
27. For a detailed discussion of the rebellion of Essex and the ideological arguments made both to defend and to accuse him, see Gajda 2012, 27–66. For Bacon's role in the trial, see Jardine and Stewart 1998, 240–47.
28. Jardine and Stewart 1998, 245–47.
29. For Bacon and Coke, see Jardine and Stewart 1998, 151, 253, 340; Zagorin 2020, 163–64, 196.
30. Butler 2015.
31. Jardine and Stewart 1998, 190.
32. Jardine and Stewart 1998, 290.
33. Jardine and Stewart 1998, 450–62.
34. Jardine and Stewart 1998, 464–66.
35. For these final years of his life, see Jardine and Stewart 1998, 473–78.
36. For analysis and scholarship on the *New Atlantis*, see Price 2018.
37. Aughterson 2002.
38. In the *Meditationes Sacrae* (1597).
39. Bacon, *New Atlantis*.
40. The name of this work, the *Novum Organum*, or the "New Organon," is a reference to a work by Aristotle on logic called the *Organon*. It is interesting that Bacon engages with the topic of what intellectual debt he owes to antiquity in a work that he has explicitly named after an ancient work.

41. Bacon, *Novum Organum* 79.
42. Bacon, *Novum Organum* 71.
43. See Hartmann 2015 for Bacon's sophisticated use of Plato in structuring historical knowledge in the *New Atlantis*.
44. Bacon, *Novum Organum* 72.
45. Hepple 2001, 109. For the Arundel collection, see Angelicoussis 2004. The Arundel collection formed the basis for the collection of Greco-Roman sculpture in the Ashmolean Museum in Oxford.
46. For Enlightenment perspectives on the ancient Greeks, see Cartledge 2009.

CHAPTER 9: THE WEST AND EMPIRE

1. Quote recorded by Giovanni Antonio Cavazzi in *Missione Evangelica*, bk. 2, 24, reproduced in Heywood 2017, 51.
2. The classic formulation of this anthropological theory is Barth 1969. For an accessible modern formulation with broader discussion, see Appiah 2018.
3. For English imperialism in the Tudor period, see Hower 2020.
4. Books about the British Empire abound, but I would recommend starting with Levine 2020 for a general introduction, and Satia 2020 for an analysis of how the British Empire has shaped our understanding of history (and vice versa).
5. There are any number of books you could read to learn about modern European imperialism, but I would start with Abernathy 2000 for an all-round basic introduction.
6. For this definition of race-making and the concept of race as a matrix, I am indebted to Ndiaye 2022 and Heng 2018. I am also grateful to the contributors to *The Cambridge Companion to Classics and Race* (Andújar et al., forthcoming), with whom I read and discussed a wide range of works on the topic as part of an online reading group.
7. Divergent approaches to race and racialisation have been identified across history (Isaac et al. 2009), including in medieval Europe (Heng 2018), the early modern period (Ndiaye 2022), and classical antiquity (McCoskey 2021; Andújar et al., forthcoming). For a discussion of the different forms of racialisation and racism in different parts of the world today, see the excellent Bonnett 2021.
8. Keevak 2011, 29.
9. Ndiaye 2022, 6. In this book, Ndiaye develops the useful idea of race as a matrix, where different factors are implicated in different ways in different times.
10. Sheth 2009, 22. In this book, Sheth argues that perhaps we should worry less about what race *is* and more about what it *does*, building on Heideggerian and Foucauldian ideas to frame race as a social technology.
11. Recent books that bring the richness and complexity of African history to a modern Western audience include French 2021; Green 2019; Gomez 2019; Fauvelle 2018. For African archaeology, see Mitchell and Lane 2013.

12. Green 2019, 39, and for the Mali more generally, see 45–67.

13. For this phase of Portuguese expansion, see Disney 2009, chap. 16.

14. For the voyages of the Chinese admiral Zheng He, see the fun Menzies 2003, and the slightly more serious and accurate Dreyer 2006.

15. For the kingdom of Kongo and its relations with the Portuguese, see Heywood 2017, 3–8; and Green 2019, chap. 5.

16. Green 2019 offers insights into the complex economies of enslavement in west Africa.

17. Heywood 2017, 19.

18. Heywood 2017, 24.

19. Heywood 2017, 27.

20. Heywood 2017, 31.

21. Heywood 2017, 29.

22. For the details of Njinga's life, I am reliant on the excellent Heywood 2017 and would recommend it heartily for anyone interested in finding out more about Njinga.

23. Heywood 2017, 15, 45.

24. Heywood 2017, 59.

25. Heywood 2017, 44.

26. Heywood 2017, 50.

27. Heywood 2017, 63–64.

28. As quoted by Father Cavazzi; for the translation, see Heywood 2017, 51.

29. Heywood 2017, 75.

30. Heywood 2017, 64

31. Heywood 2017, 65.

32. Heywood 2017, chap. 4.

33. Heywood 2017, 117.

34. Heywood 2017, 121.

35. Heywood 2017, 130.

36. Heywood 2017, 143–44.

37. Heywood 2017, 210.

38. As reported by Father Gaeta; for the translation see Heywood 2017, 188–89.

39. Heywood 2017, 236.

40. For the afterlives of Njinga, see Heywood 2017, epilogue.

41. Cavazzi, bk. 1, chap. 1:5. For the text of Cavazzi as well as notes on the manuscript, see the work of John Thornton at "John Thornton's African Texts," African American Studies, Boston University, https://www.bu.edu/afam/people/faculty/john -thornton/john-thorntons-african-texts/.

42. Cavazzi, bk. 1, chap. 1:3.

43. Cavazzi, bk. 2, chap. 8:91.

44. Herodotus in early modern travel writings: Boulègue 2012 and Varotti 2012.

45. Lupher 2002.

46. Cavazzi, bk. 2, chap. 1:1.
47. Smith 2015, chap. 6.
48. Keevak 2011.

CHAPTER 10: THE WEST AND POLITICS

1. Joseph Warren, *Boston Massacre Oration*.
2. With a few notable exceptions, scholarship on Warren is not as common or extensive as on other figures from the American revolutionary movement. Key works include Frothingham 1865, Forman 2011, and Di Spigna 2018. In this chapter, I have relied primarily on Di Spigna 2018 for the biographical details of Warren's life.
3. This phrase can be found in a letter written by Francis Rawdon-Hastings on June 20, 1776, at the time a lieutenant in the Fifth Regiment of the Grenadiers, and addressed to his uncle, the Earl of Huntingdon (Commager and Morris 1968, 130–31).
4. Allen 1993, vol. 1.
5. George Washington, letter to Lieutenant Colonel Joseph Reed, February 10, 1776.
6. Fairfax Resolves, art. 5, agreed that "it is the Opinion of this Meeting, that during our present Difficulties and Distress, no Slaves ought to be imported into any of the British Colonies on this Continent; and we take this Opportunity of declaring our most earnest Wishes to see an entire Stop for ever put to such a wicked cruel and unnatural Trade."
7. Thomas Nelson, letter to Thomas Jefferson, January 2, 1777.
8. George Washington, letter to John Hancock, March 18, 1777.
9. Fairfax Resolves, art. 17. For George Washington and enslavement, see Furstenberg 2007 and Wieneck 2003.
10. Kammen 1970.
11. The Newburgh Address, a speech delivered to army officers on March 15, 1783. Taken from: https://www.mountvernon.org/education/primary-sources-2/article/newburgh-address-george-washington-to-officers-of-the-army-march-15-1783 (last accessed October 2022).
12. General Orders, April 18, 1783.
13. Young and Nobles 2011, 144–72; Parkinson 2016.
14. Young and Nobles 2011, 172–92.
15. See Johnson's pamphlet of 1775, *Taxation No Tyranny*.
16. *African Slavery in America* (1775). Paine was to publish another pamphlet the following year in support of the American Revolution entitled *Common Sense* (1776).
17. This description comes from the memoirs of Peter Oliver, a British loyalist (Oliver [1781] 1967, 128).
18. Yet throughout his time in university, Warren seems to have courted the friendship of those deemed his social superiors—his roommates in his final two years were ranked sixth and eighth in the official class system. For Warren's time at Harvard, see Di Spigna 2018, 31–50.

19. William Gordon, a church pastor in Jamaica Plain (now a district of Boston, but at the time an agricultural area outside the city bounds), made this comment in his glowing eulogy of Warren, published in his account of the War of American Independence (Gordon 1788, vol. 2, 50).

20. John Adams, letter to Abigail Smith, April 13, 1764. For Warren's time as a doctor, see Di Spigna 2018, 51–66.

21. Boston Town Records, 1764.

22. For Warren's marriage to Elizabeth Hooton, see Di Spigna 2018, 67–71.

23. For Warren's revolutionary activities around this time, see Di Spigna 2018, 74–89.

24. *Boston Gazette*, October 7, 1765.

25. We know that Warren owned at least one enslaved person in his lifetime. A bill of sale from June 28, 1770, records Warren's purchase of one "Negro Boy" from Joshua Green, for a combination of cash and "Potter's Ware."

26. For example, "Your Folly will be as apparent as your Wickedness," Warren wrote, "you, Sir, (I write with Grief) have . . . wantonly sacrificed the Happiness of this Province to your foolish Passions." *Boston Gazette*, June 6, 1766.

27. On February 13, 1770, "The New Massachusetts Liberty Song" premiered at the Concert Hall in Boston. It took the melody of "The British Grenadiers" (a marching song favoured by imperial troops) but had acquired a new set of words—by all accounts at the hands of Joseph Warren—which transformed it instead into a radical political anthem.

28. John Adams, *Diary and Autobiography*, entry for September 6, 1769.

29. Despite claiming brevity, the pamphlet runs to some eighty-one numbered pages.

30. Di Spigna 2018, 110–13.

31. It is somewhat ironic that the Boston Tea Party was a response to a tax cut, rather than a tax rise, a fact that is often misremembered. For the real story behind the Boston Tea Party, as well as other fascinating tax tales, see Keen and Slemrod 2021.

32. Di Spigna 2018, 130–39.

33. Di Spigna 2018, 151–53.

34. Indeed Warren stayed in Boston to oversee the progress of the movement in October, when John and Samuel Adams travelled to Philadelphia for the First Continental Congress. Di Spigna 2018, 163–67.

35. Di Spigna 2018, 167–71.

36. *Boston Gazette*, May 17, 1777, 290. The three asterisks in the title of this poem stand for three missing letters of Elizabeth Warren's surname (i.e. "WAR***" stands for "WARREN"). Presumably, the reason for this was to give the Warren family a veil of anonymity, although this would have been easily penetrated by those who knew them.

37. For Warren's use of pseudonyms, see Forman 2011, 454.

38. Di Spigna 2018, 47.

39. This phenomenon is discussed in detail in Richard 1995, Shalev 2009, and Ricks 2020. For Rome in modern American political discourse, see Malamud 2009.

40. For example, the famous use of the pseudonym Publius by Alexander Hamilton (Winterer 2004).

41. Jefferson was an exception, tending more towards Greek than Roman models; see Ricks 2020.

42. Rhodes 2004.

43. Rhetorical appeals to ancient Greece and in particular to the writings of Aristotle became popular somewhat later amongst those arguing to maintain slavery as an institution. Aristotle's theory of natural slavery lent itself particularly well to justifying the continued enslavement of Africans and people of African descent; see Monoson 2011.

44. Shalev 2009, 230.

45. For the particular place of Cicero in the American revolutionary discourse, see Richard 2015.

46. Commonplace Book of Benjamin Franklin the Elder, American Antiquarian Society.

47. Nathaniel Ames, *Almanack*, 1758.

48. The exact date of this is uncertain, but it seems to have been written before January 17, 1769. Franklin's friend the Scottish surgeon Alexander Small used similar terms, writing in a letter to Franklin that "we have left your western World almost independent, and are now more afraid of your shaking us off, than of any other object what ever." Small, letter to Franklin, December 1, 1764. See also Baritz 1961 for these early uses of the terms "West" and "Western" to refer to North America.

49. Benjamin Franklin, letter to Thomas Cushing, January 5, 1773.

50. George Washington, letter to Peter Hogg, March 21, 1774.

51. John Hancock, address, Philadelphia, July 28, 1775.

52. Mercy Otis Warren, letter to John Adams, October 1775, Founders Online, National Archives, accessed October 2022, https://founders.archives.gov/documents/Adams/06-03-02-0142.

53. Philip Schuyler, letter to George Washington, July 17, 1776.

54. Malamud 2010.

55. E.g., Malamud 2009; Smil 2010.

56. For this moment, and the use of the toga by American revolutionaries, see Shalev 2009, 114ff.

57. For the toga in the Roman world, see Rothe 2019.

58. As we have seen in Chapters 4 and 7, it was characteristic of Habsburg imperial rhetoric to claim legitimacy based on the legacy of Rome, although by the time of the North American revolutionaries in the mid-eighteenth century, the Habsburgs had already been replaced on the Spanish throne by members of the House of Bourbon (the first Bourbon king of Spain, Philip V, ascended the Spanish throne in 1700).

59. Andújar and Nikoloutos 2020, 4; Lupher 2002.

60. Berruecos Frank 2022.

61. Laird 2006.
62. Feile Tomes 2015; Arbo 2018.
63. Laird 2007, 222–23.
64. For the complex engagement with the Greco-Roman past in colonial and post-colonial contexts in the Caribbean, particularly in the twentieth century, see Greenwood 2007 and 2010 for the Anglophone Caribbean; and McConnell 2013 to include discussion of the Francophone Caribbean.
65. For the inspiring yet tragic story of Louverture, see James 1989 and Hazareesingh 2020.
66. Andújar 2018, 176–77.

CHAPTER 11: THE WEST AND RACE

1. *Niobe*, from Wheatley 1773.
2. Wheatley 1773, vii.
3. See Gates 2003 for a full discussion.
4. Wheatley 1773, 124.
5. Wheatley 1773, vii.
6. See Smith 2015 for a discussion of this process more broadly; Eigen and Larrimore 2008 for the development of scientific racism amongst German Enlightenment thinkers; and Bindman 2002 for its development amongst Anglophone writers and thinkers.
7. Hume 1748, *On National Characters*, reprinted in Hume 1994; and Kant 1764, *Observations on the Feeling of the Beautiful and the Sublime*, reprinted in Kant 2011. Kant did rethink his ideas about race during his lifetime, however; see Kleingeld 2007.
8. Allen developed his argument in Allen 1994 and 1997.
9. Allen 1997, vol. 2, 239–53.
10. Allen 1997, vol. 2, 242.
11. Jefferson 1825, *Notes on the State of Virginia*, Philadelphia: H. C. Carey and I. Lea (the treatise was first published through a private printing in 1784).
12. Malamud 2016, 10.
13. This was the time of the Second Great Awakening, which saw Evangelical congregations springing up across North America and growing rapidly.
14. Such as John and Sarah Woolman; see Jackson and Kozel 2015.
15. For the life of Paul Cuffe, see Thomas 1986.
16. For the story of Amo, see Appiah 2018; and with more detail, Smith 2015.
17. See Carretta 2003 for the life of Francis Williams. Despite Williams's accomplishments, less than two decades later a new governor of Jamaica, Edward Long, was to argue in his *History of Jamaica* (1774) that black people belonged to a fundamentally different species from white people.
18. In the decades that followed, more Black writers and campaigners published notable works. See, for example, Olaudah Equiano and Ottobah Cugoano. Cugoano's *Thoughts and Sentiments on the Evil and Wicked Traffic of the Slavery and Commerce of*

the Human Species was published in 1787, and Equiano's *The Interesting Narrative of the Life of Olaudah Equiano, or Gustavus Vassa, the African* was published in 1789. It is perhaps interesting that both Equiano and Cugoano were based in Britain at the time they wrote their more explicitly political works. In contrast, the classicising poetry of Wheatley and Williams was written in the Americas.

19. For the life and work of Phillis Wheatley, see Gates 2003, essays in Shields et al. 2011, the introduction of Wheatley and Carretta 2019, and Jeffers 2020.

20. Against all the odds, these early Afro-Americans created a distinctive culture of their own in New England, for which see Piersen 1988.

21. Wheatley 1773, 68. The poem continues until page 71.

22. For the Great Awakening, see Kidd 2009.

23. Kidd 2014, 123.

24. The funerals of the murdered men attracted a crowd of thousands of disaffected Bostonians, with Wheatley and her owners likely amongst them; see Willis 2006, 165.

25. Kidd 2014, 250.

26. For the complex publication history of Wheatley's commemorative elegy for Whitefield, see Willis 2006.

27. See Greenwood 2011; Cook and Tatum 2010, 7–48.

28. Wheatley 1773, 46.

29. Wheatley 1773, 51.

30. Wheatley 1773, 65.

31. See Greenwood 2011 for a refutation of the commentators who have called her authorship into account.

32. For Wheatley's visit to London, see Robinson 1977.

33. For the significance of Boston within the revolutionary movement, see Barbier and Taylor 2017.

34. Excerpt from "To the King's Most Excellent Majesty" (1768), also published in Wheatley 1773, 17.

35. Excerpt from "To the Right Honourable William, Earl of Dartmouth" (1772), also published in Wheatley 1773, 73–75.

36. Excerpt from "To the Right Honourable."

37. *The Connecticut Gazette*, March 11, 1774.

38. Excerpt from "His Excellency General Washington" (1775).

39. Ricks 2020.

40. Excerpt from "On the Death of General Wooster" (1778).

41. For Samuel Cooper and his role in the revolutionary movement, see Akers 1978.

42. Excerpt from "To Maecenas," in Wheatley 1773, 9–12.

43. Wheatley 1773, 15–16.

44. For the history of the concept of classicism, see Schein 2007.

45. For the life and influence of Winckelmann, see Harloe 2013, pt. 1. Winckelmann is also the starting point for Marchand 1996, which investigates the emergence of Ger-

manic traditions of classical scholarship. Interestingly, Winckelmann's notions about ideal bodies and classical art also informed racial theories of the nineteenth century; see Challis 2010.

46. As argued in Harloe 2013, 107–15.
47. Winckelmann (1764) 2006, pt. 2, II.a.
48. Winckelmann (1764) 2006, pt. 2, III.c.

CHAPTER 12: THE WEST AND MODERNITY

1. William Gladstone, *Bulgarian Horrors and the Question of the East* (London: J. Murray, 1876).
2. There are literally hundreds of histories of the British Empire available, but I would recommend starting with Levine 2020 for a basic introduction. For a reflection on the role of historiography in the empire, see Satia 2020.
3. For the Industrial Revolution in Britain, see Allen 2009 for an economic discussion and Mokyr 2009 for a cultural discussion. A classic on Britain in this period is Hobsbawm 1968.
4. Trautsch 2013, 90–93.
5. See, for example, the book published by the Scottish traveller Hugh Forbes in 1863, *Poland and the Interests and Duties of Western Civilisation*, which warned against the Russian and Slavic threat.
6. Trautsch 2013, 94–95.
7. Thomas Babington Macaulay, *Minute on Indian Education* (1835). See Gogwilt 1995, 221–22.
8. Quoted in Bonnett 2004, 24–25.
9. Nassau William Senior, *A Journal Kept in Turkey and Greece in the Autumn of 1857 and the Beginning of 1858* (London: Longman, Brown, Green, Longmans, and Roberts, 1859), 226–27.
10. Senior, *A Journal Kept in Turkey and Greece*, 227.
11. Rudyard Kipling, first stanza of "The White Man's Burden" (1899).
12. This is explored sensitively in Bonnett 2004, chap. 1.
13. Johann Gaspar Spurzheim, *Outlines of the Physiognomical System* (London: Baldwin, Craddock and Joy, 1815), 58 (also quoted in Malik 1996, 88).
14. For Knox, see Bates 2010.
15. Robert Knox, *The Races of Men* (Philadelphia: Lea and Blanchard, 1850), 8.
16. Josiah Clark Nott and George R. Giddon, *Types of Mankind* (Philadelphia: J. B. Lippincott, 1854), 79.
17. Hawkins 1997, 61–81.
18. *Saturday Review*, January 16, 1864.
19. Sperber 2005.
20. For Marx, see Stedman Jones 2016.
21. Hobsbawm and Ranger 2012.

22. Cohn 2012.
23. For the development of archaeology as a discipline, see Trigger 1989.
24. For many of the biographical details of Gladstone's life, I have relied on Jenkins 2012, although this biography focuses primarily on the personal and religious aspects of his life. For Gladstone's early life and family, see Jenkins 2012, chap. 1. For the enslaving background of his father, see Quinault 2009.
25. Gladstone, *Diaries* 1, 290.
26. Quinault 2009, 366.
27. Cugoano's *Thoughts and Sentiments on the Evil and Wicked Traffic of the Slavery and Commerce of the Human Species* was published in London in 1787; and Equiano's *The Interesting Narrative of the Life of Olaudah Equiano, or Gustavus Vassa, the African* was published in 1789.
28. Quinault 2009, 367.
29. Quinault 2009, 369.
30. Quinault 2009, 386.
31. For Gladstone's ill-fated early romances, see Jenkins 2012, chap. 3; for his marriage to Catherine, see chap. 4.
32. For Gladstone's sexual urges, see Aldous 2007, 52–56; Jenkins 2012, chap. 7.
33. Isba 2003.
34. Ward Fay 2000, 203–6.
35. Kanter 2013–14.
36. Aldous 2007, 157.
37. Wrigley 2012, 68.
38. Aldous 2007, 142–51; Jenkins 2012, chap. 15.
39. Disraeli, speech at the Crystal Palace, June 24, 1872. For the rivalry between Gladstone and Disraeli, see Aldous 2007.
40. Borgstede 2011.
41. Benjamin Disraeli, *Tancred—or The New Crusade* (London: Henry Colburn, 1847).
42. Gladstone, *Studies on Homer and the Homeric Age* (Cambridge: Cambridge University Press, 2010 [1858]), vol. 2, 523.
43. Gladstone, *Address on the Place of Ancient Greece in the Providential Order of the World* (London: Gilbert Murray, 1865), 10.
44. Gladstone, *Address on the Place of Ancient Greece*, 64.
45. Gladstone, *Studies on Homer*, vol. 1, 5.
46. Mac Sweeney 2018; Vlassopoulos 2013, 172; Ross 2005.
47. Gladstone, *Studies on Homer*, vol. 1, 548.
48. Gladstone, *Studies on Homer*, vol. 2, 537.
49. Gladstone, *Address on the Place of Ancient Greece*, 4.
50. Gladstone, *Studies on Homer*, vol. 2, 532.
51. Marchand 2009, 293–300.
52. Gladstone, *Studies on Homer*, vol. 2, 530.

53. Gladstone, *Studies on Homer*, vol. 2, 525.

54. Gladstone, *Address on the Place of Ancient Greece*, 57.

55. Gladstone, *Studies on Homer*, vol. 3, 2.

56. Gladstone, *Studies on Homer*, vol. 1, 67.

57. Gladstone, *Studies on Homer*, vol. 1, 499.

58. Gladstone, *Studies on Homer*, vol. 3, 207.

59. Gladstone, *Studies on Homer*, vol. 2, 483.

60. Gladstone, *Studies on Homer*, vol. 3, 217.

61. Gladstone, *Studies on Homer*, vol. 3, 244.

62. Gladstone, *Bulgarian Horrors*, 11–12.

63. Gladstone, *Bulgarian Horrors*, 10.

64. Edward Augustus Freeman, *Ottoman Power in Europe: Its Nature, Its Growth, and Its Decline* (London: Macmillan and Co., 1877).

65. See papers in Bradley 2010, and also Hingley 2001.

66. "Our Feudatories," *Friend of India* (1861). Quoted from Vasunia 2013, 121.

67. Hegel, "On Classical Studies," lecture delivered in 1809, published in a recent edition in Hegel and Knox 1975.

68. Rebecca Futo Kennedy has traced early uses of the term "Western Civilisation," including a report for the Society for the Promotion of Collegiate and Theological Education in the United States dated 1844, and a literary review discussing a travel book from 1846. I am grateful for her guidance on this point. See Futo Kennedy 2019.

69. Gladstone, *Studies on Homer*, vol. 1, 513.

70. Bhaskar Pandurang Tarkhadkar, letter published in the *Bombay Gazette*, July 28, 1841. Quoted from Vasunia 2013, 122.

71. Vasunia 2013, 124–25.

72. Quoted from Goff 2013, 71.

73. John Collingwood Bruce, *The Roman Wall: A Description of the Mural Barrier of the North of England* (London: Longmans, Green, Reader and Dyer, 1851).

74. Malamud 2016.

75. Prins 2017.

76. Hall and Stead 2020.

CHAPTER 13: THE WEST AND ITS CRITICS

1. Said 1993, 1.

2. E.g., *The Suicide of the West* is taken as a title by both Goldberg 2018 and Koch and Smith 2006, echoing Burnham 1964. Murray 2022 blames "dishonest scholars" committing "intellectual fraud" for leading so many well-intentioned but foolish people astray by encouraging them to critique the West. A European-focused view is taken by Murray 2017.

3. Mason 2022, reporting on a speech given by Oliver Dowden, the Conservative Party chairman.

4. *The War on the West* is the title of a recent book by the British political commentator Douglas Murray (2022). The quote comes from page 13 of this book.

5. For a discussion of Ruskin's views, see Said 1993.

6. Borgstede 2011, 10–17.

7. For the end of the British Empire specifically, see Brendon 2007.

8. In Algeria, the War of Independence (1956–62) was a bloody and brutal conflict, the memory of which was so shameful and traumatic that for decades the French government kept all documents pertaining to it under a strict embargo; see Fanon 1963, "On Violence." At the other end of the spectrum, when Malta gained its independence from Britain in 1964, it did so through a completely peaceful process by mutual agreement; see Smith 2007.

9. For the Cold War, see Westad 2017.

10. For the wider global alignments during the Cold War beyond the America-Russia opposition, see Westad 2017.

11. This phrase is taken from Fukuyama's 1992 bestseller, *The Last Man and the End of History*, which did not, contrary to the implication of its title, argue that there would be no more major events or changes in world history.

12. *Out of Place* is the title of Said's autobiography, written after Said received a diagnosis of leukaemia and published in 1999.

13. I have taken the biographical details of Said's life partly from his own writings, and in particular Said 1999, but also from the excellent and meticulously researched Brennan 2021.

14. For Said's early life, see Brennan 2021, chap. 1.

15. Said 1999, 44.

16. Said 1999, 183.

17. Said 1999, 118–21.

18. Said 1999, 190.

19. Said 2000, 558.

20. Said 2000, 559. For this part of Said's life, see Brennan 2021, chap. 2.

21. Said 1999, 278. For Said's years as a student, see Brennan 2021, chap. 3.

22. Said 1999, 279.

23. Said 1999, 290.

24. For Said's marriage to Jaanus, see Brennan 2021, chap. 4.

25. Brennan 2021 points out that Said was less apolitical during his student years than his autobiography would have us believe, as he kept in touch with Middle Eastern politics.

26. Said 1970.

27. Said 2019; Brennan 2021, chap. 6.

28. Brennan 2021.

29. Said 1993, 380.

30. Said (1978) 1995, 26.

31. Said (1978) 1995, 1.
32. Said (1978) 1995, 3.
33. Said (1978) 2003, preface to the twenty-fifth-anniversary edition.
34. Said (1978) 1995, 2.
35. Warraq 2007.
36. Lewis 1990. Lewis is also credited with coining the term "clash of civilisations," which was later borrowed by Samuel Huntington for the title of his controversial book.
37. For this important subject, see Marchand 2009.
38. Nishihara 2005.
39. For Asia, see Chen 1995; for Africa, see Smail Salhi 2019.
40. Said (1978), 1995, xix.
41. Said (1978) 1995, 55.
42. Mac Sweeney 2018; Vlassopoulos 2013, 172; Ross 2005.
43. Said 1993, 407–8.
44. Said 2000, 173.
45. Issa 2018. Poem reproduced with the kind permission of Hanan Issa.

CHAPTER 14: THE WEST AND ITS RIVALS

1. Speech at the opening of the M+ centre in the West Kowloon Cultural District, November 11, 2021.
2. Healy 2021.
3. Mahbubani 2020; Strangio 2020; Frankopan 2018.
4. Address to a Joint Session of Congress and the American People, September 20, 2001, https://georgewbush-whitehouse.archives.gov/news/releases/2001/09/20010920-8.html.
5. For the Islamic State, see Filipec 2020.
6. For the economics of Daesh, see Filipec 2020, 165–83.
7. Analyses of these techniques is offered in Goertz 2021, 123–68; Lakomy 2021.
8. Sahih Muslim, bk. 041, Hadith 6294.
9. For analysis of *Dabiq* and *Rumiyah*, see Wignell et al. 2017; Lakomy 2021, 125–206.
10. "Know Your Enemy: Who Were the Safawiyyah?" *Dabiq*, no. 13 (2016): 12.
11. Flood and Elsner 2016 explores this issue further.
12. An infamous video was released online in February 2015, showing the smashing of artefacts and statues in the Mosul Museum, with most damage done in the Assyrian and Hatrene galleries. Brusaco 2016 provides an initial assessment of the damage, and Isakhan and Meskell 2019 discusses the UNESCO plan for reconstruction and regeneration after the fall of Daesh.
13. Campell 2013.
14. Cunliffe and Curini (2018) have conducted sentiment analysis on patterns of social media usage as a means of assessing the international response to these events.

15. Quote from a speech by Boris Johnson, as reported by the BBC, April 19, 2016, accessed February 26, 2022, https://www.bbc.com/news/uk-36070721.
16. Schmidt-Colinet 2019.
17. Schmidt-Colinet 2019, 42.
18. Plokhy 2017, chapter 19.
19. For the use of this phrase, see Toal 2017, chap. 2.
20. Lucas 2008.
21. The text of this essay is available on the Kremlin website: Vladimir Putin, "On the Historical Unity of Russians and Ukrainians," Kremlin, July 12, 2021, accessed February 26, 2022, http://en.kremlin.ru/events/president/news/66181.
22. For a discussion of the historical development of Russian identity and the significance of Ukraine within this, see Plokhy 2017, chap. 7; also Toal 2017.
23. Poe 2001.
24. Plokhy 2017, chap. 2.
25. Poe 2001; Kolb 2008, 17–18; Trautsch 2013.
26. Kolb 2008, 195.
27. E.g., Allison 2018.
28. For this debate in mid-twentieth-century Chinese historical scholarship, see Fan 2021. For the textbook in particular, see Fan 2021, 159.
29. For Lin Zhichun's broader activities, see Fan 2021, 87. For the discipline of "Classics" (i.e., the study of the Greco-Roman world) in China, see Brashear 1990.
30. For a Western perspective on China's historical thinking, see Stallard 2022.
31. "Athens Declaration on the Establishment of the Ancient Civilizations Forum," Ministry of Foreign Affairs of the People's Republic of China, April 24, 2017, accessed February 26, 2022, https://www.fmprc.gov.cn/mfa_eng/wjdt_665385/2649 _665393/201704/t20170428_679494.html.
32. "Kotzias in Bolivia for Ancient Civilizations Forum," *Kathimerini*, July 14, 2018, accessed February 26, 2022, https://www.ekathimerini.com/news/230701/kotzias -in-bolivia-for-ancient-civilizations-forum.
33. Wang Kaihao, "Ancient Civilizations Forum Meets in Beijing," *China Daily*, December 3, 2019, accessed February 26, 2022, https://www.chinadaily.com.cn/a/201912 /03/WS5de5aed1a310cf3e3557b79c.html.
34. "Lima Declaration, Ancient Civilizations Forum, Fourth Ministerial Meeting, 15th of December of 2020, Lima, Republic of Peru," accessed February 26, 2022, http:// www.peruthai.or.th/news.php.
35. Media3, "Acting Head of Department of International Organizations and Conferences Participates in the Fourth Ministerial Meeting of Forum of Ancient Civilizations," Republic of Iraq, Ministry of Foreign Affairs, December 20, 2020, accessed February 26, 2022, https://www.mofa.gov.iq/2020/12/?p=19956.
36. "Statement by Vahe Gevorgyan, Deputy-Minister of Foreign Affairs of Armenia, at the 5th Ministerial Meeting of the Ancient Civilizations Forum," Ministry of

Foreign Affairs of the Republic of Armenia, December 17, 2021, accessed February 26, 2022, https://www.mfa.am/en/speeches/2021/12/17/dfm-ancient_civilization _speech/11245.

37. "Athens Declaration on the Establishment of the Ancient Civilizations Forum."

38. "Spotlight: Countries Turn to Cement Cultural, Economic Ties as Ancient Civilization Forum Opens," Xinhua, April 25, 2017, accessed February 26, 2022, http://www .xinhuanet.com//english/2017-04/25/c_136232938.htm.

39. AFP, "'Ancient Civilisations' Team Up to Protect Heritage from Terrorism," *Times of Israel*, April 24, 2017, accessed February 26, 2022, https://www.timesofisrael.com /ancient-civilizations-team-up-to-protect-heritage-from-terrorism/.

40. Li 2019.

41. He 2019.

42. Chinese universities have a tradition of scholarly excellence in the study of Greco-Roman antiquity, including: Renmin, Fudan, Nanjing, Peking, Shanghai Normal University, Northeast Normal University, and Beijing Normal University. See Brashear 1990.

43. As reported by the Renmin University website: "The Conference on Spiritual Dialogue between China and Greece Was Held in Beijing," Renmin University of China, January 27, 2022, accessed February 26, 2022, https://www.ruc.edu.cn /archives/34651.

44. "New Academic Era with the Establishment of Sino-Greek Cooperation Programme," Study in Greece, October 22, 2021, accessed February 16, 2022, https:// studyingreece.edu.gr/new-academic-era-with-the-establishment-of-sino-greek -cooperation-programme.

45. "New Academic Era."

46. "The Conference on Spiritual Dialogue between China and Greece Was Held in Beijing."

47. He 2019, 432.

48. The conference website is available at the Aikaterini Laskaridis Foundation, accessed July 22, 2022, http://www.laskaridisfoundation.org/en/china-and-greece -from-ancient-civilisations-to-modern-partnerships.

49. Majende et al. 2018. The role played by cultural diplomacy, based on the idea of ancient China and ancient Greece as analogues, in strengthening the Belt and Road Initiative is highlighted in He 2019.

50. As set out expertly in Frankopan 2018.

51. He 2019; Laihui 2019; Li 2019.

52. Wang Yi, "Revitalizing the Ancient Civilisation and Jointly Constructing a Community of Shared Future for Mankind," speech at the First Ancient Civilizations Forum, Ministry of Foreign Affairs of the People's Republic of China, https://www .mfa.gov.cn/ce/ceno/eng/zgwj_1/t1456650.htm. This open acknowledgement of history as political is not a recent phenomenon in China, nor is it linked exclusively

to the Belt and Road Initiative. After all, Mao Zedong himself famously called for projects that would "make the past serve the present" (see Fan 2021, 161).

53. Speech at the opening of the M+ centre in the West Kowloon Cultural District, November 11, 2021.

54. The following details about Lam's early life have been repeated in a number of interviews and feature articles, the most accessible of which is "Hong Kong Protests: 8 Things You Might Not Know about Carrie Lam, Hong Kong's Chief Secretary," *Straits Times*, October 3, 2014, accessed February 26, 2022, https://www.straitstimes.com /asia/east-asia/hong-kong-protests-8-things-you-might-not-know-about-carrie-lam -hong-kongs-chief.

55. Lau 2016.

56. Lau 2016.

57. "Hong Kong Protests: 8 Things You Might Not Know."

58. Tong 2017.

59. Bland 2017.

60. The political development of Wong and Chow is outlined in Wong 2020.

61. "New Hong Kong Leader's Rude Nickname Portends Challenges Ahead," *Business Times*, March 27, 2017, accessed February 26, 2022, https://www.businesstimes.com .sg/government-economy/new-hong-kong-leaders-rude-nickname-portends -challenges-ahead.

62. For this stress on patriots, see "Xi Focus: Xi Stresses 'Patriots Governing Hong Kong' When Hearing Carrie Lam's Work Report," Xinhua, January 27, 2021, accessed February 26, 2022, http://www.xinhuanet.com/english/2021-01/27/c _139702049.htm.

63. Creery 2019.

64. Anne Marie Roantree and James Pomfret, "Beholden to Beijing," Reuters, December 28, 2020, accessed February 26, 2022, https://www.reuters.com/investigates /special-report/hongkong-security-lam.

65. Talk given by Carrie Lam in August 2019 to business leaders, transcribed here: Reuters Staff, "Exclusive: The Chief Executive 'Has to Serve Two Masters'—HK Leader Carrie Lam—Full Transcript," Reuters, September 12, 2019, accessed February 26, 2022, https://www.reuters.com/article/us-hongkong-protests-lam-transcript-excl -idUSKCN1VX0P7.

66. Speech at the opening of the M+ centre in the West Kowloon Cultural District, November 11, 2021.

67. "CE Addresses Business Sector on Opportunities Brought About by 14th Five-Year Plan," press release, June, 3, 2021, accessed February 26, 2022, https://www.info.gov .hk/gia/general/202106/03/P2021060300736.htm.

68. "Speech by CE at Bauhinia Culture International Forum," press release, June 16, 2022, accessed August 18, 2022, https://www.info.gov.hk/gia/general/202206/16 /P2022061600318.htm.

NOTES

CONCLUSION: THE SHAPE OF HISTORY

1. My thanks to my colleague Dr. Matthias Hoernes in Vienna for his insights and discussion on the issue of historicity and the nature of facts.

2. See the excellent Woods 2022 on politically inflected nostalgia in Britain over the centuries.

3. See Applebaum 2020 and Fukuyama 2022.

4. Among these are several prominent Anglophone classicists of the previous generation. For an example of this, see Victor Davis Hanson's book, *Why the West Has Won* (London: Faber & Faber, 2001).

5. Perhaps the most (in)famous classicist making this argument in the public eye is Dan-el Padilla Peralta; see Poser 2021. For a sense of the debates amongst classicists and their development, I would recommend reading the work of Rebecca Futo Kennedy, available online at her blog: *Classics at the Intersections* (https://rfkclassics .blogspot.com/). For intelligent discussion of the academic discipline of Classics, its development, and its complicity in Western imperialism and colonialism, see the various discussions over the course of this book but also especially: Goff 2013; Bradley 2010; Goff 2005.

REFERENCES

Abernethy, David. 2002. *The Dynamics of Global Dominance: European Overseas Empires, 1415–1980*. Illustrated ed. New Haven, CT: Yale University Press.

Adamson, Peter. 2004. "Al-Kindī and the Reception of Greek Philosophy." In *The Cambridge Companion to Arabic Philosophy*, ed. Richard C. Taylor, 32–51. Cambridge Companions to Philosophy. Cambridge: Cambridge University Press.

Adamson, Peter. 2007. *Al-Kindī*. Great Medieval Thinkers. Oxford: Oxford University Press.

Adolph, Anthony. 2015. *Brutus of Troy: And the Quest for the Ancestry of the British*. Barnsley, UK: Pen & Sword Books.

Adorno, Theodor W., and Max Horkheimer. (1972) 1997. *Dialectic of Enlightenment*. London: Verso Books.

Aerts, Willem J. 2012. "Troy in Byzantium." In *Troy: City, Homer, Turkey*, ed. Jorrit M. Kelder, Günay Uslu, and Ömer F. Şerifoğlu, 98–104. Zwolle: WBOOKS.

Agbamu, Sam. 2019. "Mare Nostrum: Italy and the Mediterranean of Ancient Rome in the Twentieth and Twenty-First Centuries." *Fascism* 8: 250–74.

Ahmad, Aijaz. 1992. *In Theory: Classes, Nations, Literatures*. London: Verso Books.

Ailes, Marianne. 2012. "Charlemagne 'Father of Europe': A European Icon in the Making." *Reading Medieval Studies* 38: 59–76.

Akers, Charles W. 1978. "Religion and the American Revolution: Samuel Cooper and the Brattle Street Church." *William and Mary Quarterly* 35 (3): 477–98.

Akrigg, Ben. 2019. *Population and Economy in Classical Athens*. Cambridge Classical Studies. Cambridge: Cambridge University Press.

Aldous, Richard. 2007. *The Lion and the Unicorn: Gladstone vs. Disraeli*. New York: W. W. Norton.

Al-Khalili, Jim. 2011. *The House of Wisdom: How Arabic Science Saved Ancient Knowledge and Gave Us the Renaissance*. New York: Penguin Books.

Al-Kindī, Yaʿqūb Ibn-Isḥāq al-Sabāh, Peter Adamson, and Peter E. Pormann. 2012. *The Philosophical Works of Al-Kindī*. Studies in Islamic Philosophy. Oxford: Oxford University Press.

Allaire, Gloria. 1995. "Tullia d'Aragona's *II Meschino Altramente Detto Il Guerrino* as Key to a Reappraisal of Her Work." *Quaderni d'italianistica* 16 (1): 33–50.

Allaire, Gloria. 1999. "From Medieval Realism to Modern Fantasy: Guerrino Meschino through the Centuries." In *Modern Retellings of Chivalric Texts*, ed. Gloria Allaire, 133–46. London: Routledge.

Allen, Archibald. 1993. *The Fragments of Mimnermus: Text and Commentary*. Palingenesia 44. Stuttgart, Germany: Steiner.

Allen, Robert C. 2009. *The British Industrial Revolution in Global Perspective*. Cambridge: Cambridge University Press.

Allen, Theodore W. 1994. *The Invention of the White Race*. Vol. 1, *Racial Oppression and Social Control*. London: Verso Books.

Allen, Theodore W. 1997. *The Invention of the White Race*. Vol. 2, *The Origin of Racial Oppression in Anglo-America*. London: Verso Books.

Allison, Graham. 2018. *Destined for War: Can America and China Escape Thucydides's Trap?* London: Scribe UK.

Al-Masūdī, Alī Ibn-al-Ḥusain, C. Barbier de Meynard, and Abel Pavet de Courteille. 1861–1917. *Maçoudi. Les prairies d'or. Texte et Traduction*. Collection d'ouvrages orientaux. Paris: Imprimerie impériale.

Ames, Christine Caldwell. 2015. *Medieval Heresies: Christianity, Judaism, and Islam*. Cambridge: Cambridge University Press.

Andùjar, Rosa, Elena Giusti, and Jackie Murray, eds. Forthcoming. *The Cambridge Companion to Classics and Race*. Cambridge: Cambridge University Press.

Andújar, Rosa, and Konstantinos P. Nikoloutsos. 2020. "Staging the European Classical in 'Latin' America: An Introduction." In *Greeks and Romans on the Latin American Stage*, ed. Rosa Andújar and Konstantinos P. Nikoloutsos, 1–15. London: Bloomsbury.

Angelicoussis, Elizabeth. 2004. "The Collection of Classical Sculptures of the Earl of Arundel, 'Father of Vertu in England.'" *Journal of the History of Collections* 16 (2): 143–59.

Angelov, Dimiter G. 2011. "The 'Moral Pieces' by Theodore II Laskaris." *Dumbarton Oaks Papers* 65–66:237–69.

Angelov, Dimiter. 2019. *The Byzantine Hellene: The Life of Emperor Theodore Laskaris and Byzantium in the Thirteenth Century*. Cambridge: Cambridge University Press.

Angelov, Dimiter, and Judith Herrin. 2012. "The Christian Imperial Tradition—Greek and Latin." In *Universal Empire: A Comparative Approach to Imperial Culture and Representation in Eurasian History,* ed. Peter Fibiger Bang and Dariusz Kołodziejczyk, 149–74. Cambridge: Cambridge University Press.

Angold, Michael. 2009. "The Greek Rump States and the Recovery of Byzantium." In *The Cambridge History of the Byzantine Empire c. 500–1492,* ed. Jonathan Shepard, 729–58. Cambridge: Cambridge University Press.

Ansary, Tamim. 2010. *Destiny Disrupted: A History of the World through Islamic Eyes.* New York: Public Affairs.

Appiah, Kwame Anthony. 2016. "There Is No Such Thing as Western Civilisation." *The Guardian,* November 9, 2016, sec. World News.

Appiah, Kwame Anthony. 2018. *The Lies That Bind: Rethinking Identity.* New York: Liveright.

Applebaum, Anne. 2020. *Twilight of Democracy: The Seductive Lure of Authoritarianism.* New York: Anchor.

Arbo, Desiree. 2018. "Plato and the Guarani Indians." *Bulletin of Latin American Research* 37 (S1): 119–31.

Asheri, David, Alan B. Lloyd, Aldo Corcella, Oswyn Murray, and Alfonso Moreno. 2007. "General Introduction." In *A Commentary on Herodotus Books I–IV,* 1–57. Oxford: Oxford University Press.

Atakuman, Çiğdem. 2008. "Cradle or Crucible: Anatolia and Archaeology in the Early Years of the Turkish Republic (1923–1938)." *Journal of Social Archaeology* 8 (2): 214–35.

Aubriet, Damien. 2013. "Mylasa et l'identité carienne." *Publications de l'Institut Français d'Études Anatoliennes* 28 (1): 189–208.

Aughterson, Kate. 2002. "Strange Things so Probably Told: Gender, Sexual Difference and Knowledge in Bacon's New Atlantis." In *Francis Bacon's New Atlantis,* ed. Bronwen Price, 156–78. Manchester: Manchester University Press.

Baer, Marc. 2021. *The Ottomans: Khans, Caesars, and Caliphs.* New York: Basic Books.

Barbier, Brooke, and Alan Taylor. 2017. *Boston in the American Revolution: A Town versus an Empire.* Cheltenham, UK: History Press.

Baritz, Loren. 1961. "The Idea of the West." *American Historical Review* 66 (3): 618–40.

Barth, Fredrik. 1969. *Ethnic Groups and Boundaries: The Social Organization of Culture Difference.* Bergen, Norway: Universitetet i Bergen.

Bates, Alan. 2010. *The Anatomy of Robert Knox: Murder, Mad Science and Medical Regulation in Nineteenth-Century Edinburgh*. Sussex, UK: Sussex Academic Press.

Beard, Mary. 2009. *The Roman Triumph*. Cambridge, MA: Harvard University Press.

Beasley, Edward. 2010. *The Victorian Reinvention of Race: New Racisms and the Problem of Grouping in the Human Sciences*. New York: Routledge.

Beaton, Roderick. 2019. *Greece: Biography of a Modern Nation*. London: Penguin.

Beaton, Roderick. 2021. *The Greeks: A Global History*. London: Faber & Faber.

Beck, Hans, and Peter Funke, eds. 2015. *Federalism in Greek Antiquity*. Cambridge: Cambridge University Press.

Bellemore, Jane. 1995. "The Wife of Sejanus." *Zeitschrift für Papyrologie und Epigraphik* 109: 255–66.

Bennison, Amira K. 2009. *The Great Caliphs: The Golden Age of the 'Abbasid Empire*. New Haven, CT: Yale University Press.

Berlin, Andrea M., and J. Andrew Overman, eds. 2003. *The First Jewish Revolt: Archaeology, History and Ideology*. London: Routledge.

Berruecos Frank, Bernardo. 2022. "Classical Traditions and Internal Colonialism in Early Eighteenth-Century Mexico: Text, Translation, and Notes on Three of Villerías' Greek Epigrams." *International Journal of the Classical Tradition* 29 (3): 281–306.

Bindman, David. 2002. *Ape to Apollo: Aesthetics and the Idea of Race in the 18th Century*. London: Reaktion Books.

Birley, Anthony R. 1997. *Hadrian: The Restless Emperor*. London: Routledge.

Bland, Ben. 2017. *Generation HK: Seeking Identity in China's Shadow*. Melbourne, Australia: Penguin.

Boeck, Elena N. 2015. *Imagining the Byzantine Past: The Perception of History in the Illustrated Manuscripts of Skylitzes and Manasses*. Cambridge: Cambridge University Press.

Bonner, Stanley. 2012. *Education in Ancient Rome: From the Elder Cato to the Younger Pliny*. London: Routledge.

Bonnett, Alastair. 2004. *The Idea of the West: Culture, Politics and History*. Basingstoke, UK: Palgrave Macmillan.

Bonnett, Alastair. 2021. *Multiracism: Rethinking Racism in Global Context*. 1st ed. Cambridge: Polity Books.

Borgstede, Simone Beate. 2011. *"All Is Race": Benjamin Disraeli on Race, Nation and Empire*. Münster, Germany: LIT Verlag.

Boulègue, Jean. 2012. "Un Écho d'Hérodote dans les Représentations Cartographiques Africaines." In *Hérodote à La Renaissance*, ed. Susanna Gambino Longo, 167–174. Turnhout, Belgium: Brepols.

Bowersock, Glen Warren. 1994. *Roman Arabia*. Cambridge, MA: Harvard University Press.

Bradley, Mark, ed. 2010. *Classics and Imperialism in the British Empire*. Oxford: Oxford University Press.

Brashear, William. 1990. "Classics in China." *The Classical Journal* 86: 73–78.

Brendon, Piers. 2007. *The Decline and Fall of the British Empire*. London: Jonathan Cape.

Brennan, Timothy. 2021. *Places of Mind: A Life of Edward Said*. London: Bloomsbury.

Briggs, John Channing. 1981. "Chapman's Seaven Bookes of the Iliades: Mirror for Essex." *Studies in English Literature, 1500–1900* 21 (1): 59–73.

Brotton, Jerry. 2006. *The Renaissance: A Very Short Introduction*. Oxford: Oxford University Press.

Brotton, Jerry. 2016. *This Orient Isle: Elizabethan England and the Islamic World*. London: Allen Lane.

Brown, Michelle P. 2003. *The Lindisfarne Gospels: Society, Spirituality and the Scribe*. Toronto: University of Toronto Press.

Brownlee, Kevin. 2007. "Dante and the Classical Poets." In *The Cambridge Companion to Dante*, ed. Rachel Jacoff, 2nd ed., 141–60. Cambridge Companions to Literature. Cambridge: Cambridge University Press.

Brucia, Margaret A. 2001. "The African-American Poet, Jupiter Hammon: A Home-Born Slave and His Classical Name." *International Journal of the Classical Tradition* 7 (4): 515.

Brusasco, Paolo. 2016. "The Assyrian Sculptures in the Mosul Cultural Museum: A Preliminary Assessment of What Was on Display Before Islamic State's Attack." *Journal of Near Eastern Studies* 75 (2): 205–48.

Bulut, Mehmet. 2001. *Ottoman-Dutch Economic Relations in the Early Modern Period 1571–1699*. Hilversum, Netherlands: Uitgeverij Verloren.

Bumke, Joachim. 1991. *Courtly Culture: Literature and Society in the High Middle Ages*. Berkeley: University of California Press.

Burckhardt, Jacob. (1860) 1945. *Die Cultur der Renaissance in Italien: ein Versuch*. Basel: Schweighauser. Translated ed. by S. G. C. Middlemore. *The Civilisation of the Renaissance in Italy*. London: Spottiswoode and Co. Citations refer to Spottiswoode edition.

Burioni, Matteo. 2010. "Vasari's Rinascita: History, Anthropology or Art Criticism?" In *Renaissance? Perceptions of Continuity and Discontinuity in Europe, c. 1300–c. 1550,* ed. P. Péporté, A. Lee, and H. Schnitker, 115–27. Leiden: Brill.

Burke, Peter. 1980. "Did Europe Exist before 1700?" *History of European Ideas* 1 (1): 21–29.

Burnham, James. 1964. *Suicide of the West: An Essay on the Meaning and Destiny of Liberalism.* New York: Encounter Books.

Buttigieg, E. 2021. "A Habsburg Thalassocracy: Habsburgs and Hospitallers in the Early Modern Mediterranean, c. 1690–1750." In *The Habsburg Mediterranean 1500–1800,* ed. Stefan Hanß and Dorothea McEwan, 99–118. Vienna: Austrian Academy of Sciences.

Butler, Todd. 2015. "The Cognitive Politics of Writing in Jacobean England: Bacon, Coke, and the Case of Edmund Peacham." *Huntington Library Quarterly* 78 (1): 21–39.

Campbell, Chris. 2022. "The Rhetoric of Hobbes's Translation of Thucydides." *Review of Politics* 84 (1): 1–24.

Campbell, Peter B. 2013. "The Illicit Antiquities Trade as a Transnational Criminal Network: Characterizing and Anticipating Trafficking of Cultural Heritage." *International Journal of Cultural Property* 20: 113–53.

Carless Unwin, Naomi. 2017. *Caria and Crete in Antiquity: Cultural Interaction between Anatolia and the Aegean.* Cambridge: Cambridge University Press.

Carretta, Vincent. 2003. "Who Was Francis Williams?" *Early American Literature* 38 (2): 213–37.

Cartledge, Paul. 2009. "Hellenism in the Enlightenment." In *The Oxford Handbook of Hellenic Studies,* ed. Phiroze Vasunia, George Boys-Stones, and Barbara Graziosi, 166–72. Oxford: Oxford University Press.

Casali, Sergio. 2010. "The Development of the Aeneas Legend." In *A Companion to Vergil's Aeneid and Its Tradition,* ed. Joseph Farrell and Michael C. J. Putnam, 37–51. Hoboken, NJ: Wiley.

Castriota, D. 2005. "Feminizing the Barbarian and Barbarizing the Feminine: Amazons, Trojans, and Persians in the Stoa Poikile." In *Periclean Athens and Its Legacy: Problems and Perspectives,* ed. J. M. Barringer and J. M. Hurwitt, 89–102. Austin: University of Texas Press.

Catlos, Brian A. 2018. *Kingdoms of Faith: A New History of Islamic Spain.* Oxford: Oxford University Press.

Challis, Debbie. 2010. "'The Ablest Race': The Ancient Greeks in Victorian Racial Theory." In *Classics and Imperialism in the British Empire*, ed. Mark Bradley. Oxford: Oxford University Press, 94–120.

Chang, Vincent K. L. 2022. "China's New Historical Statecraft: Reviving the Second World War for National Rejuvenation." *International Affairs* 98 (3): 1053–69.

Chen, Xiaomei. 1995. *Occidentalism: A Theory of Counter-Discourse in Post-Mao China*. New York and Oxford: Oxford University Press.

Chiasson, Charles C. 2003. "Herodotus' Use of Attic Tragedy in the Lydian Logos." *Classical Antiquity* 22 (1): 5–35.

Ching, Julia, and Willard G. Oxtoby, eds. 1992. *Discovering China: European Interpretations in the Enlightenment*. Library of the History of Ideas 7. Rochester, NY: University of Rochester Press.

Chrissis, Nikolaos G., Mike Carr, and Christoph Maier, eds. 2014. *Contact and Conflict in Frankish Greece and the Aegean, 1204–1453: Crusade, Religion and Trade between Latins, Greeks and Turks*. Farnham, UK: Routledge.

Cobb, Paul. 2016. *The Race for Paradise: An Islamic History of the Crusades*. Oxford: Oxford University Press.

Cohn, Bernand S. 2012. "Representing Authority in Victorian India." In *The Invention of Tradition*, ed. Eric Hobsbawm and Terence Ranger, 165–210. Cambridge: Cambridge University Press.

Cole, Joshua, and Carol Symes. 2020. *Western Civilisations*. Brief 5th ed. New York: W. W. Norton.

Colvin, Steven. 2010. "Greek Dialects in the Archaic and Classical Ages." In *A Companion to the Ancient Greek Language*, ed. Egbert J. Bakker, 200–212. Blackwell Companions to the Ancient World. Chichester, UK: Wiley-Blackwell.

Commager, Henry Steele, and Richard B. Morris. 1968. *The Spirit of Seventy-Six: The Story of the American Revolution As Told by Participants*. New York: Da Capo Press.

Conrad, Sebastian. 2012. "Enlightenment in Global History: A Historiographical Critique." *American Historical Review* 117 (4): 999–1027.

Cook, Robert Manuel. 1981. *Clazomenian sarcophagi*. Forschungen zur antiken Keramik: Reihe 2, Kerameus 3. Mainz on the Rhine: von Zabern.

Cook, William W., and James Tatum. 2010. *African American Writers and Classical Tradition*. Chicago: University of Chicago Press.

Creery, Jennifer. 2019. "Emotional Leader Carrie Lam Says She 'Sacrificed' for Hong Kong, as Police Use Tear Gas, Rubber Bullets to Clear Protests." *Hong Kong Free Press*, June 12, 2019.

Cunliffe, Emma, and Luigi Curini. 2018. "ISIS and Heritage Destruction: A Sentiment Analysis." *Antiquity* 92 (364): 1094–111.

D'Aragona, Tullia, John C. McLucas, and Julia Hairston, eds. Forthcoming. *The Wretch, Otherwise Known as Guerrino, by Tullia D'Aragona*. The Other Voice in Early Modern Europe. Toronto: University of Toronto Press.

Dardenay, Alexandra. 2010. *Les Mythes Fondateurs de Rome: Images et Politique dans l'Occident Romain*. Paris: Picard.

De Angelis, Franco, ed. 2020. *A Companion to Greeks across the Ancient World*. Vol. 158. Blackwell Companions to the Ancient World. Newark, NJ: John Wiley & Sons.

Delanty, Gerard. 1995. *Inventing Europe: Idea, Identity, Reality*. New York: St. Martin's Press.

Desmond, Marilynn. 2016. "Trojan Itineraries and the Matter of Troy." In *The Oxford History of Classical Reception in English Literature*, ed. Rita Copeland, 251–68. Oxford: Oxford University Press.

Disney, A. R. 2009. *A History of Portugal and the Portuguese Empire: From Beginnings to 1807*. Vol. 2, *The Portuguese Empire*. Cambridge: Cambridge University Press.

Di Spigna, Christian. 2018. *Founding Martyr: The Life and Death of Dr. Joseph Warren, the American Revolution's Lost Hero*. New York: Crown.

Donnellan, Lieve. 2016. "'Greek Colonization' and Mediterranean Networks: Patterns of Mobility and Interaction at Pithekoussai." *Journal of Greek Archaeology* 1: 109–48.

Dorninger, Maria E. 1997. *Gottfried von Viterbo: Ein Autor in der Umgebung der frühen Staufer*. Salzburger Beiträge 31. Stuttgart: Heinz.

Dorninger, Maria E. 2015. "Modern Readers of Godfrey." In *Godfrey of Viterbo and His Readers: Imperial Tradition and Universal History in Late Medieval Europe*, ed. Thomas Foerster, 13–36. Church, Faith and Culture in the Medieval West. Farnham, UK: Ashgate Publishing.

Doufikar-Aerts, Faustina C. W. 2016. "A Hero without Borders: 2 Alexander the Great in the Syriac and Arabic Tradition." In *Fictional Storytelling in the Medieval Eastern Mediterranean and Beyond*, ed. Bettina Krönung and Carolina Cupane, 1:190–209. Leiden: Brill.

Dreyer, Edward L. 2006. *Zheng He: China and the Oceans in the Early Ming Dynasty, 1405–1433*. New York: Pearson.

Drogin, Sara S. 2008. *Spare Me the Details!: A Short History of Western Civilisation*. Bloomington, IN: iUniverse.

Eigen, Sara, and Mark Larrimore, eds. 2006. *The German Invention of Race*. Ithaca: State University of New York Press.

Engels, Johannes. 2010. "Macedonians and Greeks." In *A Companion to Ancient Macedonia*, ed. J. Roisman and Ian Worthington, 81–98. Oxford: Wiley Blackwell.

Erskine, Andrew. 2001. *Troy Between Greece and Rome: Local Tradition and Imperial Power*. Reprint ed. Oxford: Oxford University Press.

Evrigenis, Ioannis D. 2006. "Hobbes's Thucydides." *Journal of Military Ethics* 5 (4): 303–16.

Fafinski, Mateusz. 2021. *Roman Infrastructure in Early Medieval Britain*. Amsterdam: Amsterdam University Press.

Falk, Seb. 2020. *The Light Ages: The Surprising Story of Medieval Science*. New York: W. W. Norton.

Fan, Xin. 2021. *World History and National Identity in China: The Twentieth Century*. Cambridge: Cambridge University Press.

Fanon, Franz. 1963. *The Wretched of the Earth*. New York: Grove Press.

Fauvelle, François-Xavier. 2018. *The Golden Rhinoceros: Histories of the African Middle Ages*. Princeton, NJ: Princeton University Press.

Feile Tomes, Maya. 2015. "News of a Hitherto Unknown Neo-Latin Columbus Epic, Part II: José Manuel Peramás's 'De Invento Novo Orbe Inductoque Illuc Christi Sacrificio' (1777)." *International Journal of the Classical Tradition* 22 (2): 223–57.

Fernández-Götz, Manuel, Dominik Maschek, and Nico Roymans. 2020. "The Dark Side of the Empire: Roman Expansionism between Object Agency and Predatory Regime." *Antiquity* 94 (378): 1630–39.

Field, Arthur. 1988. *The Origins of the Platonic Academy of Florence*. Princeton Legacy Library. Princeton, NJ: Princeton University Press.

Fierro, Maribel, ed. 2020. *The Routledge Handbook of Muslim Iberia*. Milton Park, UK: Taylor and Francis.

Filipec, Ondřej. 2020. *The Islamic State: From Terrorism to Totalitarian Insurgency*. London: Routledge.

Finkelstein, J. J. 1963. "Mesopotamian Historiography." *Proceedings of the American Philosophical Society* 107 (6): 461–72.

Flood, Finbarr Barry, and Jaś Elsner. 2016. "Idol-Breaking as Image-Making in the 'Islamic State.'" *Religion and Society* 7: 116–27.

Forman, Samuel A. 2011. *Dr. Joseph Warren: The Boston Tea Party, Bunker Hill, and the Birth of American Liberty.* Gretna, LA: Pelican Publishing.

Fowler, Corinne. 2021. *Green Unpleasant Land: Creative Responses to Rural England's Colonial Connections.* Leeds: Peepal Tree.

Fowler, Robert L. 1999. "Genealogical Thinking, Hesiod's Catalogue, and the Creation of the Hellenes." *Cambridge Classical Journal* 44: 1–19.

Frankopan, Peter. 2019. *The New Silk Roads: The Present and Future of the World.* London: Bloomsbury Publishing.

Frassetto, M., and D. Blanks, eds. 1999. *Western Views of Islam in Medieval and Early Modern Europe: Perception of Other.* New York: Palgrave Macmillan.

Freed, John B. 2016. *Frederick Barbarossa: The Prince and the Myth.* New Haven, CT: Yale University Press.

French, Howard W. 2021. *Born in Blackness: Africa, Africans, and the Making of the Modern World, 1471 to the Second World War.* New York: Liveright.

Frisch, Peter. 1975. *Die Inschriften von Ilion.* Vol. 3, *Inschriften griechischer Städte aus Kleinasien.* Bonn: Habelt.

Frothingham, Richard. 1865. *Life and Times of Joseph Warren.* Boston: Little, Brown.

Fuchs, Werner. 1975. "Die Bildgeschichte der Flucht des Aeneas." *Aufstieg und Niedergang der römischen Welt* 1 (4): 615–32.

Fukuyama, Francis. 2022. *Liberalism and Its Discontents.* New York: Farrar, Straus and Giroux.

Furstenberg, François. 2007. *In the Name of the Father: Washington's Legacy, Slavery, and the Making of a Nation.* Reprint ed. New York: Penguin Books.

Futo Kennedy, Rebecca. 2019. "On the History of 'Western Civilisation,' Part 1." *Classics at the Intersections* (blog). April 2019. https://rfkclassics.blogspot.com/2019/04/on-history-of-western-civilization-part.html.

Futo Kennedy, Rebecca. 2022. "Classics and 'Western Civilisation': The Troubling History of an Authoritative Narrative." In *Authority: Ancient Models, Modern Questions,* ed. Federico Santangelo and Juliana Bastos Marques 87–108. London: Bloomsbury Academic.

Gagné, Renaud. 2006. "What Is the Pride of Halicarnassus?" *Classical Antiquity* 25 (1): 1–33.

Gajda, Alexandra. 2012. *The Earl of Essex and Late Elizabethan Political Culture.* Oxford Historical Monographs. Oxford: Oxford University Press.

Galinsky, Karl. 2020. "Herakles Vajrapani, the Companion of Buddha." In *Herakles Inside and Outside the Church*, ed. Arlene L. Allan, Eva Anagnostou-Laoutides, and Emma Stafford, 315–32. Leiden: Brill.

Gates, Henry Louis, Jr. 2003. "Phillis Wheatley on Trial." *The New Yorker*, January 20, 82–87.

Giovannozzi, Delfina. 2019. "Leone Ebreo in Tullia d'Aragona's Dialogo: Between Varchi's Legacy and Philosophical Autonomy." *British Journal for the History of Philosophy* 27(4): 702–17.

Gladhill, Bill. 2009. "The Poetics of Alliance in Vergil's Aeneid." *Dictynna: Revue de Poétique Latine*, no. 6 (June).

Glassner, Jean-Jacques. 2004. *Mesopotamian Chronicles*, ed. Benjamin R. Foster. Writings from the Ancient World 19. Atlanta: Society of Biblical Literature.

Goertz, Stefan. 2021. *Der neue Terrorismus: Neue Akteure, Strategien, Taktiken und Mittel*. 2nd ed. Wiesbaden, Germany: Springer Fachmedien.

Goff, Barbara, ed. 2005. *Classics and Colonialism*. London: Duckworth.

Goff, Barbara E. 2013. *"Your Secret Language": Classics in the British Colonies of West Africa*. New York: Bloomsbury Academic.

Gogwilt, Christopher. 1995. *The Invention of the West. Joseph Conrad and the Double-Mapping of Europe and Empire*. Stanford, CA: Stanford University Press.

Goldberg, Jonah. 2018. *Suicide of the West: How the Rebirth of Tribalism, Nationalism, and Socialism Is Destroying American Democracy*. New York: Crown Forum.

Gomez, Michael. 2019. *African Dominion: A New History of Empire in Early and Medieval West Africa*. Princeton, NJ: Princeton University Press.

Goodwin, Jason. 1999. *Lords of the Horizons: A History of the Ottoman Empire*. London: Chatto and Windus.

Gordon, Andrew. 2007. "'A Fortune of Paper Walls': The Letters of Francis Bacon and the Earl of Essex." *English Literary Renaissance* 37 (3): 319–36.

Gordon, William. 1788. *The History of the Rise, Progress, and Establishment, of the Independence of the United States of America: Including an Account of the Late War; and of the Thirteen Colonies, from their Origins to That Period, by William Gordon, D.D.* New York: Hodge, Allen, and Campbell.

Graeber, David, and David Wengrow. 2021. *The Dawn of Everything: A New History of Humanity*. London: Penguin.

Graziosi, Barbara. 2015. "On Seeing the Poet: Arabic, Italian and Byzantine Portraits of Homer." *Scandinavian Journal of Byzantine and Modern Greek Studies*, no. 1 (June): 25–47.

Green, Toby. 2019. *A Fistful of Shells: West Africa from the Rise of the Slave Trade to the Age of Revolution*. London: Allen Lane.

Greenblatt, Stephen. 2012. *The Swerve: How the World Became Modern*. New York: W. W. Norton.

Greenwood, Emily. 2007. "Black Odysseys: The Homeric Odyssey in the African Diaspora since 1939." In *Classics in Post-Colonial Worlds*, ed. Lorna Hardwick and Carol Gillespie, 192–210. Oxford: Oxford University Press.

Greenwood, Emily. 2010. *Afro-Greeks: Dialogues between Anglophone Caribbean Literature and Classics in the Twentieth Century*. Classical Presences. Oxford: Oxford University Press.

Greenwood, Emily. 2011. "The Politics of Classicism in the Poetry of Phillis Wheatley." In *Ancient Slavery and Abolition: From Hobbes to Hollywood*, ed. Richard Alston, Edith Hall, and Justine McConnell, 153–80. Oxford: Oxford University Press.

Gress, David. 1998. *From Plato to NATO: The Idea of the West and Its Opponents*. New York: Free Press.

Gutas, Dimitri. 1998. *Greek Thought, Arabic Culture: The Graeco-Arabic Transla-tion Movement in Baghdad and Early 'Abbāsid Society (2nd–4th / 8th–10th Centuries)*. London: Routledge.

Hackett, Helen. 2014. "A New Image of Elizabeth I: The Three Goddesses Theme in Art and Literature." *Huntington Library Quarterly* 77 (3): 225–56.

Hairston, Julia L. 2014. "Introduction." In *The Poems and Letters of Tullia d'Aragona and Others*, ed. Julia Hairston. The Other Voice in Early Modern Europe. Toronto: Iter.

Hall, Edith. 1989. *Inventing the Barbarian: Greek Self-Definition through Tragedy*. Oxford Classical Monographs. Oxford: Clarendon Press.

Hall, Edith, and Henry Stead. 2020. *A People's History of Classics: Class and Greco-Roman Antiquity in Britain and Ireland 1689 to 1939*. London: Routledge.

Hall, Jonathan M. 1997. *Ethnic Identity in Greek Antiquity*. Cambridge: Cam-bridge University Press.

Hall, Jonathan M. 2002. *Hellenicity: Between Ethnicity and Culture*. Chicago: University of Chicago Press.

Hanink, Johanna. 2017. *The Classical Debt: Greek Antiquity in an Era of Austerity*. Illustrated ed. Cambridge, MA: Harvard University Press.

Hansen, Mogens Herman, and Thomas Heine Nielsen, eds. 2004. *An Inventory of Archaic and Classical "Poleis": An Investigation Conducted by the Copenhagen*

Polis Centre for the Danish National Research Foundation. Oxford: Oxford University Press.

Harloe, Katherine. 2013. *Winckelmann and the Invention of Antiquity: History and Aesthetics in the Age of Altertumswissenschaft*. Oxford: Oxford University Press.

Harris, Jonathan. 2003. *Byzantium and the Crusades*. London: Bloomsbury.

Harris, Jonathan. 2005. "The Debate on the Fourth Crusade." *History Compass* 2 (1).

Harris, Jonathan. 2010. *The End of Byzantium*. New Haven, CT: Yale University Press.

Hartmann, Anna-Maria. 2015. "The Strange Antiquity of Francis Bacon's New Atlantis." *Renaissance Studies* 29 (3): 375–93.

Harvey, D. 2012. *The French Enlightenment and Its Others: The Mandarin, the Savage, and the Invention of the Human Sciences*. London: Springer.

Hawkins, Mike. 1997. *Social Darwinism in European and American Thought, 1860–1945: Nature as Model and Nature as Threat*. Cambridge: Cambridge University Press.

Hazareesingh, Sudhir. 2020. *Black Spartacus: The Epic Life of Toussaint Louverture*. London: Allen Lane.

He, Xiao. 2019. "Ancient Civilisations Forum with the Belt and Road Initiative." In *Routledge Handbook of the Belt and Road*, ed. Cai Fang and Peter Nolan 430–33. London: Routledge.

Healy, Jack. 2021. "These Are the 5 People Who Died in the Capitol Riot." *The New York Times*, January 11.

Heather, Peter J. 1996. *The Goths*. The Peoples of Europe. Oxford: Blackwell.

Heather, Peter. 2009. *Empires and Barbarians: The Fall of Rome and the Birth of Europe*. Oxford: Oxford University Press.

Heather, Peter. 2017. *The Restoration of Rome: Barbarian Popes and Imperial Pretenders*. Oxford: Oxford University Press.

Hegel, Georg Wilhelm Friedrich, T. M. Know, and Richard Kroner. 1975. *Early Theological Writings, G.W.F. Hegel*. Philadelphia: University of Pennsylvania Press.

Heng, Geraldine. 2018. *The Invention of Race in the European Middle Ages*. Cambridge: Cambridge University Press.

Henrich, Joseph. 2020. *The Weirdest People in the World: How the West Became Psychologically Peculiar and Particularly Prosperous*. London: Allen Lane.

Hepple, Leslie W. 2001. "'The Museum in the Garden': Displaying Classical Antiquities in Elizabethan and Jacobean England." *Garden History* 29 (2): 109–20.

Hering, K. 2015. "Godfrey of Viterbo: Historical Writing and Imperial Legitimacy at the Early Hohenstaufen Court." In *Godfrey of Viterbo and His Readers: Imperial Tradition and Universal History in Late Medieval Europe*, ed. Thomas Foerster, 47–66. Church, Faith and Culture in the Medieval West. Farnham, UK: Ashgate Publishing.

Herrin, Judith. 2007. *Byzantium: The Surprising Life of a Medieval Empire*. Princeton, NJ : Princeton University Press.

Herrin, Judith. 2020. *Ravenna: Capital of Empire, Crucible of Europe*. Princeton, NJ: Princeton University Press.

Heywood, Linda M. 2017. *Njinga of Angola: Africa's Warrior Queen*. Cambridge, MA: Harvard University Press.

Hildebrandt, Berit. 2017. *Silk: Trade and Exchange along the Silk Roads between Rome and China in Antiquity*. Oxford: Oxbow Books.

Hill, Lisa, and Prasanna Nidumolu. 2021. "The Influence of Classical Stoicism on John Locke's Theory of Self-Ownership." *History of the Human Sciences* 34 (3–4): 3–24.

Hingley, Richard. 2001. *Roman Officers and English Gentlemen: The Imperial Origins of Roman Archaeology*. London: Routledge.

Hingley, Richard. 2005. *Globalizing Roman Culture: Unity, Diversity and Empire*. London: Routledge.

Hingley, Richard. 2019. "Assessing How Representation of the Roman Past Impacts Public Perceptions of the Province of Britain." *Public Archaeology* 18 (4): 241–60.

Hobson, John M. 2004. *The Eastern Origins of Western Civilisation*. Cambridge: Cambridge University Press.

Hobson, John M. 2020. *Multicultural Origins of the Global Economy: Beyond the Western-Centric Frontier*. Cambridge: Cambridge University Press.

Hobsbawm, Eric. 1968. *Industry and Empire*. London: Penguin Books.

Hobsbawm, Eric, and Terence Ranger, eds. 2012. *The Invention of Tradition*. Canto Classics. Cambridge: Cambridge University Press.

Horsfall, Nicholas. 1986. "The Aeneas Legend and the 'Aenied.'"*Vergilius* 32: 8–17.

Horsfall, Nicholas, ed. 2000. *A Companion to the Study of Virgil*. Leiden: Brill.

Hower, Jessica S. 2020. *Tudor Empire: The Making of Early Modern Britain and the British Atlantic World, 1485–1603*. Cham, Switzerland: Palgrave Macmillan.

Hsing, I-Tien. 2005. "Heracles in the East: The Diffusion and Transformation of His Image in the Arts of Central Asia, India, and Medieval China." *Asia Major* 18 (2): 103–54.

Hume, David. 1994. *Political Essays*. Cambridge: Cambridge University Press.

Hunt, Lucy-Anne. 2011. "A Deesis Mould in Berlin: Christian-Muslim Cultural Interchange between Iran, Syria and Mesopotamia in the Early Thirteenth Century." *Islam and Christian-Muslim Relations* 22 (2): 127–45.

Huntington, Samuel P. 1996. *The Clash of Civilisations and the Remaking of the World Order*. London: Free Press.

Huxtable, Sally-Anne, Corinne Fowler, Christo Kefalas, and Emma Slocombe. 2020. "Interim Report on the Connections between Colonialism and Properties Now in the Care of the National Trust Including Links with Historic Slavery." Swindon, UK: National Trust.

Inalcik, Halil. 2001. *The Ottoman Empire: The Classical Age 1300–1600*. London: Phoenix.

Innes, Matthew. 2000. "Teutons or Trojans? The Carolingians and the Germanic Past." In *The Uses of the Past in the Early Middle Ages*, ed. Yitzhak Hen and Matthew Innes, 227–49. Cambridge: Cambridge University Press.

Irwin, Elizabeth. 2013. "To Whom Does Solon Speak? Conceptions of Happiness and Ending Life Well in the Later Fifth Century (Hdt. 1:29–33)." In *Herodots Wege des Erzählens: Logos und Topos in den Historien*, ed. K. Geus, Elizabeth Irwin, and Thomas Poiss, 261–321. Bern, Switzerland: Peter Lang.

Isaac, Benjamin, Miriam Eliav-Feldon, and Joseph Ziegler, eds. 2009. *The Origins of Racism in the West*. Cambridge: Cambridge University Press.

Isakhan, Benjamin, and Lynn Meskell. 2019. "UNESCO's Project to 'Revive the Spirit of Mosul': Iraqi and Syrian Opinion on Heritage Reconstruction after the Islamic State." *International Journal of Heritage Studies* 25 (11): 1189–204.

Isba, Anne. 2003. "Trouble with Helen: The Gladstone Family Crisis, 1846–1848." *History* 88 (2 [290]): 249–61.

Israel, Jonathan I. 2001. *Radical Enlightenment: Philosophy and the Making of Modernity 1650–1750*. Oxford: Oxford University Press.

Israel, Jonathan I. 2006. *Enlightenment Contested: Philosophy, Modernity, and the Emancipation of Man 1670–1752*. Oxford: Oxford University Press.

Israel, Jonathan I. 2009. *A Revolution of the Mind: Radical Enlightenment and the Intellectual Origins of Modern Democracy*. Princeton, NJ: Princeton University Press.

Israel, Jonathan. 2011. *Democratic Enlightenment: Philosophy, Revolution, and Human Rights 1750–1790*. Oxford: Oxford University Press.

Issa, Hanan. 2018. *My Body Can House Two Hearts*. Bristol, UK: Burning Eye Books.

Jackson, Maurice, and Susan Kozel, eds. 2015. *Quakers and Their Allies in the Abolitionist Cause, 1754–1808*. New York: Routledge.

Jacob, Margaret C. 2001. *The Enlightenment: A Brief History with Documents*. Boston: Bedford/St. Martin's.

Jacob, Margaret C. 2019. *The Secular Enlightenment*. Princeton, NJ: Princeton University Press.

James, C. L. R. 1989. *The Black Jacobins: Toussaint L'Ouverture and the San Domingo Revolution*. New York: Vintage Books.

Jardine, Lisa. 2004. "Gloriana Rules the Waves: Or, the Advantage of Being Excommunicated (and a Woman)." *Transactions of the Royal Historical Society* 14 (14): 209–22.

Jardine, Lisa, and Alan Stewart. 1998. *Hostage to Fortune: The Troubled Life of Francis Bacon (1561–1626)*. London: Gollancz.

Jeffers, Honorée Fanonne. 2020. *The Age of Phillis*. Middletown, CT: Wesleyan University Press.

Jenkins, Roy. 2012. *Gladstone*. London: Pan Macmillan.

Johnson, Marguerite. 2012. *Boudicca*. London: A&C Black.

Jordan, William Chester. 2002. "'Europe' in the Middle Ages." In *The Idea of Europe: From Antiquity to the European Union*, ed. Anthony Pagden, 72–90. Cambridge: Cambridge University Press.

Kalb, Judith E. 2008. *Russia's Rome: Imperial Visions, Messianic Dreams, 1890–1940*. Madison: University of Wisconsin Press.

Kaldellis, Anthony. 2007. *Hellenism in Byzantium: The Transformations of Greek Identity and the Reception of the Classical Tradition*. Cambridge: Cambridge University Press.

Kaldellis, Anthony. 2019a. *Byzantium Unbound*. Leeds: Arc Humanities Press.

Kaldellis, Anthony. 2019b. *Romanland: Ethnicity and Empire in Byzantium*. Cambridge, MA: Belknap Press.

Kamil, Jill. 2013. *Christianity in the Land of the Pharaohs: The Coptic Orthodox Church*. Milton Park, UK: Taylor and Francis.

Kammen, Michael. 1970. "The Meaning of Colonization in American Revolutionary Thought." *Journal of the History of Ideas* 31 (3): 337–58.

Kant, Immanuel. 2011 [1764]. *Observations on the Feeling of the Beautiful and Sublime and Other Writings*. Cambridge and New York: Cambridge University Press.

Kanter, Douglas. 2013. "Gladstone and the Great Irish Famine." *Journal of Liberal History* 81: 8–14.

Kayaalp, Pinar. 2018. *The Empress Nurbanu and Ottoman Politics in the 16th Century: Building the Atik Valide*. Routledge Studies in Middle Eastern History 19. Milton Park, UK: Routledge.

Keen, Michael, and Joel Slemrod. 2021. *Rebellion, Rascals, and Revenue: Tax Follies and Wisdom through the Ages*. Princeton, NJ: Princeton University Press.

Keevak, Michael. 2008. *The Story of a Stele: China's Nestorian Monument and Its Reception in the West, 1625–1916*. Hong Kong: Hong Kong University Press.

Keevak, Michael. 2011. *Becoming Yellow: A Short History of Racial Thinking*. Princeton, NJ: Princeton University Press.

Kennedy, Hugh. 1996. *Muslim Spain and Portugal: A Political History of al-Andalus*. London: Routledge.

Kidd, Thomas S. 2009. *The Great Awakening: The Roots of Evangelical Christianity in Colonial America*. New Haven, CT: Yale University Press.

Kidd, Thomas S. 2014. *George Whitefield: America's Spiritual Founding Father*. New Haven, CT: Yale University Press.

Kishlansky, Mark, Patrick Geary, and Patricia O'Brien. 2006. *A Brief History of Western Civilisation: The Unfinished Legacy*. Vol. 1. 5th ed. New York: Longman Publishing.

Kleingeld, Pauline. 2007. "Kant's Second Thoughts on Race." *The Philosophical Quarterly* 57 (229): 573–92.

Koch, Richard, and Chris Smith. 2006. *Suicide of the West*. London and New York: Continuum.

Kołodziejczyk, Dariusz. 2012. "Khan, Caliph, Tsar and Imperator: The Multiple Identities of the Ottoman Sultan." In *Universal Empire: A Comparative Approach to Imperial Culture and Representation in Eurasian History*, ed. Peter Fibiger Bang and Dariusz Kołodziejczyk, 175–93. Cambridge: Cambridge University Press.

Laihui, Xie. 2019. "The Belt and Road Initiative and the Road Connecting Different Civilisations." In *Routledge Handbook of the Belt and Road*, ed. Cai Fang and Peter Nolan, 165–69. London: Routledge.

Laird, Andrew. 2006. *The Epic of America: An Introduction to Rafael Landívar and the "Rusticatio Mexicana."* London: Duckworth.

Laird, Andrew. 2007. "Latin America." In *A Companion to the Classical Tradition*, ed. Craig W. Kallendorf, 222–36. Williston, UK: John Wiley & Sons.

Łajtar, Adam, and Grzegorz Ochała. 2021. "Language Use and Literacy in Late Antique and Medieval Nubia." In *The Oxford Handbook of Ancient Nubia*, ed.

Geoff Emberling and Bruce Beyer Williams, 786–805. Oxford: Oxford University Press.

Lakomy, Miron. 2021. *Islamic State's Online Propaganda: A Comparative Analysis.* New York: Routledge.

Lape, Susan. 2010. *Race and Citizen Identity in the Classical Athenian Democracy.* Cambridge: Cambridge University Press.

Lau, Kenneth. 2016. "Lam Bares the 'Bad Records' in Her Life." *The Standard*, May 3.

Levine, Philippa. 2020. *The British Empire: Sunrise to Sunset.* 3rd ed. London: Routledge.

Lewis, Bernard. 1990. "The Roots of Muslim Rage." *The Atlantic*, September, 47–60.

Lewis, Bernard, and Benjamin Braude, eds. 1982. *Christians & Jews in the Ottoman Empire: The Functioning of a Plural Society.* Vol. 2. New York: Holmes & Meier.

Li, Xue. 2019. "Exchanges and Mutual Learning among Civilisations." In *Routledge Handbook of the Belt and Road*, ed. Cai Fang and Peter Nolan, 272–77. London: Routledge.

Lifschitz, Avi. 2016. "Rousseu's Imagined Antiquity: An Introduction." *History of Political Thought* 37: 1–7.

Low, Polly. 2008. *The Athenian Empire.* Edinburgh Readings on the Ancient World. Edinburgh: Edinburgh University Press.

Lucas, Edward. 2008. *New Cold War: Putin's Russia and the Threat to the West.* New York: St. Martin's Press.

Lupher, David A. 2002. *Romans in a New World: Classical Models in Sixteenth-Century Spanish America.* Ann Arbor: University of Michigan Press.

Ma, John, Nikolaos Papazarkadas, and Robert Parker, eds. 2009. *Interpreting the Athenian Empire.* London: Duckworth.

MacCulloch, Diarmaid. 2010. *A History of Christianity.* London: Penguin.

Mac Sweeney, Naoíse, ed. 2013. *Foundation Myths in Ancient Societies: Dialogues and Discourses.* Philadelphia: University of Pennsylvania Press.

Mac Sweeney, Naoíse. 2018. *Troy: Myth, City, Icon.* London: Bloomsbury Academic.

Mac Sweeney, Naoíse. 2021a. "Regional Identities in the Greek World: Myth and Koinon in Ionia." *Historia: Zeitschrift für Alte Geschichte* 70 (2): 268–314.

Mac Sweeney, Naoíse. 2021b. "Race and Ethnicity." In *A Cultural History of Race*, Vol. I, *Antiquity*, ed. Denise McCoskey, 103–18. London: Bloomsbury.

REFERENCES

Mahbubani, Kishore. 2020. *Has China Won?: The Chinese Challenge to American Primacy.* New York: Public Affairs.

Mairs, Rachel. 2016. *The Hellenistic Far East: Archaeology, Language and Identity in Greek Central Asia.* Berkeley: University of California Press.

Mairs, Rachel, ed. 2020. *The Graeco-Bactrian and Indo-Greek World.* London: Routledge.

Majendie, Adam, Sheridan Prasso, Kevin Hamlin, Miao Han, Faseeh Mangi, Chris Kay, Samuel Gebre, and Marcus Bensasson. 2018. "China's Empire of Money Is Reshaping Global Trade." Bloomberg.com, August 1. https://www.bloomberg.com/news/features/2018-08-01/china-s-empire-of-money-is-reshaping-lives-across-new-silk-road.

Malamud, Margaret. 2009. *Ancient Rome and Modern America.* Hoboken, NJ: Wiley.

Malamud, Margaret. 2010. "Translatio Imperii: America as the New Rome c.1900." In *Classics and Imperialism in the British Empire,* ed. Mark Bradley, 249–83. Oxford: Oxford University Press.

Malamud, Margaret. 2016. *African Americans and the Classics: Antiquity, Abolition and Activism.* London: I. B. Tauris.

Malcolm, Noel. 2019. *Useful Enemies: Islam and the Ottoman Empire in Western Political Thought, 1450–1750.* Oxford: Oxford University Press.

Malik, Kenan. 1996. *The Meaning of Race: Race, History and Culture in Western Society.* New York: New York University Press.

Malik, Kenan. 2013. "Seeing Reason: Jonathan Israel's Radical Vision." *New Humanist,* June 21.

Malkin, Irad, ed. 2001. *Ancient Perceptions of Greek Ethnicity.* Cambridge, MA: Harvard University Press.

Marchand, Suzanne L. 1996. *Down from Olympus: Archaeology and Philhellenism in Germany, 1750–1970.* Princeton, NJ: Princeton University Press.

Marchand, Suzanne L. 2009. *German Orientalism in the Age of Empire: Religion, Race, and Scholarship.* Cambridge: Cambridge University Press.

Marinella, Lucrezia, and Maria Gill Stampino. 2009. *Enrico; or, Byzantium Conquered: A Heroic Poem.* Chicago: University of Chicago Press.

Marshall, Peter. 2012. "'Rather with Papists than with Turks': The Battle of Lepanto and the Contours of Elizabethan Christendom." *Reformation* 17 (1): 135–59.

Mason, Rowena. 2022. "Tory Party Chairman Says 'Painful Woke Psychodrama' Weakening the West." *The Guardian,* February 14.

Mattingly, D. J. 2011. *Imperialism, Power, and Identity: Experiencing the Roman Empire.* Princeton, NJ: Princeton University Press.

Mazzotta, Giuseppe. 2010. "Italian Renaissance Epic." In *The Cambridge Companion to the Epic*, ed. Catherine Bates, 93–118. Cambridge: Cambridge University Press.

McConnell, Justine. 2013. *Black Odysseys: The Homeric Odyssey in the African Diaspora since 1939*. Oxford: Oxford University Press.

McCoskey, Denise, ed. 2021. *A Cultural History of Race*. Vol. 1, *In Antiquity*. London: Bloomsbury Academic.

McDaniel, Spencer. 2021. "Here's What the Costumes and Flags on Display at the Pro-Trump Insurrection Mean." *Tales of Times Forgotten* (blog). January 8. https://talesoftimesforgotten.com/2021/01/08/heres-what-the-costumes -and-flags-on-display-at-the-pro-trump-insurrection-mean.

McKenzie, Judith S., and Francis Watson. 2016. *The Garima Gospels: Early Illuminated Gospel Books from Ethiopia*. Oxford: University of Oxford Press.

McLaughlin, M. L. 1988. "Humanist Concepts of Renaissance and Middle Ages in the Tre- and Quattrocento." *Renaissance Studies* 2 (2): 131–42.

McLucas, John C. 2006. "Renaissance Carolingian: Tullia d'Aragona's Il Meschino, altramente detto Il Guerrino." *Olifant* 25 (1/2): 313–20.

McNeill, William. 1963. *The Rise of the West*. Chicago: University of Chicago Press.

Meiggs, Russell, and David Lewis. 1969. *A Selection of Greek Historical Inscriptions: To the End of the Fifth Century B.C.* Oxford: Clarendon Press.

Menzies, Gavin. 2003. *1421: The Year China Discovered the World*. London: William Morrow & Co.

Merrills, Andrew, and Richard Miles. 2010. *The Vandals*. Hoboken, NJ: Wiley.

Meserve, Margaret. 2008. *Empires of Islam in Renaissance Historical Thought*. Cambridge, MA: Harvard University Press.

Mitchell, Peter, and Paul J. Lane, eds. 2013. *The Oxford Handbook of African Archaeology*. Oxford Handbooks. Oxford: Oxford University Press.

Mitter, Rana. 2020. *China's Good War: How World War II Is Shaping a New Nationalism*. Cambridge, MA: Belknap Press.

Mokyr, Joel. 2009. *The Enlightened Economy: An Economic History of Britain, 1700–1850*. New Haven, CT: Yale University Press.

Moles, John P. 2002. "Herodotus and Athens." In *Brill's Companion to Herodotus*, ed. Egbert J. Bakker, Irene J. F. de Jong, and Hans van Wees, 33–52. Leiden: Brill.

Momigliano, Arnaldo. 1958. "The Place of Herodotus in the History of Historiography." *History* 43 (147): 1–13.

Monoson, S. Sara. 2011. "Recollecting Aristotle: Pro-Slavery Thought in Antebellum America and the Argument of *Politics* Book I." In *Ancient Slavery and*

Abolition: From Hobbes to Hollywood, ed. Richard Alston, Edith Hall, and Justine McConnell, 247–78. Oxford: Oxford University Press.

Morris, Ian. 2011. *Why the West Rules—for Now: The Patterns of History and What They Reveal about the Future.* London: Profile Books.

Morton, Nicholas. 2016. *Encountering Islam on the First Crusade.* Cambridge: Cambridge University Press.

Moyer, Ian, Adam Lecznar, and Heidi Morse, eds. 2020. *Classicisms in the Black Atlantic.* Oxford: Oxford University Press.

Munson, Rosaria Vignolo. 2014. "Herodotus and Ethnicity." In *A Companion to Ethnicity in the Ancient Mediterranean,* ed. Jeremy McInerney, 341–55. Hoboken, NJ: Wiley.

Murray, Douglas. 2017. *The Strange Death of Europe: Immigration, Identity, Islam.* London: Bloomsbury Continuum.

Murray, Douglas. 2022. *The War on the West: How to Prevail in the Age of Unreason.* London: HarperCollins.

Nakata, Sharilyn. 2012. "*Egredere O Quicumque Es:* Genealogical Opportunism and Trojan Identity in the *Aeneid.*" *Phoenix* 66 (3–4): 335–63, 467.

Ndiaye, Noémie. 2022. *Scripts of Blackness: Early Modern Performance Culture and the Making of Race.* Philadelphia: University of Pennsylvania Press.

Németh, András. 2018. *The Excerpta Constantiniana and the Byzantine Appropriation of the Past.* Cambridge: Cambridge University Press.

Neville, Leonora. 2016. *Anna Komnene: The Life and Work of a Medieval Historian.* Oxford: Oxford University Press.

Ng, Diana Y., and Molly Swetnam-Burland. 2018. *Reuse and Renovation in Roman Material Culture: Functions, Aesthetics, Interpretations.* Cambridge: Cambridge University Press.

Nicol, Donald M. 1989. *Byzantium and Venice: A Study in Diplomatic and Cultural Relations.* Cambridge: Cambridge University Press.

Nishihara, Daisuke. 2005. "Said, Orientalism, and Japan." *Alif: Journal of Comparative Poetics* 25: 241–53.

Noble, Thomas F. X., Barry Strauss, Duane Osheim, Kristen Neuschel, and Elinor Accampo. 2013. *Western Civilisation: Beyond Boundaries.* 7th ed. Boston: Cengage Learning.

Oliver, Peter. (1781) 1967. *Peter Oliver's Origin & Progress of the American Rebellion: A Tory View.* Stanford, CA: Stanford University Press.

Olson, Kelly. 2012. *Dress and the Roman Woman: Self-Presentation and Society.* London: Routledge.

Osborne, Robin, ed. 2008. *The World of Athens: An Introduction to Classical Athenian Culture*. 2nd ed. Cambridge: Cambridge University Press.

Osborne, Robin. 2015. "Unity vs. Diversity." In *The Oxford Handbook of Ancient Greek Religion*, ed. Esther Eidinow and Julia Kindt, 11–19. Oxford: Oxford University Press.

Osborne, Roger. 2008. *Civilization: A New History of the Western World*. New York: Pegasus Books.

Outram, Dorinda. 2013. *The Enlightenment*. 3rd ed. Cambridge: Cambridge University Press.

Pagden, Anthony. 2011. *Worlds at War: The 2,500-Year Struggle between East and West*. Oxford: Oxford University Press.

Parker, Grant. 2002. "*Ex Oriente Luxuria*: Indian Commodities and Roman Experience." *Journal of the Economic and Social History of the Orient* 45 (1): 40–95.

Parkinson, Robert G. 2016. *The Common Cause: Creating Race and Nation in the American Revolution*. Chapel Hill: University of North Carolina Press.

Patterson, Cynthia. 2005. "Athenian Citizenship Law." In *The Cambridge Companion to Ancient Greek Law*, ed. Michael Gagarin, 267–89. Cambridge: Cambridge University Press.

Pedani, Maria Pia. 2000. "Safiye's Household and Venetian Diplomacy." *Turcica* 32: 9–32.

Pegg, Mark Gregory. 2008. *A Most Holy War: The Albigensian Crusade and the Battle for Christendom*. Oxford: Oxford University Press.

Peirce, Leslie P. 1993. *The Imperial Harem: Women and Sovereignty in the Ottoman Empire*. New York: Oxford University Press.

Pelling, Christopher. 2012. "Tacitus and Germanicus." In *Oxford Readings in Tacitus*, ed. Rhiannon Ash, 81–313. Oxford: Oxford University Press.

Pelling, Christopher. 2019. *Herodotus and the Question Why*. Austin: University of Texas Press.

Peltonen, Markku, ed. 1996. *The Cambridge Companion to Bacon*. Cambridge: Cambridge University Press.

Perry, Marvin, Myrna Chase, James Jacob, Margaret Jacob, and Jonathan W. Daly. 2015. *Western Civilization: Ideas, Politics, and Society*. 11th ed. New York: Cengage Learning.

Petersohn, Jürgen. 1992. "Friedrich Barbarossa und Rom." In *Friedrich Barbarossa. Handlungsspielräume und Wirkungsweisen*, ed. Alfred Haverkamp, 129–146. Stuttgart: Jan Thorbecke Verlag, 129–46.

Petersohn, Jürgen. 2001. "Kaiser, Papst und römisches Recht im Hochmittelalter. Friedrich Barbarossa und Innocenz III beim Umgang mit dem Rechtsinstitut der langfristigen Verjährung." In *Mediaevalia Augiensia: Forschung zue Geschichte des Mittelalters,* ed. Jürgen Petersohn, 307–48. Stuttgart: Jan Thorbecke Verlag.

Piersen, William D. 1988. *Black Yankees: The Development of an Afro-American Subculture in Eighteenth-Century New England.* Amherst: University of Massachusetts Press.

Plassmann, Alheydis. 2006. *Origo gentis: Identitäts- und Legitimitätsstiftung in früh- und hochmittelalterlichen Herkunftserzählungen.* Berlin: De Gruyter.

Pohl, Walter, Clemens Gantner, Cinzia Grifoni, and Marianne Pollheimer-Mohaupt, eds. 2018. *Transformations of Romanness: Early Medieval Regions and Identities.* Berlin: De Gruyter.

Porter, Roy S., and Mikuláš Teich, eds. 1981. *The Enlightenment in National Context.* Cambridge: Cambridge University Press.

Poser, Rachel. 2021. "He Wants to Save Classics from Whiteness: Can the Field Survive?" *The New York Times,* February 2.

Prag, Jonathan. 2010. "Tyrannizing Sicily: The Despots Who Cried 'Carthage!'" In *Private and Public Lies,* ed. A. Turner, F. Vervaet, and J. K. On Chong-Gossard, 11:51–71. Leiden: Brill.

Price, Bronwen, ed. 2018. *Francis Bacon's New Atlantis: New Interdisciplinary Essays.* Manchester: Manchester University Press.

Prins, Yopie. 2017. *Ladies' Greek: Victorian Translations of Tragedy.* Princeton, NJ: Princeton University Press.

Prosperi, Valentina. 2019. *The Place of the Father: The Reception of Homer in the Renaissance Canon.* Leiden: Brill.

Quinault, Roland. 2009. "Gladstone and Slavery." *Historical Journal* 52 (2): 363–83.

Quinn, Josephine Crawley. Forthcoming. *How the World Made the West.* London: Bloomsbury.

Rady, Martyn. 2020. *The Habsburgs.* London: Penguin.

Reuter, Timothy. 1992. *Germany in the Early Middle Ages, c. 800–1056.* London: Longman Publishing.

Rhodes, Peter John. 2004. *Athenian Democracy.* Oxford: Oxford University Press.

Richard, Carl J. 1995. *The Founders and the Classics: Greece, Rome, and the American Enlightenment.* Cambridge, MA: Harvard University Press.

Richard, Carl J. 2015. "Cicero and the American Founders." In *Brill's Companion to the Reception of Cicero,* ed. William H. F. Altman, 124–43. Leiden: Brill.

Ricks, Thomas E. 2020. *First Principles: What America's Founders Learned from the Greeks and Romans and How That Shaped Our Country*. New York: Harper.

Rienjang, Wannaporn, and Peter Stewart, eds. 2020. *The Global Connections of Gandhāran Art: Proceedings of the Third International Workshop of the Gandhāra Connections Project, University of Oxford, 18th–19th March, 2019*. Oxford: Archaeopress.

Robinson, William H. 1977. "Phillis Wheatley in London." *CLA Journal* 21 (2): 187–201.

Rose, Charles Brian. 1997. *Dynastic Commemoration and Imperial Portraiture in the Julio-Claudian Period*. Cambridge: Cambridge University Press.

Rose, Charles Brian. 2013. *The Archaeology of Greek and Roman Troy*. Cambridge: Cambridge University Press.

Ross, Shawn A. 2005. "*Barbarophonos*: Language and Panhellenism in the *Iliad*." *Classical Philology* 100 (4): 299–316.

Rothe, Ursula. 2019. *The Toga and Roman Identity*. London: Bloomsbury Academic.

Ruffing, Kai. 2018. "Gifts for Cyrus, Tribute for Darius." In *Interpreting Herodotus*, ed. Thomas Harrison and Elizabeth Irwin, 149–61. Oxford: Oxford University Press.

Rukuni, Rugare. 2021. "Negus Ezana: Revisiting the Christianisation of Aksum." *Verbum et Ecclesia* 42 (1): 1–11.

Russell, Rinaldina. 1997. "Introduction." In *Dialogue on the Infinity of Love, by Tullia D'Aragona*, ed. Bruce Merry and Rinaldina Russell, 21–42. Chicago: University of Chicago Press.

Said, Edward W. 1970. "The Arab Portrayed." In *The Arab-Israeli Confrontation of June 1967: An Arab Perspective*, ed. Ibrahim Abu-Lughod, 1–9. Evanston, IL: Northwestern University Press.

Said, Edward W. (1978) 1995. *Orientalism*. Reprinted with a new preface. London: Penguin.

Said, Edward W. (1978) 2003. *Orientalism*. London: Penguin.

Said, Edward W. 1993. *Culture and Imperialism*. London: Vintage.

Said, Edward W. 1999. *Out of Place: A Memoir*. London: Granta Books.

Said, Edward W. 2000. *Reflections on Exile: And Other Essays*. Convergences. Cambridge, MA: Harvard University Press.

Said, Suzanne. 2001. "Greeks and Barbarians in Euripides' Tragedies: The End of Differences?" In *Greeks and Barbarians*, ed. Thomas Harrison, 62–100. Edinburgh: Edinburgh University Press.

REFERENCES

Satia, Priya. 2020. *Time's Monster: History, Conscience and Britain's Empire*. London: Allen Lane.

Schein, Seth L. 2007. "'Our Debt to Greece and Rome': Canon, Class and Ideology." In *A Companion to Classical Receptions*, ed. Lorna Hardwick and Christopher Stray, 75–85. Hoboken, NJ: Wiley.

Schmidt-Colinet, Andreas. 2019. *Kein Tempel in Palmyra!: Plädoyer gegen einen Wiederaufbau des Beltempeis*. Frankfurt am Mainz: Edition Fichter.

Schneider, Rolf Michael. 2012. "The Making of Oriental Rome: Shaping the Trojan Legend." In *Universal Empire*, ed. Peter Fibiger Bang and Dariusz Kolodziejczyk, 76–129. Cambridge: Cambridge University Press.

Seo, J. Mira. 2011. "Identifying Authority: Juan Latino, an African Ex-Slave, Professor, and Poet in Sixteenth-Century Granada." In *African Athena: New Agendas*, ed. Daniel Orrells, Gurminder K. Bhambra, and Tessa Roynon, 258–76. Oxford: Oxford University Press.

Shalev, Eran. 2009. *Rome Reborn on Western Shores: Historical Imagination and the Creation of the American Republic*. Charlottesville: University of Virginia Press.

Shepard, Alan, and Stephen D. Powell, eds. 2004. *Fantasies of Troy: Classical Tales and the Social Imaginary in Medieval and Early Modern Europe*. Toronto: Centre for Reformation and Renaissance Studies.

Sheth, Falguni A. 2009. *Toward a Political Philosophy of Race*. Albany: State University of New York Press.

Shields, John C., and Eric D. Lamore, eds. 2011. *New Essays on Phillis Wheatley*. Knoxville: The University of Tennessee Press.

Signorini, Maddalena. 2019. "Boccaccio as Homer: A Recently Discovered Self-Portrait and the 'Modern' Canon." In *Building the Canon through the Classics: Imitation and Variation in Renaissance Italy (1350–1580)*, ed. Eloisa Morra, 13–26. Leiden: Brill.

Sims-Williams, Nicholas. 2022. "The Bactrian Inscription of Jaghori: A Preliminary Reading," *Bulletin of the Asia Intitute* 30, vol. 30, 67–74.

Sinclair, Patrick. 1990. "Tacitus' Presentation of Livia Julia, Wife of Tiberius' Son Drusus." *American Journal of Philology* 111 (2): 238–56.

Sinisi, Fabrizio. 2017. "Royal Imagery on Kushan Coins: Local Tradition and Arsacid Influences." *Journal of the Economic and Social History of the Orient* 60: 818–927.

Skilliter, S. A. 1965. "Three Letters from the Ottoman 'Sultana' Safiya to Queen Elizabeth I." In *Documents from Islamic Chanceries*, ed. Samuel M. Stern, 119–57. Columbia: University of South Carolina Press.

Skinner, Quentin. 2008. *Hobbes and Republican Liberty*. Cambridge: Cambridge University Press.

Slane, Kathleen W. 2017. *Tombs, Burials, and Commemoration in Corinth's Northern Cemetery*. Princeton, NJ: American School of Classical Studies at Athens.

Smail Salhi, Zahia. 2019. *Occidentalism*. Edinburgh: Edinburgh University Press.

Smarr, Janet L. 1998. "A Dialogue of Dialogues: Tullia d'Aragona and Sperone Speroni." *Modern Language Notes* 113 (1): 204–12.

Smil, Vaclav. 2010. *Why America Is Not a New Rome*. Cambridge, MA: MIT Press.

Smith, Justin E. H. 2015. *Nature, Human Nature, and Human Difference: Race in Early Modern Philosophy*. Princeton, NJ: Princeton University Press.

Smith, Simon C. 2007. "Integration and Disintegration: The Attempted Incorporation of Malta into the United Kingdom in the 1950s." *The Journal of Imperial and Commonwealth History* 35 (1): 49–71.

Somma, Thomas P. 2010. "American Sculpture and the Library of Congress." *The Library Quarterly* 80 (4): 311–35.

Sowerby, Robin. 1992. "Chapman's Discovery of Homer." *Translation and Literature* 1: 26–51.

Sperber, Jonathan. 2005. *The European Revolutions, 1848–1851*. 2nd ed. Cambridge: Cambridge University Press.

Spielvogel, Jackson J. 2005. *Western Civilization: Combined Volume*. 6th ed. Belmont, CA: Cengage Learning.

Squire, Michael. 2011. *The Iliad in a Nutshell: Visualizing Epic on the Tabulae Iliacae*. Oxford: Oxford University Press.

Stagno, Laura, and Borja Franco Llopis, eds. 2021. *Lepanto and Beyond: Images of Religious Alterity from Genoa and the Christian Mediterranean*. Leuven, Belgium: Leuven University Press.

Stahl, A. M. 1998. *Vergil's Aeneid: Augustan Epic and Political Context*. London: Duckworth in association with the Classical Press of Wales.

Stallard, Katie. 2022. *Dancing on Bones: History and Power in China, Russia and North Korea*. Oxford: Oxford University Press.

Starr, S. Frederick. 2015. *Lost Enlightenment: Central Asia's Golden Age from the Arab Conquest to Tamerlane*. Princeton, NJ: Princeton University Press.

Stathakopoulos, Dionysios. 2014. *A Short History of the Byzantine Empire*. London: Bloomsbury.

Stedman Jones, Gareth. 2016. *Karl Marx: Greatness and Illusion*. Cambridge, MA: Harvard University Press.

Stock, Markus, ed. 2016. *Alexander the Great in the Middle Ages: Transcultural Perspectives*. Toronto: University of Toronto Press.

Stoneman, Richard. 2019. *The Greek Experience of India: From Alexander to the Indo-Greeks*. Princeton, NJ: Princeton University Press.

Strangio, Sebastian. 2020. *In the Dragon's Shadow: Southeast Asia in the Chinese Century*. New Haven, CT: Yale University Press.

Tatlock, John S. P. 1915. "The Siege of Troy in Elizabethan Literature, especially in Shakespeare and Heywood." *Proceedings of the Modern Language Association* 30 (4): 673–770.

Thomas, Lamont Dominick. 1986. *Rise to Be a People: A Biography of Paul Cuffe*. Champaign: University of Illinois Press.

Throop, Susanna A. 2018. *The Crusades*. Leeds: Kismet Press.

Toal, Gerard. 2017. *Near Abroad: Putin, the West and the Contest over Ukraine and the Caucasus*. Oxford: Oxford University Press.

Tong, Elson. 2017. "Carrie Lam and the Civil Service Part I: Not a Typical Official." *Hong Kong Free Press*, April 2.

Toohey, Peter. 1984. "Politics, Prejudice, and Trojan Genealogies: Varro, Hyginus, and Horace: *Stemmata Quid Faciunt?* Juvenal, *Sat.* 8:1." *Arethusa* 17 (1): 5–28.

Trautsch, Jasper. 2013. "The Invention of the 'West.'" *Bulletin of the German Historical Institute Washington* 53 (Fall 2013): 89–104.

Trigger, Bruce G. 1989. *A History of Archaeological Thought*. Cambridge: Cambridge University Press.

Trudell, Scott A. 2020. "An Organ for the Seraglio: Thomas Dallam's Artificial Life." *Renaissance Studies* 34 (5): 766–83.

Varner, Eric R. 2004. *Mutilation and Transformation: Damnatio Memoriae and Roman Imperial Portraiture*. Leiden: Brill.

Varotti, Carlo. 2012. "La Leggenda e La Storia: Erodoto Nella Storiografia Tra Quattrocento e Primo Cinquecento." In *Hérodote à La Renaissance*, ed. Susanna Gambino Longo, 99–125. Turnhout, Belgium: Brepols.

Varto, Emily. 2015. "Stories Told in Lists: Formulaic Genealogies as Intentional Histories." *Journal of Ancient History* 3 (2): 118–49.

Vasunia, Phiroze. 2013. *The Classics and Colonial India*. Oxford: Oxford University Press.

Villing, Alexandra, Udo Schlotzhauer, and British Museum, eds. 2006. *Naukratis: Greek Diversity in Egypt: Studies on East Greek Pottery and Exchange in the Eastern Mediterranean*. London: British Museum Press.

Vlassopoulos, Kostas. 2013. *Greeks and Barbarians*. Cambridge: Cambridge University Press.

Waibel, Paul R. 2020. *Western Civilization: A Brief History*. Hoboken, NJ: Wiley-Blackwell.

Wallace-Hadrill, Andrew. 2008. *Rome's Cultural Revolution*. Cambridge: Cambridge University Press.

Ward Fay, Peter. 2000. *The Opium War, 1840–1842: Barbarians in the Celestial Empire in the Early Part of the Nineteenth Century and the War by Which They Forced Her Gates Ajar*. Chapel Hill: University of North Carolina Press.

Warraq, Ibn. 2007. *Defending the West: A Critique of Edward Said's Orientalism*. Amherst, NY: Prometheus Books.

Waswo, Richard. 1995. "Our Ancestors, the Trojans: Inventing Cultural Identity in the Middle Ages." *Exemplaria* 7 (2): 269–90.

Weber, Loren J. 1994. "The Historical Importance of Godfrey of Viterbo." *Viator* 25: 153–96.

West, Martin L., ed. 2008. *Greek Lyric Poetry: The Poems and Fragments of the Greek Iambic, Elegiac, and Melic Poets (Excluding Pindar and Bacchylides) down to 450 B.C.* Oxford: Oxford University Press.

Westad, Odd Arne. 2017. *The Cold War: A World History*. London: Allen Lane.

Wheatley, Phillis. 1773. *Poems on Various Subjects Religious and Moral*. London: A. Bell.

Wheatley, Phillis, and Vincent Carretta. 2019. *The Writings of Phillis Wheatley*. Oxford: Oxford University Press.

Wiencek, Henry. 2003. *An Imperfect God: George Washington, His Slaves, and the Creation of America*. New York: Farrar, Straus and Giroux.

Wignell, Peter, Sabine Tan, Kay L. O'Halloran, and Rebecca Lange. 2017. "A Mixed Methods Empirical Examination of Changes in Emphasis and Style in the Extremist Magazines *Dabiq* and *Rumiyah*." *Perspectives on Terrorism* 11 (2): 2–20.

Wijma, Sara M. 2014. *Embracing the Immigrant: The Participation of Metics in Athenian Polis Religion (5th–4th Century BC)*. Stuttgart: Franz Steiner Verlag.

Willis, Patricia. 2006. "Phillis Wheatley, George Whitefield, and the Countess of Huntingdon in the Beinecke Library." *Yale University Library Gazette* 80 (3–4): 161–76.

Wilson, Peter H. 2016. *The Holy Roman Empire: A Thousand Years of Europe's History*. London: Penguin.

Winckelmann, Johann Joachim. (1764) 2006. *History of the Art of Antiquity*. Trans. Henry Francis Malgrave. Los Angeles: Getty Publications.

Winterer, Caroline. 2004. *The Culture of Classicism: Ancient Greece and Rome in American Intellectual Life, 1780–1910*. Baltimore: Johns Hopkins University Press.

Wiseman, T. P. 1995. *Remus: A Roman Myth*. Cambridge: Cambridge University Press.

Wiseman, T. P. 2004. *The Myths of Rome*. Exeter, UK: University of Exeter Press.

Wolfe, Michael. 1993. *The Conversion of Henri IV: Politics, Power, and Religious Belief in Early Modern France*. Cambridge, MA: Harvard University Press.

Wong, Joshua, Jason Y. Ng, and Ai Weiwei. 2020. *Unfree Speech: The Threat to Global Democracy and Why We Must Act, Now*. London: Penguin Books.

Wood, Ian N. 2013. *The Modern Origins of the Early Middle Ages*. Oxford: Oxford University Press.

Wood, Jennifer Linhart. 2015. "An Organ's Metamorphosis: Thomas Dallam's Sonic Transformations in the Ottoman Empire." *Journal for Early Modern Cultural Studies* 15 (4): 81–105.

Wood, Susan. 2001. *Imperial Women: A Study in Public Images, 40 B.C.–A.D. 68*. Leiden: Brill.

Woods, Hannah Rose. 2022. *Rule, Nostalgia*. London: Penguin.

Woolf, Greg. 1998. *Becoming Roman: The Origins of Provincial Civilisation in Gaul*. Cambridge: Cambridge University Press.

Wright, Elizabeth R. 2016. *The Epic of Juan Latino: Dilemmas of Race and Religion in Renaissance Spain*. Toronto: University of Toronto Press.

Wrigley, Chris. 2012. "Gladstone and Labour." In *William Gladstone. New Studies and Perspectives*, ed. Roland Quinault, Roger Swift, and Ruth Clayton Windscheffel, 51–71. London: Routledge.

Young, Alfred F., and Gregory Nobles. 2011. *Whose American Revolution Was It?: Historians Interpret the Founding*. New York: New York University Press.

Zagorin, Perez. 2020. *Francis Bacon*. Princeton, NJ: Princeton University Press.

Zanker, Paul. 1997. *Augustus und die Macht der Bilder*. 3rd ed. Munich: Beck.

Ženka, Josef. 2018. "A Manuscript of the Last Sultan of Al-Andalus and the Fate of the Royal Library of the Nasrid Sultans at the Alhambra." *Journal of Islamic Manuscripts* 9 (2–3): 341–76.

Zimmermann, Reinhard. 2001. *Roman Law, Contemporary Law, European Law: The Civilian Tradition Today*. Oxford: Oxford University Press.

RECOMMENDED READING

In this section, I am recommending only works initially written in English, as this book itself is being first published in English. For the historical development of the West, and its relationship with other regions, I would recommend Josephine Crawley Quinn's *How the World Made the West* (forthcoming). Other sensitive examinations of world history that help us move beyond the East-West conceptual binary are Peter Frankopan's *The Silk Roads: A New History of the World* (2015), and Ian Morris's *Why the West Rules—For Now* (2011).

For Herodotus, take a look at Christopher Pelling's *Herodotus and the Question Why* (2019); and for a good introduction to the ancient Greek world, see Robin Osborne's *Greek History: The Basics* (2014). It is also wonderfully enjoyable to delve into Herodotus's *Histories* themselves. The English edition that I prefer is the 2003 Penguin edition, translated by Aubrey de Sélincourt with an introduction by John Marincola. There is little that is written specifically about Livilla, but Anneliese Freisenbruch's *The First Ladies of Rome: The Women Behind the Caesars* (2010) offers a good exploration of the lives of Roman imperial women. For a general history of the Roman Empire, I would recommend Greg Woolf's *Rome: An Empire's Story* (2012).

Peter Adamson's slim but wide-ranging volume *Al-Kindī* (2007) offers an excellent overview of the man himself, but anyone wanting to learn more about the golden age of medieval Islam more generally would enjoy Amira Bennison's *The Great Caliphs: The Golden Age of the*

'Abbasid Empire (2009). A selection of essays on various aspects of Godfrey of Viterbo's life can be found in the volume edited by Thomas Foerster, *Godfrey of Viterbo and His Readers: Imperial Tradition and Universal History in Late Medieval Europe* (2015), but for a history of the Holy Roman Empire more generally, I have found Peter H. Wilson's *The Holy Roman Empire: A Thousand Years of Europe's History* (2016) very helpful. I learned about Theodore II Laskaris from Dimiter Angelov's brilliant *The Byzantine Hellene: The Life of Emperor Theodore Laskaris and Byzantium in the Thirteenth Century* (2019), but for a provocative and eye-opening take on Byzantium as a whole, I would recommend Anthony Kaldellis's *Byzantium Unbound* (2019).

The best way to find out more about Tullia D'Aragona and her poetry is through Julia L. Hairston's *The Poems and Letters of Tullia d'Aragona and Others* (2014), although Hairston and McLucas's new translation of D'Aragona's *Meschino* will hopefully soon be available. For the Renaissance more broadly, I found Jerry Brotton's *The Renaissance: A Very Short Introduction* very useful. Piecing together the scholarship on Safiye Sultan is difficult, but Margaret Meserve's *Empires of Islam in Renaissance Historical Thought* (2008) was excellent in making me think differently about interactions between the Ottoman Empire and European Christian states. Of the many books of Ottoman history that are available, I would recommend Halil Inalcik's *The Ottoman Empire: The Classical Age 1300–1600* (2001).

Much has been written about Francis Bacon, but I found Lisa Jardine and Alan Stewart's *Hostage to Fortune: The Troubled Life of Francis Bacon* (1998) particularly helpful. There are even more books available on the Enlightenment, but I found myself making use of Margaret C. Jacob's *The Enlightenment: A Brief History with Documents* (2001). The excellent *Njinga of Angola: Africa's Warrior Queen* (2017) by Linda Heywood was my exciting and reliable guide for the life of Njinga of Angola, but for wider historical context I found Toby Green's *A Fistful of Shells: West Africa from the Rise of the Slave Trade to the Age of Revolution* (2019) to be both shocking and enlightening.

For the life of Joseph Warren, I would recommend Christian Di Spigna's *Founding Martyr: The Life and Death of Dr. Joseph Warren, the American Revolution's Lost Hero* (2018), but for the politicised classicism of the founding fathers, I turned to Thomas E. Ricks's *First Principles: What America's Founders Learned from the Greeks and Romans and How That Shaped Our Country* (2020). There is now an excellent body of literature available on the life of Phillis Wheatley, but perhaps the first book I would turn to would be the critical new edition of her poetry edited by Vincent Caretta and published in 2019 under the title *The Writings of Phillis Wheatley*. For the problematic politics of the American Revolution, my eyes were opened by *Whose American Revolution Was It?: Historians Interpret the Founding* (2011) by Alfred F. Young and Gregory Nobles. Out of the many biographies available for William Gladstone, I most enjoyed Richard Aldous's *The Lion and the Unicorn: Gladstone vs Disraeli* (2009); and of the many books available on the British Empire, I would recommend Priya Satia's *Time's Monster: History, Conscience and Britain's Empire* (2020).

An excellent new biography of Edward Said by Timothy Brennan, *Places of Mind: A Life of Edward Said* (2021), makes for wonderful reading, and Kwame Anthony Appiah's *The Lies That Bind: Rethinking Identity* (2018) is an accessible as well as brilliant rethinking of culture and identity in the modern world that builds on postcolonial thinking such as that of Said. It is far too early to know whether biographies of Carrie Lam will eventually become available, but books that challenged my thinking about China and the global balance of power include Peter Frankopan's *The New Silk Roads* (2019) and Kishore Mahbubani's *Has China Won?: The Chinese Challenge to American Primacy* (2020).

LIST OF IMAGES

LIST OF IMAGES

INDEX

INDEX

Henrique, Infante of Portugal (Henry the
  Navigator), 204
Henry IV, King of France, 153, 157
Henry VI, Holy Roman Emperor, 82, 94, 96
Henry VIII, King of England, 200
Heracleitus of Ephesus, 117
Heracles (Herakles, Hercules), 41, 63
Herodotus, *13*
  on Athenian democracy, 238
  and Byzantine scholarship, 61
  and colonial-era ethnography, 218
  and complexity of civilisational identity, 23–26,
    35–37, 306
  and definitions of Greekness, 360n33
  as "father of history," 14–22
  and modern cultural values, 352, 353
  modern translations of, 358n2
  and origin myth of Western Civilisation, 346
  and Said's *Orientalism*, 312
  and Sophocles, 359–60n22
  and writing of *Histories*, 30–35
Hildegard of Bingen, 57
Histories (Herodotus), 14–15, 16, 17–21, 30, 32,
  34–36, 359n22
Hobbes, Thomas, 178, 179, 195, 237
Hohenstaufen dynasty, 81–84, 88, 90–91,
  95–96, 99
Holy League, 155, 172–73
Holy Roman Empire
  and Christian Eurocentrism, 107–8
  and confessional conflict in Europe, 156–57
  and Godfrey of Viterbo's scholarship, 81, 83–89,
    95, 98–100
  and Greco-Roman cultural influences, 129–31
  and imperial competition, 201
  See also specific emperors
Homer, 7, 36, 117, 118, 120, 122–23, 130, 262, 287,
  311, 352
Hong Kong, 280, 316–18, 334–43, 350
Horton, James Africanus Beale, 291
humanism, 125–26, 177, 270
Hume, David, 250, 253
Hunayn ibn Ishāq, 66–67, 69
Huntingdon, Selina Hastings, Countess of, 257,
  262, 263
Huntington, Samuel, 16, 58, 330
Hutchinson, Thomas, 247
Hyginus, 43

Iceni tribe, 42, 292
Iliad (Homer), 7, 39, 117, 168, 170, 285, 287, 311
Ilium, 38, 39. *See also* Troy and Trojan lineage
Il Meschino (The Wretch), 136, 140–41, 143–47
Imbangalas, 209, 212–14, 217
India, 18, 119, 144–45, 203, 290–91
Ionians, 17, 32, 33

Iraq, 66, 320–21, 330
Ireland, 200, 226, 276, 280, 282
Islam and Muslims
  and al-Kindi's scholarship, 73
  and confessional conflict in Europe, 154,
    165, 172
  and the Crusades, 121
  and extent of Byzantine Empire, 57
  and Greco-Roman cultural influences, 127, 347
  and inheritance of Classical civilisation, 72–76
  Islamic theology, 73
  and Islamophobia, 146–47, 173, 312
  and modern Islamist movements, 296, 319–23,
    343, 387n12
  and origin myth of Western Civilisation, 10
  and Ottoman civilisational identity, 166
  and Renaissance literature, 145
  and Said's *Orientalism*, 310
Islamic State of Iraq and Syria ("Daesh"), 296, 319,
  320–23, 343, 387n12
Isocrates, 25, 29
Israel, 300–301, 303–4
Issa, Hanan, 314–15
Italy, 42, 59–60, 83, 97, 116, 131, 142, 153, 156, 218, 269
'Izz al-Dīn Kaykāwūs II, Sultan of the Seljuks,
  114, 118

Jaanus, Marie, 303, 304
James I of England (James VI of Scotland), 170,
  176, 185–86, 195–96, 201
January 6, 2001, U.S. Capitol riot, 4, 54, 316–17,
  318, 357n9
Japan, 202, 269, 310
Jefferson, Thomas, 104, 228, 244, 252
Jesuits, 211, 244
Jiménez de Cisneros, Francisco (Cardinal
  Cisneros), 132
John III Doukas Vatatzes, Emperor of the East, 112
John of Austria, 172
Johnson, Samuel, 229
Jones, Inigo, 196
Juvenal, 41, 44

Kant, Immanuel, 180, 250, 374n9
Kasa (Imbangala war captain), 212–13
Kiluanje kia Samba, Ngola of Ndongo, 206
Knox, Robert, 272–73
Komnene, Anna, 61, 118
Kongo, 204, 206, 214, 218
Kotzias, Nikos, 330

Lam, Carrie, *316*, 318, 334–42, 343, 350
Landívar, Rafael, 244
Latin culture
  and Bacon's *New Atlantis*, 194
  and "clash of civilisations" thesis, 310

INDEX

INDEX

INDEX

Trojan War, 15, 24, 36, 39, 44, 96, 168
Troy Games, 43
Trumbull, John, 246
Trump, Donald, 4, 54, 317
Tudor dynasty, 168, 200
Turks (Turchi), 145, 166, 288

Ukraine, 7, 324–25
United Kingdom. *See* Britain and the United
    Kingdom; England
United States of America
    and Chinese model of cultural inheritance, 329
    and establishment of racial hierarchy, 251, 348
    and grand narrative of Western Civilisation,
        266, 290, 348
    and ideology of American revolutionary
        movements, 243–46
    and imperial competition, 269
    and January 6 Capitol riot, 4, 54, 317–18, 358n9
    and modern geopolitical conflict, 319
    and "new Rome" rhetoric, 240, 245
    and Njinga's cultural legacy, 216
    and origin myth of Western Civilisation, 4
    political logic of founders, 228–29
    Warren's legacy in founding of, 224–25
    Warren's role in founding, 230–35
    See also American War of Independence
Urban III, Pope, 84, 100

Vajrapani, 63
Varchi, Benedetto, 139–40
Varro, 43
Vasari, Giorgio, 128–29, 147, 148, 172
Venice, 96, 108, 109, 162, 173
Verdelot, Philippe, 134
Victoria, Queen of England, 276
Victor IV, Antipope, 85
Virgil, 44–45, 129, 256, 262
Voltaire, 83–84, 181

Wang Yi, 329, 333
War on Terror, 7, 104, 320
Warren, Elizabeth, 235
Warren, Joseph, 223
    background and education, 230–31, 378n18
    and complexity of civilisational identity, 306,
        353

death of, 246
and demographics of colonial America, 226
and ideology of American revolutionary
    movement, 249
and modern conceptions of Western
    Civilisation, 298
oration and rhetorical skills, 223–25, 235–43
role in American Revolution, 231–35, 243–44,
    258–59
slaves owned by, 379n25
and theories of civilisational inheritance, 343
and Wheatley's writings, 262
Warren, Mercy Otis, 240
Wars of Religion, 153
Washington, George, 228, 240, 244, 261
West-Eastern Divan Orchestra, 305
Wheatley, Phillis, 247
    background and education of, 253–58
    and complexity of civilisational identity, 307
    court case establishing authorship of,
        247–49
    death of, 264
    and grand narrative of Western
        Civilisation, 348
    and modern conceptions of Western
        Civilisation, 298
    and politics of colonial America, 258–64
    and Western ideas on race, 249
Whitefield, George, 255, 257, 259
Wilberforce, William, 279
William I, Prince of Orange, 153–54, 157
William of Rubruck, 107
Williams, Francis, 253
Winckelmann, Johann Joachim, 265
The Wisdom of the Ancients (Bacon), 194
Wong, Joshua, 340
Woolf, Virginia, 143
Wooster, David, 261

Xerxes I, King of Persia, 17, 20, 39
Xi'an Stele, 107
Xi Jinping, 7, 330, 332

Yeats, W. B., 275
Yunan, 74–75

Zheng He, 204

ABOUT THE AUTHOR

Naoíse Mac Sweeney is a professor of classical archaeology at the University of Vienna, having previously held posts at both Leicester and Cambridge Universities, and has been a researcher at Harvard's Center for Hellenic Studies. She has won numerous academic awards for her work on classical antiquity and origin myths, her previous book on Troy was short-listed for a major prize, and she has appeared on BBC television and radio.